taste of home.
GRANDMA'S
favorites

taste of home
B O O K S

taste of home

A TASTE OF HOME/READER'S DIGEST BOOK
© 2012 Reiman Media Group, LLC
5400 S. 6oth St., Greendale WI 53129
All rights reserved.

Taste of Home and Reader's Digest are registered trademarks of The Reader's Digest Association, Inc.

EDITORIAL

EDITOR-IN-CHIEF	Catherine Cassidy
EXECUTIVE EDITOR, PRINT AND DIGITAL BOOKS	Stephen C. George
CREATIVE DIRECTOR	Howard Greenberg
EDITORIAL SERVICES MANAGER	Kerri Balliet
EDITOR	Janet Briggs
ASSOCIATE CREATIVE DIRECTOR	Edwin Robles Jr.
ART DIRECTOR	Jessie Sharon
CONTENT PRODUCTION MANAGER	Julie Wagner
CONTRIBUTING LAYOUT DESIGNER	Holly Patch
LAYOUT DESIGNER	Catherine Fletcher
COPY CHIEF	Deb Warlaumont Mulvey
COPY EDITORS	Joanne Weintraub, Alysse Gear
RECIPE EDITOR	Mary King
RECIPE CONTENT MANAGER	Colleen King
RECIPE TESTING	Taste of Home Test Kitchen
FOOD PHOTOGRAPHY	Taste of Home Photo Studio
EXECUTIVE ASSISTANT	Marie Brannon
EDITORIAL ASSISTANT	Marilyn Iczkowski

BUSINESS

VICE PRESIDENT, PUBLISHER	Jan Studin, jan_studin@rd.com
REGIONAL ACCOUNT DIRECTOR	Donna Lindskog, donna_lindskog@rd.com
EASTERN ACCOUNT DIRECTOR	Joanne Carrara
EASTERN ACCOUNT MANAGER	Kari Nestor
ACCOUNT MANAGER	Gina Minerbi
MIDWEST & WESTERN ACCOUNT DIRECTOR	Jackie Fallon
MIDWEST ACCOUNT MANAGER	Lorna Phillips
MICHIGAN SALES REPRESENTATIVE	Linda C. Donaldson
SOUTHWESTERN ACCOUNT REPRESENTATIVE	Summer Nilsson
CORPORATE DIGITAL AND INTEGRATED SALES DIRECTOR, N.A.	Steve Sottile
ASSOCIATE MARKETING DIRECTOR, INTEGRATED SOLUTIONS	Katie Gaon Wilson
DIGITAL SALES PLANNER	Tim Baarda
GENERAL MANAGER, TASTE OF HOME COOKING SCHOOLS	Erin Puariea
DIRECT RESPONSE ADVERTISING	Katherine Zito, David Geller Associates
VICE PRESIDENT, CREATIVE DIRECTOR	Paul Livornese
EXECUTIVE DIRECTOR, BRAND MARKETING	Leah West
SENIOR MARKETING MANAGER	Vanessa Bailey
ASSOCIATE MARKETING MANAGER	Betsy Connors
VICE PRESIDENT, MAGAZINE MARKETING	Dave Fiegel

READER'S DIGEST NORTH AMERICA

VICE PRESIDENT, BUSINESS DEVELOPMENT	Jonathan Bigham
PRESIDENT, BOOKS AND HOME ENTERTAINING	Harold Clarke
CHIEF FINANCIAL OFFICER	Howard Halligan
VP, GENERAL MANAGER, READER'S DIGEST MEDIA	Marilynn Jacobs
CHIEF CONTENT OFFICER, MILWAUKEE	Mark Jannot
CHIEF MARKETING OFFICER	Renee Jordan
VICE PRESIDENT, CHIEF SALES OFFICER	Mark Josephson
GENERAL MANAGER, MILWAUKEE	Frank Quigley
VICE PRESIDENT, CHIEF CONTENT OFFICER	Liz Vaccariello

THE READER'S DIGEST ASSOCIATION, INC.

PRESIDENT AND CHIEF EXECUTIVE OFFICER	Robert E. Guth

For other Taste of Home books and products, visit us at *tasteofhome.com*.

For more Reader's Digest products and information, visit
rd.com (in the United States) or *rd.ca* (in Canada).

INTERNATIONAL STANDARD BOOK NUMBER	978-1-61765-134-2
LIBRARY OF CONGRESS CONTROL NUMBER	2012948152

COVER PHOTOGRAPHY

PHOTOGRAPHER	Jim Wieland
SENIOR FOOD STYLIST	Kathryn Conrad
SET STYLIST	Melissa Haberman

PICTURED ON FRONT COVER Top: Fried Chicken with Pan Gravy, page 164; Peanut Butter Cookies, page 269; Spaghetti 'n' Meatballs, page 149; main: Streusel-Topped Apple Cheesecake, page 241
PICTURED ON BACK COVER Top: Hearty Potato Soup, page 60; Breakfast Bread Pudding, page 41; Center: Chicken Cheese Lasagna, page 162; Bottom: Mom's Peach Pie, page 248; Roasted Chicken with Rosemary, page 171
PICTURED ON SPINE Tasty Tossed Salad, page 65

Printed in China.
1 3 5 7 9 10 8 6 4 2

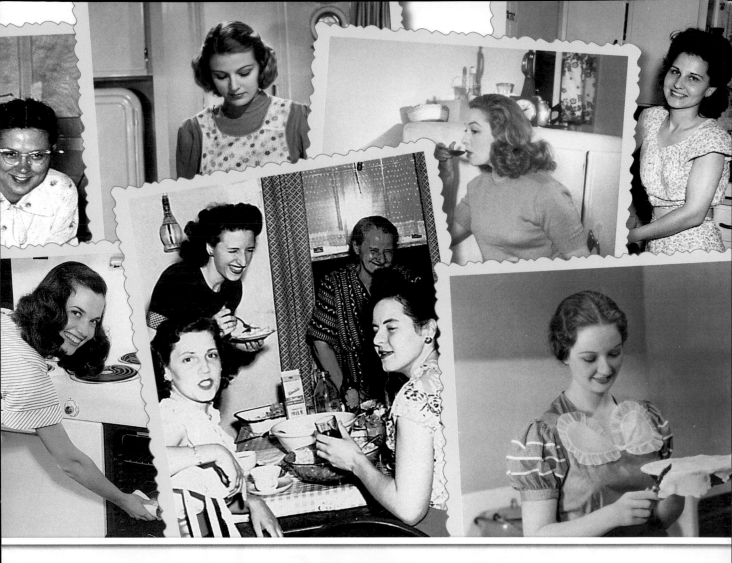

TABLE OF CONTENTS

Snacks & Beverages 4

Breakfast & Brunch.. 22

Soups 42

Salads.. 62

Side Dishes 80

Breads.. 102

Beef 130

Poultry.. 152

Pork, Ham & Sausage.. 178

Seafood & Meatless Main Dishes 200

Cakes & Cheesecakes.. 220

Pies.. 244

Cookies & Bars.. 264

Desserts.. 286

Indexes 302

SNACKS & BEVERAGES

Deviled Eggs with Bacon

These yummy deviled eggs went over so well at our summer cookouts, I started making them for holiday dinners as well. Everyone likes the addition of crumbled bacon.

—BARBARA REID MOUNDS, OKLAHOMA

YIELD: 2 DOZEN.

- 12 **hard-cooked eggs**
- ⅓ **cup mayonnaise**
- 3 **bacon strips, cooked and crumbled**
- 3 **tablespoons finely chopped red onion**
- 3 **tablespoons sweet pickle relish**
- ¼ **teaspoon smoked paprika**

1. Cut eggs in half lengthwise. Remove yolks; set whites aside. In a small bowl, mash yolks. Add the mayonnaise, bacon, onion and relish; mix well. Stuff into egg whites. Refrigerate until serving. Sprinkle with paprika.

Pepperoni Pizza Spread

Loaded with popular pizza ingredients, this cheesy concoction is wonderful on crackers of all kinds.

—CONNIE MILINOVICH CUDAHY, WISCONSIN

YIELD: 6 CUPS.

- 2 **cups (8 ounces) shredded part-skim mozzarella cheese**
- 2 **cups (8 ounces) shredded cheddar cheese**
- 1 **cup mayonnaise**
- 1 **cup chopped pimiento-stuffed olives**
- 1 **cup chopped pepperoni**
- 1 **can (6 ounces) ripe olives, drained and chopped**
- 1 **can (4 ounces) mushroom stems and pieces, drained and chopped**
- ½ **cup chopped onion**
- ½ **cup chopped green pepper**

Crackers, breadsticks and/or French bread

1. In a large bowl, combine the first nine ingredients. Transfer to an 11-in. x 7-in. baking dish. Bake, uncovered, at 350° for 25-30 minutes or until edges are bubbly and lightly browned. Serve with crackers, breadsticks and/or French bread.

Strawberry Citrus Slushies

Ordinary juice is just fine most of the time, but when you have guests in the morning, try something special. Pretty and refreshing, this festive drink will delight everyone at the table.

—TASTE OF HOME TEST KITCHEN

YIELD: 5 SERVINGS.

STRAWBERRY PUREE
- ½ **cup frozen unsweetened sliced strawberries, thawed**
- 2 **tablespoons confectioners' sugar**
- 2 **tablespoons water**

CITRUS SLUSH
- ¾ **cup sugar**
- ¾ **cup water**
- ¾ **cup lemon juice**
- ⅔ **cup orange juice**
- 4½ **cups ice cubes**

1. Place the strawberries, confectioners' sugar and water in a blender. Cover and process until blended; transfer to a small bowl. Cover and chill until serving.

2. In a small saucepan, bring sugar and water to a boil. Cook and stir until sugar is dissolved. Remove from the heat; cool to room temperature.

3. Just before serving, place the lemon juice, orange juice, ice cubes and sugar syrup in a blender. Cover and process until it reaches a slushy consistency. Divide strawberry puree among four chilled glasses. Top with citrus slush. Serve immediately.

Cheese Rye Appetizers

I enjoy serving this canape at family gatherings. The topping can be mixed ahead of time and refrigerated. Just before serving, spread cheese mixture on bread and bake. Even kids like it.

—JOYCE DYKSTRA LANSING, ILLINOIS

YIELD: 2½ DOZEN.

2 cups (8 ounces) shredded Swiss cheese
1 cup mayonnaise
1 can (4¼ ounces) chopped ripe olives
4 bacon strips, cooked and crumbled
¼ cup chopped green onions
1½ teaspoons minced fresh parsley or ½ teaspoon dried parsley flakes
30 slices snack rye bread

1. In a small bowl, combine first six ingredients. Spread a rounded tablespoonful over each slice of bread. Place on an ungreased baking sheet. Bake at 450° for 6-8 minutes or until the cheese is melted.

Blizzard Party Mix

This sweet-salty combo is sure to be popular. It's perfect for a party, munching at home or giving away as a gift.

—KELLEY SCOTT PARMA, OHIO

YIELD: 6 CUPS.

- 2 **cups Corn Chex**
- 2 **cups miniature pretzels**
- 1 **cup dry roasted peanuts**
- 20 **caramels, coarsely chopped**
- 1 **package (10 to 12 ounces) white baking chips**

1. In a large bowl, combine the first four ingredients. In a microwave, melt chips; stir until smooth. Pour over cereal mixture and toss to coat.

2. Immediately spread onto waxed paper-lined baking sheet; let stand until set, about 20 minutes.

3. Break into pieces. Store in an airtight container.

Artichoke Spinach Dip in a Bread Bowl

Baking the dip in the actual bread shell makes a very attractive dish, and it's so easy to clean up. Every time I serve my dip, people can't believe how healthy and veggie-filled it is.

—ELLA HOMEL CHICAGO, ILLINOIS

YIELD: 4 CUPS.

- 3 **jars (7½ ounces each) marinated quartered artichoke hearts, drained and chopped**
- 1 **cup grated Parmesan cheese**
- ¾ **cup mayonnaise**
- 3 **green onions, sliced**
- 1 **can (4 ounces) chopped green chilies, drained**
- 1 **package (10 ounces) frozen chopped spinach, thawed and squeezed dry**
- 1 **cup (4 ounces) shredded Swiss cheese**
- 1 **round loaf (1 pound) rye or pumpernickel bread**

1. In a large bowl, combine the first seven ingredients. Cut a thin slice off the top of bread. Hollow out the bottom half, leaving a ½-in. shell. Cut removed bread into 1-in. cubes.

2. Place cubes on an ungreased baking sheet. Broil 6 in. from the heat for 2-3 minutes or until golden, stirring once.

3. Place bread shell on an ungreased baking sheet. Spoon dip into bread shell. Bake, uncovered, at 350° for 20-25 minutes or until heated through. Serve with bread cubes.

Editor's Note: *Reduced-fat or fat-free mayonnaise is not recommended for this recipe. If any of the dip does not fit in bread shell, bake, uncovered, in a greased small baking dish until heated through.*

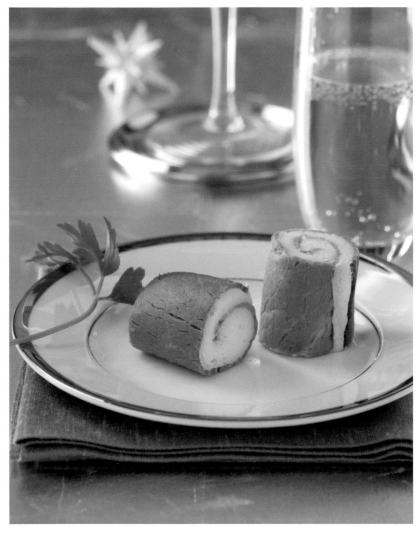

Easy Elephant Ears

You'll love the classic cinnamon-sugar flavor of these crispy bite-size treats. Even more, you'll love that they call for just three ingredients and are so simple to assemble.

—**BOB ROSE** WAUKESHA, WISCONSIN

YIELD: ABOUT 2½ DOZEN.

- 1 package (17.3 ounces) frozen puff pastry, thawed
- ½ cup sugar
- 2 teaspoons ground cinnamon

1. On a lightly floured surface, roll one sheet of puff pastry into an 11-in. x 8-in. rectangle. Combine sugar and cinnamon; sprinkle half of mixture over pastry.

2. Working from the short sides, roll up dough jelly-roll style toward the center. With a sharp knife, cut roll into ½-in. slices. Place on parchment paper-lined baking sheets. Repeat with remaining pastry and sugar mixture.

3. Bake at 375° for 12-15 minutes or until crisp and golden brown. Remove from pans to wire racks.

Roast Beef Spirals

This savory appetizer is simple, addictive and a nice change of pace from familiar tortilla pinwheels.

—**MARCIA ORLANDO** BOYERTOWN, PENNSYLVANIA

YIELD: 4 DOZEN.

- 2 packages (8 ounces each) cream cheese, softened
- 2 garlic cloves, minced
- 1 teaspoon ground ginger
- 6 thin slices deli roast beef

1. In a small bowl, beat the cream cheese, garlic and ginger until blended. Spread over beef slices; roll up.

2. Wrap each in plastic wrap; refrigerate for at least 2 hours or until firm. Cut into 1-in. slices.

Cinnamon-Raisin Granola

This granola recipe makes a great late-night snack. I like that it's nutritious, too.

—**TAMMY NEUBAUER** IDA GROVE, IOWA

YIELD: 12 SERVINGS.

- 4 cups old-fashioned oats
- 1 cup flaked coconut
- ¼ cup packed brown sugar
- ¼ cup canola oil
- ¼ cup honey
- 1 teaspoon ground cinnamon
- 1½ teaspoons vanilla extract
- 1 cup raisins

1. In a large bowl, combine oats and coconut; set aside. In a saucepan, combine the brown sugar, oil, honey and cinnamon; bring to a boil. Remove from the heat and stir in vanilla. Pour over oat mixture; stir to coat. Spread in a large shallow baking pan.

2. Bake at 350° for 15-20 minutes, stirring occasionally. Cool. Add raisins. Store in an airtight container.

During warm weather, Grandma would roll lemons back and forth between her hands. Then she'd cut those fragrant lemons in half and twist them on a glass juicer. I could hardly wait as she added sugar, water and ice and stirred up a big pitcher of lemonade!

—**SHIRLEY MIER-MAY**
OLYMPIA, WASHINGTON

Tangy Meatballs

These hearty meatballs are a family favorite and a big hit wherever they go! In their delicious barbecue sauce, they're a perfect dish to pass along and also work well as hors d'oeuvres.

—**JANE BARTA** ST. THOMAS, NORTH DAKOTA

YIELD: 12 SERVINGS.

- 2 eggs
- 2 cups quick-cooking or rolled oats
- 1 can (12 ounces) evaporated milk
- 1 cup chopped onion
- 2 teaspoons salt
- ½ teaspoon pepper
- ½ teaspoon garlic powder
- 3 pounds lean ground beef (90% lean)

SAUCE
- 2 cups ketchup
- 1½ cups packed brown sugar
- ½ cup chopped onion
- 1 to 2 teaspoons liquid smoke
- ½ teaspoon garlic powder

1. In a large bowl, beat eggs. Add oats, milk, onion, salt, pepper and garlic powder. Add the ground beef; mix well. Shape into 1½-in. balls. Place meatballs on greased racks in shallow baking pans. Bake, uncovered, at 375° for 30 minutes; drain.

2. Place all of the meatballs in one of the pans. In a saucepan, bring all sauce ingredients to a boil. Pour over meatballs. Return to the oven and bake, uncovered, for 20 minutes or until meatballs are done.

Cheesy Sun Crisps

These crisps have a great cheesy flavor perfect for snacking.
—**MARY DETWEILER** MIDDLEFIELD, OHIO

YIELD: 32 SERVINGS.

- 2 **cups (8 ounces) shredded cheddar cheese**
- ½ **cup grated Parmesan cheese**
- ½ **cup butter, softened**
- 3 **tablespoons water**
- 1 **cup all-purpose flour**
- ¼ **teaspoon salt**
- 1 **cup quick-cooking oats**
- ⅔ **cup roasted salted sunflower kernels**

1. In a bowl, combine cheddar and Parmesan cheeses, butter and water until well mixed. Combine flour and salt; add to cheese mixture. Stir in oats and sunflower kernels. Knead dough until it holds together. Shape into a 12-in. roll. Cover with plastic wrap; chill for 4 hours or overnight.

2. Let stand at room temperature for 10 minutes before cutting into ⅛-in. slices. Place on greased foil-lined baking sheets. Bake at 400° for 8 to 10 minutes or until edges are golden. Slide crackers and foil off baking sheets to wire racks to cool.

Chunky Salsa

My fresh-tasting salsa is wonderfully chunky. If you like it hotter, add more habanero peppers; if you prefer a mild salsa, add fewer.
—**DANA HAYES** CANTON, OHIO

YIELD: 7 PINT JARS.

- 5 **pounds tomatoes**
- 4 **large green peppers, chopped**
- 3 **large onions, chopped**
- 2 **large sweet red peppers, chopped**
- 2 **habanero peppers, seeded and finely chopped**
- 1 **cup white vinegar**
- 1 **can (6 ounces) tomato paste**
- 3 **teaspoons salt**

1. Fill a Dutch oven two-thirds with water; bring to a boil. Score an X on the bottom of each tomato. Using a slotted spoon, place tomatoes, one at a time, in boiling water for 30-60 seconds. Remove tomatoes and immediately plunge in ice water. Discard peel; chop tomatoes.

2. In a stockpot, combine the remaining ingredients. Stir in tomatoes. Bring to a boil over medium-high heat. Reduce heat; simmer, uncovered, for 15-20 minutes or until desired thickness.

3. Carefully ladle hot mixture into hot 1-pint jars, leaving ½-in. headspace. Remove air bubbles; wipe rims and adjust lids. Process for 15 minutes in a boiling-water canner.

Editor's Note: *We recommend wearing disposable gloves when cutting hot peppers. Avoid touching your face. The processing time listed is for altitudes of 1,000 feet or less. For altitudes up to 3,000 feet, add 5 minutes; 6,000 feet, add 10 minutes; 8,000 feet, add 15 minutes; 10,000 feet, add 20 minutes.*

Spiced Pecans

These crunchy pecans are a family-favorite treat to munch on anytime and are very nice to serve when you have company.

—MIRIAM HERSCHBERGER HOLMESVILLE, OHIO

YIELD: 4 CUPS.

- 1 egg white
- 1 teaspoon cold water
- 4 cups (about 1 pound) pecan halves
- ½ cup sugar
- ½ teaspoon ground cinnamon
- ¼ teaspoon salt

1. In a small bowl, lightly beat egg white. Add water; beat until frothy but not stiff. Add pecans; stir until well coated. Combine the sugar, cinnamon and salt. Sprinkle over pecans; toss to coat.

2. Spread in a 15-in. x 10-in. x 1-in. greased baking pan. Bake at 250° for 1 hour, stirring occasionally.

Easy Hummus

Using sun-dried tomato salad dressing instead of tahini adds a new dimension of flavor to this nutritious predinner snack.

—JEANNETTE JEREMIAS KITCHENER, ONTARIO

YIELD: 1½ CUPS.

- 1 can (15 ounces) garbanzo beans or chickpeas, rinsed and drained
- ½ cup sun-dried tomato salad dressing
- 2 garlic cloves, minced
- Baked pita chips or assorted fresh vegetables

1. In a food processor, combine the beans, salad dressing and garlic. Cover and process for 30 seconds or until smooth. Serve with chips.

Cozy Hot Chocolate

Steaming mugs of this smooth, chocolaty drink make a comforting treat anytime, especially during the colder months.

—MARIE HATTRUP SPARKS, NEVADA

YIELD: 2 SERVINGS.

- 2 tablespoons baking cocoa
- 2 tablespoons sugar
- ¼ cup water
- 2 cups 2% milk
- ½ teaspoon vanilla extract
- ¼ cup whipped cream
- Ground cinnamon, optional

1. In a small saucepan, mix the cocoa and sugar; add water and stir until smooth. Bring to a boil, stirring constantly. Boil for 1 minute. Reduce heat; stir in milk and heat through.

2. Remove from the heat and stir in vanilla. Pour into 2 cups; top with whipped cream and sprinkle with cinnamon if desired.

Cozy Hot Mocha: Reduce milk to 1 cup. Add 1 cup strong brewed coffee. Proceed as directed.

Maple Hot Chocolate: Omit whipped cream and cinnamon. Add 1 tablespoon butter to cocoa mixture before bringing it to a boil. Add 3 large marshmallows with the milk and heat until marshmallows are melted. Add ½ teaspoon maple flavoring with the vanilla. Pour into mugs and top with additional marshmallows.

Banana Brunch Punch

A cold glass of refreshing punch really brightens a brunch or other gathering. It's nice to serve a beverage like this that's more special than plain juice. With bananas, orange juice and lemonade, it can add tropical flair to a winter day.

—MARY ANNE MCWHIRTER PEARLAND, TEXAS

YIELD: 60-70 SERVINGS (10 QUARTS).

- 6 medium ripe bananas
- 1 can (12 ounces) frozen orange juice concentrate, thawed
- ¾ cup thawed lemonade concentrate
- 3 cups warm water, divided
- 2 cups sugar, divided
- 1 can (46 ounces) pineapple juice, chilled
- 3 bottles (2 liters each) lemon-lime soda, chilled
- Orange slices, optional

1. In a blender, cover and process the bananas, orange juice and lemonade until smooth. Remove half of the mixture and set aside. Add 1½ cups warm water and 1 cup sugar to blender; blend until smooth.

2. Place in a large freezer container. Repeat with remaining banana mixture, water and sugar; add to container. Cover and freeze until solid.

3. One hour before serving, remove punch base from freezer. Just before serving, place in a large punch bowl. Add pineapple juice and soda; stir until well blended. Garnish with orange slices if desired.

Mini Hamburgers

I guarantee these delicious little burgers will be the first snack cleared from your table. These hearty snacks are perfect for Sunday afternoon football games and teen parties. The mini buns are actually store-purchased pan dinner rolls available everywhere.
—**JUDY LEWIS** STERLING HEIGHTS, MICHIGAN

YIELD: 40 SERVINGS.

½ cup chopped onion
1 tablespoon butter
1 egg, lightly beaten
¼ teaspoon seasoned salt
¼ teaspoon ground sage
¼ teaspoon salt
⅛ teaspoon pepper
1 pound ground beef
40 mini rolls, split

8 ounces process American cheese slices, cut into 1½-inch squares, optional
40 dill pickle slices, optional

1. In a large skillet, saute onion in butter. Transfer to large bowl; add egg and seasonings. Crumble beef over mixture and mix well. Spread over bottom halves of the rolls; replace tops. Place on baking sheets; cover with foil.

2. Bake at 350° for 20 minutes or until a meat thermometer reads 160° and juices run clear. If desired, place a cheese square and pickle on each hamburger; replace tops and foil and return to the oven for 5 minutes.

BLT Bites

These quick hors d'oeuvres may be mini, but their bacon and tomato flavor is full size. I serve them at parties, brunches and picnics, and they're always a hit...even my kids love them.

—**KELLIE REMMEN** DETROIT LAKES, MINNESOTA

YIELD: 16-20 APPETIZER SERVINGS.

- 16 to 20 cherry tomatoes
- 1 pound sliced bacon, cooked and crumbled
- ½ cup mayonnaise
- ⅓ cup chopped green onions
- 3 tablespoons grated Parmesan cheese
- 2 tablespoons snipped fresh parsley

1. Cut a thin slice off of each tomato top. Scoop out and discard pulp. Invert the tomatoes on a paper towel to drain.

2. In a small bowl, combine the remaining ingredients. Spoon into tomatoes. Refrigerate for several hours.

Sweet Minglers

This snack mix is perfect for a late-night treat or a pick-me-up any time of the day. I sometimes take a batch to work, and it's always eaten up quickly. It's a slightly different cereal snack because of the chocolate and peanut butter.

—**MARY OBEILIN** SELINSGROVE, PENNSYLVANIA

YIELD: ABOUT 6 CUPS.

- 1 cup (6 ounces) semisweet chocolate chips
- ¼ cup creamy peanut butter
- 6 cups Corn or Rice Chex
- 1 cup confectioners' sugar

1. In a large microwave-safe bowl, melt chocolate chips on high for 30 seconds. Stir; microwave 30 seconds longer or until the chips are melted. Stir in peanut butter. Gently stir in cereal until well coated; set aside.

2. Place confectioners' sugar in a 2-gallon plastic storage bag. Add cereal mixture and shake until well coated. Store in an airtight container in the refrigerator.

Editor's Note: *This recipe was tested in a 1,100-watt microwave.*

Sweet Gingered Chicken Wings

I first enjoyed this delicious chicken dish many years ago when I attended a class on using honey in cooking. When I prepare this recipe for a party, it's one of the first dishes to disappear.

—DEBBIE DOUGAL ROSEVILLE, CALIFORNIA

YIELD: 2 DOZEN.

- 1 **cup all-purpose flour**
- 2 **teaspoons salt**
- 2 **teaspoons paprika**
- ¼ **teaspoon pepper**
- 24 **chicken wings**

SAUCE

- ¼ **cup honey**
- ¼ **cup thawed orange juice concentrate**
- ½ **teaspoon ground ginger**

Minced fresh parsley, optional

1. In a large resealable plastic bag, combine the flour, salt, paprika and pepper. Add chicken wings, a few at a time; seal bag and toss to coat.

2. Place wings on a large greased baking sheet. Bake at 350° for 30 minutes. Remove from the oven and drain.

3. Combine the honey, orange juice concentrate and ginger; brush generously over chicken wings. Reduce heat to 325°.

4. Bake for 30-40 minutes or until chicken juices run clear, basting occasionally with more sauce. Sprinkle with parsley before serving if desired.

Buttermilk Shakes

These creamy, rich shakes taste just like liquid cheesecake! It's so easy to whip up a couple of satisfying servings.

—GLORIA JARRETT LOVELAND, OHIO

YIELD: 2 SERVINGS.

- 1 **pint vanilla ice cream**
- 1 **cup buttermilk**
- 1 **teaspoon grated lemon peel**
- ½ **teaspoon vanilla extract**
- 1 **drop lemon extract**

1. Place all ingredients in a blender container. Cover and process on high until smooth. Pour into glasses. Refrigerate any leftovers.

How my grandma managed to turn out the good food she did on a woodstove is beyond me. I guess, like everything else, practice makes perfect. Most everything she cooked was what she raised on the farm. For a special treat, she parched corn. She placed ears of corn in the oven and left them until they became crispy and brown. That corn tasted wonderful.

—SHELBY TEANEY ROCKY MOUNT, MISSOURI

Mini Apple Pizzas

My four children are now grown, but they still enjoy snacking on these sweet little pizzas...and so do my five grandchildren. We use fresh apples from the small orchard on our dairy farm, and they're so easy to make. The warm cinnamon flavor and light crust make them delicious!

—**HELEN LAMB** SEYMOUR, MISSOURI

YIELD: 10 SERVINGS.

- 1 **tube refrigerator biscuits (about 10 biscuits)**
- ½ **cup packed brown sugar**
- 2 **tablespoons all-purpose flour**
- 1 **teaspoon ground cinnamon**
- 2 **medium tart apples, peeled and shredded**
- 1 **cup (4 ounces) shredded cheddar cheese, optional**

1. Roll or pat biscuits into 3½-in. circles; place on a lightly greased baking sheet. In a bowl, combine brown sugar, flour and cinnamon. Add apples and mix well; spoon rounded tablespoonfuls onto biscuits.

2. Bake at 350° for 15-20 minutes or until edges begin to brown. If desired, sprinkle each pizza with 1 tablespoon cheese. Serve warm.

> I remember Grandma's moist spice cakes. She'd bake on Monday, and even several days later her cakes were still fresh. I think they stayed moist because she used real cream, butter and the juice of canned fruits.
>
> —**GEORGE BURKE** BONNERDALE, ARKANSAS

Fresh Vegetable Dip

This cool and creamy dip is a real family favorite for snacking, especially when paired with fresh garden vegetables. It's also perfect for parties.

—**DENISE GOEDEKEN**
PLATTE CENTER, NEBRASKA

YIELD: 8 SERVINGS.

- 1½ **cups (12 ounces) sour cream**
- ¾ **cup mayonnaise**
- 1 **tablespoon dried minced onion**
- 1 **teaspoon dill weed**
- 1 **teaspoon dried parsley flakes**
- 1 **teaspoon garlic salt**
- **Dash Worcestershire sauce**
- **Fresh vegetables**

1. In a small bowl, combine sour cream, mayonnaise, onion, dill, parsley, garlic salt and Worcestershire sauce. Chill for at least 1 hour. Serve with fresh vegetables.

Aunt Frances' Lemonade

My sister and I spent a week each summer with our Aunt Frances, who always had this thirst-quenching lemonade in a stoneware crock in the refrigerator. It tastes so much like fresh citrus and makes a refreshing drink after a hot day of running around.

—DEBBIE REINHART NEW CUMBERLAND, PENNSYLVANIA

YIELD: 12-16 SERVINGS (1 GALLON).

5 lemons
5 limes
5 oranges
3 quarts water
1½ to 2 cups sugar

1. Squeeze the juice from four of the lemons, limes and oranges; pour into a gallon container.

2. Thinly slice the remaining fruit and set aside for garnish. Add water and sugar; mix well. Store in the refrigerator. Serve over ice with fruit slices.

Puffed Wheat Balls

My Grandma Hunt is almost 90 years old and she still makes her famous Puffed Wheat Balls by the dozen whenever she comes over. Her 82 grandchildren and 168 great-grandchildren all love them.

—LUCILE PROCTOR PANGUITCH, UTAH

YIELD: 2½ TO 3 DOZEN.

12	**cups unsweetened puffed wheat cereal**
2	**cups packed brown sugar**
1	**cup light corn syrup**
2	**tablespoons butter**
1	**cup evaporated milk**
⅓	**cup sugar**

1. Place cereal in a large bowl; set aside.

2. In a heavy saucepan, bring brown sugar and corn syrup to a boil. Add butter. Combine evaporated milk and sugar; add to boiling mixture. Cook until candy thermometer reads 240° (soft-ball stage). Pour over cereal and stir to coat. Shape into 2-in. balls.

Editor's Note: *We recommend that you test your candy thermometer before each use by bringing water to a boil; the thermometer should read 212°. Adjust your recipe temperature up or down based on your test.*

Homemade Orange Refresher

Family and friends will thank you for serving this cool, tangy orange drink on warm evenings. It tastes a little like orange sherbet.

—IOLA EGLE BELLA VISTA, ARKANSAS

YIELD: 4 SERVINGS.

    1 can (6 ounces) frozen orange juice concentrate, thawed
    ⅓ cup sugar
    ½ cup instant nonfat dry milk powder
    2 teaspoons vanilla extract
    ¾ cup cold water
    10 to 12 ice cubes
Orange slices and mint, optional

1. In a blender, combine the first five ingredients; cover and process on high speed until smooth. Add the ice cubes, a few at a time, blending until slushy. Serve in chilled glasses. Garnish with the orange slices and mint if desired. Serve immediately.

Editor's Note: *For a fancy glass edge, invert glass and dip into orange juice and then sugar; let dry 1 hour before filling glass.*

Tater-Dipped Veggies

Deep-fried vegetables are terrific, but it's not always convenient to prepare them for company. Here's a recipe that produces the same deliciously crisp results in the oven. Serve with your favorite ranch-style dressing as a dip.

—EARLEEN LILLEGARD PRESCOTT, ARIZONA

YIELD: 6-8 SERVINGS.

    1 cup instant potato flakes
    ⅓ cup grated Parmesan cheese
    ½ teaspoon celery salt
    ¼ teaspoon garlic powder
    ¼ cup butter, melted and cooled
    2 eggs
    4 to 5 cups raw bite-size vegetables (mushrooms, peppers, broccoli, cauliflower, zucchini and/or parboiled carrots)
Prepared ranch salad dressing or dip, optional

1. In a small bowl, combine potato flakes, Parmesan cheese, celery salt, garlic powder and butter. In another bowl, beat eggs. Dip vegetables, one at a time, into egg, then into potato mixture; coat well.

2. Place on an ungreased baking sheet. Bake at 400° for 20-25 minutes. Serve with dressing or dip if desired.

> My grandma and grandpa lived on a farm in Arkansas. My cousins and I liked to visit them. We'd climb up into the loft of the barn where Grandpa stored his peanut crop. Then we'd sit in the middle of the peanut vines and eat raw peanuts until we were about to burst!
>
> **—JEAN HAYGOOD** MINDEN, LOUISIANA

Caramel Corn

For years I've taken this snack to our church retreat. I take it in two containers—one for each night—so it doesn't all disappear the first night. Other church members tell us that if we can't attend, we should just send the caramel corn.

—NANCY BREEN CANASTOTA, NEW YORK

YIELD: 48 SERVINGS
(1 CUP PER SERVING).

    12 quarts plain popped popcorn
    1   pound peanuts
    2   cups butter, cubed
    2   pounds brown sugar
    ½   cup dark corn syrup
    ½   cup molasses

1. Place popcorn in two large bowls. Stir ½ pound nuts into each bowl. In a Dutch oven, combine the remaining ingredients. Bring to a boil over medium heat; cook and stir for 5 minutes.

2. Pour half of syrup over each bowl of popcorn and stir to coat. Transfer coated popcorn into a large roasting pan. Bake at 250° for 1 hour. Remove from the oven and break apart while warm. Cool. Store in airtight containers.

Jungle Float

This fun float lets kids (and adults, too) be the masters of their own creations. What a tasty way to experiment!

—TASTE OF HOME TEST KITCHEN

YIELD: 1 SERVING.

- 3 **tablespoons chocolate syrup**
- 3 **scoops chocolate or vanilla ice cream**
- 1 **cup chilled club soda**

Optional toppings: sliced banana, honey-roasted peanuts, cut-up peanut butter cups, animal crackers, whipped cream and maraschino cherries

1. Place 2 tablespoons chocolate syrup in a tall glass. Add ice cream and remaining chocolate syrup. Top with club soda. Garnish with toppings of your choice. Serve immediately.

Crisp and Nutty Mix

On those busy days when running on the track or running to class, this mixture of dried fruit, cereal, nuts and more is the ultimate combination for munching.

—MIKE TCHOU PEPPER PIKE, OHIO

YIELD: 2 QUARTS.

- 1 **cup Wheat Chex**
- 1 **cup Multi Grain Cheerios**
- 1 **cup reduced-fat Triscuits, broken**
- 1 **cup yogurt-covered pretzels**
- ½ **cup blanched almonds**
- ½ **cup dried apples, chopped**
- ½ **cup dried banana chips**
- ½ **cup dried blueberries**
- ½ **cup salted cashews**
- ½ **cup dark chocolate M&M's**
- ⅓ **cup finely shredded unsweetened coconut**
- ⅓ **cup sunflower kernels**
- ⅓ **cup salted pumpkin seeds or pepitas**

1. In a large bowl, combine all ingredients. Store in an airtight container.

Editor's Note: *Look for unsweetened coconut in the baking or health food section.*

Mock Champagne

Everyone can join in the toast with this light and refreshing drink. It tastes just like Champagne, complete with bubbles!

—PAM ION GAITHERSBURG, MARYLAND

YIELD: 8 SERVINGS.

- 3 **cups white grape juice, divided**
- 2 **cans (12 ounces each) ginger ale, chilled**
- ½ **cup club soda, chilled**

Orange slices and sliced fresh strawberries

1. Pour 2 cups juice into ice cube trays; freeze until set.

2. Transfer ice cubes to a pitcher; add remaining juice. Slowly stir in ginger ale and club soda. Garnish with oranges and strawberries. Serve immediately.

Horseradish Cheese Spread

I got the recipe for this zippy, irresistible cheese spread from a friend. It makes a creamy, delicious evening snack.

—CONNIE SIMON DURAND, MICHIGAN

YIELD: 4 CUPS.

- 2 **pounds process American cheese, cubed**
- ½ **cup prepared horseradish**
- ⅓ **cup mayonnaise**
- 1 **teaspoon hot pepper sauce**

¼ **teaspoon garlic salt**
¼ **teaspoon Worcestershire sauce**

1. Melt cheese in the top of a double boiler over simmering water until smooth. Add remaining ingredients and stir until smooth. Spoon into containers and refrigerate. Serve with crackers or raw vegetables.

Olive-Stuffed Celery

My grandmother taught both me and my mom this appetizer recipe. We always serve it at Christmas and Thanksgiving. The stuffing is so yummy that even if you don't normally care for the ingredients on their own, you'll love the end result.

—STACY POWELL SANTA FE, TEXAS

YIELD: 2 DOZEN.

- 1 **dill pickle spear plus 1 teaspoon juice**
- 3 **sweet pickles plus 1 teaspoon juice**
- 6 **pitted ripe olives plus 1 teaspoon juice**
- 6 **pimiento-stuffed olives plus 1 teaspoon juice**
- 1 **package (8 ounces) cream cheese, softened**
- ⅓ **cup Miracle Whip**
- ¼ **teaspoon salt**
- ¼ **cup finely chopped pecans, toasted**
- 6 **celery ribs, cut into 2-inch pieces**

1. Finely chop the pickles and olives; set aside. In a small bowl, beat the cream cheese, Miracle Whip, juices and salt until blended. Stir in the pickles, olives and pecans.

2. Transfer to a small resealable plastic bag. Cut a small hole in the corner of the bag; pipe or stuff into celery sticks. Store in the refrigerator.

BREAKFAST & BRUNCH

Overnight Raisin French Toast

This recipe came from a colleague years ago and has become a potluck, brunch and family favorite! My staff used to ask for it every holiday. I love the convenience of great make-ahead recipes and this is one I turn to all the time. I like to sprinkle it with cinnamon and sugar when removing it from the oven.

—STEPHANIE WEAVER SLIGO, PENNSYLVANIA

YIELD: 12 SERVINGS.

- 1 loaf (1 pound) cinnamon-raisin bread, cubed
- 1 package (8 ounces) cream cheese, cubed
- 8 eggs, lightly beaten
- 1½ cups half-and-half cream
- ½ cup sugar
- ½ cup maple syrup
- 2 tablespoons vanilla extract
- 1 tablespoon ground cinnamon
- ⅛ teaspoon ground nutmeg

1. Place half of the bread cubes in a greased 13-in. x 9-in. baking dish. Top with cream cheese and remaining bread.

2. In a large bowl, whisk the remaining ingredients. Pour over top. Cover and refrigerate overnight.

3. Remove from the refrigerator 30 minutes before baking. Cover and bake at 350° for 30 minutes. Uncover; bake 15-20 minutes longer or until a knife inserted near the center comes out clean.

Polynesian Parfaits

Pack one of these refreshing, tropical treats in a plastic container to take with you. They're great for lunch boxes, too.
—JANICE MITCHELL AURORA, COLORADO

YIELD: 4 SERVINGS.

- 2 cups (16 ounces) pineapple yogurt
- 1 tablespoon sugar
- ⅛ teaspoon ground nutmeg
- 1 cup granola without raisins
- 1 can (11 ounces) mandarin oranges, drained
- ¾ cup unsweetened pineapple tidbits
- ⅓ cup fresh raspberries

1. Combine the yogurt, sugar and nutmeg; spoon into four dishes. Top with granola and fruit.

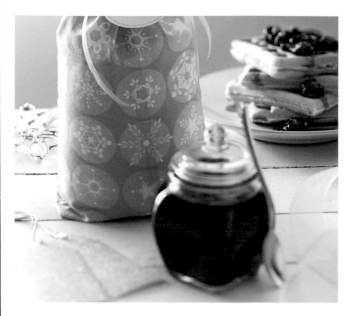

Cherry Syrup

My mom and grandma have been making this fruity syrup to serve with fluffy waffles and pancakes ever since I was a little girl. Now I make it for my sons, who love it as much as me!

—**SANDRA HARRINGTON** NIPOMO, CALIFORNIA

YIELD: 3 CUPS.

- 1 package (12 ounces) frozen pitted dark sweet cherries, thawed
- 1 cup water
- 2½ cups sugar
- 2 tablespoons butter
- ½ teaspoon almond extract
- Dash ground cinnamon

1. Bring cherries and water to a boil in a small saucepan. Reduce heat; simmer, uncovered, for 20 minutes.

2. Add sugar and butter; cook and stir until sugar is dissolved. Remove from the heat; stir in extract and cinnamon. Cool; transfer to airtight containers. Store in the refrigerator for up to 2 weeks.

Elephant Ears

Reaction from those who eat them makes them worth the effort!

—**SUZANNE MCKINLEY** LYONS, GEORGIA

YIELD: 15 SERVINGS.

- 1 package (¼ ounce) active dry yeast
- 1 cup warm water (110° to 115°)
- 1 cup warm milk (110° to 115°)
- 3 tablespoons sugar
- 1 tablespoon salt
- 3 tablespoons shortening
- 4 to 4½ cups all-purpose flour
- Oil for deep-fat frying
- GLAZE
- ½ cup sugar
- 1 teaspoon ground cinnamon

1. Dissolve yeast in water. Add milk, sugar, salt, shortening and 2 cups flour; beat until smooth. Stir in enough remaining flour to form a soft dough.

2. On a floured surface, knead until smooth and elastic, 6-8 minutes. Place in a greased bowl; turn once to grease top. Cover and let rise in a warm place until doubled, about 1 hour.

3. Punch down and shape into 15 ovals, 5½ in. round by ⅛ in. thick. Heat 3-4 in. of oil to 375° in deep-fat fryer. Fry ovals, one at a time, 3 minutes per side or until golden brown. Drain. Mix sugar and cinnamon; sprinkle over warm pastries.

Peanut Butter & Jelly Waffles

Don't count out the grown-ups when it comes to craving these golden-brown waffles flavored with peanut butter and just a sprinkling of cinnamon. These are guaranteed crowd-pleasers!

—**HELENA GEORGETTE MANN** SACRAMENTO, CALIFORNIA

YIELD: 10 WAFFLES.

- 1¼ cups all-purpose flour
- 3 tablespoons sugar
- 1 tablespoon baking powder
- ¼ teaspoon baking soda
- ¼ teaspoon ground cinnamon
- 2 eggs, separated
- 1¼ cups milk
- ⅓ cup peanut butter
- 3 tablespoons butter, melted
- Jelly of your choice

1. In a large bowl, combine the flour, sugar, baking powder, baking soda and cinnamon. In another bowl, whisk the egg yolks, milk, peanut butter and butter; stir mixture into dry ingredients just until moistened.

2. In a small bowl, beat egg whites until stiff peaks form; fold into batter. Bake in a preheated waffle iron according to manufacturer's directions until golden brown. Serve with jelly.

To freeze: Arrange waffles in a single layer on sheet pans. Freeze overnight or until frozen. Transfer to a resealable plastic freezer bag. Waffles may be frozen for up to 2 months.

To use frozen waffles: Reheat the waffles in a toaster. Serve with jelly.

Hash Brown Quiche

We love to have guests stay with us, and this is a great dish to serve for breakfast. To save time in the morning, I make the hash brown crust and chop the ham, cheese and peppers the night before.

—**JAN PETERS** CHANDLER, MINNESOTA

YIELD: 6 SERVINGS.

    3   cups frozen loose-pack shredded hash browns, thawed
    ⅓   cup butter, melted
    1   cup diced fully cooked ham
    1   cup (4 ounces) shredded cheddar cheese
    ¼   cup diced green pepper
    2   eggs
    ½   cup milk
    ½   teaspoon salt
    ¼   teaspoon pepper

1. Press hash browns between paper towel to remove excess moisture. Press onto the bottom and up the sides of an ungreased 9-in. pie plate. Drizzle with butter. Bake at 425° for 25 minutes.

2. Combine the ham, cheese and green pepper; spoon over crust. In a small bowl, beat eggs, milk, salt and pepper. Pour over all. Reduce heat to 350°; bake for 25-30 minutes or until a knife inserted near the center comes out clean. Let stand for 10 minutes before cutting.

Ambrosia Fruit

You can capture the flavor of fresh fruit any time of year with this recipe. With its combination of canned pineapple, fresh apples and flaky coconut, it's the perfect dish to rely on no matter the season.

—**MARSHA RANSOM** SOUTH HAVEN, MICHIGAN

YIELD: 6 SERVINGS.

    1   can (20 ounces) pineapple tidbits
    ¼   cup packed brown sugar
    ½   teaspoon grated orange peel
    2   medium oranges
    2   medium unpeeled apples, diced
    1   tablespoon flaked coconut

1. Drain pineapple, reserving ¼ cup juice in a saucepan, set pineapple aside. Add brown sugar and orange peel to the juice; heat until sugar dissolves. Peel and section oranges into a large bowl, reserving any juice; add the apples and pineapple. Add pineapple juice mixture and stir gently. Chill. Just before serving, sprinkle with coconut.

Feather-Light Muffins

Your family will likely gobble up these airy muffins; they won a blue ribbon at our county fair. Pretty as well as tasty, their hint of spice will brighten any breakfast.

—**SONJA BLOW** NIXA, MISSOURI

YIELD: 8-10 MUFFINS.

    ⅓   cup shortening
    ½   cup sugar
    1   egg
    1½ cups cake flour
    1½ teaspoons baking powder
    ½   teaspoon salt
    ¼   teaspoon ground nutmeg
    ½   cup milk
TOPPING
    ½   cup sugar
    1   teaspoon ground cinnamon
    ½   cup butter, melted

1. In a bowl, cream shortening, sugar and egg. Combine dry ingredients; add to creamed mixture alternately with milk. Fill greased muffin cups two-thirds full.

2. Bake at 325° for 20-25 minutes or until golden. Let cool for 3-4 minutes. Meanwhile, combine sugar and cinnamon in a small bowl. Roll warm muffins in melted butter, then in sugar mixture. Serve warm.

Cinnamon Coffee Cake

I love the excellent texture of this old-fashioned streusel-topped coffee cake. I find that everyone enjoys it. The pleasing vanilla flavor enriched by sour cream will remind you of breakfast at Grandma's!

—ELEANOR HARRIS CAPE CORAL, FLORIDA

YIELD: 16-20 SERVINGS.

1	cup butter, softened
2¾	cups sugar, divided
4	eggs
2	teaspoons vanilla extract
3	cups all-purpose flour
1	teaspoon baking soda
1	teaspoon salt
2	cups (16 ounces) sour cream
2	tablespoons ground cinnamon
½	cup chopped walnuts

1. In a large bowl, cream butter and 2 cups sugar until light and fluffy. Add eggs, one at a time, beating well after each addition. Beat in vanilla. Combine flour, baking soda and salt; add alternately with sour cream, beating just enough after each addition to keep batter smooth.

2. Spoon a third of batter into a greased 10-in. tube pan. Combine cinnamon, nuts and remaining sugar; sprinkle a third over batter in pan. Repeat layers two more times. Bake at 350° for 60-65 minutes or until a toothpick inserted near the center comes out clean. Cool for 15 minutes before removing from pan to a wire rack to cool completely.

Crunchy Granola

This crisp, lightly sweet mixture is great just eaten out of hand or as an ice cream topping. My husband and I grow wheat, barley and canola.

—LORNA JACOBSEN
ARROWWOOD, ALBERTA

YIELD: 10 CUPS.

- ⅔ cup honey
- ½ cup canola oil
- ⅓ cup packed brown sugar
- 2 teaspoons vanilla extract
- 4 cups old-fashioned oats
- 1 cup sliced almonds
- 1 cup flaked coconut
- ½ cup sesame seeds
- ½ cup salted sunflower kernels
- 2 cups raisins

1. In a small saucepan, combine the honey, oil and brown sugar; cook and stir over medium heat until sugar is dissolved. Remove from the heat; stir in vanilla.

2. In a bowl, combine oats, almonds, coconut, sesame seeds and sunflower kernels. Add honey mixture, stirring until evenly coated. Spread onto two ungreased baking pans.

3. Bake at 300° for 20 minutes, stirring frequently. Stir in the raisins. Bake 10 minutes longer. Cool, stirring occasionally. Store the granola in an airtight container.

Overnight Apple French Toast

My in-laws own and operate an orchard, so we have an abundance of fruit fresh from the trees. This dish includes fresh apples, apple jelly and applesauce all in one recipe. It's a warm, hearty breakfast for busy days.

—DEBRA BLAZER HEGINS, PENNSYLVANIA

YIELD: 9 SERVINGS.

- 1 cup packed brown sugar
- ½ cup butter, cubed
- 2 tablespoons light corn syrup
- 2 large tart apples, peeled and sliced ¼ inch thick
- 3 eggs
- 1 cup milk
- 1 teaspoon vanilla extract
- 9 slices day-old French bread (¾ inch thick)

SYRUP
- 1 cup applesauce
- 1 jar (10 ounces) apple jelly
- ½ teaspoon ground cinnamon
- ⅛ teaspoon ground cloves

1. In a small saucepan, cook brown sugar, butter and syrup until thick, about 5-7 minutes. Pour into an ungreased 13-in. x 9-in. baking pan; arrange apples on top.

2. In a large bowl, beat eggs, milk and vanilla. Soak bread slices in the egg mixture for 1 minute; place over apples. Cover and refrigerate overnight.

3. Remove from the refrigerator 30 minutes before baking. Bake, uncovered, at 350° for 35-40 minutes.

4. Meanwhile combine syrup ingredients in a medium saucepan; cook and stir until hot. Serve with French toast.

Hearty Egg Scramble

Scrambled eggs with meat and potatoes for breakfast is always a satisfying choice. Switch up the veggies to your family's liking.
—**MARSHA RANSOM** SOUTH HAVEN, MICHIGAN

YIELD: 6 SERVINGS.

- ⅓ cup chopped onion
- ¼ cup chopped green pepper
- ¼ cup butter, cubed
- 2 medium potatoes, peeled, cooked and cubed
- 1½ cups julienned fully cooked ham
- 6 eggs
- 2 tablespoons water
- Dash pepper

1. In a large skillet, saute the onion and green pepper in butter until crisp-tender. Add the potatoes and ham; cook and stir for 5 minutes.

2. In a large bowl, whisk the eggs, water and pepper; pour over ham mixture. Cook and stir over medium heat until eggs are completely set.

Sheepherder's Breakfast

My sister-in-law always made this delicious breakfast dish when we were camping. Served with toast, juice and milk or coffee, it's a sure hit with the breakfast crowd! One-dish casseroles like this were a big help while I was raising my nine children. Now I've passed this recipe on to them.
—**PAULETTA BUSHNELL** ALBANY, OREGON

YIELD: 10 SERVINGS.

- 1 pound sliced bacon, diced
- 1 medium onion, chopped
- 32 ounces frozen shredded hash brown potatoes, thawed
- 10 eggs
- Salt and pepper to taste
- 2 cups (8 ounces) shredded cheddar cheese, optional
- Chopped fresh parsley

1. In a large skillet, cook bacon and onion over medium heat until bacon is crisp. Drain all but ½ cup of the drippings. Add hash browns to skillet; mix well.

2. Cook over medium heat for 10 minutes, turning when browned. Make 10 "wells" evenly spaced in hash browns. Place one egg in each well. Sprinkle with salt and pepper. Sprinkle with cheese if desired.

3. Cover and cook over low heat for about 10 minutes or until eggs are set. Garnish with parsley; serve immediately.

Sweet Broiled Grapefruit

I was never a fan of grapefruit until I had it broiled at a Florida restaurant—it was so tangy and delicious! I finally got the recipe and now make it often for husband Ron, myself and our children and grandchildren.
—**TERRY BRAY** AUBURNDALE, FLORIDA

YIELD: 2 SERVINGS.

- 1 large grapefruit
- 2 tablespoons butter, softened
- 2 tablespoons sugar
- ½ teaspoon ground cinnamon
Maraschino cherry for garnish, optional

1. Cut each grapefruit in half. With a sharp knife, cut around the membrane in the center of each half and discard. Cut around each section to loosen fruit.

2. Place 1 tablespoon butter in the center of each half. Combine sugar and cinnamon; sprinkle over each. Place on a baking pan. Broil 4 in. from heat until butter is melted and sugar is bubbly. Garnish with a cherry if desired. Serve immediately.

Overnight Blueberry Coffee Cake

This cake, made with our own berries, stars at "Welcome to Washington" breakfasts I serve summer company.
—**MARIAN PLATT** SEQUIM, WASHINGTON

YIELD: 9 SERVINGS.

- 1 egg
- ½ cup plus 2 tablespoons sugar, divided
- 1¼ cups all-purpose flour
- 2 teaspoons baking powder
- ¾ teaspoon salt
- ⅓ cup milk
- 3 tablespoons butter, melted
- 1 cup fresh blueberries

1. In a bowl, beat egg and ½ cup sugar. Combine flour, baking powder and salt; add alternately with milk to sugar mixture, beating well after each addition. Stir in butter. Fold in berries.

2. Pour batter into greased 8-in. square baking pan; sprinkle with the remaining sugar. Cover and chill overnight. Remove from the refrigerator 30 minutes before baking. Bake at 350° for 30-35 minutes.

Stuffed Apricot French Toast

In our family, this special recipe is often served for our Christmas Day brunch. I was always looking for something unique to serve, and this rich, colorful dish made my dreams come true. It tastes so good!

—DEB LELAND THREE RIVERS, MICHIGAN

YIELD: 8 SERVINGS.

- 1 **package (8 ounces) cream cheese, softened**
- 1½ **teaspoons vanilla extract, divided**
- ½ **cup finely chopped walnuts**
- 1 **loaf (1½ pounds) French bread**
- 4 **eggs**
- 1 **cup heavy whipping cream**
- ½ **teaspoon ground nutmeg**
- 1 **jar (12 ounces) apricot preserves**
- ½ **cup orange juice**

1. In a bowl, beat cream cheese and 1 teaspoon vanilla until fluffy. Stir in nuts; set aside.

2. Cut bread into 1½-in. slices; cut a pocket in the top of each slice. Fill each pocket with about 2 tablespoons cream cheese mixture. In another bowl, beat eggs, cream, nutmeg and remaining vanilla. Dip both sides of bread into egg mixture, being careful not to squeeze out the filling.

3. Cook on a lightly greased griddle until lightly browned on both sides. Place on an ungreased baking sheet; bake at 325° for 15-20 minutes or until a knife inserted near the middle comes out clean.

4. Meanwhile, combine preserves and orange juice in a small saucepan; heat through. Drizzle over hot French toast.

Sausage Gravy

This savory sausage gravy is a specialty among country folks in our area. It's best served over fresh, hot biscuits. It makes a real "stick to the ribs" dish that we always enjoy, and carries a traditional flavor that can showcase locally produced sausage.

—MRS. J. N. STINE ROANOKE, VIRGINIA

YIELD: 4-6 SERVINGS.

- 1 **pound sage-flavored bulk pork sausage**
- 2 **tablespoons finely chopped onion**
- 6 **tablespoons all-purpose flour**
- 1 **quart milk**
- ½ **teaspoon poultry seasoning**
- ½ **teaspoon ground nutmeg**
- ¼ **teaspoon salt**

Dash Worcestershire sauce
Dash hot pepper sauce
Biscuits

1. Crumble sausage into a large saucepan; cook over medium-low heat. Add onion; cook and stir until transparent. Drain, discarding all but 2 tablespoons of drippings.

2. Stir in flour; cook over medium-low heat about 6 minutes or until mixture bubbles and turns golden. Stir in milk. Add seasonings; cook, stirring, until thickened.

3. To serve, slice biscuits and spoon gravy over halves.

Oh-So-Good Oatmeal

Add extra nutrition to fiber-rich oatmeal by adding chopped apple with the peel and chopped almonds. My two boys demand seconds! At 1½ cups per serving, it's hearty and filling; and at zero cholesterol, what's not to love?
—**DANIELLE PEPA** ELGIN, ILLINOIS

YIELD: 4 SERVINGS.

　3　**cups water**
　2　**medium tart apples, chopped**
1½　**cups old-fashioned oats**
Dash salt
　¼　**cup packed brown sugar**
　½　**teaspoon ground cinnamon**
　½　**teaspoon vanilla extract**
　¼　**cup chopped almonds**
**Maple syrup and/or fat-free milk,
　optional**

1. In a large saucepan over medium heat, bring water to a boil. Add the apples, oats and salt; cook and stir for 5 minutes.

2. Remove from the heat; stir in the brown sugar, cinnamon and vanilla. Cover and let stand for 2 minutes. Sprinkle each serving with almonds. Serve with maple syrup and/or milk if desired.

Grandma's Cinnamon Rolls

The secret to these rolls is the brown sugar sauce they're baked in. I serve them as dinner rolls as well as for a special breakfast treat.
—**DELLA TALBERT** HOWARD, COLORADO

YIELD: 15 ROLLS.

DOUGH
　1　**package (¼ ounce) active dry yeast**
　¼　**cup sugar, divided**
　1　**cup warm water (110° to 115°), divided**
　2　**tablespoons butter, softened**
　1　**egg**
　1　**teaspoon salt**
3¼　**to 3¾ cups all-purpose flour**
TOPPING
　1　**cup heavy whipping cream**
　1　**cup packed brown sugar**
FILLING
　½　**cup sugar**
　2　**teaspoons ground cinnamon**
　½　**cup butter, softened**

1. In a large bowl, dissolve yeast and ½ teaspoon sugar in ¼ cup warm water. Let stand for 5 minutes. Add the remaining sugar and water, butter, egg, salt and 1½ cups of flour; beat until smooth. Stir in enough remaining flour to form a soft dough.

2. Turn onto a lightly floured surface; knead until smooth and elastic, about 6-8 minutes. Place in a greased bowl, turning once to grease top. Cover and let rise in a warm place until doubled, about 1 hour.

3. Meanwhile, combine topping ingredients; pour into a greased 13-in. x 9-in. baking pan; set aside. Combine filling ingredients; set aside.

4. Punch dough down and turn onto a lightly floured surface. Roll into a 15-in. x 8-in. rectangle; spread filling over dough. Roll up from the long side. Seal seam. Slice into 15 rolls; place with cut side down over topping. Cover and let rise until nearly doubled, about 30-45 minutes.

5. Bake at 375° for 25 minutes or until golden brown. Cool 3 minutes; invert pan onto a serving plate.

Cream Cheese Coffee Cake

These impressive loaves really sparkle on the buffet. You can't just eat one slice of this treat.

—MARY ANNE MCWHIRTER PEARLAND, TEXAS

YIELD: 20-24 SERVINGS.

1 cup (8 ounces) sour cream
½ cup sugar
½ cup butter, cubed
1 teaspoon salt
2 packages (¼ ounce each) active
   dry yeast
½ cup warm water (110° to 115°)
2 eggs, lightly beaten
4 cups all-purpose flour

FILLING
2 packages (8 ounces each) cream
   cheese, softened
¾ cup sugar
1 egg, lightly beaten
2 teaspoons vanilla extract
⅛ teaspoon salt

GLAZE
2½ cups confectioners' sugar
¼ cup milk
1 teaspoon vanilla extract
Toasted sliced almonds, optional

1. In a small saucepan, combine the sour cream, sugar, butter and salt. Cook over medium-low heat, stirring constantly, for 5-10 minutes or until well blended. Cool to room temperature.

2. In a large bowl, dissolve yeast in warm water. Add sour cream mixture and eggs. Beat until smooth. Gradually stir in flour to form a soft dough (dough will be very soft). Cover and refrigerate overnight.

3. Punch dough down. Turn dough onto a floured surface; knead 5-6 times. Divide into fourths. Roll each piece into a 12-in. x 8-in. rectangle. In a large bowl, combine the filling ingredients until well blended. Spread over each rectangle to within 1 in. of edges.

4. Roll up jelly-roll style, starting with a long side; pinch seams and ends to seal. Place seam side down on greased baking sheets. Cut six X's on top of loaves. Cover and let rise until nearly doubled, about 1 hour.

5. Bake at 375° for 20-25 minutes or until golden brown. Remove from pans to wire racks to cool. In a bowl, combine confectioners' sugar, milk and vanilla; drizzle over warm loaves. Sprinkle with almonds if desired. Store in the refrigerator.

Caramel-Pecan Monkey Bread

You can either cut this bread into generous slices, or let everyone pick off the gooey pieces themselves. No one can resist this tender, caramel-coated bread.

—TASTE OF HOME TEST KITCHEN

YIELD: 1 LOAF (20 SERVINGS).

- 1 package (¼ ounce) active dry yeast
- ¼ cup water (110° to 115°)
- 1¼ cups warm 2% milk (110° to 115°)
- ⅓ cup butter, melted
- ¼ cup sugar
- 2 eggs
- 1 teaspoon salt
- 5 cups all-purpose flour

CARAMEL
- ⅔ cup packed brown sugar
- ¼ cup butter, cubed
- ¼ cup heavy whipping cream

ASSEMBLY
- ¾ cup chopped pecans
- 1 cup sugar
- 1 teaspoon ground cinnamon
- ½ cup butter, melted

1. In a large bowl, dissolve yeast in warm water. Add the milk, butter, sugar, eggs, salt and 3 cups flour. Beat on medium speed for 3 minutes. Stir in enough of the remaining flour to form a firm dough.

2. Turn onto a floured surface; knead until smooth and elastic, about 6-8 minutes. Place in a greased bowl, turning once to grease the top. Cover and refrigerate overnight.

3. For caramel, in a small saucepan, bring the brown sugar, butter and cream to a boil. Cook and stir for 3 minutes. Pour half into a greased 10-in. fluted tube pan; sprinkle with half of the pecans.

4. Punch dough down; shape into 40 balls (about 1¼-in. diameter). In a shallow bowl, combine sugar and cinnamon. Place melted butter in another bowl. Dip balls in butter, then roll in sugar mixture.

5. Place 20 balls in the tube pan; top with remaining caramel and pecans. Top with remaining balls. Cover and let rise until doubled, about 45 minutes.

6. Bake at 350° for 30-35 minutes or until golden brown. (Cover loosely with foil if top browns too quickly.) Cool for 10 minutes before inverting onto a serving plate. Serve warm.

Sweet Potato Muffins

This is my own recipe, and I make it often. My five grandchildren think these are a delicious treat.

—CHRISTINE JOHNSON RICETOWN, KENTUCKY

YIELD: 2 DOZEN.

- 2 cups self-rising flour
- 2 cups sugar
- 2 teaspoons ground cinnamon
- 1 egg
- 2 cups cold mashed sweet potatoes (without added butter or milk)
- 1 cup canola oil

GLAZE
- 1 cup confectioners' sugar
- 2 tablespoons plus 1½ teaspoons 2% milk
- 1½ teaspoons butter, melted
- 1 teaspoon vanilla extract
- ½ teaspoon ground cinnamon

1. In a small bowl, combine the flour, sugar and cinnamon. In another bowl, whisk the egg, sweet potatoes and oil. Stir into dry ingredients just until moistened.

2. Fill greased muffin cups two-thirds full. Bake at 375° for 15-18 minutes or until a toothpick comes out clean. Cool for 5 minutes before removing from pans to wire racks. In a small bowl, combine glaze ingredients; drizzle over warm muffins.

Editor's Note: *As a substitute for each cup of self-rising flour, place 1½ teaspoons baking powder and ½ teaspoon salt in a measuring cup. Add all-purpose flour to measure 1 cup.*

Banana Chip Pancakes

Perfect for weekends or a birthday-morning special, these fluffy pancakes can be flavor-adjusted to your heart's content! One of my kids eats the plain banana pancakes, another likes just chocolate chips added, and a third one goes for the works.

—**CHRISTEEN PRZEPIOSKI** NEWARK, CALIFORNIA

YIELD: 12 PANCAKES.

- 2 cups biscuit/baking mix
- 1 egg
- 1 cup milk
- 1 cup mashed ripe bananas
- ¾ cup swirled milk chocolate and peanut butter chips

Maple syrup and additional swirled milk chocolate and peanut butter chips, optional

1. Place biscuit mix in a large bowl. Combine the egg, milk and bananas; stir into biscuit mix just until moistened. Stir in chips.

2. Pour batter by ¼ cupfuls onto a greased hot griddle; turn when bubbles form on top. Cook until the second side is golden brown. Serve with syrup and additional chips if desired.

Sausage Hash

I created this recipe by trying to work with what I had in the refrigerator. Regular or spicy sausage can be used, and red potatoes make it more colorful.

—**KARI CAVEN** POST FALLS, IDAHO

YIELD: 2 SERVINGS.

- ½ pound bulk pork sausage
- 2½ cups cubed cooked potatoes
- 1 cup thinly sliced sweet onion
- 1 cup sliced fresh mushrooms
- 2 tablespoons butter
- ¼ teaspoon salt
- ¼ teaspoon pepper

1. In a large heavy skillet over medium heat, cook the sausage until no longer pink; drain and set aside.

2. In the same skillet, cook the potatoes, onion and mushrooms in butter until potatoes are lightly browned. Stir in the sausage, salt and pepper; heat through.

Apple Fritters

My kids love these fritters year-round, but I get even more requests in the fall when there are plenty of apples in season. I like to serve them as a special breakfast treat when they host friends for sleepovers.

—**KATIE BEECHY** SEYMOUR, MISSOURI

YIELD: 40 FRITTERS.

- 2½ cups all-purpose flour
- ½ cup nonfat dry milk powder
- ⅓ cup sugar
- 2 teaspoons baking powder
- 1 teaspoon salt
- 2 eggs
- 1 cup water
- 2 cups chopped peeled apples

Oil for deep-fat frying
Sugar

1. In a large bowl, combine first five ingredients. Whisk eggs and water; add to the dry ingredients just until moistened. Fold in apples.

2. In an electric skillet, heat oil to 375°. Drop batter by teaspoonfuls, a few at a time, in hot oil. Fry until golden brown, about 1½ minutes on each side. Drain on paper towels. Roll warm fritters in sugar. Serve warm.

Delicious Potato Doughnuts

I first tried these tasty treats at my sister's house and thought they were the best I've ever had. They're easy to make, and the fudge frosting tops them off well.

—PAT DAVIS BEULAH, MICHIGAN

YIELD: 4 DOZEN.

2 cups hot mashed potatoes (with added milk and butter)
2½ cups sugar
2 cups buttermilk
2 eggs, lightly beaten
2 tablespoons butter, melted
2 teaspoons baking soda
2 teaspoons baking powder
1 teaspoon salt
1 teaspoon ground nutmeg
6½ to 7 cups all-purpose flour
Oil for deep-fat frying
FAST FUDGE FROSTING
3¾ cups confectioners' sugar
½ cup baking cocoa

¼ teaspoon salt
⅓ cup boiling water
⅓ cup butter, melted
1 teaspoon vanilla extract

1. In a large bowl, combine the potatoes, sugar, buttermilk and eggs. Stir in the butter, baking soda, baking powder, salt, nutmeg and enough of the flour to form a soft dough. Turn onto a lightly floured surface; pat out to ¾-in. thickness. Cut with a 2½-in. floured doughnut cutter.

2. In an electric skillet, heat 1 in. of oil to 375°. Fry the doughnuts for 2 minutes on each side or until browned. Place on paper towels.

3. For frosting, combine the confectioners' sugar, cocoa and salt in a large bowl. Stir in the water, butter and vanilla. Dip tops of warm doughnuts in frosting.

Spinach Bacon Quiche

My versatile dish fits nicely into a menu for brunch or supper.
The colorful pie slices easily.

—**LOIS SUNDHEIM** FAIRVIEW, MONTANA

YIELD: 6 SERVINGS.

- 4 eggs
- 2 cups milk
- 1¼ cups shredded cheddar cheese, divided
- ¼ cup finely chopped onion
- 4 bacon strips, cooked and crumbled
- ½ teaspoon salt
- ½ teaspoon ground mustard
- ¼ teaspoon paprika
- 1 package (10 ounces) frozen chopped spinach, cooked and drained
- 1 unbaked pastry shell (9 inches)

1. In a large bowl, beat eggs; whisk in milk, 1 cup cheese, onion, bacon, salt, mustard and paprika. Add spinach. Pour into pie shell. Sprinkle with the remaining cheese. Bake at 400° for 40 minutes or until a knife inserted halfway between the center and the edge comes out clean.

Jellied Biscuits

These biscuits are a pleasure to serve because they look so lovely with the colorful jelly.

—**MARSHA RANSOM** SOUTH HAVEN, MICHIGAN

YIELD: ABOUT 1 DOZEN.

- 2 cups all-purpose flour
- 4 teaspoons baking powder
- 2 teaspoons sugar
- ½ teaspoon salt
- ½ teaspoon cream of tartar
- ½ cup shortening
- ¾ cup milk
- ⅓ cup jelly

1. In a bowl, combine the flour, baking powder, sugar, salt and cream of tartar. Cut in shortening until the mixture resembles coarse crumbs. Add milk; stir quickly with a fork just until mixed. Drop by rounded tablespoonfuls onto a greased baking sheet. Make a deep thumbprint in tops; fill each with 1 teaspoon of jelly. Bake at 450° for 10-12 minutes or until browned.

Scrambled Egg Casserole

There's nothing nicer than a delicious egg dish you can prepare the night before so you're not "scrambling" when guests arrive. With satisfying ingredients like ham and a creamy cheese sauce, this dish is really special.

—**MARY ANNE MCWHIRTER** PEARLAND, TEXAS

YIELD: 6-8 SERVINGS.

- ½ cup butter, divided
- 2 tablespoons all-purpose flour
- ½ teaspoon salt
- ⅛ teaspoon pepper
- 2 cups milk
- 1 cup (4 ounces) shredded process American cheese
- 1 cup cubed fully cooked ham
- ¼ cup sliced green onions
- 12 eggs, beaten
- 1 jar (4 ounces) sliced mushrooms, drained
- 1½ cups soft bread crumbs

Additional sliced green onions, optional

1. In a large saucepan, melt 2 tablespoons butter. Whisk in the flour, salt and pepper until smooth. Gradually stir in milk. Bring to a boil. Cook and stir for 2 minutes or until thickened and bubbly. Remove from the heat. Stir in cheese; set aside.

2. In a large skillet, saute the ham and onions in 3 tablespoons butter until onions are tender. Add eggs; cook and stir until eggs are almost set. Stir in mushrooms and cheese sauce. Transfer to a greased 11-in. x 7-in. baking dish. Melt remaining butter; toss with bread crumbs. Sprinkle over top. Cover and refrigerate for 2-3 hours or overnight.

3. Remove from the refrigerator 30 minutes before baking. Bake, uncovered, at 350° for 25-30 minutes or until top is golden brown. Sprinkle with additional green onions if desired.

Buttermilk Pecan Waffles

I like cooking with buttermilk. These nutty, golden waffles are my husband's favorite breakfast, so we enjoy them often. They're as easy to prepare as regular waffles, but their unique taste makes them exceptional.
—**EDNA HOFFMAN** HEBRON, INDIANA

YIELD: 7 WAFFLES
(ABOUT 8 INCHES EACH).

- 2 **cups all-purpose flour**
- 1 **tablespoon baking powder**
- 1 **teaspoon baking soda**
- ½ **teaspoon salt**
- 4 **eggs**
- 2 **cups buttermilk**
- ½ **cup butter, melted**
- 3 **tablespoons chopped pecans**

1. In a large bowl, combine the flour, baking powder, baking soda and salt; set aside.

2. In a large bowl, beat eggs until light. Add buttermilk; mix well. Add dry ingredients and beat until batter is smooth. Stir in butter.

3. Pour about ¾ cup batter onto a lightly greased preheated waffle iron. Sprinkle with a few pecans. Bake according to the manufacturer's directions until golden brown. Repeat until batter and pecans are gone.

Ham 'n' Cheese Pie

There's no need to make a crust for this delicious and easy quiche. My family and friends love it for dinner, brunch or any other time.
—**IRIS POSEY** ALBANY, GEORGIA

YIELD: 6-8 SERVINGS.

- 1 **cup diced fully cooked ham**
- ¾ **cup shredded Swiss cheese**
- 5 **bacon strips, cooked and crumbled**
- ¾ **cup shredded sharp cheddar cheese**
- 3 **tablespoons chopped onion**
- 3 **tablespoons chopped green pepper**
- 1 **cup milk**
- ¼ **cup biscuit/baking mix**
- 2 **eggs**
- ¼ **teaspoon salt**
- ⅛ **teaspoon pepper**

1. In a greased 10-in. quiche dish or pie plate, layer the ham, Swiss cheese, bacon, cheddar cheese, onion and green pepper. Place remaining ingredients in blender in the order given; cover and process for 35-40 seconds. Pour over the meat, cheese and vegetables; do not stir.

2. Bake, uncovered at 350° for 30-35 minutes or until set and lightly browned. Let stand for 5 minutes before cutting.

Quiche Lorraine

Ideal for a brunch or luncheon, this classic recipe highlights a delicious meal. Try serving a wedge with fresh fruit of the season and homemade muffins for a plate that will look as good as the food tastes!

—**MARCY CELLA** L'ANSE, MICHIGAN

YIELD: 6 SERVINGS.

CRUST
- 2 **cups sifted all-purpose flour**
- ½ **teaspoon salt**
- ¾ **cup butter-flavored shortening**
- 3 **to 4 tablespoons cold water**

FILLING
- 12 **bacon strips, cooked and crumbled**
- 4 **eggs**
- 2 **cups half-and-half cream**
- ¼ **teaspoon salt**
- ⅛ **teaspoon ground nutmeg**
- 1¼ **cups shredded Swiss cheese**

1. Combine flour and salt in a bowl. Cut in shortening with a pastry blender until mixture resembles coarse crumbs. Add water, a little at a time, until dough comes away from the bowl. Form dough into a ball. Divide in half.

2. On a lightly floured surface, roll half of dough to fit a 9-in. pie plate; transfer to pie plate. Trim and flute edges. Chill. Wrap remaining dough; chill or freeze for another use.

3. For filling, sprinkle crumbled bacon into the chilled pie crust. In a bowl, beat eggs, cream, salt and nutmeg. Stir in cheese. Pour into crust.

4. Bake at 425° for 15 minutes. Reduce temperature to 325°; continue to bake for 30 to 40 minutes or until a knife inserted near the center comes out clean. Let stand 10 minutes before cutting.

Zucchini Scramble

I like this recipe because I can change it through the year as other fresh vegetables become available. It also makes a tasty light lunch or dinner.

—**BETTY CLAYCOMB**
ALVERTON, PENNSYLVANIA

YIELD: 4-6 SERVINGS.

- 2 **to 3 small zucchini (about 1 pound), sliced**
- 1 **medium onion, chopped**
- 2 **tablespoons butter**

Salt and pepper to taste
- 6 **to 8 eggs, beaten**
- ½ **cup shredded cheddar cheese**

Tomato wedges, optional

1. In a skillet, saute zucchini and onion in butter until tender. Season with salt and pepper. Add the eggs; cook and stir until set. Sprinkle with cheese. Remove from the heat; cover until cheese melts. Serve with tomato wedges if desired.

Apple-Topped Oatcakes

During the week we have quick breakfasts, but on Saturday I like to make something special. This is one of our favorite recipes because the oatcakes and apple topping are a tasty, wholesome combination. They also can be made ahead so a hungry family doesn't have to wait long.

—LOIS HOFMEYER AURORA, ILLINOIS

YIELD: 6-8 SERVINGS.

- 1½ cups hot milk
- ¾ cup old-fashioned oats
- 1 egg, lightly beaten
- 2 tablespoons canola oil
- 2 tablespoons molasses
- 1 cup all-purpose flour
- 1½ teaspoons baking powder
- ¾ teaspoon ground cinnamon
- ¼ teaspoon ground ginger
- ¼ teaspoon baking soda
- ¼ teaspoon salt
- 3 egg whites

LEMON APPLES

- 2 tablespoons butter
- 5 medium tart apples, peeled and sliced
- 1 tablespoon lemon juice
- 1 teaspoon grated lemon peel
- ½ cup sugar
- 1 tablespoon cornstarch
- ⅛ teaspoon ground nutmeg

1. In a large bowl, combine milk and oats; let stand for 5 minutes. Stir in the egg, oil and molasses. Combine dry ingredients; stir into oat mixture just until moistened. Beat egg whites until soft peaks form; fold gently into batter. Set aside.

2. Heat the butter in a skillet until foamy. Add the apples, lemon juice and peel; cook, uncovered, for 8-10 minutes, stirring occasionally.

3. Meanwhile, cook oatcakes. Pour batter by ¼ cupfuls onto a hot greased griddle. Cook until bubbles form; turn and cook until browned on other side.

4. For apples, combine sugar, cornstarch and nutmeg; add to apple mixture and cook 2 minutes longer or until tender. Serve warm over oatcakes.

Breakfast Biscuit Cups

The first time I made these biscuit cups, my husband and his assistant basketball coach came in as I was pulling them out of the oven. They loved them!

—DEBRA CARLSON COLUMBUS JUNCTION, IOWA

YIELD: 8 SERVINGS.

- ⅓ pound bulk pork sausage
- 1 tablespoon all-purpose flour
- ⅛ teaspoon salt
- ½ teaspoon pepper, divided
- ¾ cup plus 1 tablespoon 2% milk, divided
- ½ cup frozen cubed hash brown potatoes, thawed
- 1 tablespoon butter
- 2 eggs
- ⅛ teaspoon garlic salt
- 1 can (16.3 ounces) large refrigerated flaky biscuits
- ½ cup shredded Colby-Monterey Jack cheese

1. In a large skillet, cook sausage over medium heat until no longer pink; drain. Stir in the flour, salt and ¼ teaspoon pepper until blended; gradually add ¾ cup milk. Bring to a boil; cook and stir for 2 minutes or until thickened. Remove from the heat and set aside.

2. In another large skillet over medium heat, cook potatoes in butter until tender. Whisk the eggs, garlic salt and remaining milk and pepper; add to skillet. Cook and stir until almost set.

3. Press each biscuit onto the bottom and up the sides of eight ungreased muffin cups. Spoon the egg mixture, half of the cheese and sausage into cups; sprinkle with remaining cheese.

4. Bake at 375° for 18-22 minutes or until golden brown. Cool for 5 minutes before removing from pan. Serve immediately or allow to cool completely. Tightly wrap individual biscuit cups in foil; freeze for up to 3 months.

To use one frozen biscuit cup: Unwrap; microwave on high for 50-60 seconds or until heated through.

Pork Patties

These patties provide a taste bud wake-up call with a variety of herbs and spices. To save some time, combine all the seasonings the night before, then stir in the ground pork just before frying in the morning.

—LOIS FETTING NELSON, WISCONSIN

YIELD: 6 SERVINGS.

- 1 pound lean ground pork
- 2 tablespoons water
- 1½ teaspoons salt
- ½ teaspoon dried sage
- ¼ teaspoon pepper
- ¼ teaspoon ground nutmeg
- ¼ teaspoon dried thyme

Pinch of ground ginger

1. In a bowl, combine all of the ingredients; mix well. Shape into six patties. Fry in a skillet until meat is browned and cooked through.

Breakfast Bread Pudding

I assemble this dish the day before our grandchildren visit. It gives me more time for fun with them!

—ALMA ANDREWS LIVE OAK, FLORIDA

YIELD: 6-8 SERVINGS.

- 12 slices white bread
- 1 package (8 ounces) cream cheese, cubed
- 12 eggs
- 2 cups milk
- ⅓ cup maple syrup
- ¼ teaspoon salt

1. Remove and discard crusts from bread; cut bread into cubes. Toss lightly with cream cheese cubes; place in a greased 13-in. x 9-in. baking pan. In a large bowl, beat eggs. Add milk, syrup and salt; mix well. Pour over bread mixture. Cover and refrigerate 8 hours or overnight.

2. Remove from refrigerator 30 minutes before baking. Bake, uncovered, at 375° for 40-45 minutes or until a knife inserted near the center comes out clean. Let stand 5 minutes before cutting.

SOUPS

Creamy Vegetable Soup

I tasted this delicious soup in a restaurant, and when I couldn't persuade the chef to share the recipe, I began to experiment on my own. Finally, I came up with this blend, which is very close to what I'd tasted. The secret ingredient, I think, is sweet potatoes!

—**AUDREY NEMETH** MT. VERNON, MAINE

YIELD: 12-16 SERVINGS (4 QUARTS).

- 1 **large onion, chopped**
- ¼ **cup butter**
- 3 **medium sweet potatoes, peeled and chopped**
- 3 **medium zucchini, chopped**
- 1 **bunch broccoli, chopped**
- 2 **cartons (32 ounces each) chicken broth**
- 2 **medium potatoes, peeled and shredded**
- 1 **teaspoon celery seed**
- 1 **to 2 teaspoons ground cumin**
- 2 **teaspoons salt**
- 1 **teaspoon pepper**
- 2 **cups half-and-half cream**

1. In a stockpot, saute onion in butter until transparent but not browned. Add the sweet potatoes, zucchini and broccoli; saute lightly for 5 minutes or until crisp-tender. Stir in the broth; simmer for a few minutes. Add the potatoes and seasonings; cook 10 minutes longer or until the vegetables are tender. Stir in the cream and heat through.

Three-Bean Soup

When I was growing up, my mother prepared many different soups, each seasoned just right. She often made this colorful combination that's chock-full of harvest-fresh goodness. It showcases an appealing assortment of beans, potatoes, carrots and spinach.

—**VALERIE LEE** SNELLVILLE, GEORGIA

YIELD: 12 SERVINGS (ABOUT 3 QUARTS).

- 1 **medium onion, chopped**
- 1 **tablespoon canola oil**
- 3 **small potatoes, peeled and cubed**
- 2 **medium carrots, sliced**
- 3 **cans (14½ ounces each) chicken or vegetable broth**
- 3 **cups water**
- 2 **tablespoons dried parsley flakes**
- 2 **teaspoons dried basil**
- 1 **teaspoon dried oregano**
- 1 **garlic clove, minced**
- ½ **teaspoon pepper**
- 1 **can (15½ ounces) great northern beans, rinsed and drained**
- 1 **can (15 ounces) pinto beans, rinsed and drained**
- 1 **can (15 ounces) garbanzo beans or chickpeas, rinsed and drained**
- 3 **cups chopped fresh spinach**

1. In a Dutch oven, saute onion in oil. Add the next nine ingredients. Simmer, uncovered, until vegetables are tender. Add beans and spinach; heat through.

Italian-Style Onion Soup

On a chilly winter's day, warm everyone from head to toe with a steaming pot of this veggie soup. Each bowlful is crowned with a slice of cheesy tomato-topped toast.

—**DEBBIE MILLER** OLDSMAR, FLORIDA

YIELD: 5 SERVINGS.

- 2 tablespoons butter
- 1 tablespoon olive oil
- 6 medium sweet onions, thinly sliced (about 6 cups)
- ½ teaspoon minced fresh rosemary
- ¼ teaspoon salt, divided
- ¼ teaspoon pepper, divided
- 6 cups beef broth
- ½ cup white wine or additional beef broth
- 1 tablespoon balsamic vinegar
- 1 cup grape tomatoes, quartered
- ½ cup fresh basil leaves, thinly sliced
- ¼ cup grated Parmesan cheese
- ½ teaspoon garlic powder
- 5 slices day-old French bread (1½ inches thick), toasted
- 5 slices part-skim mozzarella cheese

1. In a Dutch oven over medium heat, melt butter with the oil. Add the onions, rosemary, ⅛ teaspoon salt and ⅛ teaspoon pepper. Cook for 30 minutes or until lightly browned, stirring occasionally. Add the broth, wine and vinegar; heat through.

2. Meanwhile, in a small bowl, combine the tomatoes, basil, Parmesan cheese, garlic powder and remaining salt and pepper. Spoon tomato mixture over bread slices; top with mozzarella. Place on a baking sheet.

3. Broil 3-4 in. from the heat for 2-3 minutes or until the cheese is melted. Ladle the soup into bowls; top with toast. Serve immediately.

Tomato Soup with Cheese Tortellini

Tortellini gives this garden-fresh tomato soup an extra stick-to-your-ribs bonus. It's a staple on my family's table.

—**SUSAN PECK** REPUBLIC, MISSOURI

YIELD: 8 SERVINGS (2 QUARTS).

- 1 large onion, chopped
- 1 tablespoon butter
- 2 pounds plum tomatoes, seeded and quartered
- 3 cups reduced-sodium chicken broth or vegetable broth
- 1 can (8 ounces) tomato sauce
- 1 tablespoon minced fresh basil
- ¼ teaspoon salt

Dash pepper
- 1 cup dried cheese tortellini
- ⅓ cup shredded Parmesan cheese

1. In a large saucepan, saute the onion in butter until tender. Add the tomatoes, broth, tomato sauce, basil, salt and pepper. Bring to a boil. Reduce heat; cover and simmer for 30 minutes. Cool slightly.

2. Cook tortellini according to package directions; drain well and set aside. In a blender, cover and process soup in batches until smooth. Return to the saucepan; add tortellini and heat through. Garnish with cheese.

Country Italian Soup

My mom gave me this recipe a few years back, and it quickly became a family favorite. It's so rustic and flavorful, and loaded with veggies.

—**KIM L'HOTE** VIOLA, WISCONSIN

YIELD: 10 SERVINGS (2½ QUARTS).

- 1 pound bulk Italian sausage
- 1 large onion, sliced
- 2 celery ribs, sliced
- 2 garlic cloves, minced
- 5 cups water
- 2 medium potatoes, peeled and chopped
- 1 can (14½ ounces) diced tomatoes, undrained
- 2 medium carrots, sliced
- 2 teaspoons salt
- 1 teaspoon dried basil
- 1 teaspoon dried thyme
- ½ teaspoon dried oregano
- ½ teaspoon pepper
- ¼ teaspoon cayenne pepper, optional
- 1 bay leaf
- 2 medium zucchini, sliced

1. In a Dutch oven, cook the sausage, onion and celery over medium heat until meat is no longer pink; drain. Add garlic; cook 1 minute longer.

2. Add the water, potatoes, tomatoes, carrots and seasonings. Bring to a boil. Reduce heat; cover and simmer for 15 minutes. Stir in the zucchini; simmer 8-10 minutes longer or until the vegetables are tender. Discard the bay leaf.

Cheesy Chicken Chowder

I like to serve this hearty chowder with garlic bread and a salad. It's a wonderful dish to prepare when company drops in. The rich, mild flavor and tender chicken and vegetables appeal even to children and picky eaters.

—**HAZEL FRITCHIE** PALESTINE, ILLINOIS

YIELD: 6-8 SERVINGS.

- 3 cups chicken broth
- 2 cups diced peeled potatoes
- 1 cup diced carrots
- 1 cup diced celery
- ½ cup diced onion
- 1½ teaspoons salt
- ¼ teaspoon pepper
- ¼ cup butter, cubed
- ⅓ cup all-purpose flour
- 2 cups milk
- 2 cups (about 8 ounces) shredded cheddar cheese
- 2 cups diced cooked chicken

1. In a 4-quart saucepan, bring chicken broth to a boil. Reduce heat; add the potatoes, carrots, celery, onion, salt and pepper. Cover and simmer for 12-15 minutes or until vegetables are tender.

2. Meanwhile, melt butter in a medium saucepan; stir in flour until smooth. Gradually stir in the milk. Bring to a boil over medium heat; cook and stir for 2 minutes or until thickened. Reduce heat; add cheese, stirring until melted; add to broth along with chicken. Cook and stir until heated through.

Chicken Soup with Spaetzle

Here's a new and interesting twist to traditional chicken soup. Everyone who samples it can't resist the delicious soup paired with homemade spaetzle.
—**ELAINE LANGE** GRAND RAPIDS, MICHIGAN

YIELD: 8-10 SERVINGS (2 ½ QUARTS).

- 1 broiler/fryer chicken (2 to 3 pounds), cut into pieces
- 2 tablespoons canola oil
- 8 cups chicken broth
- 2 bay leaves
- ½ teaspoon dried thyme
- ¼ teaspoon pepper
- 1 cup sliced carrots
- 1 cup sliced celery
- ¾ cup chopped onion
- 1 garlic clove, minced
- ⅓ cup medium pearl barley
- 2 cups sliced fresh mushrooms

SPAETZLE
- 1¼ cups all-purpose flour
- ⅛ teaspoon baking powder
- ⅛ teaspoon salt
- 1 egg, lightly beaten
- ¼ cup water
- ¼ cup 2% milk

1. In a stockpot or Dutch oven, brown chicken pieces in oil. Add the broth, bay leaves, thyme and pepper. Bring to a boil; skim foam. Reduce heat; cover and simmer for 45-60 minutes or until chicken is tender. Remove chicken and set aside until cool enough to handle. Remove meat from bones; discard bones and skin and cut chicken into bite size pieces. Cool broth and skim off fat.

2. Return chicken to broth along with the carrots, celery, onion, garlic and barley. Bring to a boil. Reduce heat; cover and simmer for 35 minutes. Add mushrooms and simmer 8-10 minutes longer. Discard bay leaves.

3. In a small bowl, combine first three spaetzle ingredients. Stir in the egg, water and milk; blend well. Drop batter by ½ teaspoonfuls into simmering soup. Cook for 10 minutes.

French Onion Soup

I adapted a basic recipe to copy the onion soup served at my favorite restaurant. No matter what my entree, I always ordered the soup. Now I can make it at home. It can be a meal in itself or an impressive beginning to a full-course meal.
—**BARBARA BRUNNER**
STEELTON, PENNSYLVANIA

YIELD: 2 SERVINGS.

- 2 medium onions, chopped
- 1 teaspoon sugar
- 6 tablespoons butter, divided
- 1 tablespoon all-purpose flour
- ⅛ teaspoon pepper
- Dash ground nutmeg
- 2½ cups beef or vegetable broth
- 2 tablespoons grated Parmesan cheese
- 2 slices French bread (1 inch thick)
- 4 slices provolone cheese

1. In a large saucepan, saute onions and sugar in 3 tablespoons of butter until golden brown. Stir in the flour, pepper and nutmeg until blended. Gradually stir in the broth. Bring to a boil; cook and stir for 2 minutes. Reduce heat; cover and simmer for 30 minutes. Stir in Parmesan cheese.

2. Meanwhile, in a large skillet, melt remaining butter; add bread. Cook until golden brown on both sides. Ladle soup into two oven-proof bowls. Place a slice of cheese in each bowl; top with bread and remaining cheese. Bake at 375° for 10 minutes or until the cheese is bubbly.

Gnocchi Chicken Minestrone

My Italian heritage—and my mother, who was an excellent soup maker—inspired my take on minestrone. Using frozen gnocchi saves time and adds extra heartiness to this chunky soup.

—BARBARA ESTABROOK RHINELANDER, WISCONSIN

YIELD: 8 SERVINGS (2¾ QUARTS).

1¼ pounds chicken tenderloins, cut into ½-inch pieces
¾ teaspoon dried oregano
¼ teaspoon salt
¼ teaspoon pepper
2 tablespoons olive oil, divided
1 each small green, sweet red and yellow peppers, finely chopped
1 medium zucchini, finely chopped
1 cup chopped fresh baby portobello mushrooms
⅓ cup chopped red onion
⅓ cup chopped prosciutto or deli ham
4 garlic cloves, minced
2 cans (14½ ounces each) chicken broth
1 can (14½ ounces) Italian diced tomatoes, undrained
¾ cup canned white kidney or cannellini beans, rinsed and drained
½ cup frozen peas
3 tablespoons tomato paste
1 package (16 ounces) potato gnocchi
½ cup shredded Asiago cheese
8 fresh basil leaves, thinly sliced

1. Sprinkle chicken with oregano, salt and pepper. In a Dutch oven, saute chicken in 1 tablespoon oil until no longer pink. Remove from the pan and set aside.

2. In the same pan, cook the peppers, zucchini, mushrooms and onion in remaining oil until tender. Add prosciutto and garlic; cook 1 minute longer. Add the broth, tomatoes, beans, peas, tomato paste and chicken. Bring to a boil. Reduce heat; simmer, uncovered, for 20 minutes, stirring occasionally.

3. Meanwhile, cook gnocchi according to package directions. Drain; stir into the soup. Garnish each serving with cheese and basil.

Editor's Note: *Look for potato gnocchi in the pasta or frozen foods section.*

Italian Wedding Soup

You don't have to be Italian to love this easy-to-make soup! I find it's very popular when I serve it, and makes a great meal with hot crusty Italian bread or garlic bread.

—MARY SHEETZ CARMEL, INDIANA

YIELD: 9 SERVINGS (2¼ QUARTS).

- 2 **eggs, lightly beaten**
- ½ **cup dry bread crumbs**
- ¼ **cup minced fresh parsley**
- 2 **tablespoons grated Parmesan cheese**
- 1 **tablespoon raisins, finely chopped**
- 3 **garlic cloves, minced**
- ¼ **teaspoon crushed red pepper flakes**
- ½ **pound lean ground beef (90% lean)**
- ½ **pound bulk spicy pork sausage**
- 2 **cartons (32 ounces each) reduced-sodium chicken broth**
- ½ **teaspoon pepper**
- 1½ **cups cubed rotisserie chicken**
- ⅔ **cup uncooked acini di pepe pasta**
- ½ **cup fresh baby spinach, cut into thin strips**

Shredded Parmesan cheese, optional

1. In a large bowl, combine the first seven ingredients. Crumble beef and sausage over mixture and mix well. Shape into ½-in. balls.

2. In a Dutch oven, brown the meatballs in small batches; drain. Add the broth and pepper; bring to a boil. Reduce heat; simmer, uncovered, for 10 minutes. Stir in chicken and pasta; cook 5-7 minutes longer or until pasta is tender. Stir in the spinach; cook until wilted. Sprinkle with shredded Parmesan cheese if desired.

Knoephla Soup

While I was growing up, my mom would make this traditional German soup. It tasted so good on chilly fall days. Knoephla (pronounced nip-fla) Soup is still a warm and comforting meal.

—LORRAINE MEYERS WILLOW CITY, NORTH DAKOTA

YIELD: 8-10 SERVINGS (2½ QUARTS).

- ½ **cup butter, cubed**
- 3 **medium potatoes, peeled and cubed**
- 1 **small onion, grated**
- 3 **cups milk**
- 6 **cups water**
- 6 **teaspoons chicken bouillon granules or 3 vegetable bouillon cubes**

KNOEPHLA
- 1½ **cups all-purpose flour**
- 1 **egg, beaten**
- 5 **to 6 tablespoons milk**
- ½ **teaspoon salt**

Minced fresh parsley, optional

1. In a large skillet, melt butter; cook potatoes and onion for 20-25 minutes or until tender. Add the milk; heat through but do not boil. Set aside. In a Dutch oven, bring water and bouillon to a boil.

2. Combine the first four knoephla ingredients to form a stiff dough. Roll into a ½-in. rope; cut into ¼-in. pieces. Drop into boiling broth. Reduce heat; cover and simmer for 10 minutes. Add the potato mixture; heat through. Sprinkle with parsley if desired.

Rocky Ford Chili

When my brother and sister were in grade school in little Rocky Ford, Colorado, this satisfying chili dish was served in the school cafeteria. My siblings described it to my mother so she could duplicate it at home. We all enjoy preparing it for our own families now.

—**KAREN SIKORA** PHOENIX, ARIZONA

YIELD: 4 SERVINGS.

- 2 cans (14.3 ounces each) chili with beans
- 1 package (10 ounces) frozen corn
- 4 cups corn chips
- 1 cup shredded lettuce
- 1 cup (4 ounces) shredded Mexican cheese blend
- 1 can (2¼ ounces) sliced ripe olives, drained
- ¼ cup sour cream
- ¼ cup salsa

1. In a large microwave-safe bowl, cook chili and corn on high for 2-4 minutes or until heated through. Place corn chips in four large soup bowls; top with chili mixture, lettuce, cheese, olives, sour cream and salsa.

Editor's Note: *This recipe was tested in a 1,100-watt microwave.*

Mushroom Barley Soup

Here's a hearty soup that is delicious and full of vegetables. I like to eat it with warm bread smothered in butter.

—**CONSTANCE SULLIVAN** OCEANSIDE, CALIFORNIA

YIELD: 12 SERVINGS (3 QUARTS).

- ½ cup dried great northern beans
- 1 pound sliced fresh mushrooms
- 2 cups chopped onions
- 1 medium leek (white portion only), sliced
- 2 tablespoons butter
- 1 to 2 garlic cloves, minced
- 2 cartons (32 ounces each) chicken broth
- 3 celery ribs, thinly sliced
- 3 large carrots, chopped
- ½ cup medium pearl barley
- 2 teaspoons dried parsley flakes
- 1½ teaspoons salt
- 1 bay leaf
- ¼ teaspoon white pepper

1. Soak beans according to package directions. In a large skillet, cook the mushrooms, onions and leek in butter over medium heat until tender. Add garlic; cook 1 minute longer.

2. Transfer to a 6-quart slow cooker. Drain and rinse beans, discarding liquid. Add the beans, broth, celery, carrots, barley, parsley, salt, bay leaf and pepper. Cover and cook on low for 5-6 hours or until beans and vegetables are tender. Discard bay leaf.

Mulligatawny Soup

I learned to cook and bake from my mom and grandmother, and always try to use fresh fruits, vegetables and herbs. This is a delicious and satisfying soup, which I make with leftover chicken, turkey and sometimes beef, pork or lamb. My family enjoys this on a crisp fall or winter day.

—MARY ANN MARINO WEST PITTSBURGH, PENNSYLVANIA

YIELD: 8 SERVINGS (2 QUARTS).

- 1 carton (32 ounces) chicken broth
- 1 can (14½ ounces) diced tomatoes
- 2 cups cubed cooked chicken
- 1 large tart apple, peeled and chopped
- ¼ cup finely chopped onion
- ¼ cup chopped carrot
- ¼ cup chopped green pepper
- 1 tablespoon minced fresh parsley
- 2 teaspoons lemon juice

- 1 teaspoon salt
- 1 teaspoon curry powder
- ½ teaspoon sugar
- ¼ teaspoon pepper
- 2 whole cloves

1. In a 3- or 4-qt. slow cooker, combine all ingredients. Cover and cook on low for 6-8 hours or until vegetables are tender. Discard cloves.

Hearty Minestrone

Packed with sausage and veggies, this soup is not only nutritious, it's also a great way to put your garden bounty to use.

—**DONNA SMITH** FAIRPORT, NEW YORK

YIELD: 9 SERVINGS.

- 1 pound bulk Italian sausage
- 2 cups sliced celery
- 1 cup chopped onion
- 6 cups chopped zucchini
- 1 can (28 ounces) diced tomatoes, undrained
- 1½ cups chopped green pepper
- 1½ teaspoons Italian seasoning
- 1½ teaspoons salt
- 1 teaspoon dried oregano
- 1 teaspoon sugar
- ½ teaspoon dried basil
- ¼ teaspoon garlic powder

1. In a large saucepan, cook the sausage until no longer pink. Remove with a slotted spoon to paper towel to drain, reserving 1 tablespoon of drippings. Saute celery and onion in drippings for 5 minutes. Add sausage and remaining ingredients; bring to a boil. Reduce heat; cover and simmer for 20-30 minutes or until the vegetables are tender.

Spinach Garlic Soup

During the years I owned and operated a deli, this was one of the most popular soups I served.

—**MARILYN PARADIS** WOODBURN, OREGON

YIELD: 4-6 SERVINGS.

- 1 package (10 ounces) fresh spinach, trimmed and coarsely chopped
- 4 cups chicken broth
- ½ cup shredded carrots
- ½ cup chopped onion
- 8 garlic cloves, minced
- ⅓ cup butter, cubed
- ¼ cup all-purpose flour
- ¾ cup heavy whipping cream
- ¼ cup milk
- ½ teaspoon pepper
- ⅛ teaspoon ground nutmeg

1. In a 5-qt. Dutch oven, bring spinach, broth and carrots to a boil. Reduce heat; simmer for 5 minutes, stirring occasionally. Remove from heat; cool to lukewarm.

2. Meanwhile, in a large skillet, saute the onion and garlic in butter until onion is soft, about 5-10 minutes. Add flour; cook and stir over low heat for 3-5 minutes. Add to spinach mixture. Cool slightly.

3. Puree in small batches in a blender until finely chopped. Place in a large saucepan. Add the cream, milk, pepper and nutmeg; heat through but do not boil.

Creamy Carrot Soup

When I set this creamy soup on the table, people are amazed by the bright carrot color and are hooked by the deliciously different flavor. A hint of rosemary adds a nice spark to a slightly sweet soup.

—**GRACE YASKOVIC** LAKE HIAWATHA, NEW JERSEY

YIELD: 10 SERVINGS (2½ QUARTS).

- 1 cup chopped onion
- ¼ cup butter, cubed
- 4½ cups sliced fresh carrots
- 1 large potato, peeled and cubed
- 2 cans (14½ ounces each) chicken broth
- 1 teaspoon ground ginger
- 2 cups heavy whipping cream
- 1 teaspoon dried rosemary, crushed
- ½ teaspoon salt
- ⅛ teaspoon pepper

1. In a Dutch oven, saute onion in butter until tender. Add the carrots, potato, broth and ginger. Cover and cook over medium heat for 30 minutes or until the vegetables are tender. Cool for 15 minutes.

2. In a blender, cover and puree the vegetable mixture in batches. Return all to the pan; stir in the cream, rosemary, salt and pepper. Cook over low heat until heated through.

Five-Bean Soup

One of my family's favorite soups, this tasty recipe was one I discovered years ago. Served with a salad and bread or rolls, it makes a savory supper.

—LYNNE DODD MENTOR, OHIO

YIELD: 14 SERVINGS (3½ QUARTS).

- 5 packages (16 ounces each) dried beans: lima, great northern, kidney, pinto and split peas (enough for four batches of soup)

For one batch of soup
- 3 tablespoons minced chives
- 1 teaspoon dried savory
- 1 teaspoon salt, optional
- ½ teaspoon ground cumin
- ½ teaspoon pepper
- 1 bay leaf
- 3 beef bouillon cubes
- 2½ quarts water
- 1 can (14½ ounces) stewed tomatoes

1. Combine beans; divide into four even batches, about 3¾ cups each.

To make one batch of soup:

2. Wash one batch of beans. Place in a stockpot; add enough water to cover. Bring to a boil; cook for 3-4 minutes. Remove from the heat; cover and let stand 1 hour.

3. Tie spices in a cheesecloth bag. Drain and rinse beans. Return to stockpot; add bouillon, spices and water. Bring to a boil. Reduce heat; cover and simmer 1½ hours or until beans are tender, stirring occasionally. Discard spice bag. Add tomatoes and heat through.

Mushroom and Potato Chowder

My daughter shared this delightful recipe with me. Its rich broth, big mushroom taste and medley of vegetables make this chowder a little different from ordinary mushroom soup.

—ROMAINE WETZEL
RONKS, PENNSYLVANIA

YIELD: 4-6 SERVINGS.

- ½ cup chopped onion
- ¼ cup butter, cubed
- 2 tablespoons all-purpose flour
- 1 teaspoon salt
- ½ teaspoon pepper
- 3 cups water
- 1 pound fresh mushrooms, sliced
- 1 cup chopped celery
- 1 cup diced peeled potatoes
- ½ cup chopped carrots
- 1 cup half-and-half cream
- ¼ cup grated Parmesan cheese

1. In a stockpot, saute onion in butter until tender. Add the flour, salt and pepper; stir to make a smooth paste. Gradually add the water, stirring constantly. Bring to a boil; cook and stir for 1 minute. Add the mushrooms, celery, potatoes and carrots. Reduce heat; cover and simmer for 30 minutes or until vegetables are tender. Add cream and Parmesan cheese; heat through (do not boil).

Old-World Tomato Soup

This hearty soup has been in our family for four generations, and I've never seen another recipe like it. Each spoonful brings back memories.

—LINDA PANDOLFO
EAST HADDAM, CONNECTICUT

YIELD: 16-20 SERVINGS.

- 3   quarts water
- 4   bone-in beef short ribs (2 pounds)
- 2   to 3 meaty soup bones, beef shanks or short ribs (about 2 pounds)
- 1   can (28 ounces) diced tomatoes, undrained
- 3   celery ribs, halved
- 1   large onion, quartered
- ½   cup chopped fresh parsley, divided
- 1   tablespoon salt
- 1½   teaspoons pepper
- 4   carrots, cut into 1-inch pieces
- 2   parsnips, peeled and quartered
- 2   cups (16 ounces) sour cream
- ½   cup all-purpose flour
- ½   teaspoon ground nutmeg, optional
- 1   package (8 ounces) egg noodles, cooked and drained

1. In a stockpot, combine water, ribs, soup bones, tomatoes, celery, onion, ¼ cup parsley, salt and pepper. Cover and simmer for 2 hours. Add carrots and parsnips; cover and simmer for 1 hour or until the meat and vegetables are tender.

2. With a slotted spoon, remove meat, bones and vegetables. Strain broth and skim off fat; return all but 1 cup broth to stockpot. Set reserved broth aside. Remove meat from the bones; dice and return to stockpot. Discard celery and onion. Cut parsnips, carrots and tomatoes into ½-in. pieces and return to pot. Add the remaining parsley.

3. In a large bowl, combine the sour cream, flour, nutmeg if desired and reserved broth; stir into soup. Add noodles. Cook and stir until thickened and heated through (do not boil).

Potato Cheese Soup

My father was Swiss, so cheese has been a basic food in our family as long as I can remember. With its big cheese taste, you'll want to prepare this soup often. A steaming bowl plus a salad and a slice of bread makes a wonderful light meal.

—CAROL SMITH NEW BERLIN, WISCONSIN

YIELD: 6 SERVINGS (1½ QUARTS).

- 3   medium potatoes (about 1 pound), peeled and quartered
- 1   small onion, finely chopped
- 1   cup water
- 1   teaspoon salt
- 3   cups milk
- 3   tablespoons butter, melted
- 2   tablespoons all-purpose flour
- 2   tablespoons minced fresh parsley
- ⅛   teaspoon white pepper
- 1   cup (4 ounces) shredded Swiss cheese

1. In a large saucepan, bring potatoes, onion, water and salt to a boil. Reduce heat; cover and simmer until potatoes are tender. Do not drain; mash slightly. Stir in milk.

2. Meanwhile, in a small bowl, blend the butter, flour, parsley and pepper; stir into the potato mixture. Bring to a boil over medium heat. Cook and stir for 2 minutes. Remove from the heat; add cheese and stir until almost melted.

Grandma almost always had a pot of soup simmering on the woodstove. When my brother and I came in from sledding, we'd get a bowl, and sometimes Grandma would ask all the neighbor kids in for soup. Hoboes would stop by for a bowl, too. Grandma fed her soup to anyone who was hungry, any time, day or night.

—JOE SNYDER BELLEVUE, WASHINGTON

Grandma's Chicken 'n' Dumpling Soup

I've enjoyed making this rich soup for over 40 years. Every time I serve it, I remember my grandma, who was very special to me and was known as a great cook.

—PAULETTE BALDA PROPHETSTOWN, ILLINOIS

YIELD: 12 SERVINGS (3 QUARTS).

- 1 broiler/fryer chicken (3½ to 4 pounds), cut up
- 2¼ quarts cold water
- 5 chicken bouillon cubes
- 6 whole peppercorns
- 3 whole cloves
- 1 can (10¾ ounces) condensed cream of chicken soup, undiluted
- 1 can (10¾ ounces) condensed cream of mushroom soup, undiluted
- 1½ cups chopped carrots
- 1 cup fresh or frozen peas
- 1 cup chopped celery
- 1 cup chopped peeled potatoes
- ¼ cup chopped onion
- 1½ teaspoons seasoned salt
- ¼ teaspoon pepper
- 1 bay leaf

DUMPLINGS

- 2 cups all-purpose flour
- 4 teaspoons baking powder
- 1 teaspoon salt
- ¼ teaspoon pepper
- 1 egg, beaten
- 2 tablespoons butter, melted
- ¾ to 1 cup milk

Snipped fresh parsley, optional

1. Place the chicken, water, bouillon, peppercorns and cloves in a stockpot. Cover and bring to a boil; skim foam. Reduce heat; cover and simmer 45-60 minutes or until chicken is tender. Strain broth; return to stockpot.

2. Remove chicken and set aside until cool enough to handle. Remove meat from bones; discard bones and skin and cut chicken into chunks. Cool broth and skim off fat.

3. Return chicken to stockpot with soups, vegetables and seasonings; bring to a boil. Reduce heat; cover and simmer for 1 hour. Uncover; increase heat to a gently boil. Discard bay leaf.

4. For dumplings, combine dry ingredients in a medium bowl. Stir in egg, butter and enough milk to make a moist, stiff batter. Drop by teaspoonfuls into soup. Cover and cook without lifting the lid for 18-20 minutes. Sprinkle with parsley if desired.

Vegetable Beef Soup

When we come in from playing in the snow, I serve this warming, economical soup. Because the recipe makes a lot, you'll have plenty to freeze or to share with friends.

—NANCY SODERSTROM
ROSEVILLE, MINNESOTA

YIELD: 18-20 SERVINGS (6 QUARTS).

- 1 boneless beef chuck roast (2½ to 3 pounds)
- 4 quarts water
- 1 cup medium pearl barley
- 1½ cups chopped onion
- 1½ cups chopped celery
- 1 teaspoon salt
- 1 teaspoon pepper
- 1 can (28 ounces) diced tomatoes, undrained
- 1½ cups chopped carrots
- 1 package (16 ounces) frozen mixed vegetables
- ¼ cup minced fresh parsley
- ½ teaspoon dried basil
- ¼ teaspoon dried thyme
- ¼ teaspoon garlic salt

1. Place roast in a large Dutch oven. Add the water, barley, onion, celery, salt and pepper; bring to a boil. Reduce heat; cover and simmer for 1¼ hours or until meat is tender.

2. Remove the meat; cool. Cut into bite-size pieces. Skim fat from broth. Add beef and remaining ingredients; bring to a boil. Reduce heat; cover and simmer for 45 minutes or until the vegetables are tender.

Creamy Squash Soup

I make my smooth, full-flavored soup featuring whatever winter squash is available.

—GAYLE LEWIS YUCAIPA, CALIFORNIA

YIELD: 6-8 SERVINGS.

- 3 bacon strips
- 1 cup finely chopped onion
- 2 garlic cloves, minced
- 2 cups mashed cooked winter squash
- 2 tablespoons all-purpose flour
- 1 can (12 ounces) evaporated milk, divided
- 3 cups chicken broth
- ½ teaspoon curry powder
- ½ teaspoon salt
- ¼ teaspoon pepper
- ⅛ teaspoon ground nutmeg
Sour cream, optional

1. In a large saucepan or Dutch oven, cook bacon over medium heat until crisp. Remove to paper towels; crumble and set aside. Drain all but 1 tablespoon drippings; saute onion and garlic in drippings until tender.

2. In a blender or food processor, puree squash, flour, ⅓ cup milk and onion mixture; add to pan. Add the broth, curry powder, salt, pepper, nutmeg and remaining milk; bring to a boil over medium heat. Boil for 2 minutes. Top servings with a dollop of sour cream if desired. Sprinkle with bacon.

Beef Noodle Soup

This takes minutes—but tastes like it simmered all day.

—MARGERY BRYAN MOSES LAKE, WASHINGTON

YIELD: 6-8 SERVINGS (2 QUARTS).

- 1 pound ground beef
- ½ cup chopped onion
- 2 cans (14½ ounces each) Italian stewed tomatoes
- 2 cans (10½ ounces each) beef broth
- 1 can (15 ounces) mixed vegetables, drained
- 1 teaspoon salt
- ¼ teaspoon pepper
- 1 cup uncooked medium egg noodles

1. In a Dutch oven, cook beef and onion over medium heat until meat is no longer pink; drain.

2. Add the tomatoes, broth, vegetables and seasonings. Bring to a boil; add the noodles. Reduce heat to medium-low; cover and cook for 10-15 minutes to until noodles are tender.

Scotch Broth

Early in winter, I make up big pots of this hearty soup to freeze in plastic containers. Then I can bring out one or two containers at a time. I heat the frozen soup in a saucepan on low all morning. By lunchtime, it's hot and ready to serve!

—ANN MAIN MOOREFIELD, ONTARIO

YIELD: 6-8 SERVINGS (2 QUARTS).

- 2 pounds meaty beef soup bones (beef shanks or short ribs)
- 8 cups water
- 6 whole peppercorns
- 1½ teaspoons salt
- 1 cup chopped carrots
- 1 cup chopped turnips
- 1 cup chopped celery
- ½ cup chopped onion
- ¼ cup medium pearl barley

1. In a stockpot, combine soup bones, water, peppercorns and salt. Cover and simmer for 2½ hours or until the meat comes easily off the bones.

2. Remove bones. Strain broth; cool and chill. Skim off fat. Remove meat from bones; dice. Place the meat, broth and remaining ingredients in stockpot. Bring to a boil. Reduce heat; cover and simmer about 1 hour or until vegetables and barley are tender.

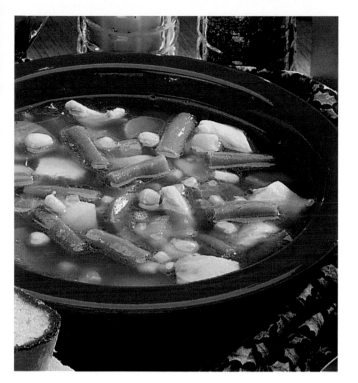

Basic Turkey Soup

I cook up a batch of this rich broth using a turkey carcass, then add my favorite vegetables and sometimes noodles to this soup.

—**KATIE KOZIOLEK** HARTLAND, MINNESOTA

YIELD: 8-10 SERVINGS.

TURKEY BROTH

- 1 leftover turkey carcass
- 8 cups water
- 1 teaspoon chicken bouillon granules
- 1 celery rib with leaves
- 1 small onion, halved
- 1 carrot
- 3 whole peppercorns
- 1 garlic clove
- 1 teaspoon seasoned salt
- 1 teaspoon dried thyme

TURKEY VEGETABLE SOUP

- 8 cups turkey broth
- 2 teaspoons chicken bouillon granules
- ½ to ¾ teaspoon pepper
- 4 cups sliced carrots, celery, green beans and/or other vegetables
- ¾ cup chopped onion
- 4 cups diced cooked turkey

1. Place all broth ingredients in a large stockpot; cover and bring to a boil. Reduce heat; simmer for 25 minutes. Strain broth; discard bones and vegetables. Cool; skim fat. Use immediately for turkey vegetable soup or refrigerate and use within 24 hours.

2. For soup, combine the broth, bouillon, pepper, vegetables and onion in a large stockpot. Cover and simmer for 15-20 minutes or until the vegetables are tender. Add turkey and heat through.

Dumpling Vegetable Soup

Fabulous rice dumplings give a homemade touch to this speedy soup that takes advantage of canned goods, frozen vegetables and dry soup mix. My mom found this to be a quick, nourishing all-in-one-pot meal, and so do I.

—**PEGGY LINTON** COBOURG, ONTARIO

YIELD: 6-8 SERVINGS (2 QUARTS).

- ½ pound ground beef
- 4 cups water
- 1 can (28 ounces) diced tomatoes, undrained
- 1 package (10 ounces) frozen mixed vegetables
- 1 envelope onion soup mix
- ½ teaspoon dried oregano
- ¼ teaspoon pepper

RICE DUMPLINGS

- 1¼ cups all-purpose flour
- 1 teaspoon baking powder
- ½ teaspoon salt
- 1 tablespoon shortening
- ⅓ cup cooked rice, room temperature
- 1 tablespoon minced fresh parsley
- 1 egg, lightly beaten
- ½ cup milk

1. In a Dutch oven, cook beef over medium heat until no longer pink; drain. Add the water, tomatoes, vegetables, soup mix, oregano and pepper; bring to a boil. Reduce heat; cover and simmer for 30-40 minutes or until the vegetables are tender.

2. For dumplings, combine the flour, baking powder and salt in a bowl. Cut in shortening until the mixture resembles coarse crumbs. Add rice and parsley; toss. In a small bowl, combine egg and milk. Stir into rice mixture just until moistened.

3. Drop the dough by teaspoonfuls onto the simmering soup. Cover and simmer for 15 minutes or until a toothpick inserted in a dumpling comes out clean (do not lift lid while simmering).

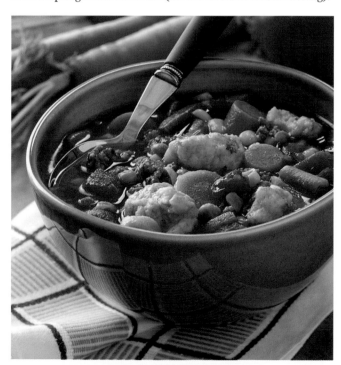

Broccoli Soup

This thick, creamy soup has wonderful broccoli flavor with just a hint of nutmeg. When it comes to broccoli recipes, this is one of my favorites.

—MARION TIPTON PHOENIX, ARIZONA

YIELD: 4 SERVINGS.

- 4 **cups chicken broth**
- 2 **to 2½ pounds fresh broccoli spears, cut into florets**
- ½ **cup chopped green onions**
- 1 **tablespoon canola oil**
- ¼ **cup all-purpose flour**
- 1 **teaspoon salt**
- ¼ **teaspoon ground nutmeg**
- ⅛ **teaspoon pepper**
- 1 **cup half-and-half cream**

1. In a large saucepan, bring broth to a boil; add broccoli. Reduce heat; cover and simmer until broccoli is tender, about 10 minutes.

2. Meanwhile, in a small skillet, saute the onions in oil until tender; stir into the broth. Remove from heat; cool 10-15 minutes. Puree soup in small batches in a blender or food processor until smooth.

3. In the saucepan, combine flour, salt, nutmeg and pepper. Slowly add cream, stirring constantly. Gradually stir in broccoli mixture. Bring to a boil over medium heat. Coook and stir for 2 minutes or until thickened.

Creamy Corn Chowder

Corn really stars in this delectable recipe—it hits the spot whenever you crave a rich, hearty soup. I make it each year for a luncheon at our church's flea market, where it's always a big seller.

—CAROL SUNDQUIST ROCHESTER, NEW YORK

YIELD: 6-8 SERVINGS (2 QUARTS).

- 2 **chicken bouillon cubes**
- 1 **cup hot water**
- 5 **bacon strips**
- 1 **cup chopped green pepper**
- ½ **cup chopped onion**
- ¼ **cup all-purpose flour**
- 3 **cups milk**
- 1½ **cups fresh or frozen whole kernel corn**
- 1 **can (14¾ ounces) cream-style corn**
- 1½ **teaspoons seasoned salt**
- ¼ **teaspoon salt**
- ⅛ **teaspoon white pepper**
- ⅛ **teaspoon dried basil**

1. Dissolve bouillon in water; set aside. In a large Dutch oven, cook bacon over medium heat until crisp. Remove bacon to paper towels to drain; crumble and set aside.

2. In a large skillet, saute green pepper and onion in the drippings until tender. Add flour; cook and stir until smooth. Gradually stir in milk and dissolved bouillon. Bring to a boil; cook and stir for 2 minutes or until thickened. Add corn and seasonings. Cook for 10 minutes or until heated through. Sprinkle with bacon.

Tomato Dill Bisque

My family really enjoys this soup when we make it from our garden tomatoes. When those tomatoes are plentiful, I make a big batch (without mayonnaise) and freeze it. Then we can enjoy it even after the garden is gone for the season.

—SUSAN BRECKBILL LINCOLN UNIVERSITY, PENNSYLVANIA

YIELD: 5 SERVINGS (5 CUPS).

- 2 medium onions, chopped
- 1 garlic clove, minced
- 2 tablespoons butter
- 2 pounds tomatoes, peeled and chopped
- ½ cup water
- 1 chicken bouillon cube
- 1 teaspoon sugar
- 1 teaspoon dill weed
- ½ teaspoon salt
- ¼ teaspoon pepper
- ½ cup mayonnaise, optional

1. In a large saucepan, saute onions and garlic in butter until tender. Add the tomatoes, water, bouillon, sugar and seasonings. Cover and simmer 10 minutes or until tomatoes are tender. Remove from heat; cool slightly.

2. Place tomato mixture in a blender, cover and process until pureed. Return to saucepan. If creamy soup is desired, stir in mayonnaise. Cook and stir over low heat until heated through. Serve warm.

Savory Cheese Soup

This delicious soup recipe was shared by a friend and instantly became a hit with my husband. Its big cheese flavor blends wonderfully with the flavor of the vegetables. I first served this creamy soup as part of a holiday meal, but now we enjoy it throughout the year.

—DEE FALK STROMSBURG, NEBRASKA

YIELD: 4 SERVINGS.

- ¼ cup chopped onion
- 3 tablespoons butter
- ¼ cup all-purpose flour
- ¼ teaspoon salt
- ⅛ teaspoon garlic powder
- ⅛ teaspoon pepper
- 2 cups 2% milk
- 1 can (14½ ounces) chicken or vegetable broth
- ½ cup shredded carrot
- ½ cup finely chopped celery
- 1½ cups (6 ounces) shredded cheddar cheese
- ¾ cup shredded part-skim mozzarella cheese

Minced chives, optional

1. In a large saucepan, saute onion in butter until tender. Add the flour, salt, garlic powder and pepper; stir until smooth. Gradually add milk; bring to a boil over medium heat. Cook and stir for 2 minutes or until thickened.

2. Meanwhile, in a small saucepan, bring broth to a boil. Add the carrot and celery; simmer for 5 minutes or until vegetables are tender. Add to the milk mixture and stir until blended. Add cheeses. Cook and stir until melted (do not boil). Garnish with chives if desired.

Hearty Potato Soup

Having grown up on a dairy farm in Holland, I love our country life here in Idaho's "potato country." My favorite potato soup originally called for heavy cream and bacon fat, but I've trimmed it down.
—**GLADYS DE BOER** CASTLEFORD, IDAHO

YIELD: 8-10 SERVINGS (ABOUT 2½ QUARTS).

- 6 **medium potatoes, peeled and sliced**
- 2 **carrots, chopped**
- 6 **celery ribs, chopped**
- 8 **cups water**
- 1 **onion, chopped**
- 6 **tablespoons butter, cubed**
- 6 **tablespoons all-purpose flour**
- 1 **teaspoon salt**
- ½ **teaspoon pepper**
- 1½ **cups 2% milk**

1. In a Dutch oven, cook the potatoes, carrots and celery in water until tender, about 15-20 minutes. Drain, reserving liquid and setting vegetables aside.

2. In the same pan, saute onion in butter until tender. Stir in the flour, salt and pepper; gradually add milk. Bring to a boil, cook and stir for 2 minutes or until thickened. Gently stir in cooked vegetables. Add 1 cup or more of reserved cooking liquid until soup is desired consistency.

U.S. Senate Bean Soup

Chock-full of ham, beans and celery, this hearty soup makes a wonderful meal at any time of year. Freeze the bone from a holiday ham until you're ready to make soup. Plus, once prepared, it freezes well for a great make-ahead supper!

—**ROSEMARIE FORCUM** HEATHSVILLE, VIRGINIA

YIELD: 8-10 SERVINGS (2½ QUARTS).

- 1 **pound dried great northern beans**
- 1 **meaty ham bone or 2 smoked ham hocks**
- 3 **medium onions, chopped**
- 3 **garlic cloves, minced**
- 3 **celery ribs, chopped**
- ¼ **cup minced fresh parsley**
- 1 **cup mashed potatoes or ⅓ cup instant potato flakes**

Salt and pepper to taste
Minced parsley or chives

1. Rinse and sort beans. Place beans in a Dutch oven or stockpot; add water to cover by 2 in. Bring to a boil; boil for 2 minutes. Remove from the heat; cover and let stand for 1 to 4 hours or until beans are softened.

2. Drain and rinse beans, discarding liquid. In a large Dutch oven or stockpot, bring the beans, ham bone and 3 quarts water to boil. Reduce heat; cover and simmer for 2 hours.

3. Skim fat if necessary. Add the onions, garlic, celery, parsley, potatoes, salt and pepper; simmer 1 hour longer.

4. Set aside ham bones until cool enough to handle. Remove meat from bones; discard bones. Cut meat into bite-size pieces and return to Dutch oven. Heat through. Sprinkle with parsley or chives.

The scent of dill takes me back to Grandma's kitchen. She always spent much time tending the coal cookstove and the pot of dill-flavored chicken soup, which seemed to be constantly simmering on the back burner.

—**HELEN CATHERINE SMITH** TAMPA, FLORIDA

Stuffed Roast Pepper Soup

After sampling a similar soup at a summer resort, my daughter and I experimented to create this version. Using a colorful variety of peppers gives it plenty of eye appeal.

—**BETTY VIG** VIROQUA, WISCONSIN

YIELD: 14-16 SERVINGS (4 QUARTS).

- 2 **pounds ground beef**
- ½ **medium onion, chopped**
- 6 **cups water**
- 8 **beef bouillon cubes**
- 2 **cans (28 ounces each) diced tomatoes, undrained**
- 2 **cups cooked rice**
- 2 **teaspoon salt**
- ½ **teaspoon pepper**
- ½ **teaspoon paprika**
- 3 **green, sweet yellow or red peppers, seeded and chopped**

1. In a large Dutch oven, cook ground beef and onion over medium heat, until the meat is no longer pink and onion is tender; drain. Add water, bouillon cubes, tomatoes, rice and seasonings. Bring to a boil; reduce heat and simmer, covered, for 1 hour.

2. Add peppers; cook, uncovered, for 10-15 minutes or just until tender.

SALADS

Seven-Layer Gelatin Salad

Here's an eye-catching salad that my mother makes for Christmas dinner each year. You can choose different flavors to make other color combinations for specific holidays or other gatherings.

—**JAN HEMNESS** STOCKTON, MISSOURI

YIELD: 15-20 SERVINGS.

>   7 packages (3 ounces each) assorted flavored gelatin
> 4½ cups boiling water, divided
> 4½ cups cold water, divided
>   1 can (12 ounces) evaporated milk, divided
>   1 carton (8 ounces) frozen whipped topping, thawed
> **Fresh mint, sliced strawberries and kiwifruit, optional**

1. In a small bowl, dissolve one package of gelatin in ¾ cup boiling water. Add ¾ cup cold water; stir. Spoon into a 13-in. x 9-in. dish coated with cooking spray. Chill until set but not firm, about 40 minutes.

2. In another bowl, dissolve another package of gelatin in ½ cup boiling water. Add ½ cup cold water and ½ cup milk; stir. Spoon over the first layer. Chill until set but not firm, about 40 minutes.

3. Repeat five times, alternating plain gelatin layers with creamy gelatin layers. Chill each layer until set but not firm before spooning next layer on top. Refrigerate the entire salad overnight. Just before serving, spread top with the whipped topping. Cut into squares to serve. Garnish with mint and fruit if desired.

Editor's Note: *This recipe takes time to prepare since each layer must be set before the next layer is added.*

Banana Fruit Compote

My mother used to make this recipe when I was a child. My four kids always eat more fruit when I serve it up this way.

—**MAXINE OTIS** HOBSON, MONTANA

YIELD: 2 SERVINGS.

>   1 cup apricot nectar, divided
> **Dash to ⅛ teaspoon ground cloves**
> **Dash to ⅛ teaspoon ground cinnamon**
>   1 tablespoon cornstarch
>   2 tablespoons lemon juice
>   1 firm banana, cut into ½-inch slices
>   4 fresh strawberries, sliced
>   1 kiwifruit, halved and thinly sliced

1. In a small saucepan, bring ¾ cup apricot nectar, cloves and cinnamon to a boil. Combine the cornstarch and remaining apricot nectar until smooth; gradually whisk into nectar mixture. Return to a boil; cook and stir for 1-2 minutes or until thickened . Remove from heat; stir in the lemon juice. Cool.

2. Stir in the banana, strawberries and kiwi. Cover and refrigerate for at least 1 hour before serving.

Tasty Tossed Salad

My mom got this recipe from a friend; it's a re-creation of a salad at a favorite restaurant. It's crisp, crunchy and colorful, with a slightly sweet homemade dressing everyone will enjoy.

—EMILY DENNIS HANCOCK, MICHIGAN

YIELD: 6 SERVINGS.

2 **cups torn iceberg lettuce**
1 **cup fresh cauliflowerets**
1 **cup fresh broccoli florets**
1 **cup shredded carrots**
⅓ **cup chopped red onion**
6 **bacon strips, cooked and crumbled**
1 **cup (4 ounces) shredded cheddar cheese**

DRESSING

¾ **cup mayonnaise**
3 **tablespoons sugar**
3 **tablespoons lemon juice**

1. In a large salad bowl, combine the lettuce, cauliflower, broccoli, carrots, onion and bacon. Top with cheese.

2. In a bowl, combine the mayonnaise, sugar and lemon juice. Pour over lettuce mixture and toss to coat.

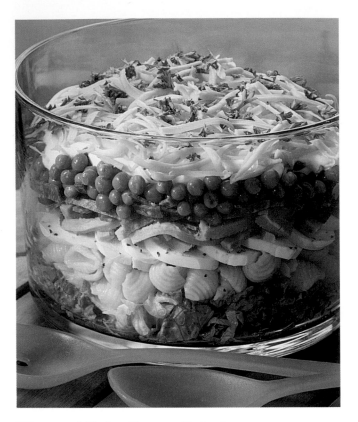

Creamy German Potato Salad

My mom's recipe for potato salad has been a staple in our family for years. The whipping cream makes it taste like no other.

—TRACY ZETTELMEIER MUKWONAGO, WISCONSIN

YIELD: 13 SERVINGS (¾ CUP EACH).

- 4½ **pounds red potatoes (about 18 medium)**
- ½ **pound bacon strips, diced**
- 1 **medium onion, chopped**
- 4 **teaspoons all-purpose flour**
- ¾ **cup sugar**
- ¾ **cup cider vinegar**
- 1 **cup heavy whipping cream**

1. Cut potatoes into ½-in. cubes; place in a stockpot and cover with water. Bring to a boil. Reduce heat; cover and simmer for 10-12 minutes or until tender.

2. In a Dutch oven, cook bacon over medium heat until crisp. Using a slotted spoon, remove to paper towels; drain, reserving 5 tablespoons drippings. Set bacon aside.

3. In the same pan, saute onion in drippings until tender. Stir in flour until blended. Gradually stir in sugar and vinegar. Bring to a boil; cook and stir for 2 minutes until thickened.

4. Remove from the heat; gradually whisk in cream. Set aside. Drain potatoes. Transfer to a large bow; add reserved onion mixture and bacon. Stir gently to coat. Serve warm.

Hearty Eight-Layer Salad

I'm a great-grandmother and have been making this satisfying salad for years. It's my most requested recipe for family gatherings. It's simple to make ahead of time and looks lovely with all of its tasty layers. Dijon mustard gives a nice kick to the dressing.

—NOREEN MEYER MADISON, WISCONSIN

YIELD: 10 SERVINGS.

- 1½ **cups uncooked small pasta shells**
- 1 **tablespoon canola oil**
- 3 **cups shredded lettuce**
- 3 **hard-cooked eggs, sliced**
- ¼ **teaspoon salt**
- ⅛ **teaspoon pepper**
- 1 **cup julienned fully cooked ham**
- 1 **cup julienned hard salami**
- 1 **package (10 ounces) frozen peas, thawed**
- 1 **cup mayonnaise**
- ¼ **cup sour cream**
- ¼ **cup chopped green onions**
- 2 **teaspoons Dijon mustard**
- 1 **cup (4 ounces) shredded Colby or Monterey Jack cheese**
- 2 **tablespoons minced fresh parsley**

1. Cook macaroni according to package directions; drain and rinse with cold water. Drizzle with oil; toss to coat.

2. Place the lettuce in a 2½-qt. glass serving bowl; top with macaroni and eggs. Sprinkle with salt and pepper. Layer with ham, salami and peas. Combine mayonnaise, sour cream, green onions and mustard. Spread over the top. Cover and refrigerate for several hours or overnight.

3. Just before serving, sprinkle with cheese and parsley.

Watercress with Fennel & Berries

I like to experiment when I'm cooking. This surprising combination of watercress and fennel creates a fresh-tasting summer salad, which was a success with my family.
—**JIM RUDE** JANESVILLE, WISCONSIN

YIELD: 6 SERVINGS.

 4 **cups watercress**
 1 **cup thinly sliced fennel bulb**
 ½ **cup fresh blueberries**
 ¼ **cup chopped fennel fronds**
 ¼ **cup pistachios, toasted**
 ⅓ **cup refrigerated spinach salad dressing with bacon**
 1 **tablespoon orange juice**
 1 **teaspoon grated orange peel**
 1 **teaspoon teriyaki sauce**

1. In a salad bowl, combine the first five ingredients. In a small bowl, whisk the remaining ingredients. Drizzle over salad; toss to coat. Serve immediately.

Editor's Note: *This recipe was tested with Marie's brand salad dressing.*

Sweet 'n' Creamy Coleslaw

My grandmother taught me how to make the dressing for this coleslaw when I was very young. It's not too tart and not too sweet. Sometimes I make 8 gallon jars a week at the restaurant where I work! It gets lots of compliments.
—**DENISE ELDER** HANOVER, ONTARIO

YIELD: 32 (¾-CUP) SERVINGS.

 ½ **cup plus 2 tablespoons sugar**
 2¼ **teaspoons all-purpose flour**
 2¼ **teaspoons cornstarch**
 1 **teaspoon ground mustard**
 ½ **teaspoon salt**
 ½ **teaspoon pepper**
 ½ **cup plus 2 tablespoons cider vinegar**
 ½ **cup water**
 1 **egg, lightly beaten**
 ½ **cup milk**
 ¼ **cup packed brown sugar**
 ½ **cup half-and-half cream**
 2 **cups mayonnaise**
 3 **medium heads cabbage (6 to 7 pounds), shredded**
 2 **medium carrots, shredded**
 2 **celery ribs, chopped**
 7 **green onions, thinly sliced**

1. In a large saucepan, combine the sugar, flour, cornstarch, mustard, salt and pepper. Gradually stir in vinegar and water. Add egg and milk. Cook and stir until mixture comes to a boil. Cook 2 minutes longer or until slightly thickened. Cool to room temperature, stirring several times.

2. In a large bowl, combine the brown sugar and cream. Stir in mayonnaise. Add cooked dressing; mix well. In several large bowls, combine the cabbage, carrots, celery and green onions. Add dressing and toss to coat.

Gazpacho Salad

Here's a beautiful and tasty way to use garden vegetables. This fresh, savory salad is great to make ahead and take to a potluck later, after the flavors have had a chance to blend. It's sure to be a success!

—**FLORENCE JACOBY**
GRANITE FALLS, MINNESOTA

YIELD: 10-12 SERVINGS.

- 4 tomatoes, diced and seeded
- 2 cucumbers, peeled and diced
- 2 green peppers, seeded and diced
- 1 medium onion, diced
- 1 can (2¼ ounces) sliced ripe olives, drained
- 1 teaspoon salt
- ½ teaspoon pepper

DRESSING
- ½ cup olive oil
- ¼ cup white vinegar
- Juice of 1 lemon (about ¼ cup)
- 1 tablespoon chopped fresh parsley
- 2 garlic cloves, minced
- 2 teaspoons chopped green onions
- ½ teaspoon salt
- ¼ teaspoon ground cumin

1. In a 1½-quart bowl, layer one-third to one-half of the tomatoes, cucumbers, green peppers, onion, olives, salt and pepper. Repeat layers two or three more times.

2. In a small bowl, combine all dressing ingredients. Pour over vegetables. Cover and chill several hours or overnight. Serve with a slotted spoon.

Summer Squash Salad

This is a colorful and tasty alternative to coleslaw. Like most gardeners, we usually have an abundance of squash and zucchini in summer, so this dish is inexpensive to prepare and a great way to put this fresh produce to use.

—**DIANE HIXON** NICEVILLE, FLORIDA

YIELD: 12-16 SERVINGS.

- 4 cups julienned zucchini
- 4 cups julienned yellow squash
- 2 cups sliced radishes
- 1 cup canola oil
- ⅓ cup cider vinegar
- 2 tablespoons Dijon mustard
- 2 tablespoons snipped fresh parsley
- 1½ teaspoons salt
- 1 teaspoon dill weed
- ½ teaspoon pepper

1. In a large bowl, toss the zucchini, squash and radishes. In a small bowl, whisk the remaining ingredients. Pour over vegetables. Cover and refrigerate for at least 2 hours.

Pineapple Gelatin Salad

My family enjoys this lovely layered salad in the summer with grilled hamburgers. Although I haven't used the recipe long, it's already become a favorite. A good friend shared it with me, and every time I make it, I think of her.

—**SUSAN KIRBY** TIPTON, INDIANA

YIELD: 12-16 SERVINGS.

- 1 can (20 ounces) crushed pineapple
- 1 package (6 ounces) lemon gelatin
- 3 cups boiling water
- 1 package (8 ounces) cream cheese, softened
- 1 carton (16 ounces) frozen whipped topping, thawed
- ¾ cup sugar
- 3 tablespoons lemon juice
- 3 tablespoons water
- 2 tablespoons all-purpose flour
- 2 egg yolks, lightly beaten

1. Drain pineapple, reserving juice. Dissolve gelatin in boiling water; add pineapple. Pour into a 13-in. x 9-in. dish; chill until almost set, about 45 minutes.

2. In a bowl, beat cream cheese and whipped topping until smooth. Carefully spread over gelatin; chill for 30 minutes. Meanwhile, in a saucepan over medium heat, combine sugar, lemon juice, water, flour, egg yolks and reserved pineapple juice; bring to a boil, stirring constantly. Cook for 1 minute or until thickened. Cool. Carefully spread over cream cheese layer. Chill for at least 1 hour.

Corn Bread Layered Salad

My mother's corn bread salad is so complete, it can be a meal in itself. The recipe has been in our family for years and is great for potlucks or large family gatherings.

—**JODY MILLER** OKLAHOMA CITY, OKLAHOMA

YIELD: 6-8 SERVINGS.

- 1 package (8½ ounces) corn bread/muffin mix
- 6 green onions, chopped

- 1 medium green pepper, chopped
- 1 can (15¼ ounces) whole kernel corn, drained
- 1 can (15 ounces) pinto beans, rinsed and drained
- ¾ cup mayonnaise
- ¾ cup sour cream
- 2 medium tomatoes, seeded and chopped
- ½ cup shredded cheddar cheese

1. Prepare and bake corn bread according to package directions. Cool on a wire rack.

2. Crumble corn bread into a 2-qt. glass serving bowl. Layer with onions, green pepper, corn and beans.

3. In a small bowl, combine mayonnaise and sour cream; spread over the vegetables. Sprinkle with tomatoes and cheese. Refrigerate until serving.

Garden Bean Salad

My mother gave me this crunchy bean salad recipe many years ago, and I often take it to covered-dish dinners. It looks especially attractive served in a glass bowl to show off the colorful vegetables.

—**BERNICE MCFADDEN** EATON, OHIO

YIELD: 12-16 SERVINGS.

- 1 can (16 ounces) kidney beans, rinsed and drained
- 2 cans (15¼ ounces each) lima beans
- 1 can (14½ ounces) cut green beans
- 1 can (14½ ounces) cut wax beans, drained
- 1 can (15 ounces) garbanzo beans or chickpeas, rinsed and drained
- 1 large green pepper, chopped
- 3 celery ribs, chopped
- 1 jar (2 ounces) sliced pimientos, drained
- 1 bunch green onions, sliced
- 2 cups white vinegar
- 2 cups sugar
- ½ cup water
- 1 teaspoon salt

1. Drain all beans; place in a large bowl. Add the green pepper, celery, pimientos and green onions; set aside. Bring remaining ingredients to a boil in a heavy saucepan; boil for 5 minutes. Remove from heat and immediately pour over vegetables.

2. Refrigerate the salad several hours or overnight. Serve with a slotted spoon.

Favorite Broccoli Salad

"Fresh-tasting...so colorful...delicious dressing." Those are some of the compliments I get when I serve this broccoli salad with a meal or take it to a church dinner. Although I have many other good salad recipes, I'm especially fond of this one.

—ESTHER SHANK HARRISONBURG, VIRGINIA

YIELD: 6-8 SERVINGS.

- 1 bunch broccoli, separated into florets
- 1 head cauliflower, separated into florets
- 8 bacon strips, cooked and crumbled
- 1 cup chopped seeded tomatoes
- ⅓ cup chopped onion
- 2 hard-cooked eggs, sliced
- 1 cup mayonnaise
- ⅓ cup sugar
- 2 tablespoons cider vinegar

1. In a large salad bowl, combine the broccoli, cauliflower, bacon, tomatoes, onion and eggs; set aside.

2. In another bowl, combine the mayonnaise, sugar and vinegar. Just before serving, pour dressing over salad and toss to coat.

Tomato Basil Salad

Tomatoes team up with red onion and fresh basil in a pleasant salad.

—JOYCE BROWN GENESEE, IDAHO

YIELD: 2 SERVINGS.

- 6 tomato slices (¼ inch thick)
- 6 red onion slices
- 2 tablespoons olive oil
- 4 teaspoons red wine vinegar
- 2 tablespoons chopped fresh basil
- 1 teaspoon sugar

1. Place tomatoes in a shallow dish; top each slice with an onion. In a small jar with tight-fitting lid, combine remaining ingredients; shake well. Pour over tomatoes and onions. Cover and refrigerate for at least 1 hour.

Lime Gelatin Salad

I've made this refreshing recipe hundreds of times! It can be a salad or dessert. When I take it to a potluck, it's always one of the first things to disappear.

—**LOUISE HARDING** NEWBURGH, NEW YORK

YIELD: 16-20 SERVINGS.

- 1 package (6 ounces) lime gelatin
- 1 cup boiling water
- 1 package (8 ounces) cream cheese, softened
- ½ teaspoon vanilla extract
- 1 can (15 ounces) mandarin oranges, drained
- 1 can (8 ounces) crushed pineapple, drained
- 1 cup lemon-lime soda
- ½ cup chopped pecans
- 1 carton (8 ounces) frozen whipped topping, thawed, divided

1. Dissolve gelatin in water. In a bowl, beat cream cheese until fluffy. Stir in gelatin mixture and beat until smooth. Stir in vanilla, oranges, pineapple, soda and pecans. Chill until mixture mounds slightly when dropped from a spoon.

2. Fold in three-fourths of the whipped topping. Pour into a 13-in. x 9-in. dish. Refrigerate for 3-4 hours or until firm. Cut into squares; garnish with the remaining whipped topping.

> Grandma would make the most delicious dishes from so little. One of my favorites was "old field lettuce" picked behind the house and wilted with a cooked creamy-white dressing. It was a delightful taste that I haven't experienced since.
>
> —**JACK ZINN** LONG BEACH, NORTH CAROLINA

Overnight Coleslaw

This has been a very popular salad from my recipe box for a long, long time! Before I retired, when my office had a covered-dish get-together, I was always asked to bring my tangy coleslaw. My family loves it, too.

—**FERN HAMMOCK** GARLAND, TEXAS

YIELD: 12-16 SERVINGS.

- 12 cups shredded cabbage (1 medium head)
- 1 green pepper, chopped
- 1 medium red onion, chopped
- 2 carrots, shredded
- 1 cup sugar

DRESSING

- 2 teaspoons sugar
- 1 teaspoon ground mustard
- 1 teaspoon celery seed
- 1 teaspoon salt
- 1 cup white vinegar
- ¾ cup canola oil

1. In a large bowl, combine first four ingredients. Sprinkle with sugar; set aside.

2. In a large saucepan, combine dressing ingredients; bring to a boil. Remove from the heat and pour over vegetables; toss to coat.

3. Cover and refrigerate overnight. Stir well before serving. Serve with a slotted spoon.

Special Potato Salad

Vinegar and yogurt give this salad a refreshing tang that's unlike typical potato salads with heavy dressings. My family loves the crispness of the onion and celery and the heartiness that comes from the eggs and crumbled bacon.

—PAGE ALEXANDER BALDWIN CITY, KANSAS

YIELD: 6-8 SERVINGS.

    2½ pounds red potatoes
    2   tablespoons red wine vinegar
    1   tablespoon olive oil
    1   tablespoon Dijon mustard
    ½   teaspoon dried basil
    ½   teaspoon pepper
    ¼   teaspoon salt
    ½   cup plain yogurt
    ¼   cup sour cream
    1   teaspoon garlic salt
    ¾   cup chopped red onion
    ½   cup diced celery
    4   bacon strips, cooked and crumbled
    2   hard-cooked eggs, chopped

1. In a saucepan, cook potatoes in boiling salted water until tender. Meanwhile, in a large bowl, combine the vinegar, oil, mustard, basil, pepper and salt. Drain potatoes; cut into 1-in. chunks and add to vinegar and oil mixture while still warm. Toss to coat; cool completely.

2. In another bowl, combine yogurt, sour cream and garlic salt. Add onion, celery, bacon and eggs; mix well. Add to potato mixture; toss gently. Cover and chill for several hours.

Summer Apple Salad

It is a good thing this serves 12 because my family can't get enough of it! The salad tastes great, looks nice on the table and combines a mixture of healthy fruits and vegetables with a sweet dressing—a deliciously different idea.

—KIM STOLLER SMITHVILLE, OHIO

YIELD: 12 SERVINGS.

    3   medium tart red apples, diced
    ¾   cup pineapple tidbits, drained
    1½ cups sliced celery
    1   cup grape halves
    1   medium carrot, shredded
    ½   cup coarsely chopped almonds
    ¾   cup sour cream
    1   tablespoon sugar
    ½   teaspoon lemon juice

1. In a large salad bowl, combine the apples, pineapple, celery, grapes, carrot and almonds. In a small bowl, combine the sour cream, sugar and lemon juice. Add to the apple mixture and toss to coat. Chill.

Molded Peach Gelatin

The outstanding orange color of this gelatin makes it a perfect addition to any Halloween party table. It's a convenient do-ahead dish when preparing for a busy day.

—BETTY HOWARD WHEELER, TEXAS

YIELD: 4-6 SERVINGS.

    1   can (15¼ ounces) sliced peaches
    ½   cup sugar
    ¼   to ½ teaspoon ground nutmeg
    1   package (3 ounces) peach or orange gelatin

1. Drain peaches, reserving juice; add enough water to juice to measure 1 cup. Place peaches in a blender. Cover and process until smooth; set aside.

2. In a large saucepan, combine the sugar, nutmeg and reserved juice mixture. Bring to a boil over medium heat; cook and stir for 1 minute or until sugar is dissolved. Remove from the heat; stir in gelatin until dissolved. Stir in the peach puree.

3. Pour mixture into a 3-cup mold coated with cooking spray. Refrigerate the salad until set. Just before serving, unmold onto a serving plate.

Emily's Spinach Salad

I've always loved eating spinach—it's grown here in our area. When I saw an announcement of a spinach cooking contest, I made up this recipe to enter. I was delighted when my colorful, tangy salad took the grand prize!
—**EMILY FIELDS** SANTA ANA, CALIFORNIA

YIELD: 6-8 SERVINGS.

⅔ cup canola oil
¼ cup red wine vinegar
2 teaspoons lemon juice
2 teaspoons soy sauce
1 teaspoon sugar
1 teaspoon ground mustard
½ teaspoon curry powder
½ teaspoon salt
½ teaspoon seasoned pepper
¼ teaspoon garlic powder

1 package (10 ounces) fresh spinach, torn
5 bacon strips, cooked and crumbled
2 hard-cooked eggs, sliced

1. In a small bowl, whisk the first 10 ingredients; set aside. Place spinach in a large salad bowl.

2. Just before serving, whisk dressing again and drizzle over spinach; toss gently. Garnish with bacon and egg slices.

Pat's Potato Salad

I developed this recipe while working at a restaurant. We wanted a salad that would complement a barbecue sandwich and use up day-old baked potatoes. It keeps well and tastes even better after it's chilled.

—PATRICIA MAUL
BARTLESVILLE, OKLAHOMA

YIELD: 12-16 SERVINGS.

- 12 medium red potatoes, cooked, peeled and cubed
- 1 medium red onion, chopped
- 1 cup chopped fresh parsley
- 1½ cups mayonnaise
- 1 cup (8 ounces) sour cream
- ¼ cup sugar
- ¼ cup vinegar
- 4 teaspoons ground mustard
- 1 teaspoon salt

1. In a large bowl, combine potatoes, onion and parsley. In a small bowl, combine the remaining ingredients. Pour dressing over the potatoes and mix well. Refrigerate at least 1 hour before serving. Salad can be prepared a day ahead.

Layered Fruit Salad

Fresh fruit is layered into an appealing salad that's a welcome side dish not only in summer but all year long.

—PAGE ALEXANDER BALDWIN CITY, KANSAS

YIELD: 8 SERVINGS.

- ½ cup orange juice
- ¼ cup lemon juice
- ¼ cup packed brown sugar
- ½ teaspoon grated orange peel
- ½ teaspoon grated lemon peel
- 1 cinnamon stick (3 inches)
- 2 cups fresh or drained canned pineapple chunks
- 1 cup seedless red grapes
- 2 medium bananas, sliced
- 2 medium oranges, sectioned
- 1 medium grapefruit, sectioned
- 1 pint fresh strawberries, sliced
- 2 medium kiwifruit, peeled and sliced

1. In a large saucepan, combine the juices, sugar, peels and cinnamon stick; bring to a boil. Reduce heat; simmer, uncovered, for 5 minutes. Remove from the heat; cool completely.

2. Meanwhile, layer fruit in a glass serving bowl. Remove cinnamon stick from the sauce; pour sauce over fruit. Cover and refrigerate for several hours.

Vegetable Pasta Salad

This light, multicolored salad is an original. When I serve it at potlucks, I'm always asked for the recipe. It's also a standby for the snowbirds who gather with us in Arizona each winter.

—KATHY CROW CORDOVA, ALASKA

YIELD: 16-18 SERVINGS.

- 12 ounces spiral pasta, cooked and drained
- 6 green onions, thinly sliced
- 1 to 2 small zucchini, thinly sliced
- 2 cups frozen broccoli and cauliflower, thawed and drained
- 1½ cups thinly sliced carrots, parboiled
- 1 cup thinly sliced celery
- ½ cup frozen peas, thawed
- 1 jar (2¼ ounces) sliced ripe olives, drained
- 1 jar (6 ounces) marinated artichoke hearts, drained and quartered

DRESSING
- ½ cup mayonnaise
- ½ cup bottled Italian salad dressing
- ½ cup sour cream
- 1 tablespoon prepared mustard
- ½ teaspoon Italian seasoning

1. In a large bowl, combine pasta, onions, zucchini, broccoli and cauliflower, carrots, celery, peas, olives and artichoke hearts. In a small bowl, combine dressing ingredients. Pour over pasta and vegetables and toss. Cover and refrigerate for at least 1 hour.

Curried Walnut Rice Salad

As a busy wife and mother of eight, I'm always on the lookout for appetizing and nutritious recipes. With its mild curry flavor, nutty crunch and veggie garnish, this one easily passed my test!

—RHODA WENGER PILOT MOUNTAIN, NORTH CAROLINA

YIELD: 10 SERVINGS.

- 1¾ cups brown rice, cooked and cooled
- 1 medium cucumber, diced
- ½ cup chopped onion
- 1 large carrot, shredded

- 1 tablespoon minced fresh parsley
- 3 tablespoons fat-free mayonnaise
- 2 tablespoons canola oil
- 1 tablespoon lemon juice
- 2 teaspoons honey
- 1 teaspoon curry powder
- 2 garlic cloves, minced
- 1 teaspoon salt
- ¼ teaspoon pepper
- ½ cup chopped walnuts, toasted
- 4 medium tomatoes, cut into wedges

1. In a large bowl, combine the first five ingredients. In another bowl, whisk mayonnaise, oil, lemon juice, honey, curry powder, garlic, salt and pepper; stir into rice mixture. Just before serving, stir in nuts. Garnish with tomatoes.

Caesar Salad

Here's a great salad to perk up any spring or summer meal. The zesty dressing provides a fresh burst of flavor with each bite.

—SCHELBY THOMPSON CAMDEN WYOMING, DELAWARE

YIELD: 6-8 SERVINGS.

- 1 large bunch romaine, torn
- ¾ cup olive oil
- 3 tablespoons red wine vinegar
- 1 teaspoon Worcestershire sauce
- ½ teaspoon salt
- ¼ teaspoon ground mustard
- 1 large garlic clove, minced
- ½ fresh lemon

Dash pepper
- ¼ to ½ cup shredded Parmesan cheese

Caesar-flavored or garlic croutons

1. Place lettuce in a large salad bowl. Combine the next six ingredients in a blender; process until smooth. Pour over lettuce and toss to coat.

2. Squeeze lemon over lettuce. Sprinkle with pepper, cheese and croutons.

Sweet and Tangy Pasta Salad

I'm a retired farmwife and one of 16 children. I learned lots about cooking from my mother. This recipe is my version of her pasta salad.

—**JUNE HERKE** WATERTOWN, SOUTH DAKOTA

YIELD: 16 SERVINGS.

1 package (16 ounces) spiral pasta
1 medium cucumber, finely chopped
1 jar (8 ounces) whole baby corn, drained and cut into ½-inch pieces
1 jar (7½ ounces) marinated artichoke hearts, drained
1 cup sliced pimiento-stuffed olives
1 cup sliced ripe olives
½ cup finely chopped sweet red pepper
¼ cup finely chopped onion

DRESSING
1 cup canola oil
1 cup cider vinegar
1 cup sugar
½ teaspoon pepper
2 tablespoons minced fresh parsley

1. Cook pasta according to package directions. Meanwhile, in a large bowl, combine the cucumber, corn, artichokes, olives, red pepper and onion. Drain pasta and rinse in cold water; stir into vegetable mixture.

2. In a small bowl, whisk the dressing ingredients. Pour over salad; toss to coat. Cover and refrigerate for at least 2 hours. Serve with a slotted spoon.

Greens with Vinaigrette

This pretty salad topped with a sweet and savory dressing is a refreshing addition to any meal. It's a perfect example of how Mother could turn even simple ingredients into something special.
—NANCY DUTY JACKSONVILLE, FLORIDA

YIELD: 6 SERVINGS (ABOUT ⅔ CUP VINAIGRETTE).

- 6 **cups torn romaine**
- 1 **cup sliced radishes**
- ⅓ **cup olive oil**
- ¼ **cup honey**
- 2 **teaspoons white wine vinegar**
- 1½ **teaspoons lemon juice**
- 1 **teaspoon Dijon mustard**
- 1 **teaspoon poppy seeds**
- 2 **garlic cloves, minced**
- **Dash hot pepper sauce**
- **Pinch sugar**
- **Salt and pepper to taste**

1. In a large bowl, combine the romaine and radishes. In a jar with tight-fitting lid, combine the remaining ingredients; shake well. Just before serving, pour the vinaigrette over salad; toss to coat.

Cheddar-Almond Lettuce Salad

Sugared almonds and a honey-mustard dressing make this salad a real standout. In fact, I keep slivered almonds in my freezer just so I can whip it up on the spur of the moment. For more nutrition, color or variety, I sometimes add broccoli and tomatoes.
—JULIA MUSSER LEBANON, PENNSYLVANIA

YIELD: 9 SERVINGS.

- ½ **cup slivered almonds**
- 3 **tablespoons sugar**
- 9 **cups torn romaine**
- 2 **hard-cooked eggs, sliced**
- 1 **cup (4 ounces) shredded cheddar cheese**

HONEY-MUSTARD DRESSING
- ¼ **cup sugar**
- 2 **tablespoons white vinegar**
- 2 **tablespoons honey**
- 1 **tablespoon lemon juice**
- ½ **teaspoon onion powder**
- ½ **teaspoon celery seed**
- ½ **teaspoon ground mustard**
- ½ **teaspoon paprika**
- ¼ **teaspoon salt**
- ½ **cup canola oil**

1. In a small heavy skillet, combine almonds and sugar. Cook and stir over medium heat for 5-6 minutes or until nuts are coated and golden. Spread onto foil to cool. Divide romaine among salad plates; top with eggs and cheese.

2. In a blender, combine the sugar, vinegar, honey, lemon juice, onion powder, celery seed, mustard, paprika and salt. While processing, gradually add oil in a steady stream. Drizzle over salads; sprinkle with almonds.

Southwestern Rice Salad

The recipe for this delicious salad has been in my family for years. My mother used to bring it to many different functions, and I'm carrying on her tradition.

—**RUTH BIANCHI** APPLE VALLEY, MINNESOTA

YIELD: 12 SERVINGS.

- 1⅓ cups water
- ⅔ cup uncooked long grain rice
- ¾ cup chopped green pepper
- ½ cup chopped red onion
- 1 medium carrot, chopped
- 1 tablespoon canola oil
- 3 garlic cloves, minced
- 1 package (16 ounces) frozen corn, thawed
- 1 can (15 ounces) black beans, rinsed and drained
- 2 medium plum tomatoes, chopped
- 1 cup salted peanuts
- ⅓ cup minced fresh cilantro
- ⅔ cup olive oil
- ⅓ cup lemon juice
- ½ to 1½ teaspoons cayenne pepper
- ½ teaspoon ground cumin

1. In a large saucepan, bring water and rice to a boil. Reduce heat; cover and simmer for 15 minutes. Remove from the heat. Let stand for 5 minutes or until rice is tender. Rinse rice with cold water and drain. Place in a large bowl.

2. In a small skillet, saute the green pepper, onion and carrot in oil until crisp-tender. Add garlic; cook 1 minute longer. Add to rice. Stir in the corn, beans, tomatoes, peanuts and cilantro.

3. In a small bowl, combine the oil, lemon juice, cayenne and cumin. Pour over the rice mixture; stir to coat. Cover and refrigerate until serving.

Tomato Spinach Salad

When I serve my fresh spinach tossed with a creamy dill dressing, I receive plenty of compliments. The recipe is a longtime favorite.
—**RUTH SEITZ** COLUMBUS JUNCTION, IOWA

YIELD: 6-8 SERVINGS.

- ½ cup mayonnaise
- ½ cup grated Parmesan cheese
- ¼ cup milk
- 1½ teaspoons dill weed
- 1½ teaspoons dried minced onion
- 1½ teaspoons lemon-pepper seasoning
- 1 package (10 ounces) fresh spinach, torn
- 2 cups cherry tomatoes

1. In a jar with tight-fitting lid, combine first six ingredients; shake well. Refrigerate for at least 1 hour. Just before serving, combine spinach and tomatoes in a large salad bowl. Shake dressing; drizzle over salad and toss.

Editor's Note: *If the dressing thickens, thin with additional milk if desired.*

Ruby Red Raspberry Salad

A refreshing and attractive side dish, this salad adds a festive touch to any table. Children especially like this slightly sweet salad.
—**MARGE CLARK** WEST LEBANON, INDIANA

YIELD: 12-16 SERVINGS.

- 1 package (3 ounces) raspberry gelatin
- 2 cups boiling water, divided
- 1 package (10 ounces) frozen sweetened raspberries
- 1½ cups sour cream
- 1 package (3 ounces) cherry gelatin
- 1 can (20 ounces) crushed pineapple, drained
- 1 can (14 ounces) whole-berry cranberry sauce
- Mayonnaise and mint sprigs, optional

1. Dissolve raspberry gelatin in 1 cup boiling water. Add raspberries and stir until berries are thawed and separated. Pour into a 13-in. x 9-in. dish; chill until set.

2. Carefully spread with sour cream; chill. Dissolve cherry gelatin in remaining boiling water. Add pineapple and cranberry sauce; mix well. Allow to thicken slightly.

3. Carefully spoon over sour cream mixture; chill. If desired, garnish with mayonnaise and mint.

Dilly Bean Potato Salad

Green beans, dill pickles and a refreshing Italian-style dressing perk up this potato salad. My Irish grandmother made it for family gatherings. Even though I've changed it a bit, Nanny always comes to mind when I dish it up.

—MARGUERITE NOVICKE VINELAND, NEW JERSEY

YIELD: 14-16 SERVINGS.

- 1 **pound fresh green beans, trimmed**
- 4 **pounds red potatoes**
- 1 **medium red onion, thinly sliced and separated into rings**
- 1 **medium Vidalia or sweet onion, thinly sliced and separated into rings**
- 1 **cup chopped celery**
- 8 **dill pickles, sliced**
- 2 **tablespoons snipped fresh dill or 2 teaspoons dill weed**
- 2 **tablespoons minced fresh parsley**
- 4 **garlic cloves, minced**

VINAIGRETTE
- ¾ **cup olive oil**
- ⅓ **to ½ cup tarragon vinegar**
- 1 **envelope Italian salad dressing mix**
- 2 **tablespoons sugar**
- 1 **teaspoon salt**
- 1 **teaspoon pepper**

Celery salt and seasoned salt to taste

1. Place 1 in. of water and beans in a skillet; bring to a boil. Reduce heat. Cover and simmer for 8-10 minutes or until crisp-tender; drain and set aside.

2. Meanwhile, place potatoes in a large saucepan or Dutch oven and cover with water. Bring to a boil. Reduce heat. Cover and cook for 15-20 minutes or until tender; drain and cool.

3. Cut potatoes into ¼-in. slices; transfer to a large bowl. Add the onions, celery, pickles, dill, parsley and garlic.

4. In a jar with a tight-fitting lid, combine the vinaigrette ingredients; shake well. Drizzle over potato mixture. Add beans; gently toss.

After he finished lunch, Grandpa would say to Grandma, "That was the best meal I ever ate!" Then, turning to me, he'd say, "Your grandmother has cooked me 16,425 meals so far and every one of them has been delicious!"

—SUZANNE BEARD KINGS MOUNTAIN, NORTH CAROLINA

Festive Fruit Salad

Everyone who tries this refreshing, beautiful salad loves it. My bowl always comes home empty when I take it to a party or cookout. The recipe is an excellent way to take advantage of fresh fruit at its best.

—GAIL SELLERS SAVANNAH, GEORGIA

YIELD: 16-20 SERVINGS.

- 1 **medium fresh pineapple**
- 3 **medium apples (red, yellow and green), cubed**
- 1 **small cantaloupe, cubed**
- 1 **large firm banana, sliced**
- 1 **pint strawberries, halved**
- 1 **pint blueberries**
- 4 **cups seedless red and green grapes**
- 3 **kiwifruit, peeled and sliced**

DRESSING
- 1 **package (3 ounces) cream cheese, softened**
- ½ **cup confectioners' sugar**
- 2 **teaspoons lemon juice**
- 1 **carton (8 ounces) frozen whipped topping, thawed**

Additional berries for garnish, optional

1. Peel and core pineapple; cut into cubes. Place in a 3- or 4-qt. glass serving bowl. Stir in remaining fruit.

2. In a large bowl, beat cream cheese until fluffy. Gradually add sugar and lemon juice and mix well. Fold in the whipped topping.

3. Spread over fruit. Garnish with additional berries if desired. Store leftovers in the refrigerator.

SIDE DISHES

Root for Winter Vegetables

This medley is an updated version of a recipe my mom had while growing up. It's my favorite way to prepare veggies and is marvelous with a batch of hot rolls.

—JULIE BUTLER PUYALLUP, WASHINGTON

YIELD: 13 SERVINGS (¾ CUP EACH).

1 whole garlic bulb
3 tablespoons olive oil, divided
1 pound fresh beets
3 medium parsnips
2 small rutabagas
2 medium turnips
4 medium carrots
2 large red onions, cut into wedges
1 teaspoon salt
15 whole peppercorns
3 bay leaves
½ cup white wine or vegetable broth
½ cup vegetable broth
2 tablespoons butter

1. Remove papery outer skin from garlic (do not peel or separate cloves). Cut top off garlic bulb. Brush with ½ teaspoon oil. Wrap bulb in heavy-duty foil.

2. Peel the beets, parsnips, rutabagas, turnips and carrots; cut into 2-in. pieces. Place in a large bowl; add the onions, salt, peppercorns, bay leaves and remaining oil. Toss to coat.

3. Transfer to three greased 15-in. x 10-in. x 1-in. baking pans. Place garlic on one of the pans.

4. Bake at 400° for 35 minutes or until garlic is softened, stirring once. Remove garlic; set aside to cool. Drizzle wine and broth over vegetables. Bake vegetables 20-30 minutes longer or until tender. Squeeze softened garlic over vegetables; dot with butter. Transfer to a serving platter.

Summer Risotto

My mom always made this hearty dish to use up late-summer garden vegetables. Often, I'll add sauteed mushrooms and serve it as an entree with crusty bread and a salad.

—SHIRLEY HODGE BANGOR, PENNSYLVANIA

YIELD: 12 SERVINGS.

- 5½ to 6 cups reduced-sodium chicken broth
- 1 small onion, finely chopped
- 2 tablespoons olive oil
- 1 tablespoon butter
- 2 cups uncooked arborio rice
- 3 large tomatoes, chopped
- 2 cups fresh or frozen corn, thawed
- ½ cup crumbled feta cheese
- 2 tablespoons minced fresh thyme or 2 teaspoons dried thyme
- 2 tablespoons minced fresh rosemary or 2 teaspoons dried rosemary, crushed
- 2 tablespoons minced fresh basil or 2 teaspoons dried basil
- ¼ teaspoon salt
- ¼ teaspoon pepper
- Shredded Parmesan cheese

1. In a large saucepan, heat broth and keep warm. In a large skillet, saute onion in oil and butter until tender. Add rice; cook and stir for 2-3 minutes or rice is until lightly browned. Stir in 1 cup warm broth. Cook and stir until all the liquid is absorbed.

2. Add remaining broth, ½ cup at a time, stirring constantly. Allow the liquid to be absorbed between additions. Cook until risotto is creamy and rice is almost tender (total cooking time will be about 20 minutes).

3. Add tomatoes, corn, feta cheese, herbs, salt and pepper; heat through. Sprinkle with Parmesan cheese. Serve immediately.

Succotash

You can't get more Southern than succotash. This recipe comes from my mother, who was a fantastic cook. Her dish made her famous with everyone who ever tasted it.

—ROSA BOONE MOBILE, ALABAMA

YIELD: 12-16 SERVINGS.

- 1 smoked ham hock (about 1½ pounds)
- 4 cups water
- 1 can (28 ounces) diced tomatoes, undrained
- 1½ cups frozen lima beans, thawed
- 1 package (10 ounces) crowder peas, thawed or 1 can (15½ ounces) black-eyed peas, drained
- 1 package (10 ounces) frozen corn, thawed
- 1 medium green pepper, chopped
- 1 medium onion, chopped
- ⅓ cup ketchup
- 1½ teaspoons salt
- 1½ teaspoons dried basil
- 1 teaspoon rubbed sage
- 1 teaspoon paprika
- ½ teaspoon pepper
- 1 bay leaf
- 1 cup sliced fresh or frozen okra

1. In a Dutch oven or large saucepan, simmer ham hock in water for 1½ hours or until tender. Cool; remove meat from the bone and return to pan. (Discard bone and broth or save for another use.) Add the tomatoes, beans, peas, corn, green pepper, onion, ketchup and seasonings. Simmer, uncovered, for 45 minutes. Add okra; simmer, uncovered, 15 minutes longer. Discard bay leaf before serving.

Maple Baked Beans

My mother's baked beans were always a hit. You'll get a touch of heat from the chopped jalapeno pepper. Once you make it, you'll know it off the top of your head—it's just a half-cup of this and a half-cup of that!

—**NADINE BRISSEY** JENKS, OKLAHOMA

YIELD: 8 SERVINGS.

- 3 cans (15 ounces each) pork and beans
- ½ cup finely chopped onion
- ½ cup chopped green pepper
- ½ cup ketchup
- ½ cup maple syrup
- 2 tablespoons finely chopped seeded jalapeno pepper
- ½ cup crumbled cooked bacon

1. In a 3-qt. slow cooker, combine the first six ingredients. Cover and cook on low for 6-8 hours or until vegetables are tender. Just before serving, stir in bacon.

Editor's Note: *Wear disposable gloves when cutting hot peppers; the oils can burn skin. Avoid touching your face.*

Sage Dressing for Chicken

My family just loves this chicken stuffed with delicious sage dressing. They always ask for seconds.

—**BOBBIE TALBOTT** VENETA, OREGON

YIELD: 6 SERVINGS.

- 2 cups unseasoned dry bread cubes
- ½ cup chopped onion
- ¼ cup chopped fresh parsley
- 3 tablespoons chopped fresh sage or 1 tablespoon rubbed dried sage
- 1 egg, beaten

- ½ to ¾ cup chicken broth
- 1 roasting chicken (3 to 4 pounds)
Melted butter, optional

1. In a large bowl, combine bread cubes, onion, parsley, sage and the egg. Add enough broth until stuffing is moistened and holds together. Stuff loosely into chicken. Fasten with skewers to close.

2. Place with breast side up on a shallow rack in roasting pan. Brush with butter if desired. Bake, uncovered, at 375° for 1¾ to 2¼ hours or until juices run clear. Baste several times with pan juices or butter.

Onion Potato Pancakes

When Grandma prepared potato pancakes, she used an old-fashioned grater, which was great for potatoes but not for knuckles! With homemade applesauce, this side dish complements a meal so well. I made these pancakes for my family and often served them as a main dish for light suppers.

—**JOAN HUTTER** WARWICK, RHODE ISLAND

YIELD: 6-8 SERVINGS (12 PANCAKES).

- 2 eggs
- 1 medium onion, quartered
- 2 tablespoons all-purpose flour
- ¾ teaspoon salt
- ¼ teaspoon pepper
- ¼ teaspoon baking powder
- 4 medium potatoes, peeled and cubed (about 1½ pounds)
- 2 tablespoons chopped fresh parsley
- 3 to 4 tablespoons vegetable oil

1. In a blender or food processor, place the eggs, onion, flour, salt, pepper, baking powder and ½ cup of potatoes. Cover and process on high until smooth. Add parsley and remaining potatoes; cover and pulse 2-4 times until potatoes are chopped.

2. Pour 1 to 2 tablespoons oil onto a hot griddle or skillet. Pour batter by ⅓ cupfuls onto griddle; flatten slightly to a 4-in. to 5-in. diameter. Cook over medium heat until golden on both sides. Add oil as needed until all pancakes are cooked.

Broccoli Bake

This tasty side dish is always a big hit when my son, daughter-in-law and granddaughter come for dinner or when I'm hosting a shower or party. At Easter, it's a great way to use up hard-cooked eggs!

—CAROLYN GRIFFIN MACON, GEORGIA

YIELD: 6 SERVINGS.

- 2 packages (10 ounces each) frozen cut broccoli
- ½ cup chopped onion
- 1 tablespoon butter
- 1 can (10¾ ounces) condensed cream of mushroom soup, undiluted
- ½ teaspoon ground mustard
- ½ teaspoon salt
- 4 hard-cooked eggs, chopped
- 1½ cups (6 ounces) shredded cheddar cheese
- 1 can (2.8 ounces) french-fried onions

1. Cook broccoli according to package directions; drain and set aside. In a skillet or saucepan, saute onion in butter until tender. Stir in soup, mustard and salt; heat until bubbly. In a 1½-qt. baking dish, arrange half of broccoli; top with half the eggs, half the cheese and half the mushroom sauce. Repeat layers. Bake at 350° for 20 minutes. Sprinkle onions on top and bake 5 minutes longer.

Tomato Dumplings

The wonderful fresh tomato taste of the sauce complements these light, savory dumplings. They make a perfect side dish for a meal with beef. My family enjoys them very much.

—LUCILLE TUCKER CLINTON, ILLINOIS

YIELD: 6 SERVINGS.

- ½ cup finely chopped onion
- ¼ cup finely chopped green pepper
- ¼ cup finely chopped celery
- ¼ cup butter
- 1 bay leaf
- 1 can (28 ounces) diced tomatoes, undrained
- 1 tablespoon brown sugar
- ½ teaspoon dried basil
- ½ teaspoon salt
- ¼ teaspoon pepper

DUMPLINGS

- 1 cup all-purpose flour
- 1½ teaspoons baking powder
- ½ teaspoon salt
- 1 tablespoon cold butter
- 1 tablespoon snipped fresh parsley
- ⅔ cup milk

1. In large skillet, saute the onion, green pepper and celery in butter until tender. Add bay leaf, tomatoes, brown sugar, basil, salt and pepper; cover and simmer for 5-10 minutes.

2. Meanwhile, for the dumplings, combine flour, baking powder and salt in a bowl. Cut in butter. Add parsley and milk; stir just until mixed.

3. Drop by tablespoonfuls onto the simmering tomato mixture, making six mounds; cover tightly and simmer for 12-15 minutes or until a toothpick inserted into one of the dumplings comes out clean. Discard the bay leaf. Serve immediately.

Paprika Potatoes

These tasty potatoes are golden and crusty on the outside and tender on the inside. I've served them with many kinds of meat. When a meal needs a homey, comforting touch, I whip up a batch.

—RUTH ANDREWSON
LEAVENWORTH, WASHINGTON

YIELD: 4-6 SERVINGS.

> 4 large potatoes, peeled, cooked and quartered
> 3 tablespoons butter
> ½ teaspoon paprika

1. In a large skillet, slowly saute the potatoes in butter until golden brown, about 10-15 minutes. Sprinkle with the paprika.

As a young girl, I felt privileged when my grandmother asked me to shop for her. I walked to the creamery for some butter and then stopped by the meat market to buy 25 cents worth of German bologna. I'd proudly carry them back to my grandma's house in a little basket.

—HELEN DILLSON
HIXSON, TENNESSEE

Cheese Potato Puff

I enjoy entertaining and always look for recipes I can make ahead of time. I got this satisfying potato recipe from my mother-in-law. It's wonderful because I can prepare it the night before. It also contains basic ingredients that everyone loves, like milk and cheddar cheese.

—BEVERLY TEMPLETON GARNER, IOWA

YIELD: 8-10 SERVINGS.

> 12 medium potatoes, peeled (about 5 pounds)
> 1 teaspoon salt, divided
> ¾ cup butter, cubed
> 2 cups (8 ounces) shredded cheddar cheese
> 1 cup milk
> 2 eggs, beaten
> Minced chives, optional

1. Place potatoes in a Dutch oven; cover with water. Add ½ teaspoon salt; cook until tender. Drain; mash potatoes until smooth.

2. In a large saucepan, cook and stir the butter, cheese, milk and remaining salt until smooth. Stir into the potatoes; fold in the eggs. Pour into a greased 3-qt. baking dish.

3. Bake, uncovered, at 350° for 40 minutes or until puffy and golden brown. Sprinkle with chives if desired.

2. Pour into a greased 11-in. x 7-in. baking dish. Bake, uncovered, at 350° for 45 minutes or until almost set.

3. In a small bowl, combine topping ingredients; sprinkle over casserole. Return to the oven for 5-10 minutes or until bubbly.

Corn and Bacon Casserole

Corn is my three boys' favorite vegetable, so we eat a lot of it. My husband, Bob, and our sons really enjoy it.

—**MARCIA HOSTETTER** CANTON, NEW YORK

YIELD: 6-8 SERVINGS.

- 6 bacon strips
- ½ cup chopped onion
- 2 tablespoons all-purpose flour
- 2 garlic cloves, minced
- ½ teaspoon salt
- ½ teaspooon pepper
- 1 cup (8 ounces) sour cream
- 3½ cups fresh or frozen whole kernel corn
- 1 tablespoon chopped fresh parsley
- 1 tablespoon minced chives

1. In a large skillet, cook the bacon over medium heat until crisp. Drain, reserving 2 tablespoon of drippings. Crumble bacon; set aside.

2. Saute onion in drippings until tender. Add flour, garlic, salt and pepper. Cook and stir until bubbly; cook and stir 1 minute more. Remove from the heat and stir in sour cream until smooth. Add corn, parsley and half of the bacon; mix well.

3. Pour into a 1-qt. baking dish. Sprinkle with remaining bacon. Bake, uncovered, at 350° for 20-25 minutes or until heated through. Sprinkle with chives.

Butternut Squash Bake

If I ask our two girls what to fix for a special meal, they always request this dish. I discovered this slightly sweet, crunchy-topped casserole at a church dinner years ago. Now I take it to potluck dinners and come home with an empty dish!

—**JULIE JAHN** DECATUR, INDIANA

YIELD: 6-8 SERVINGS.

- ⅓ cup butter, softened
- ¾ cup sugar
- 2 eggs
- 1 can (5 ounces) evaporated milk
- 1 teaspoon vanilla extract
- 2 cups mashed cooked butternut squash

TOPPING
- ½ cup crisp rice cereal
- ¼ cup packed brown sugar
- ¼ cup chopped pecans
- 2 tablespoons butter, melted

1. In a large bowl, cream butter and sugar until fluffy. Beat in the eggs, milk and vanilla. Stir in squash (mixture will be thin).

Delicious Corn Pudding

This old-fashioned dish has been part of our family meals for years, and we've shared it at many gatherings.

—P. MARCHESI ROCKY POINT, NEW YORK

YIELD: 8 SERVINGS.

- 4 eggs, separated
- 2 tablespoons butter, melted and cooled
- 1 tablespoon sugar
- 1 tablespoon brown sugar
- 1 teaspoon salt
- ½ teaspoon vanilla extrsact
- Dash each ground cinnamon and nutmeg
- 2 cups fresh or frozen corn
- 1 cup half-and-half cream
- 1 cup milk

1. In a bowl, beat yolks until lemon-colored, 5-8 minutes. Add the butter, sugars, salt, vanilla, cinnamon and nutmeg; mix well. Add corn. Stir in cream and milk. In a small bowl, beat egg whites on high speed until stiff; fold into yolk mixture.

2. Pour into a greased 1½-qt. baking dish. Bake, uncovered, at 350° for 35 minutes or until a knife inserted near the center comes out clean. Cover loosely with foil during the last 10 minutes of baking if top browns too quickly.

Caraway Sauerkraut

Over the years, I've learned that cooking with herbs and spices is fun and rewarding. With sauerkraut, bacon and caraway, this side dish really reflects my German heritage.

—TRUDI JOHNSON HIXSON, TENNESSEE

YIELD: 18-20 SERVINGS.

- 6 bacon strips, chopped
- 1 medium onion, chopped
- 2 bags or jars (32 ounces each) sauerkraut, rinsed and drained
- 1 tablespoon caraway seeds
- 2 cups water
- 1 large potato, peeled and shredded

1. In a 5-qt. Dutch oven, cook bacon and onion over medium heat for 8-9 minutes or until onion is golden brown. Stir in sauerkraut and caraway. Add water; bring to a boil. Reduce heat; cover and simmer for 1½ hours, stirring occasionally. Add potato. Cook for 20 minutes or until potato is tender.

Norwegian Parsley Potatoes

I love to use parsley in many dishes, and it suits the fresh taste of small red potatoes well. Even though these potatoes are easy to prepare, they look fancy and are great with baked ham.

—EUNICE STOEN DECORAH, IOWA

YIELD: 6-8 SERVINGS.

- 2 pounds small red new potatoes
- ½ cup butter, cubed
- ¼ cup chopped fresh parsley
- ¼ teaspoon dried marjoram

1. Cook potatoes in boiling salted water for 15 minutes or until tender. Cool slightly. With a sharp knife, remove one narrow strip of skin around the middle of each potato. In a large skillet, melt butter; add parsley and marjoram. Add the potatoes and stir gently until coated and heated through.

Creamed Peas

I can still taste these wonderful peas in Mama's delicious white sauce. Our food was generally pretty plain during the week, so I thought the sauce made the peas extra fancy and fitting for a Sunday meal.

—IMOGENE HUTTON BROWNWOOD, TEXAS

YIELD: 3-4 SERVINGS.

- 1 package (10 ounces) frozen peas
- 1 tablespoon butter
- 1 tablespoon all-purpose flour
- ¼ teaspoon salt
- ⅛ teaspoon pepper
- ½ cup milk
- 1 teaspoon sugar

1. Cook peas according to package directions. Meanwhile, in a small saucepan, melt the butter. Stir in the flour, salt and pepper until blended; gradually add milk and sugar. Bring to a boil; cook and stir for 1-2 minutes or until thickened. Drain peas; stir into the sauce and heat through.

Easy Grilled Squash

This is one of my favorite ways to use butternut squash, which I love not just for its flavor but also because it's full of vitamin A. I usually make this when I am grilling steak or chicken.

—ESTHER HORST MONTEREY, TENNESSEE

YIELD: 4 SERVINGS.

- 3 tablespoons olive oil
- 2 garlic cloves, minced
- ¼ teaspoon salt
- ¼ teaspoon pepper
- 1 small butternut squash, peeled and cut lengthwise into ½-inch slices

1. In a small bowl, combine the oil, garlic, salt and pepper. Brush over squash slices.

2. Grill squash, covered, over medium heat or broil 4 in. from the heat for 4-5 minutes on each side or until tender.

Asparagus with Sesame Butter

The first fresh asparagus is a delightful springtime treat. This light butter sauce lets the asparagus flavor come through, and the sprinkling of sesame seeds adds a delicate crunch. It's a simple yet delicious dish.

—EUNICE STOEN DECORAH, IOWA

YIELD: 6-8 SERVINGS.

- 2 **pounds fresh asparagus**
- 1 **cup boiling water**
- ½ **teaspoon salt**
- 1 **tablespoon cornstarch**
- ¼ **cup cold water**
- ¼ **cup butter, cubed**
- 3 **tablespoons sesame seeds, toasted**

1. Place asparagus spears in a large skillet; add boiling water and salt. Cook for 5-7 minutes or until tender. Remove the asparagus and keep warm. Drain cooking liquid, reserving ½ cup in a small saucepan.

2. Combine cornstarch and cold water; stir into liquid. Cook and stir over medium heat until thickened and bubbly; cook and stir 1 minute more. Stir in the butter until melted. Spoon over asparagus; sprinkle with sesame seeds and serve immediately.

Herbed Rice Pilaf

I've relied on this savory side dish for years. We especially enjoy it in summer alongside a grilled entree.

—JERI DOBROWSKI BEACH, NORTH DAKOTA

YIELD: 6 SERVINGS.

- 1 **cup uncooked long grain rice**
- 1 **cup chopped celery**
- ¾ **cup chopped onion**
- ¼ **cup butter**
- 2½ **cups water**
- 1 **package (2 to 2½ ounces) dry chicken noodle soup mix**

- 2 **tablespoons minced fresh parsley**
- ½ **teaspoon dried thyme**
- ¼ **teaspoon rubbed sage**
- ¼ **teaspoon pepper**
- 1 **tablespoon chopped pimientos, optional**

1. In a large skillet, cook the rice, celery and onion in butter, stirring constantly, until rice is browned. Stir in the next six ingredients; bring to a boil.

2. Reduce heat; cover and simmer for 15 minutes. Stir in the pimientos if desired. Remove from the heat and let stand, covered, for 10 minutes.

Creamed Onions

This is my absolute favorite dish of my mom's. The onions have a mild flavor, and there's plenty of the rich creamy sauce. The sweetness makes it a nice complement to beef tenderloin.

—DENISE BITNER REEDSVILLE, PENNSYLVANIA

YIELD: 8-10 SERVINGS.

- 6 **large onions, sliced**
- 1 **cup butter**
- 2 **teaspoons all-purpose flour**
- 2 **teaspoons salt**
- ½ **teaspoon white pepper**
- 2 **cups milk**

1. In a large skillet or Dutch oven, saute onions in butter until tender and golden brown, about 25 minutes. Remove with a slotted spoon. Add flour, salt and pepper to skillet; stir until smooth. Gradually stir in milk until blended.

2. Bring to a boil; cook and stir for 2 minutes or until sauce is thickened. Reduce heat to medium. Return onions to the pan; heat through.

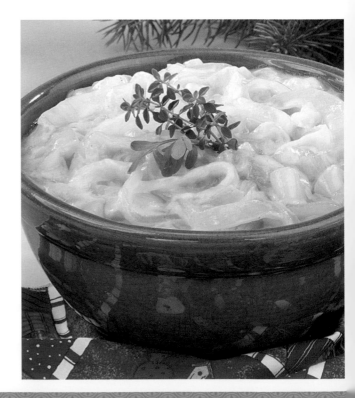

German-Style Spinach

Grandma's Austrian heritage comes through in her spinach dish. It's tasty and always looks so pretty on the plate. We children never had to be told to eat our spinach at Grandma's house!

—**JOAN HUTTER** WARWICK, RHODE ISLAND

YIELD: 8 SERVINGS.

- 2 packages (10 ounces each) frozen chopped spinach
- 1 large onion, chopped
- 2 garlic cloves, minced
- 2 tablespoons butter
- 6 bacon strips, cooked and crumbled
- ½ teaspoon ground nutmeg
- ½ teaspoon salt
- Pepper to taste

1. Cook spinach according to package directions. Drain well and set aside. Saute onion and garlic in butter in a large skillet until tender. Stir in the spinach, bacon, nutmeg, salt and pepper; heat through.

Mashed Horseradish Potatoes

Instead of the ordinary garlic mashed potatoes, this unusual—but delicious— recipe calls for prepared horseradish. My family requests it every Thanksgiving, and it is also great with roast beef.

—**CYNTHIA GOBELI** NORTON, OHIO

YIELD: 6-8 SERVINGS.

- 6 medium potatoes, peeled and cubed
- ¼ cup butter, melted
- ¾ teaspoon salt
- ⅛ teaspoon pepper
- ½ cup sour cream
- 2 tablespoons prepared horseradish

1. Place potatoes in a large saucepan and cover with water. Bring to a boil. Reduce heat and cook for 10 minutes or until tender; drain.

2. Add the butter, salt and pepper. Mash potatoes. Beat in the sour cream and horseradish.

When Mom fried potatoes, she would moisten bread under the faucet, squeeze out the water, then break the bread into the potatoes. It would fry up brown and crunchy. When I got married, I made potatoes the same way. When my daughter got married, so did she.

Not long ago, Mom came for a visit. She decided to fry potatoes. I was stunned when she did not add the bread to the pan. When I asked where the bread was, she said she didn't know what I was talking about. So I explained that when I was a child in the early 1940s, she always fried potatoes that way. She started to laugh. She told me the only reason she did that was because we didn't have enough potatoes!

—**JUDIE DUMONT** WALTON, INDIANA

Party Potatoes

These creamy potatoes can be prepared the day before and then stored in the refrigerator until you're ready to pop them in the oven. The garlic powder and chives add zip, and the shredded cheese adds color.

—**SHARON MENSING** GREENFIELD, IOWA

YIELD: 10-12 SERVINGS.

- 4 cups mashed potatoes (about 8 to 10 large) or 4 cups prepared instant potatoes
- 1 cup (8 ounces) sour cream
- 1 package (8 ounces) cream cheese, softened
- 1 teaspoon minced chives
- ¼ teaspoon garlic powder
- ¼ cup dry bread crumbs
- 1 tablespoon butter, melted
- ½ cup shredded cheddar cheese

1. In a large bowl, combine potatoes, sour cream, cream cheese, chives and garlic powder. Tranfer to a greased 2-qt. baking dish. Combine the bread crumbs with the butter; sprinkle over the potatoes.

2. Bake at 350° for 50 to 60 minutes. Sprinkle with the cheese and serve immediately.

Hungarian Noodle Side Dish

I first served this rich casserole at a women's meeting at church. Everyone liked it and many of the ladies wanted the recipe. The original recipe was from a friend, but I changed it a bit to suit our tastes.

—**BETTY SUGG** AKRON, NEW YORK

YIELD: 8-10 SERVINGS.

- 3 chicken bouillon cubes
- ¼ cup boiling water
- 1 can (10¾ ounces) condensed cream of mushroom soup, undiluted
- ½ cup chopped onion
- 2 tablespoons Worcestershire sauce
- 2 tablespoons poppy seeds
- ⅛ to ¼ teaspoon garlic powder
- ⅛ to ¼ teaspoon hot pepper sauce
- 2 cups (16 ounces) 4% cottage cheese
- 2 cups (16 ounces) sour cream
- 1 package (16 ounces) medium noodles, cooked and drained
- ¼ cup shredded Parmesan cheese

Paprika

1. In a large bowl, dissolve bouillon in water. Add the next six ingredients; mix well. Stir in cottage cheese, sour cream and noodles and mix well.

2. Pour into a greased 2½-qt. baking dish. Sprinkle with the Parmesan cheese and paprika. Cover and bake at 350° for 45 minutes or until heated through.

Scalloped Pineapple Casserole

My family can't get enough of this sweet and satisfying side dish. The casserole disappears quickly whenever I prepare it.

—JUDY HOWLE COLUMBUS, MISSISSIPPI

YIELD: 6 SERVINGS.

- ¾ **cup butter, softened**
- 1¼ **cups sugar**
- 3 **eggs**
- 1 **can (20 ounces) crushed pineapple, well drained**
- 1½ **teaspoons lemon juice**
- 4 **cups firmly packed cubed white bread (crusts removed)**

1. In a large bowl, cream butter and sugar until light and fluffy. Add eggs, one at a time, beating well after each addition. Stir in the pineapple and lemon juice. Gently fold in bread cubes.

2. Spoon into a greased 2-qt. baking dish. Bake, uncovered, at 350° for 40 to 45 minutes or until the top is lightly golden. Serve warm.

Harvard Beets

My beets are a pretty accompaniment to any meal and have wonderful flavor. Even those who normally shy away from beets will gobble these up.

—JEAN ANN PERKINS NEWBURYPORT, MARYLAND

YIELD: 4-6 SERVINGS.

- 1 **can (16 ounces) sliced beets**
- ¼ **cup sugar**
- 1½ **teaspoons cornstarch**
- 2 **tablespoons cider vinegar**
- 2 **tablespoons orange juice**
- 1 **tablespoon grated orange peel**

1. Drain beets, reserving 2 tablespoons juice; set beets and juice aside. In a saucepan, combine sugar and cornstarch. Add vinegar, orange juice and beet juice; bring to a boil. Reduce heat and simmer for 3-4 minutes or until thickened. Add beets and orange peel; heat through.

Continental Zucchini

Zucchini are big and plentiful here, and people often joke about using them up before they multiply! Even with so much zucchini to go around, everyone enjoys it prepared this way.

—MARTHA FEHL BROOKVILLE, INDIANA

YIELD: 6 SERVINGS.

- 1 **tablespoon canola oil**
- 1 **pound zucchini (about 3 small), cubed**
- 1 **to 2 garlic cloves, minced**
- 1 **jar (2 ounces) diced pimientos, drained**
- 1 **can (15¼ ounces) whole kernel corn, drained**
- 1 **teaspoon salt, optional**
- ¼ **teaspoon lemon-pepper seasoning**
- ½ **cup shredded part-skim mozzarella cheese**

1. Heat oil in a large skillet. Saute zucchini and garlic for 3 to 4 minutes. Add pimientos, corn, salt if desired and lemon-pepper; cook and stir for 2-3 minutes or until the zucchini is tender. Sprinkle with cheese and heat until the cheese is melted.

Stuffed Baked Potatoes

My whole family, from the smallest grandchild on up, loves these special potatoes. I prepare them up to a week in advance, wrap them well and freeze. The flavorful filling will go nicely with your favorite meat dish.

—MARGE CLARK WEST LEBANON, INDIANA

YIELD: 6 SERVINGS.

- 3 large baking potatoes (1 pound each)
- 1½ teaspoons canola oil, optional
- ½ cup sliced green onions
- ½ cup butter, cubed, divided
- ½ cup half-and-half cream
- ½ cup sour cream
- 1 teaspoon salt
- ½ teaspoon white pepper
- 1 cup (4 ounces) shredded cheddar cheese
Paprika

1. Scrub and pierce potatoes. Rub with oil if desired. Bake at 400° for 50-75 minutes or until tender. When cool enough to handle, cut each potato in half lengthwise. Scoop out pulp, leaving a thin shell; set aside.

2. In a small skillet, saute onions in ¼ cup butter until tender. In a large bowl, mash potato pulp. Stir in the onion mixture, cream, sour cream, salt and pepper. Fold in the cheese. Stuff into potato shells.

3. Place on a baking sheet. Melt remaining butter; drizzle over potatoes. Sprinkle with paprika. Bake at 375° for 20 minutes or until heated through.

Editor's Note: *Potatoes may be stuffed ahead of time and refrigerated or frozen. Allow additional time for reheating.*

Ranch Stuffed Baked Potatoes: Stir 1 to 2 tablespoons ranch salad dressing mix into sour cream before adding to mashed potatoes. Fold in 3 crumbled cooked bacon strips along with the cheese.

Tex-Mex Stuffed Baked Potatoes: Omit green onions and ¼ cup butter. Stir in 1 can (4 ounces) chopped green chilies (drained). Substitute pepper Jack cheese for the cheddar. Sprinkle with chili powder instead of paprika.

Herb-Stuffed Baked Potatoes: Add 2 tablespoons each minced chives and fresh parsley with the onions. Susbtitute mozzarella for the cheddar.

Broccoli-Stuffed Baked Potatoes: Omit green onions. Saute 2 cups fresh broccoli florets and ½ cup chopped onion in ¼ cup butter. Stir into mashed potatoes.

Western Beans

I've made these zesty beans many times for picnics and potlucks. They're hearty and zippy with chili pepper and the extra flavor of lentils in the bean mix. I sometimes make them ahead of time and heat right before serving.

—ARTHUR MORRIS WASHINGTON, PENNSYLVANIA

YIELD: 8-10 SERVINGS.

- 4 bacon strips, diced
- 1 large onion, chopped
- 1⅓ cups water
- ⅓ cup dried lentils, rinsed
- 2 tablespoons ketchup
- 1 teaspoon garlic powder
- ¾ teaspoon chili powder
- ½ teaspoon ground cumin
- ¼ teaspoon dried red pepper flakes
- 1 bay leaf
- 1 can (14½ ounces) diced tomatoes, undrained
- 1 can (15 ounces) pinto beans, drained
- 1 can (16 ounces) kidney beans, drained

1. Lightly fry bacon in a heavy 3-qt. saucepan. Add onion; cook until transparent. Stir in remaining ingredients. Cook over medium heat for 45 minutes or until lentils are tender, stirring once or twice. Remove bay leaf before serving.

Special Garden Medley

My mother used to make this in large batches to can for our family 60 years ago. Now I make it for my freezer.

—NORMA COATS PETERSBURG, TENNESSEE

YIELD: 6 SERVINGS.

- 2 **celery ribs, chopped**
- 1 **large onion, chopped**
- 1 **medium sweet yellow or green pepper, chopped**
- ¼ **cup water**
- 4 **cups chopped seeded peeled tomatoes (about 9 medium)**
- 4½ **teaspoons sugar**
- 1 **teaspoon salt**

1. In a large saucepan, combine the celery, onion, yellow pepper and water. Bring to a boil. Reduce heat; cover and simmer for 20 minutes or until tender.

2. Stir in the tomatoes, sugar and salt; cook 6-8 minutes longer or until heated through.

Zesty Carrot Bake

For a fun vegetable dish, try tender carrots in a sauce that gets a little extra punch from horseradish. With a crunchy crumb topping and comforting sauce, it will tempt even those who usually don't care for cooked carrots.

—GRACE YASKOVIC
LAKE HIAWATHA, NEW JERSEY

YIELD: 6 SERVINGS.

- 1 **pound carrots, cut into ½-inch slices**
- 2 **tablespoons finely chopped onion**
- ¾ **cup mayonnaise**
- ⅓ **cup water**
- 1 **tablespoon prepared horseradish**
- ¼ **teaspoon pepper**
- ½ **cup dry bread crumbs**
- 2 **tablespoons butter, melted**
- ½ **cup shredded sharp cheddar cheese**

1. On stovetop or microwave, cook the carrots until tender. Transfer to a 1-qt. baking dish; set aside.

2. In a small bowl, combine the next five ingredients. Pour over carrots. Combine bread crumbs and butter; sprinkle over top. Bake, uncovered, at 350° for 25-30 minutes. Sprinkle with cheese. Bake 2-3 minutes longer or until cheese is melted.

Creamy Sweet Potatoes

I took my mother's delicious sweet potato casserole recipe and gave it a new twist by adding the tempting taste of orange. The flavors are wonderful together and made this delightful dish a family favorite.

—NORMA POOLE AUBURNDALE, FLORIDA

YIELD: 10-12 SERVINGS.

- 5 pounds sweet potatoes, peeled and cooked
- 4 eggs, lightly beaten
- ½ cup orange juice
- ½ cup butter, softened
- ½ cup sugar
- 1 teaspoon vanilla extract
- ½ teaspoon ground nutmeg
- Dash salt
- Marshmallows

1. In a large bowl, mash the sweet potatoes. Add the eggs, orange juice, butter, sugar, vanilla, nutmeg and salt and mix well. Transfer to a greased 3-qt. baking dish.

2. Bake at 350° for 35-40 minutes or until set. Top with the marshmallows; bake about 5-10 minutes longer or until the marshmallows just begin to puff and melt.

Broccoli-Pasta Side Dish

I love to fix new recipes for my husband, Robert, and our children. With garlic and cheese, this is a tasty way to get kids to eat broccoli.

—JUDI LACOURSE MESA, ARIZONA

YIELD: 4-6 SERVINGS.

- 2½ pounds fresh broccoli
- 2 garlic cloves, minced
- ⅓ cup olive oil
- 1 tablespoon butter
- 1 teaspoon salt
- ¼ teaspoon pepper
- Pinch cayenne pepper
- 8 ounces linguine or thin spaghetti, cooked and drained
- Grated Romano or Parmesan cheese

1. Cut florets and tender parts of broccoli stems into bite-size pieces. In a large skillet, saute broccoli with garlic, oil, butter, salt, pepper and cayenne over medium heat for about 10 minutes or until just tender, stirring frequently. Place hot pasta in a serving dish; top with the broccoli mixture. Sprinkle with cheese.

2. Cut eggplant into ½-in. cubes. Transfer to a large skillet; saute in oil until lightly browned. Add onions and zucchini; cook 3 minutes. Add garlic; cook 1 minute longer. Add the tomatoes, celery, parsley, basil, pepper and remaining salt; bring to a boil. Reduce heat; cover and simmer for 10 minutes. Remove from the heat; stir in Romano cheese.

3. Pour into a greased 13-in. x 9-in. baking dish. Combine crumbs and butter; sprinkle on top. Bake, uncovered, at 375° for 15 minutes. Sprinkle with the mozzarella cheese. Bake 5 minutes longer or until cheese is melted.

Peas with Mushrooms

My savory side dish has a fresh taste, even though it's made with convenient frozen peas.

—MARY DENNIS BRYAN, OHIO

YIELD: 4 SERVINGS.

- ½ **pound fresh mushrooms, sliced**
- ? **tablespoons sliced green onions**
- 1 **tablespoon butter**
- ¼ **teaspoon dried marjoram**
- ¼ **teaspoon salt, optional**
- ⅛ **teaspoon pepper**
Dash ground nutmeg
- 1 **package (10 ounces) frozen peas, cooked**

1. In a skillet over medium heat, saute the mushrooms and onions in butter for 3-5 minutes. Add marjoram, salt if desired, pepper and nutmeg; mix well. Add peas and heat through.

Garden Casserole

In summer, I fill this delicious cheesy casserole with lots of vegetables and herbs from my garden. It features a sunny medley of eggplant, zucchini and tomatoes.

—PHYLLIS HICKEY BEDFORD, NEW HAMPSHIRE

YIELD: 12 SERVINGS.

- 2 **pounds eggplant, peeled**
- 5 **teaspoons salt, divided**
- ¼ **cup olive oil**
- 2 **medium onions, finely chopped**
- 2 **medium zucchini, sliced ½ inch thick**
- 2 **garlic cloves, minced**
- 5 **medium tomatoes, peeled and chopped**
- 2 **celery ribs, sliced**
- ¼ **cup minced fresh parsley**
- ¼ **cup minced fresh basil or 1 tablespoon dried basil**
- ½ **teaspoon pepper**
- ½ **cup grated Romano cheese**
- 1 **cup seasoned bread crumbs**
- 2 **tablespoons butter, melted**
- 1 **cup (4 ounces) shredded part-skim mozzarella cheese**

1. Cut eggplant into ½-in.-thick slices; sprinkle both sides with 3 teaspoons salt. Place in a deep dish; cover and let stand for 30 minutes. Rinse with cold water; drain and dry on paper towels.

Mushroom Rice Medley

We would never hear the end of it if we failed to have my grandmother's mushroom rice dish on the table for any family gathering. It's the dish my dad requests most often.

—SUE MULLIS SHARON, WISCONSIN

YIELD: 6 SERVINGS.

3 cups water
½ cup uncooked brown rice
½ cup uncooked wild rice
1 teaspoon chicken bouillon granules
1 teaspoon dried oregano
½ pound sliced bacon, diced
½ pound sliced fresh mushrooms
1 small onion, chopped
¼ teaspoon salt, optional

1. In a large saucepan, combine the water, brown rice, wild rice, bouillon and oregano. Bring to a boil. Reduce heat; cover and simmer for 50-60 minutes or until rice is tender.

2. In a large skillet, cook bacon over medium heat until crisp. Using a slotted spoon, remove to paper towels. Drain, reserving 2 tablespoons drippings. In the drippings, saute mushrooms and onion until tender. Stir in rice and bacon; heat through. Season with salt if desired.

Finnish Cauliflower

After my Finnish grandmother passed away, I found a large index card in a box of her trinkets. I had the writing translated, and it turned out to be this festive casserole.

—**JUDY BATSON** TAMPA, FLORIDA

YIELD: 8 SERVINGS.

- 2 **cups cubed day-old rye bread**
- 1 **small head cauliflower, cut into florets**
- 2 **tablespoons butter**
- 1 **teaspoon caraway seeds**
- 3 **cups (12 ounces) shredded sharp cheddar cheese**
- 4 **eggs, beaten**
- 1 **cup flat beer or nonalcoholic beer**
- 1 **teaspoon ground mustard**
- ½ **teaspoon ground coriander**
- ¼ **teaspoon pepper**

1. Place bread in a 15-in. x 10-in. x 1-in. baking pan; bake at 300° for 15-20 minutes or until crisp. In a large skillet, saute cauliflower in butter with the caraway seeds until tender. Remove from the heat; stir in bread and cheese. Transfer to a greased 11-in. x 7-in. baking dish.

2. In a small bowl, whisk the eggs, beer, mustard, coriander and pepper. Pour over bread mixture. Bake at 350° for 30-35 minutes or until a knife inserted near the center comes out clean.

Parmesan Noodles

The special blend of flavors in this cheesy side dish makes it a good addition to any meal. It's a nice change of pace from regular pasta and cheese dishes.

—**ELIZABETH EWAN** CLEVELAND, OHIO

YIELD: 8 SERVINGS.

- 2 **packages (3 ounces each) cream cheese, softened**
- ½ **cup butter, softened, divided**
- 2 **tablespoons minced fresh parsley**
- 1 **teaspoon dried basil**
- ½ **teaspoon lemon-pepper seasoning**
- ⅔ **cup boiling water**
- 1 **garlic clove, minced**
- 6 **cups hot cooked thin noodles**
- ⅔ **cup grated Parmesan cheese, divided**

Additional parsley, optional

1. In a small bowl, combine the cream cheese, 2 tablespoons butter, parsley, basil and lemon-pepper. Stir in water; keep warm.

2. In a saucepan, saute the garlic in remaining butter for 1 minute or until golden brown.

3. Place noodles in a serving bowl; top with garlic mixture. Sprinkle with half of the Parmesan cheese; toss lightly. Spoon the cream sauce over noodles and sprinkle with the remaining Parmesan cheese. Garnish with parsley if desired.

Broccoli Rice Casserole

When I was little, serving this dish was the only way my mother could get me to eat broccoli. It's an excellent recipe and very good with poultry.

—JENNIFER FULLER
BALLSTON SPA, NEW YORK

YIELD: 8 SERVINGS.

- 1½ **cups water**
- ½ **cup butter, cubed**
- 1 **tablespoon dried minced onion**
- 2 **cups uncooked instant rice**
- 1 **package (16 ounces) frozen chopped broccoli, thawed**
- 1 **can (10¾ ounces) condensed cream of mushroom soup, undiluted**
- 1 **jar (8 ounces) process cheese sauce**

1. In a large saucepan, bring the water, butter and onion to a boil. Stir in rice. Remove from the heat; cover and let stand for 5 minutes or until water is absorbed.

2. Stir in the broccoli, soup and cheese sauce. Transfer broccoli mixture to a greased 2-qt. baking dish. Bake, uncovered, at 350° for 30-35 minutes or until bubbly.

Spaetzle Dumplings

It takes only minutes to make my tender homemade noodles. They are a natural accompaniment to chicken. You can enjoy them with chicken gravy or simply eat them buttered and sprinkled with parsley.

—PAMELA EATON MONCLOVA, OHIO

YIELD: 6 SERVINGS.

- 2 **cups all-purpose flour**
- 4 **eggs, lightly beaten**
- ⅓ **cup 2% milk**
- 2 **teaspoons salt**
- 8 **cups water**
- 1 **tablespoon butter**

1. In a large bowl, stir the flour, eggs, milk and salt until smooth (dough will be sticky). In a large saucepan, bring water to a boil. Pour dough into a colander or spaetzle maker coated with cooking spray; place over boiling water.

2. With a wooden spoon, press dough until small pieces drop into boiling water. Cook for 2 minutes or until dumplings are tender and float. Remove with a slotted spoon; toss with butter.

Potato Gnocchi

My Italian mother remembers her own mother making these dumplings for special occasions. She still has the bowl Grandma mixed the dough in, which will someday be passed down to me.

—TINA REPAK MIRILOVICH JOHNSTOWN, PENNSYLVANIA

YIELD: 6-8 SERVINGS.

4	medium potatoes, peeled and quartered
1	egg, lightly beaten
1½	teaspoons salt, divided
1¾ to 2	cups all-purpose flour
3	quarts water

Spaghetti sauce, warmed

1. Place potatoes in a saucepan and cover with water. Bring to a boil. Reduce heat; cover and cook for 15-20 minutes or until tender. Drain and mash.

2. Place 2 cups mashed potatoes in a large bowl (save any remaining mashed potatoes for another use). Stir in egg and 1 teaspoon salt. Gradually beat in flour until blended (dough will be firm and elastic).

3. Turn onto a lightly floured surface; knead 15 times. Roll into ½-in.-wide ropes. Cut ropes into 1-in. pieces. Press down with a lightly floured fork.

4. In a Dutch oven, bring water and remaining salt to a boil. Add gnocchi in small batches, cook for 8-10 minutes or until gnocchi float to the top and are cooked through. Remove with a slotted spoon. Serve immediately with spaghetti sauce.

Zucchini Mozzarella Medley

I love fresh vegetables, especially zucchini, and this recipe of my mother-in-law's is one of my favorite ways to prepare it.

—JENNIFER YODER AMBERG, WISCONSIN

YIELD: 4 SERVINGS.

3	cups sliced zucchini
1	cup sliced onion
½	teaspoon dried basil
¼	teaspoon dried oregano
⅛	teaspoon salt
3	tablespoons butter
1	garlic clove, minced
1	medium tomato, cut into 12 wedges
1	cup (4 ounces) shredded part-skim mozzarella cheese

1. In a large skillet, saute the zucchini, onion and seasonings in butter until crisp-tender. Add garlic; cook 1 minute longer.

2. Gently stir in tomato wedges; sprinkle with cheese. Remove from the heat; cover and let stand for 1-2 minutes or until the cheese is melted.

BREADS

Grandma's Honey Muffins

I can remember Grandma Wheeler making these delicious muffins—we'd eat them nice and warm, fresh from the oven! She was a "pinch of this" and "handful of that" kind of cook, so getting the ingredient amounts correct for the recipe was a challenge. Now it's a family treasure!

—**DARLIS WILFER** WEST BEND, WISCONSIN

YIELD: 1 DOZEN.

    2   cups all-purpose flour
    ½   cup sugar
    3   teaspoons baking powder
    ½   teaspoon salt
    1   egg
    1   cup 2% milk
    ¼   cup butter, melted
    ¼   cup honey

1. In a large bowl, combine the flour, sugar, baking powder and salt. In a small bowl, combine the egg, milk, butter and honey. Stir into dry ingredients just until moistened.

2. Fill greased or paper-lined muffin cups three-fourths full. Bake at 400° for 15-18 minutes or until a toothpick inserted near the center comes out clean. Remove from pan to a wire rack. Serve warm.

Cheese Straws

The first recipe I learned to make was cheese straws. My grandmother helped my twin sister and me make these fun snacks when we were only 5 or 6 years old.
—**SHERI VERO** OCALA, FLORIDA

YIELD: ABOUT 4 ½ DOZEN.

    2   cups all-purpose flour
    ½   cup butter, softened
    4   cups (16 ounces) shredded cheddar cheese
Salt and pepper to taste
Paprika or garlic salt, optional

1. In a food processor, combine the flour, butter and cheese. Cover and process until well blended. Divide into four portions; shape each into a ball. Roll between pieces of waxed paper or plastic wrap into 7-in. x 5-in. rectangles.

2. Cut into 5-in. x ½-in. strips. Place on ungreased baking sheets. Sprinkle with salt, pepper and paprika or garlic salt if desired.

3. Bake at 425° for 10-12 minutes or lightly browned. Remove to wire racks to cool.

Chocolate Chip Cherry Bread

Chips, cherries, bananas, pecans—Mom's quick bread is packed full of goodies. For my wedding reception, we baked a triple batch of the wonderful bread!

—**TERRI COLGROVE** ASHLAND, WISCONSIN

YIELD: 1 LOAF (16 SLICES).

- 2   **cups all-purpose flour**
- 1   **cup sugar**
- 2½ **teaspoons baking powder**
- ½   **teaspoon salt**
- 2   **eggs**
- 1   **cup mashed ripe bananas**
- ½   **cup butter, melted**
- ½   **cup 60% cacao bittersweet chocolate baking chips**
- ¼   **cup chopped pecans**
- ¼   **cup chopped maraschino cherries**

1. In a large bowl, combine the flour, sugar, baking powder and salt. Combine the eggs, bananas and butter; stir into dry ingredients just until moistened. Fold in the chocolate chips, pecans and cherries.

2. Transfer to a greased 9-in. x 5-in. loaf pan. Bake at 350° for 45-50 minutes or until a toothpick inserted near the center comes out clean. Cool for 10 minutes before removing from pan to a wire rack.

Mom's Buttermilk Biscuits

Rich buttermilk biscuits baking in the oven will bring back warm memories of your own mom's kitchen. These have a classic old-fashioned flavor that's stood the test of time. You can make them with little effort.

—**JUDITH RUSH** KATY, TEXAS

YIELD: 1 DOZEN.

- 2   **cups all-purpose flour**
- 2¼ **teaspoons baking powder**
- ¾   **teaspoon salt**
- ¼   **teaspoon baking soda**
- ⅓   **cup shortening**
- ¾   **cup buttermilk**

1. In a large bowl, combine the dry ingredients. Cut in shortening until mixture resembles coarse crumbs. Stir in buttermilk just until moistened.

2. Turn onto a lightly floured surface. Roll to ½-in. thickness; cut with a floured 2½-in. biscuit cutter. Place 1 in. apart on an ungreased baking sheet. Bake at 450° for 8-10 minutes or until golden brown. Serve warm.

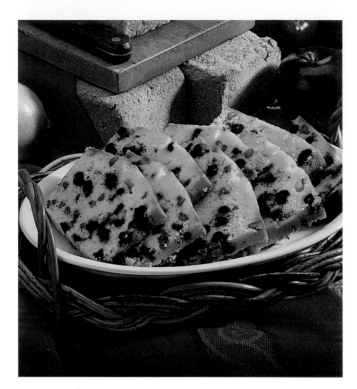

Lemon Blueberry Bread

Of all the quick breads we had growing up, this beautifully glazed berry-studded loaf is the best!

—JULIANNE JOHNSON GROVE CITY, MINNESOTA

YIELD: 1 LOAF (16 SLICES).

⅓ cup butter, melted
1 cup sugar
3 tablespoons lemon juice
2 eggs
1½ cups all-purpose flour
1 teaspoon baking powder
½ teaspoon salt
½ cup milk
1 cup fresh or frozen blueberries
½ cup chopped nuts
2 tablespoons grated lemon peel
GLAZE
2 tablespoons lemon juice
¼ cup sugar

1. In a large bowl, beat the butter, sugar, lemon juice and eggs. Combine the flour, baking powder and salt; stir into the egg mixture alternately with milk, beating well after each addition. Fold in the blueberries, nuts and lemon peel.

2. Transfer to a greased 8-in. x 4-in. loaf pan. Bake at 350° for 60-70 minutes or until a toothpick inserted near the center comes out clean. Cool for 10 minutes before removing from pan to a wire rack.

3. Combine the glaze ingredients; drizzle over warm bread. Cool completely.

Editor's Note: *If using frozen blueberries, use without thawing to avoid discoloring the batter.*

Irish Soda Bread

This bread is prepared much like a biscuit. Mix the dough just until moist to keep it tender.

—GLORIA WARCZAK CEDARBURG, WISCONSIN

YIELD: 6-8 SERVINGS.

2 cups all-purpose flour
2 tablespoons brown sugar
1 teaspoon baking powder
1 teaspoon baking soda
½ teaspoon salt
3 tablespoons butter
2 eggs
¾ cup buttermilk
⅓ cup raisins

1. In a large bowl, combine flour, brown sugar, baking powder, baking soda and salt. Cut in butter until crumbly. In a small bowl, whisk 1 egg and buttermilk. Stir into flour mixture just until moistened. Fold in raisins.

2. Knead on a floured surface for 1 minute. Shape into a round loaf; place on a greased baking sheet. Cut a ¼-in.-deep cross in top of loaf. Beat remaining egg; brush over loaf.

3. Bake at 375° for 30-35 minutes or until golden brown.

Caraway Irish Soda Bread: Add 1 to 2 tablespoons caraway seeds to the dry ingredients.

Pop-Up Rolls

For lightly sweet, biscuit-like rolls that are anything but dry, you can't beat simple Pop-Up Rolls. With just four basic ingredients that are mixed in one bowl, these easy-to-make rolls are great alongside just about everything.

—JUDY BRINEGAR LIBERTY, NORTH CAROLINA

YIELD: 9 ROLLS.

1½ cups self-rising flour
¾ cup milk
3 tablespoons sugar
1½ tablespoons mayonnaise

1. In a large bowl, stir together all ingredients until thoroughly combined. Fill greased muffin cups half full. Bake at 375° for 18-20 minutes or until lightly browned. Serve warm.

Editor's Note: *As a substitute for 1½ cups self-rising flour, place 2¼ teaspoons baking powder and 3/4 teaspoon salt in a measuring cup. Add all-purpose flour to measure 1 cup. Combine with an additional 1/2 cup all-purpose flour.*

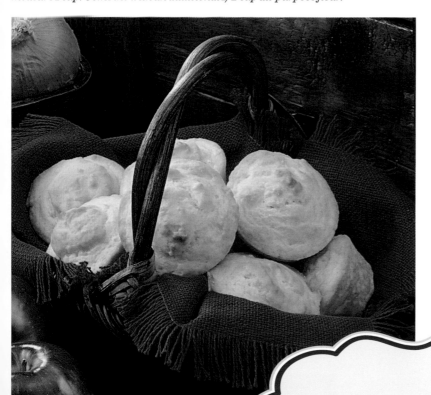

Apricot Walnut Bread

Orange juice and oat bran add flavor and texture to this quick bread.

—DIANE HIXON NICEVILLE, FLORIDA

YIELD: 1 LOAF.

4 egg whites
⅔ cup water
½ cup orange juice
¼ cup canola oil
1 teaspoon vanilla extract
¾ cup uncooked oat bran hot cereal
½ cup chopped dried apricots
1¼ cups all-purpose flour
½ cup packed brown sugar
1 teaspoon baking powder
½ teaspoon baking soda
¼ cup chopped walnuts

1. In a bowl, combine the egg whites, water, orange juice, oil and vanilla. Stir in the oat bran and apricots. Combine the flour, brown sugar, baking powder and baking soda; stir into apricot mixture just until moistened. Fold in walnuts.

2. Pour into a greased 8-in. x 4-in. loaf pan. Bake at 350° for 50-55 minutes or a toothpick inserted near the center comes out clean. Cool for 10 minutes before removing from pan to a wire rack.

> My grandmother made a doughnut-shaped bread that she called "pretzel buck." She would deep-fry it like doughnuts and sprinkle cinnamon and sugar on it. You can't buy bread that tastes as good as that old pretzel buck.
>
> **—DAVID KIDD** WATERFORD, MICHIGAN

Cheddar-Dill Bread

With soup and salad, this savory cheese bread makes a terrific meal.

—**KAREN GARDINER** EUTAW, ALABAMA

YIELD: 1 LOAF.

- 2 **cups self-rising flour**
- 1 **tablespoon sugar**
- ¼ **cup cold butter, cubed**
- 1 **cup (4 ounces) shredded sharp cheddar cheese**
- 2 **teaspoons dill weed**
- 1 **egg**
- ¾ **cup milk**

1. In a large bowl, combine flour and sugar. Cut in butter until crumbly; stir in the cheese and dill. In a small bowl, beat egg and milk; pour into dry ingredients and stir just until moistened. (Batter will be very thick.)

2. Pour into a greased 8-in. x 4-in. loaf pan. Bake at 350° for 35-40 minutes or until a toothpick comes out clean. Cool in pan for 10 minutes before removing to a wire rack.

Editor's Note: *As a substitute for each cup of self-rising flour, place 1½ teaspoons baking powder and 1/2 teaspoon salt in a measuring cup. Add all-purpose flour to measure 1 cup.*

Glazed Cinnamon Biscuits

I often make this easy, delicious variation of glazed cinnamon rolls for our family as a breakfast treat on weekends.

—**SUE GRONHOLZ** BEAVER DAM, WISCONSIN

YIELD: 1 DOZEN.

- 2 **cups all-purpose flour**
- 4 **teaspoons baking powder**
- ½ **teaspoon salt**
- 6 **tablespoons butter, divided**
- ¾ **cup milk**
- ¼ **cup sugar**
- 1 **teaspoon ground cinnamon**

GLAZE

- 1 **cup confectioners' sugar**
- 1 **tablespoon butter, melted**
- 5 **to 6 teaspoons milk**
- ⅛ **teaspoon vanilla extract**

1. In a large bowl, combine dry ingredients. Cut in 4 tablespoons of butter until mixture resembles coarse crumbs. Stir in milk just until moistened.

2. Turn onto a lightly floured surface; knead gently 8 to 10 times. Roll into an 11-in. x 8-in. rectangle about ½ in. thick. Melt remaining butter; brush 1 tablespoon over dough. Combine sugar and cinnamon; sprinkle over butter. Roll up jelly-roll style, starting with long edge. Cut into 12 equal slices. Place with cut side down in a greased 8-in. square baking pan. Brush with remaining butter.

3. Bake at 450° for 18 to 20 minutes or until golden brown. Cool for 5 minutes. Combine glaze ingredients; spread over warm biscuits. Serve immediately.

Raspberry Lemon Muffins

These are my all-time favorite muffins, and I have a hard time eating just one. They're pretty, tangy and delectable.

—**SHARON SHINE** BRADFORD, PENNSYLVANIA

YIELD: 18 SERVINGS.

- 2 **cups all-purpose flour**
- 1 **cup sugar**
- 1 **tablespoon baking powder**
- ½ **teaspoon salt**
- 2 **eggs, lightly beaten**
- 1 **cup half-and-half cream**
- ½ **cup canola oil**
- 1 **teaspoon lemon extract**
- 1½ **cups fresh or frozen raspberries**

1. In a large bowl, combine flour, sugar, baking powder and salt. Combine the eggs, cream, oil and lemon extract; stir into dry ingredients just until moistened. Fold in raspberries.

2. Spoon into 18 greased or paper-lined muffin cups. Bake at 400° for 18 to 20 minutes or until a toohpick comes out clean.

Editor's Note: *If using frozen raspberries, use without thawing to avoid discoloring the batter.*

Chocolate Mini Loaves

Rich and moist, these luscious mini breads will remind you of pound cake. Slice them for snacking or to serve as dessert with a cup of coffee or tea.

—ELIZABETH DOWNEY EVART, MICHIGAN

YIELD: 5 MINI LOAVES (6 SLICES EACH).

½ cup butter, softened
⅔ cup packed brown sugar
1 cup (6 ounces) semisweet
  chocolate chips, melted
2 eggs
2 teaspoons vanilla extract
2½ cups all-purpose flour
1 teaspoon baking powder
1 teaspoon baking soda
1½ cups applesauce
½ cup miniature semisweet
  chocolate chips
GLAZE
½ cup semisweet chocolate chips
1 tablespoon butter
5 teaspoons water
½ cup confectioners' sugar
¼ teaspoon vanilla extract
Dash salt

1. In a large bowl, cream butter and brown sugar until light and fluffy. Beat in the melted chocolate chips, eggs and vanilla. Combine the flour, baking powder and baking soda; add to creamed mixture alternately with applesauce just until moistened. Fold in miniature chips.

2. Divide batter among five greased 5¾-in. x 3-in. x 2-in. loaf pans, about 1 cup in each. Bake at 350° for 30-40 minutes or until a toothpick inserted near the center comes out clean. Cool for 10 minutes before removing from pans to wire racks to cool completely.

3. For glaze, combine the chocolate chips, butter and water in a saucepan; cook and stir over low heat until chocolate is melted. Remove from the heat; stir in confectioners' sugar, vanilla and salt until smooth. Drizzle over cooled loaves.

Editor's Note: *Two 8-in. x 4-in. x 2-in. loaf pans may be used; bake for 50-55 minutes.*

Blueberry Streusel Muffins

What a joy to set out a basket of these moist blueberry muffins topped with a super streusel on the bake sale table. People rave when they taste them for the first time.

—MARY ANNE MCWHIRTER PEARLAND, TEXAS

YIELD: 1 DOZEN.

- ¼ cup butter, softened
- ⅓ cup sugar
- 1 egg
- 1 teaspoon vanilla extract
- 2⅓ cups all-purpose flour
- 4 teaspoons baking powder
- ½ teaspoon salt
- 1 cup milk
- 1½ cups fresh or frozen blueberries

STREUSEL

- ½ cup sugar
- ⅓ cup all-purpose flour
- ½ teaspoon ground cinnamon
- ¼ cup cold butter

1. In a large bowl, cream the butter and sugar. Beat in egg and vanilla; mix well. Combine the flour, baking powder and salt; add to creamed mixture alternately with milk. Fold in the blueberries.

2. Fill 12 greased or paper-lined muffin cups two-thirds full. In a small bowl, combine the sugar, flour and cinnamon; cut in the butter until crumbly. Sprinkle over the muffins. Bake at 375° for 25-30 minutes or until browned. Cool for 5 minutes before removing to a wire rack. Serve warm.

Editor's Note: *If using frozen blueberries, use without thawing to avoid discoloring the batter.*

Pumpkin Bread

You'll love this deliciously spicy, pumpkin-rich quick bread. I keep my freezer stocked with home-baked goodies. This one is always a winner with our harvest crew.

—JOYCE JACKSON BRIDGETOWN, NOVA SCOTIA

YIELD: 1 LOAF (16 SLICES).

- 1⅔ cups all-purpose flour
- 1½ cups sugar
- 1 teaspoon baking soda
- 1 teaspoon ground cinnamon
- ¾ teaspoon salt
- ½ teaspoon baking powder
- ½ teaspoon ground nutmeg
- ¼ teaspoon ground cloves
- 2 eggs

- 1 **cup canned pumpkin**
- ½ **cup canola oil**
- ½ **cup water**
- ½ **cup chopped walnuts**
- ½ **cup raisins, optional**

1. In a large small bowl, combine the flour, sugar, baking soda cinnamon, salt, baking powder, nutmeg and cloves. In a small bowl, whisk the eggs, pumpkin, oil, and water. Stir into dry ingredients just until moistened. Fold in walnuts and raisins if desired.

2. Pour into a greased 9-in. x 5-in. loaf pan. Bake at 350° for 65-70 minutes or until a toothpick inserted in the center comes out clean. Cool in pan for 10 minutes before removing to a wire rack.

Poppy Seed Bread

This moist, rich bread is so delicious—it's very popular in our area. It gets golden brown and looks great sliced for a buffet. I also like to make miniature loaves to give as gifts.

—**FAYE HINTZ** SPRINGFIELD, MISSOURI

YIELD: 2 LOAVES.

- 3 **cups all-purpose flour**
- 2¼ **cups sugar**
- 1½ **tablespoons poppy seeds**
- 3 **teaspoons baking powder**
- 1½ **teaspoons salt**
- 3 **eggs, lightly beaten**
- 1½ **cups milk**
- 1 **cup canola oil**
- 1½ **teaspoons vanilla extract**
- 1½ **teaspoons almond extract**
- 1½ **teaspoons butter flavoring**

GLAZE

- ¾ **cup sugar**
- ¼ **cup orange juice**
- ½ **teaspoon vanilla extract**
- ½ **teaspoon almond extract**
- ½ **teaspoon butter flavoring**

1. In a large bowl, combine first five ingredients. Add eggs, milk, oil, extracts and flavoring. Pour into two greased 8-in. x 4-in. loaf pans. Bake at 350° for 60-65 minutes or until a toothpick comes out clean. Cool completely in pans.

2. In a saucepan, bring glaze ingredients to a boil. Pour over bread in pans. Cool for 5 minutes before removing from pans to wire racks to cool completely.

Dutch Apple Bread

My fruity streusel-topped bread is delightful for brunch. This is a great make-ahead treat that freezes well, too.

—**JUNE FORMANEK** BELLE PLAINE, IOWA

YIELD: 1 LOAF.

- ½ **cup butter, softened**
- 1 **cup sugar**
- 2 **eggs**
- 1 **teaspoon vanilla extract**
- 2 **cups all-purpose flour**
- 1 **teaspoon baking soda**
- ½ **teaspoon salt**
- ⅓ **cup buttermilk**
- 1 **cup chopped peeled apple**
- ⅓ **cup chopped walnuts**

TOPPING

- ⅓ **cup all-purpose flour**
- 2 **tablespoons sugar**
- 2 **tablespoons brown sugar**
- ½ **teaspoon ground cinnamon**
- 3 **tablespoons butter**

1. In a bowl, cream butter and sugar. Beat in eggs and vanilla. Combine flour, baking soda and salt; stir into the creamed mixture alternately with buttermilk. Fold in apple and nuts.

2. Pour into a greased 9-in. x 5-in. loaf pan. For topping, combine the first four ingredients; cut in butter until crumbly. Sprinkle over batter. Bake at 350° for 55-60 minutes or until a toothpick comes out clean.. Cool in pan for 10 minutes; remove to a wire rack.

Apple Bran Muffins

My mom taught me how to make these moist, tasty muffins. The recipe makes a big batch, so you can freeze the extras or share with co-workers, family or friends.
—**KELLY KIRBY** WESTVILLE, NOVA SCOTIA

YIELD: 2 DOZEN.

- 3 **cups all-purpose flour**
- 2 **teaspoons baking powder**
- 2 **teaspoons ground cinnamon**
- 1 **teaspoon salt**
- ½ **teaspoon baking soda**
- ¼ **teaspoon ground nutmeg**
- 1½ **cups 2% milk**
- 4 **eggs**
- ⅔ **cup packed brown sugar**
- ½ **cup canola oil**
- 2 **teaspoons vanilla extract**
- 3 **cups All-Bran**
- 2 **cups shredded peeled tart apples**
- 1 **cup chopped walnuts**
- 1 **cup raisins**

1. In a large bowl, combine first six ingredients. In another bowl, combine the milk, eggs, brown sugar, oil and vanilla. Stir into dry ingredients just until moistened. Fold in remaining ingredients.

2. Fill greased or paper-lined muffin cups three-fourths full. Bake at 350° for 18-22 minutes or until a toothpick inserted in muffin comes out clean. Cool for 5 minutes before removing from pans to wire racks.

Cranberry Nut Bread

Whenever I serve slices of this favorite treat, someone asks for the recipe. It's a moist, dark holiday bread chock-full of old-fashioned spicy goodness.
—**MAXINE SMITH** OWANKA, SOUTH DAKOTA

YIELD: 2 LOAVES (16 LOAVES EACH).

- 2½ **cups halved fresh or frozen cranberries, divided**
- ⅔ **cup sugar**
- 2 **teaspoons grated orange peel**
- 2¼ **cups all-purpose flour**
- ¾ **cup packed light brown sugar**
- 1 **tablespoon baking soda**
- 2 **teaspoons ground cinnamon**
- ½ **teaspoon salt**
- ¼ **teaspoon ground cloves**
- 2 **eggs, lightly beaten**
- ¾ **cup sour cream**
- ¼ **cup butter, melted**
- 1 **cup chopped pecans**

1. In a large saucepan, combine 1½ cups cranberries, sugar and orange peel. Bring to a boil; reduce heat and cook for 6-8 minutes or until the cranberries are softened. Remove from the heat; stir in the remaining berries and set aside.

2. In a large bowl, combine the flour, brown sugar, baking soda, cinnamon, salt and cloves. Combine the eggs, sour cream and butter; stir into dry ingredients just until blended. Fold in cranberries and pecans.

3. Pour into two greased 8-in. x 4-in. loaf pans. Bake at 350° for 55-60 minutes or until a toothpick inserted near the center comes out clean. Cool in pan for 10 minutes before removing to a wire rack to cool completely.

Bacon Swiss Bread

I'm a busy mom, so I'm always looking for fast and easy recipes. These savory slices of jazzed-up French bread are great with soup and salad. My daughter and her friends liked to snack on them instead of pizza.

—**SHIRLEY MILLS** TULSA, OKLAHOMA

YIELD: 10 SERVINGS.

    1   loaf (1 pound) French bread (20 inches)
    ⅔ cup butter, softened
    ⅓ cup chopped green onions
    4   teaspoons prepared mustard
    5   slices process Swiss cheese
    5   bacon strips

1. Cut bread into 1-in.-thick slices, leaving slices attached at bottom. In a bowl, combine the butter, onions and mustard; spread on both sides of each slice of bread. Cut each cheese slice diagonally into four triangles; place between the slices of bread. Cut bacon in half widthwise and then lengthwise; drape a piece over each slice.

2. Place the loaf on a double thickness of heavy-duty foil. Bake at 400° for 20-25 minutes or until bacon is crisp.

Corn Bread Squares

This inexpensive cornbread will disappear as fast as you can make it. It is always fluffy and moist.

—**MARCIA SALISBURY** WAUKESHA, WISCONSIN

YIELD: 9 SERVINGS.

    1   cup all-purpose flour
    1   cup yellow cornmeal
    ¼ cup sugar
    2   teaspoons baking powder
    ¾ teaspoon salt
    2   eggs, lightly beaten
    1   cup 2% milk
    ¼ cup canola oil

1. In a bowl, combine flour, cornmeal, sugar, baking powder and salt. Add eggs, milk and oil. Beat just until moistened.

2. Spoon into a greased 8-in. square baking pan. Bake at 400° for 20-25 minutes or until a toothpick inserted near the center comes out clean. Serve warm.

Nutty Apple Muffins

I teach quick-bread making for 4-H, and I'm always on the lookout for good new recipes. My sister-in-law shared this recipe with me for a slightly different kind of muffin. With apples and coconut, each bite is moist, chewy and tasty.

—**GLORIA KAUFMANN** ORRVILLE, OHIO

YIELD: 1½ DOZEN.

    1½ cups all-purpose flour
    1½ teaspoons baking powder
    ¾ teaspoon salt
    ½ teaspoon ground nutmeg
    ¼ teaspoon baking soda
    2   eggs
    ¾ cup sugar
    ⅓ cup canola oil
    3   tablespoons milk
    1½ cups diced peeled apples
    1   cup chopped walnuts
    ¾ cup flaked coconut

1. In a large bowl, combine the flour, baking powder, salt, nutmeg and baking soda. In another bowl, beat the eggs, sugar, oil and milk. Stir in the apples, nuts and coconut. Stir into dry ingredients just until moistened.

2. Fill 18 greased muffin cups three-fourths full. Bake at 350° for 20-25 minutes or until a toothpick comes out clean. Cool in pan for 10 minutes before removing to a wire rack.

My favorite memory of childhood was visiting my great-grandmother. She cooked on a huge, old wood-burning cookstove. She rose every morning at 4 a.m. no matter the weather. After she got that stove going, she'd start baking hot biscuits for breakfast. I don't think anything was ever as wonderful as waking up to the smell of a batch of her fresh hot biscuits.

—PEGGY NELSON CAMBRIDGE, MARYLAND

Orange Date Bread

I loved visiting my aunt—she was an excellent baker, and her kitchen always smelled great. With her inspiration, I now bake this moist, yummy bread every holiday season.

—JOANN WOLFE SUNLAND, CALIFORNIA

YIELD: 32 SERVINGS.

- 1 cup butter, softened
- 2 cups sugar
- 3 eggs, beaten
- 4 cups all-purpose flour
- 1 teaspoon baking soda
- 1 teaspoon salt
- 1⅓ cups buttermilk
- 1 cup chopped walnuts
- 1 cup chopped dates
- 1 tablespoon grated orange peel

GLAZE
- ¼ cup orange juice
- ½ cup sugar
- 2 tablespoons grated orange peel

1. In a bowl, cream butter and sugar. Add the eggs; mix well. Combine flour, baking soda and salt; add to creamed mixture alternately with buttermilk. Fold in nuts, dates and orange peel.

2. Pour into two greased and floured 8-in. x 4-in. loaf pans. Bake at 350° for 60-65 minutes or until done. Combine glaze ingredients; spoon half over hot bread. Cool for 10 minutes. Remove from pans; spoon remaining glaze over bread.

Mexican Corn Bread

This tasty corn bread is easy to mix up. I serve it often with a meal or hearty bowl of soup as an alternative to rolls. Cheddar cheese makes it especially flavorful, and the diced peppers add nice color.

—ESTHER SHANK HARRISONBURG, VIRGINIA

YIELD: 8-10 SERVINGS.

- 1 cup yellow cornmeal
- ⅓ cup all-purpose flour
- 2 tablespoons sugar
- 2 teaspoons baking powder
- 1 teaspoon salt
- ½ teaspoon baking soda
- 2 eggs
- 1 cup buttermilk
- 1 can (8¼ ounces) cream-style corn
- ⅓ cup canola oil
- ⅓ cup chopped onion
- 2 tablespoons chopped green pepper
- ½ cup shredded cheddar cheese

1. In a large bowl, combine the first six ingredients. Whisk together the eggs, buttermilk, corn, oil, onion and green pepper. Stir into dry ingredients just until moistened. Fold in cheese.

2. Pour into a greased 10-in. ovenproof skillet or 9-in. square baking pan. Bake at 350° for 30-35 minutes or until a toothpick inserted near the center comes out clean. Serve warm.

Lemon Bread

You'll often find me baking this sunshiny-sweet bread in the kitchen when company's due. It has a texture like pound cake.

—KATHY SCOTT LINGLE, WYOMING

YIELD: 1 LOAF (12 SLICES).

- ½ **cup butter, softened**
- 1 **cup sugar**
- 2 **eggs**
- 2 **tablespoons lemon juice**
- 1 **tablespoon grated lemon peel**
- 1½ **cups all-purpose flour**
- 1 **teaspoon baking powder**
- ⅛ **teaspoon salt**
- ½ **cup 2% milk**

GLAZE
- ½ **cup confectioners' sugar**
- 2 **tablespoons lemon juice**

1. In a large bowl, cream butter and sugar until light and fluffy. Beat in the eggs, lemon juice and peel. Combine the flour, baking powder and salt; gradually stir into creamed mixture alternately with milk, beating well after each addition.

2. Pour into a greased 8-in. x 4-in. loaf pan. Bake at 350° for 45 minutes or until a toothpick inserted near the center comes out clean.

3. Combine glaze ingredients. Remove bread from pan; immediately drizzle with glaze. Cool on a wire rack.

Fluffy Whole Wheat Biscuits

This golden biscuit recipe is my favorite. They turn out just scrumptious— light and tasty!

—RUTH ANN STELFOX
RAYMOND, ALBERTA

YIELD: 1 DOZEN.

- 1 **cup all-purpose flour**
- 1 **cup whole wheat flour**
- 4 **teaspoons baking powder**
- 1 **tablespoon sugar**
- ¾ **teaspoon salt**
- ¼ **cup cold butter, cubed**
- 1 **cup milk**

1. In a medium bowl, combine flours, baking powder, sugar, and salt; mix well. Cut in the butter until mixture resembles coarse crumbs. Stir in milk just until moistened.

2. Turn out onto a lightly floured surface; knead gently 8 to 10 times. Roll to ¾-in. thickness; cut with a 2½-in. biscuit cutter and place on an ungreased baking sheet. Bake at 450° for 10-12 minutes or until lightly browned. Serve warm.

Nutty Sweet Potato Biscuits

Back in the 1920s and '30s, Mom always had something good for us to eat when we got home from school. She often left a plate of these warm wonderful biscuits waiting for us. What a treat!

—**INDIA THACKER** CLIFFORD, VIRGINIA

YIELD: 18 SERVINGS.

- 2¾ cups all-purpose flour
- 4 teaspoons baking powder
- 1¼ teaspoons salt
- ½ teaspoon ground cinnamon
- ½ teaspoon ground nutmeg
- ¾ cup chopped nuts
- 2 cups mashed sweet potatoes
- ¾ cup sugar
- ½ cup butter, melted
- 1 teaspoon vanilla extract

1. In a large bowl, combine flour, baking powder, salt, cinnamon, nutmeg and nuts. In another bowl, combine sweet potatoes, sugar, butter and vanilla; add to flour mixture and mix well.

2. Turn onto a lightly floured surface; knead slightly. Roll dough to ½-in. thickness. Cut with a 2½-in. biscuit cutter and place on lightly greased baking sheets. Bake at 450° for 12 minutes or until golden brown.

Buttery Crescents

This rich dough makes a soft and very tender roll because it is prepared with milk and eggs.

—**LYNNE PETERSON** SALT LAKE CITY, UTAH

YIELD: 3 DOZEN.

- 2 packages (¼ ounce each) active dry yeast
- 2 cups warm milk (110° to 115°)
- 2 eggs, lightly beaten
- ¼ cup butter, melted and cooled
- 3 tablespoons sugar
- 1 teaspoon salt
- 6½ to 7 cups all-purpose flour
- Additional melted butter, optional

1. In a large bowl, dissolve yeast in milk. Add eggs, butter, sugar, salt and 4 cups flour; beat until smooth. Add enough remaining flour to form a soft dough. Turn onto a floured surface; knead until smooth and elastic, about 6-8 minutes.

2. Place in a greased bowl, turning once to grease top. Cover and let rise in a warm place until doubled, about 1 hour.

3. Punch the dough down and divide in thirds. Roll each portion into a 12-in. circle; cut each circle into 12 wedges. Roll up wedges from the wide end and place with pointed end down on greased baking sheets. Cover and let rise until doubled, about 30 minutes.

4. Bake at 400° for 12-14 minutes or until golden brown. Brush with butter if desired.

Muenster Bread

With a layer of cheese peeking out of every slice, this beautiful round loaf is definitely worth the effort.

—**MELANIE MERO** IDA, MICHIGAN

YIELD: 1 LOAF (16 SLICES).

- 2 **packages (¼ ounce each) active dry yeast**
- 1 **cup warm milk (110° to 115°)**
- ½ **cup butter, softened**
- 2 **tablespoons sugar**
- 1 **teaspoon salt**
- 3¼ to 3¾ **cups all-purpose flour**
- 1 **egg plus 1 egg yolk**
- 4 **cups (1 pound) shredded Muenster cheese**
- 1 **egg white, beaten**

1. In a large bowl, dissolve yeast in warm milk. Add the butter, sugar, salt and 2 cups flour; beat until smooth. Stir in enough remaining flour to form a soft dough.

2. Turn onto a floured surface; knead until smooth and elastic, about 6-8 minutes. Place in a greased bowl, turning once to grease top. Cover and let rise in a warm place until doubled, about 1 hour.

3. In a large bowl, beat egg and yolk; stir in cheese. Punch down dough; roll into a 16-in. circle.

4. Place in a greased 9-in. round baking pan, letting dough drape over the edges. Spoon the cheese mixture into center of dough. Gather dough up over filling in 1½-in. pleats. Gently squeeze pleats together at top and twist to make a top knot. Allow to rise 10-15 minutes.

5. Brush loaf with egg white. Bake at 375° for 40-45 minutes. Cool on a wire rack for 20 minutes. Serve warm.

Honey Wheat Bread

My recipe produces two beautiful, high loaves that have wonderful texture and slice well. The tempting aroma of this bread baking can cut the chill from a cold winter day.

—**DOROTHY ANDERSON** OTTAWA, KANSAS

YIELD: 2 LOAVES.

- 2½ to 3 **cups all-purpose flour**
- 3½ **cups whole wheat flour, divided**
- 2 **packages (¼ ounce each) active dry yeast**
- 1 **cup milk**
- 1¼ **cups water**
- ¼ **cup honey**
- 3 **tablespoons butter**
- 1 **tablespoon salt**

1. In a bowl, combine 2 cups all-purpose flour, 2 cups whole wheat flour and yeast. In a saucepan, heat milk, water, honey, butter and salt to 120°-130°; add to flour mixture. Blend on low speed until moistened; beat on medium for 3 minutes. Gradually stir in remaining whole wheat flour and enough of the remaining all-purpose flour to form a soft dough.

2. Turn onto a floured surface; knead until smooth and elastic, about 6-8 minutes. Place in a greased bowl, turning once to grease top. Cover and let rise in a warm place until doubled, about 1 hour.

3. Punch dough down. Shape into two loaves; place in 2 greased 8-in. x 4-in. loaf pans. Cover and let rise until doubled, about 1 hour. Bake at 375° for 40-45 minutes. Remove from pans to cool on wire racks.

Sour Cream Yeast Rolls

Tender, soft rolls are the perfect finishing touch for any meal. I think they represent genuine home comfort, especially since they were Mom's recipe.

—CHRISTINE FRAZIER AUBURNDALE, FLORIDA

YIELD: 1 DOZEN.

2½ to 3 cups all-purpose flour
2 tablespoons sugar
1 package (¼ ounce) active dry yeast
1 teaspoon salt
1 cup (8 ounces) sour cream
¼ cup water
3 tablespoons butter, divided
1 egg

1. In a large bowl, combine 1½ cups flour, sugar, yeast and salt. In a small saucepan, heat sour cream, water and 2 tablespoons butter to 120°-130°; add to dry ingredients. Beat on medium speed for 2 minutes. Add egg and ½ cup flour; beat 2 minutes longer. Stir in enough remaining flour to form a soft dough.

2. Turn onto a floured surface; knead until smooth and elastic, about 6-8 minutes. Place in a greased bowl, turning once to grease the top. Cover and let rise in a warm place until doubled, about 1 hour.

3. Punch dough down. Turn onto a lightly floured surface; divide into 12 pieces. Shape each into a ball. Place in a greased 13-in. x 9-in. baking pan. Cover and let rise until doubled, about 30 minutes.

4. Bake at 375° for 25-30 minutes or until golden brown. Melt the remaining butter; brush over rolls. Remove from pan to a wire rack.

Danish Julekage

Cardamom and lots of fruit enliven this unique holiday bread. The recipe was handed down from my grandmother, who came to the United States from Denmark when she was 16 years old.

—PHYLLIS LEVENDUSKY OSAGE, IOWA

YIELD: 2 LOAVES.

- 2 packages (¼ ounce each) active dry yeast
- ¼ cup warm water (110° to 115°)
- 2 cups warm milk (110° to 115°)
- 1 cup sugar
- ½ cup butter, softened
- 1 tablespoon shortening
- 2 teaspoons salt
- 1 teaspoon ground cardamom
- 3 eggs, beaten
- 8½ to 9 cups all-purpose flour
- 1 cup raisins
- 1 cup chopped candied fruit

FILLING
- 2 tablespoons butter, melted
- ¼ cup sugar

TOPPING
- ¼ cup sugar
- 2 tablespoons all-purpose flour
- ½ teaspoon ground cardamom
- 2 tablespoons cold butter

1. In a bowl, dissolve yeast in warm water. Add milk, sugar, butter, shortening, salt, cardamom, eggs and 4 cups flour; beat until smooth. Stir in raisins, candied fruit and enough remaining flour to form a soft dough.

2. Turn onto a floured surface; knead until smooth and elastic, about 6-8 minutes. Place in a greased bowl, turning once to grease top. Cover and let rise in a warm place until doubled, about 1¼ hours.

3. Punch dough down. Turn onto a lightly floured surface; divide in half. Roll each portion into a 12-in. x 9-in. rectangle. Brush with butter and sprinkle with sugar to within ½-in. of edges. Roll up, jelly-roll style, starting with a long side; pinch seams to seal and tuck ends under. Place, seam side down, in two greased 9-in. x 5-in. loaf pans. Cover and let rise until doubled, about 45 minutes.

4. For topping, combine the sugar, flour and cardamom; cut in butter until mixture resembles coarse crumbs. Sprinkle over loaves. Bake at 350° for 50-60 minutes or until golden brown. Remove from pans to cool on wire racks.

Poteca Nut Roll

You'll need a large surface to roll out the dough for this classic Yugoslavian treat.

—ANTHONY SETTA
SAEGERTOWN, PENNSYLVANIA

YIELD: 1 COFFEE CAKE.

- 1 package (¼ ounce) active dry yeast
- ¼ cup warm water (110° to 115°)
- ¾ cup warm milk (110° to 115°)
- ¼ cup sugar
- 1 teaspoon salt
- 1 egg, lightly beaten
- ¼ cup shortening
- 3 to 3½ cups all-purpose flour

FILLING
- ½ cup butter, softened
- 1 cup packed brown sugar
- 2 eggs, lightly beaten
- 1 teaspoon vanilla extract
- 1 teaspoon lemon extract, optional
- 4 cups ground or finely chopped walnuts

2% milk
Confectioners' sugar icing, optional

1. In a large bowl, dissolve yeast in warm water. Add the milk, sugar, salt, egg, shortening, and 1½ cups flour; beat until smooth. Add enough remaining flour to form a soft dough.

2. Turn onto a floured surface; knead until smooth and elastic, about 6-8 minutes. Place in a greased bowl, turning once to grease top. Cover and let rise in a warm place until doubled, about 1 hour.

3. Punch down. Turn onto a lightly floured surface; roll into a 30-in. x 20-in. rectangle. In a bowl, combine the butter, brown sugar, eggs, vanilla, lemon extract if desired and nuts. Add about ½ cup milk until mixture reaches spreading consistency. Spread over rectangle to within 1 in. of edges.

4. Roll up jelly-roll style, starting with a long side; pinch seams and ends to seal. Place on a greased baking sheet; shape into a tight spiral. Cover and let rise until nearly doubled, about 1 hour.

5. Bake at 350° for 35 minutes or until golden brown. Remove from pan to a wire rack to cool. If desired, combine confectioners' sugar and enough milk to make a thin glaze; brush over roll.

Cheese Twists

These impressive loaves take a little time to prepare, but they're well worth the effort. I've used the recipe for several years. I love making bread—there's no better way to work out life's little frustrations and with such yummy results!

—**MICHELLE BERAN** CLAFLIN, KANSAS

YIELD: 2 LOAVES.

      3¼ cups all-purpose flour
      2   packages (¼ ounce each) active dry yeast
   1½   cups buttermilk
      ¾   cup butter
      ½   cup sugar
      ½   teaspoon salt
      5   eggs
   3½   to 4 cups whole wheat flour, divided
      2   cups (8 ounces) shredded cheddar cheese

1. In a large bowl, combine all-purpose flour and yeast. In a saucepan, heat buttermilk, butter, sugar and salt to 120°-130°; add to flour mixture. Blend on low speed until moistened. Add eggs; beat on low for 30 seconds. Beat on high for 3 minutes. Stir in enough whole wheat flour to make a soft dough.

2. Turn onto a floured surface; knead until smooth and elastic, about 6-8 minutes. Place in a greased bowl, turning once to grease top. Cover and let rise in a warm place until nearly doubled, about 1 hour.

3. Punch dough down; divide in half. On a lightly floured surface, roll each into a 12-in. x 9-in. rectangle. Cut each into three 12-in. x 3-in. strips. Combine cheese with 2 tablespoons of remaining whole wheat flour; sprinkle ⅓ cup down center of each strip. Bring long edges together over cheese and pinch to seal. Place three strips seam side down on greased baking sheets. Braid strips together; secure ends. Cover and let rise until doubled, about 45 minutes.

4. Bake at 375° for 20-25 minutes or until golden. Immediately remove from baking sheets to wire racks; cool.

Apple Raisin Bread

I've been making this bread for many years. It smells so good in the oven and tastes even better. I make bread almost every Saturday, and it doesn't stay around long with our sons home from college in the summer.

—**PERLENE HOEKEMA** LYNDEN, WASHINGTON

YIELD: 3 LOAVES.

      2   packages (¼ ounce each) active dry yeast
   1½   cups warm water (110° to 115°), divided
      1   teaspoon sugar
      3   eggs, beaten
      1   cup applesauce
      ½   cup honey
      ½   cup canola oil
      2   teaspoons salt
      8   to 9 cups all-purpose flour
   1½   cups diced peeled apples
   1½   cups raisins
      2   tablespoons lemon juice
      2   tablespoons cornmeal
   GLAZE
      1   egg, beaten
   Sugar

1. In a small bowl, combine yeast, ½ cup water and sugar; set aside. In a large bowl, combine eggs, applesauce, honey, oil, salt and remaining water; mix well. Stir in yeast mixture. Gradually add enough flour to form a soft dough.

2. Knead on a floured surface until smooth and elastic, about 10 minutes. Place dough in a greased bowl; turn once to grease top. Cover and rise in a warm place until doubled, about 1 hour.

3. Punch down; turn over in bowl. Cover and let rise 30 minutes. In a small bowl, combine apples, raisins and lemon juice. Divide dough into three parts; knead a third of the apple mixture into each part. Shape each into round flat balls. Place each in a greased 8-in. round baking pan that has been sprinkled with cornmeal. Cover and let rise until doubled, about 1 hour.

4. Brush each loaf with egg and sprinkle with sugar. Bake at 350° for 30 to 35 minutes or until bread sounds hollow when tapped.

Homemade Egg Bread

People rave about this tender, delicate bread every time I serve it.

—JUNE MULLINS LIVONIA, MISSOURI

YIELD: 2 LOAVES.

2 packages (¼ ounce each) active dry yeast
½ cup warm water (110° to 115°)
1½ cups warm milk (110° to 115°)
¼ cup sugar
1 tablespoon salt
3 eggs, beaten
¼ cup butter, softened
7 to 7½ cups all-purpose flour
1 egg yolk
2 tablespoons water
Sesame seeds

1. Dissolve yeast in warm water. Add milk, sugar, salt, eggs, butter and 3½ cups flour; mix well. Stir in enough remaining flour to form a soft dough.

2. On a floured surface, knead until smooth and elastic, 6-8 minutes. Place in greased bowl; turn once to grease top. Cover and let rise in warm place until doubled, 1½ to 2 hours.

3. Punch down. Cover and let rise until almost doubled, about 30 minutes. Divide into six portions. On a floured surface, shape each into a 14-in.-long rope. For each loaf, braid three ropes together on greased baking sheet; pinch ends to seal. Cover and let rise until doubled, about 50 minutes.

4. Beat egg yolk and water; brush over loaves. Sprinkle with sesame seeds. Bake at 375° for 30-35 minutes.

Caraway Rye Bread

This pretty round bread's Old World flavor is so comforting and delicious. Just the right amount of caraway flavors the rye.

—CONNIE MOORE MEDWAY, OHIO

YIELD: 1 LOAF.

2 packages (¼ ounce each) active dry yeast
1½ cups warm water (110° to 115°), divided
3 tablespoons molasses
3 tablespoons butter, melted
1 tablespoon caraway seeds
1 teaspoon salt
1½ to 2 cups all-purpose flour
1¼ cups whole wheat flour
1 cup rye flour

1. In a large bowl, dissolve yeast in ½ cup warm water. Add molasses, butter, caraway, salt and remaining water; mix well. Combine flours; add 3 cups to batter. Beat until smooth. Add enough remaining flour to form a firm dough.

2. Turn onto a floured surface; knead until smooth and elastic, 6-8 minutes. Place in greased bowl, turning once to grease top. Cover and let rise in a warm place until doubled, about 1 hour.

3. Punch dough down; shape into a round loaf. Place on a greased baking sheet. Cover and let rise until doubled, about 30 minutes.

4. Bake at 375° for 20-25 minutes or until golden brown.

Grandma's Orange Rolls

Our children and grandchildren love these fine-textured sweet rolls. We have our own orange, lime and grapefruit trees, and it's such a pleasure to go out and pick fruit for the rolls right off the tree.

—**NORMA POOLE** AUBURNDALE, FLORIDA

YIELD: 2½ DOZEN.

- 1 package (¼ ounce) active dry yeast
- ¼ cup warm water (110° to 115°)
- 1 cup warm 2% milk (110° to 115°)
- ¼ cup shortening
- ¼ cup sugar
- 1 teaspoon salt
- 1 egg, lightly beaten
- 3½ to 3¾ cups all-purpose flour

FILLING
- 1 cup sugar
- ½ cup butter, softened
- 2 tablespoons grated orange peel

GLAZE
- 1 cup confectioners' sugar
- 4 teaspoons butter, softened
- ½ teaspoon lemon extract
- 4 to 5 teaspoons 2% milk

1. In a large bowl, dissolve yeast in water. Add the milk, shortening, sugar, salt, egg and 3 cups flour. Beat until smooth. Stir in enough remaining flour to form a soft dough.

2. Knead on a lightly floured surface until smooth and elastic, about 6-8 minutes. Place in a greased bowl, turning once to grease top. Cover and let rise in a warm place until doubled, about 1 hour. Meanwhile, in a small bowl, combine filling ingredients; set aside.

3. Punch dough down; divide in half. Roll each half into a 15-in. x 10-in. rectangle. Spread half the reserved filling on each rectangle. Roll up, jelly-roll style, starting with a long end. Cut each into 15 rolls.

4. Place in two greased 11-in. x 7-in. baking pans. Cover and let rise until doubled, about 45 minutes.

5. Bake at 375° for 20-25 minutes or until lightly browned. In a small bowl, combine the confectioners' sugar, butter, extract and enough milk to achieve desired consistency; spread over the warm rolls.

Whole Wheat Refrigerator Rolls

This recipe is easy and versatile. I like to mix up the dough beforehand and let it rise in the refrigerator.

—**SHARON MENSING** GREENFIELD, IOWA

YIELD: 2 DOZEN.

- 2 packages (¼ ounce each) active dry yeast
- 2 cups warm water (110° to 115°)
- ½ cup sugar
- 1 egg
- ¼ cup canola oil
- 2 teaspoons salt
- 4½ to 5 cups all-purpose flour, divided
- 2 cups whole wheat flour

1. In a large bowl, dissolve yeast in warm water. Add the sugar, egg, oil, salt and 3 cups all-purpose flour. Beat on medium speed for 3 minutes. Stir in whole wheat flour and enough remaining all-purpose flour to make a soft dough.

2. Turn out onto a lightly floured surface. Knead until smooth and elastic, about 6-8 minutes. Place in a greased bowl, turning once to grease top. Cover and let rise until doubled or cover and refrigerate overnight.

3. Punch dough down and form into 24 dinner-size rolls. Place on greased baking sheets for plain rolls or knots, or in greased muffin tins for cloverleaf rolls. Cover and let rise until doubled, about 1 hour for dough prepared the same day or 1-2 hours for refrigerated dough.

4. Bake at 375° for 10-12 minutes or until light golden brown. Serve warm. If desired, dough may be kept up to 4 days in the refrigerator. Punch down daily.

Country White Bread

Any time is the right time for a comforting slice of homemade bread. These loaves are especially nice since the crust stays so tender. This recipe is my husband Nick's favorite. He makes most of the bread at our house.
—**JOANNE SHEW CHUK** ST. BENEDICT, SASKATCHEWAN

YIELD: 2 LOAVES (16 SLICES EACH).

- 2 **packages (¼ ounce each) active dry yeast**
- 2 **cups warm water (110° to 115°)**
- ½ **cup sugar**
- 2 **teaspoons salt**
- 2 **eggs, lightly beaten**
- ¼ **cup canola oil**
- 6½ **to 7 cups all-purpose flour**

1. In a large bowl, dissolve yeast in warm water. Add the sugar, salt, eggs, oil and 3 cups of flour; beat until smooth. Stir in enough remaining flour to form a soft dough.

2. Turn onto a floured surface; knead until smooth and elastic, about 6-8 minutes. Place in a greased bowl, turning once to grease top. Cover and let rise in a warm place until doubled, about 1 hour.

3. Punch dough down. Divide in half and shape into loaves. Place in two greased 9-in. x 5-in. loaf pans. Cover and let rise until doubled, about 1 hour.

4. Bake at 375° for 25-30 minutes or until golden brown. Remove from pans to cool on wire racks.

Herbed Country White Bread: Stir in 2 tablespoons dried parsley flakes,1 tablespoon dried basil, 1 teaspoon each dried oregano and thyme and ½ teaspoon garlic powder along with the 3 cups of flour.

Angel Biscuits

My biscuit recipe combines both yeast bread and quick bread techniques for fantastic results—a light, airy biscuit.
—**FAYE HINTZ** SPRINGFIELD, MISSOURI

YIELD: 2½ DOZEN.

- 2 **packages (¼ ounce each) active dry yeast**
- ¼ **cup warm water (110° to 115°)**
- 2 **cups warm buttermilk (110° to 115°)**
- 5 **cups all-purpose flour**
- ⅓ **cup sugar**
- 2 **teaspoons salt**
- 2 **teaspoons baking powder**
- 1 **teaspoon baking soda**
- 1 **cup shortening**

Melted butter

1. Dissolve yeast in warm water. Let stand 5 minutes. Stir in the buttermilk; set aside. In a large bowl, combine the flour, sugar, salt, baking powder and baking soda. Cut in shortening with a pastry blender until mixture resembles coarse meal. Stir in yeast mixture.

2. Turn out onto a lightly floured surface; knead lightly 3-4 times. Roll into a ½-in. thickness. Cut with a 2½-in. biscuit cutter. Place on a lightly greased baking sheet. Cover and let rise in a warm place about 1½ hours.

3. Bake at 450° for 8-10 minutes until golden brown. Lightly brush tops with melted butter. Serve warm.

ICING

- ½ cup confectioners' sugar
- ¼ teaspoon vanilla extract
- 2 to 3 teaspoons 2% milk

1. In a large bowl, dissolve yeast in warm water. Add the milk, sugar, butter, eggs, salt and 2 cups flour; beat on low speed for 3 minutes. Stir in enough of remaining flour to form a soft dough.

2. Turn onto a floured surface; knead until smooth and elastic, about 6-8 minutes. Place in a greased bowl, turning once to grease top. Cover and let rise in a warm place until doubled, about 1 hour.

3. Meanwhile, in a small bowl, beat all the filling ingredients until fluffy; set aside.

4. Punch dough down. Turn onto a lightly floured surface; roll into a 14-in. x 12-in. rectangle. Place on a greased baking sheet. Spread filling down center third of rectangle. On each long side, cut 1-in.-wide strips, 3 in. into center. Starting at one end, fold alternating strips at an angle across filling. Seal ends. Cover and let rise for 30 minutes.

5. Bake at 375° for 25-30 minutes or until golden brown. Cool on a wire rack. Combine confectioners' sugar, vanilla and enough milk to achieve drizzling consistency; drizzle over warm bread.

Butternut Squash Bread

Squash gives the loaves a pretty golden color. One pound of squash yields about 1 cup mashed.

—AGNES MILLER MARSHALL, ILLINOIS

YIELD: 3 LOAVES.

- 2 packages (¼ ounce each) active dry yeast
- ½ cup warm water (110° to 115°)
- 1¼ cups mashed cooked butternut squash
- 1 cup warm milk (110° to 115°)
- 2 eggs, beaten
- ⅓ cup butter, melted
- ⅓ cup sugar
- 1 teaspoon salt
- 7 to 7½ cups all-purpose flour

1. In a large bowl, dissolve yeast in warm water. Add the squash, milk, eggs, butter, sugar and salt; mix well. Gradually add 3½ cups flour; beat until smooth. Add enough remaining flour to form a soft dough.

2. Turn onto a floured surface; knead until smooth and elastic, about 6-8 minutes. Place in a greased bowl, turning once to grease top. Cover and let rise in a warm place until doubled, about 1 hour.

3. Punch dough down. Shape into three loaves; place in greased 8-in. x 4-in. loaf pans. Cover and let rise until doubled, about 30 minutes.

4. Bake at 375° for 25-30 minutes or until tops are golden. Remove from pans to cool on wire racks.

Lemon Cheese Braid

This recipe came from my mom, who is an excellent cook. Although the bread is fairly simple to make, when you finish you'll feel a definite sense of accomplishment because it not only tastes delicious but looks so impressive.

—GRACE DICKEY HILLSBORO, OREGON

YIELD: 12-14 SERVINGS.

- 1 package (¼ ounce) active dry yeast
- 3 tablespoons warm water (110° to 115°)
- ⅓ cup 2% milk
- ¼ cup sugar
- ¼ cup butter, melted
- 2 eggs
- ½ teaspoon salt
- 3 to 3½ cups all-purpose flour

FILLING

- 2 packages (one 8 ounces, one 3 ounces) cream cheese, softened
- ½ cup sugar
- 1 egg
- 1 teaspoon grated lemon peel

Easy Potato Rolls

After I discovered this recipe, it became a mainstay for me. I make the dough ahead of time when company is coming, and I try to keep some in the refrigerator to make for "hay hands" on our cattle ranch.

—JEANETTE MCKINNEY BELLEVIEW, MISSOURI

YIELD: 45 SERVINGS.

> 2 packages (¼ ounce each) active dry yeast
> 1⅓ cups warm water (110° to 115°), divided
> ⅔ cup sugar
> ⅔ cup shortening
> 2 eggs
> 1 cup mashed potatoes
> 2½ teaspoons salt
> 6 to 6½ cups all-purpose flour

1. In a small bowl, dissolve yeast in ⅔ cup warm water. In a large bowl, cream sugar and shortening until light and fluffy. Add the eggs, potatoes, salt, yeast mixture, remaining water and 2 cups flour. Beat until smooth. Add enough remaining flour to form a soft dough.

2. Shape into a ball; do not knead. Place in a greased bowl, turning once to grease top. Cover and let rise in a warm place until doubled, about 1 hour.

3. Punch dough down; divide into thirds. Shape each portion into 15 balls and arrange in three greased 9-in. round baking pans. Cover and let rise until doubled, about 30 minutes.

4. Bake at 375° for 20-25 minutes or until golden brown. Remove from pans to cool on wire racks.

Honey Party Buns

I use this recipe often for church get-togethers. Finger sandwiches are popular at these events, so I make these small golden buns and add sandwich toppings. They're a big hit with everyone.

—RUTH LINSCOTT MILLFIELD, OHIO

YIELD: 4-5 DOZEN.

> 1 cup butter, cut into pieces
> ½ cup honey
> 2 cups boiling water
> 2 packages (¼ ounce each) active dry yeast
> ⅓ cup warm water (110° to 115°)
> 2 eggs, beaten
> 1 teaspoon baking powder
> 1 teaspoon salt
> 3½ cups whole wheat flour
> 4 to 4½ cups all-purpose flour
> Sliced ham, cheese and lettuce, optional

1. Place butter and honey in a large bowl; pour the boiling water over and set aside to cool to 110°-115°. In a small bowl, dissolve yeast in warm water; set aside. To honey mixture, add eggs, baking powder and salt. Add yeast mixture and whole wheat flour; beat until smooth. Stir in enough all-purpose flour to form a soft dough.

2. Turn onto a floured surface; knead until smooth and elastic, about 8-10 minutes. Place in a greased bowl, turning once to grease top. Cover and let rise in a warm place until doubled, about 1 hour.

3. Punch the dough down; divide in half. On a lightly floured surface, roll each half to ½-in. thickness; cut with a 2½-in. cutter. Place on greased baking sheets. Cover and let rise in a warm place until doubled, about 1 hour.

4. Bake at 350° for 15-20 minutes or until golden brown. Remove from pans to cool on wire racks. Make into small sandwiches, if desired, by filling with ham, cheese and lettuce, or serve plain.

Grandma Russell's Bread

I remember as a child always smelling fresh homemade bread and rolls whenever I walked into Grandma's house. The warm slices were delicious and melted in my mouth!

—JANET POLITO NAMPA, IDAHO

YIELD: 2 LOAVES OR 2 DOZEN ROLLS.

1 package (¼ ounce) active dry yeast
⅓ cup warm water (110° to 115°)
½ cup sugar, divided
1 cup milk
½ cup butter, cubed
1 tablespoon salt
1 cup mashed potatoes
2 eggs, beaten
5½ to 6 cups all-purpose flour

CINNAMON FILLING
¼ cup butter, melted
¾ cup sugar
1 tablespoon ground cinnamon

1. In a large bowl, combine the yeast, warm water and 1 teaspoon sugar; set aside. In a saucepan, heat milk, butter, salt and remaining sugar until butter is melted. Remove from the heat; stir in potatoes until smooth. Cool to lukewarm; add eggs and mix well.

2. To yeast mixture, add the potato mixture and 5 cups flour. Stir in enough remaining flour to make a soft dough. Turn onto a floured surface and knead until smooth and elastic, about 6-8 minutes. Place in a greased bowl, turning once to grease top. Cover and let rise in a warm place until doubled, about 1½ hours.

3. Punch down and divide in half.

For white bread: Shape two loaves and place in greased 8-in. x 4-in. loaf pans.

For cinnamon bread: Roll each half into a 16-in. x 8-in. rectangle. Brush with melted butter; combine sugar and cinnamon and sprinkle over butter. Starting at the narrow end, roll up into a loaf, sealing the edges and ends. Place in greased 8-in. x 4-in. loaf pans.

For cinnamon rolls: Roll each half into an 18-in. x 12-in. rectangle. Brush with melted butter; sprinkle with cinnamon-sugar. Starting at the narrow end, roll up and seal edges and ends. Cut each into 12 pieces of 1½ in. Place in greased 9-in. round baking pans.

4. Cover and let rise until doubled. Bake loaves at 375° for 20 minutes; bake rolls at 375° for 25-30 minutes. Cover with foil if they brown too quickly.

Cinnamon Twists

These delightful golden twists are perfect as part of a holiday meal. The brown sugar and cinnamon give them a delicate spicy flavor. It's a good thing the recipe makes a big batch because people can rarely eat just one.

—JANET MOOBERRY PEORIA, ILLINOIS

YIELD: 4 DOZEN.

- 1 package (¼ ounce) active dry yeast
- ¾ cup warm water (110° to 115°), divided
- 4 to 4½ cups all-purpose flour
- ¼ cup sugar
- 1½ teaspoons salt
- ½ cup warm 2% milk (110° to 115°)
- ¼ cup butter, softened
- 1 egg

FILLING
- ¼ cup butter, melted
- ½ cup packed brown sugar
- 4 teaspoons ground cinnamon

1. In a large bowl, dissolve yeast in ¼ cup warm water. Add 2 cups of flour, sugar, salt, milk, butter, egg and remaining water; beat on medium speed for 3 minutes. Stir in enough remaining flour to form a soft dough.

2. Turn onto a floured surface; knead until smooth and elastic, about 6-8 minutes. Place in a greased bowl, turning once to grease top. Cover and let rise in a warm place until doubled, about 1 hour.

3. Punch down dough. Roll into a 16-in. x 12-in. rectangle. Brush with butter. Combine brown sugar and cinnamon; sprinkle over butter. Let dough rest for 6 minutes. Cut lengthwise into three 16-in. x 4-in. strips. Cut each strip into sixteen 4-in. x 1-in. pieces. Twist and place on greased baking sheets. Cover and let rise until doubled, about 30 minutes.

4. Bake at 350° for 15 minutes or until golden brown.

English Muffin Bread

This recipe is even faster than most batter breads because it has only one rising time. If you can't use both loaves right away, freeze one for later.

—JANE ZIELINSKI ROTTERDAM JUNCTION, NEW YORK

YIELD: 2 LOAVES.

- 5 cups all-purpose flour, divided
- 2 packages (¼ ounce each) active dry yeast
- 1 tablespoon sugar
- 2 teaspoons salt
- ¼ teaspoon baking soda
- 2 cups warm milk (120° to 130°)
- ½ cup warm water (120° to 130°)
Cornmeal

1. In a large bowl, combine 2 cups flour, yeast, sugar, salt and baking soda. Add warm milk and water; beat on low speed for 30 seconds, scraping bowl occasionally. Beat on high speed for 3 minutes.

2. Stir in remaining flour (batter will be stiff). Do not knead. Grease two 8-in. x 4-in. loaf pans. Sprinkle pans with cornmeal. Spoon batter into the pans and sprinkle cornmeal on top. Cover and let rise in a warm place until doubled, about 45 minutes.

3. Bake at 375° for 35 minutes or until golden brown. Remove from pans immediately and cool on wire racks. Slice and toast.

Italian Easter Bread

It is an Italian tradition to make this sweet, golden braid at Easter. This family heirloom recipe came from my mother-in-law, who received it from her mother. If you're not a fan of raisins, the bread is just as wonderful without them.

—KATHI WEST CANTON, MICHIGAN

YIELD: 2 LOAVES.

- 2 packages (¼ ounce each) active dry yeast
- 3 tablespoons warm water (110° to 115°)
- 1⅓ cups warm milk (110° to 115°)
- ⅔ cup sugar
- ⅔ cup butter, softened
- 1¼ teaspoons salt
- 2 eggs
- 3 teaspoons anise extract
- 6 to 6½ cups all-purpose flour
- ⅔ cup raisins
- 1 egg white, beaten
- 1 tablespoon water

1. In a large bowl, dissolve yeast in warm water. Add the milk, sugar, butter and salt; mix well. Add eggs, extract and 2 cups flour; beat until smooth. Stir in enough remaining flour to form a soft dough.

2. Turn onto a floured surface; knead until smooth and elastic, about 8-10 minutes. Place in a greased bowl, turning once to grease the top. Cover and let rise in a warm place until doubled, about 1 hour.

3. Punch dough down. Turn onto a lightly floured surface; sprinkle with raisins and knead in. Divide in half. Divide each portion into thirds. Shape each into a 14-in. rope. Place three ropes on a greased baking sheet and braid; pinch ends to seal and tuck under. Repeat with remaining dough. Cover and let rise until doubled, about 45 minutes.

4. Whisk egg white and water; brush over braids. Bake at 325° for 35-40 minutes or until golden brown. Remove from pans to wire racks to cool.

Rustic Apple-Raisin Bread

A flavorful blend of apples, raisins and caraway seeds makes this crusty loaf a savory specialty! Try it toasted with melted butter for a mouthwatering treat.

—MELISSA NEWMAN DANVILLE, PENNSYLVANIA

YIELD: 2 LOAVES (8 SLICES EACH).

- 1 package (¼ ounce) active dry yeast
- ¼ cup warm water (110° to 115°)
- 1 cup unsweetened applesauce
- ½ cup warm fat-free milk (110° to 115°)
- 2 tablespoons sugar
- 2 tablespoons butter, softened
- 1 teaspoon salt
- 1 egg, separated
- 4 to 4½ cups all-purpose flour
- 1 cup raisins
- 1 teaspoon caraway seeds
- 1 tablespoon cold water

1. In a large bowl, dissolve the yeast in warm water. Add the applesauce, milk, sugar, butter, salt, egg yolk and 2 cups flour; beat until smooth. Stir in enough remaining flour to form a firm dough. Stir in raisins and caraway seeds.

2. Turn onto a lightly floured surface; knead until smooth and elastic, about 6-8 minutes. Place in a bowl coated with cooking spray, turning once to coat top. Cover and let rise in a warm place until doubled, about 1 hour.

3. Punch the dough down. Turn onto a lightly floured surface; divide in half. Shape each portion into a ball. Place 4 in. apart on a baking sheet coated with cooking spray. Pat into 6-in. round loaves. Cover loaves and let rise until almost doubled, about 45 minutes.

4. In a small bowl, beat egg white and cold water; brush over loaves. Bake at 375° for 30-35 minutes or until golden brown. Cool on a wire rack.

Sally Lunn Batter Bread

The tantalizing aroma of this golden loaf baking always draws people into my mother's kitchen. With its circular shape, it's a pretty bread, too. I've never seen it last more than 2 hours once it's out of the oven!

—JEANNE VOSS ANAHEIM HILLS, CALIFORNIA

YIELD: 12-16 SERVINGS.

- 1 **package (¼ ounce) active dry yeast**
- ½ **cup warm water (110° to 115°)**
- 1 **cup warm milk (110° to 115°)**
- ½ **cup butter, softened**
- ¼ **cup sugar**
- 2 **teaspoon salt**
- 3 **eggs**
- 5½ **to 6 cups all-purpose flour**

HONEY BUTTER
- ½ **cup butter, softened**
- ½ **cup honey**

1. In a large bowl, dissolve yeast in warm water. Add the milk, butter, sugar, salt, eggs and 3 cups flour; beat until smooth. Stir in enough remaining flour to form a soft dough.

2. Do not knead. Place in a greased bowl, turning once to grease the top. Cover and let rise in a warm place until doubled, about 1 hour.

3. Stir the dough down. Spoon into a greased and floured 10-in. tube pan. Cover and let rise until doubled, about 1 hour.

4. Bake at 400° for 25-30 minutes or until golden brown. Remove from pan to a wire rack to cool.

5. Combine the honey butter ingredients until smooth. Serve with bread.

Parmesan-Ranch Pan Rolls

My mom showed me how to make her delicious pan rolls. They're great for feeding a crowd and you won't even see a crumb left over. Mom used her own bread dough recipe, but frozen dough is my shortcut.

—TRISHA KRUSE EAGLE, IDAHO

YIELD: 1½ DOZEN.

- 2 **loaves (1 pound each) frozen bread dough, thawed**
- 1 **cup grated Parmesan cheese**
- ½ **cup butter, melted**
- 1 **envelope buttermilk ranch salad dressing mix**
- 1 **small onion, finely chopped**

1. On a lightly floured surface, divide dough into 18 portions; shape each into a ball. In a small bowl, combine cheese, butter and ranch dressing mix.

2. Roll balls in cheese mixture; arrange in two greased 9-in. square baking pans. Sprinkle with onion. Cover and let rise in a warm place until doubled, about 45 minutes.

3. Bake at 350° for 20-25 minutes or until golden brown. Remove from the pans to wire racks.

BEEF

Peppered Ribeye Steaks

A true Southerner to the core, I love to cook—especially on the grill. This recipe is one of my favorites! The seasoning rub makes a wonderful marinade, and nothing beats the summertime taste of these flavorful grilled steaks.

—**SHARON BICKETT** CHESTER, SOUTH CAROLINA

YIELD: 8 SERVINGS.

- 4 **beef ribeye steaks (1½ inches thick)**
- 1 **tablespoon olive oil**
- 1 **tablespoon garlic powder**
- 1 **tablespoon paprika**
- 2 **teaspoons dried gound thyme**
- 2 **teaspoons dried ground oregano**
- 1½ **teaspoons pepper**
- 1 **teaspoon salt**
- 1 **teaspoon lemon-pepper seasoning**
- 1 **teaspoon cayenne pepper**
- 1 **teaspoon crushed red pepper flakes**

Orange slices, optional
Parsley sprigs, optional

1. Brush steaks lightly with oil. In a small bowl, combine all seasonings. Sprinkle seasonings over steaks and press into both sides. Cover and chill for 1 hour.

2. Grill, covered, over medium heat or broil 4 in. from the heat for 7-8 minutes on each side or until meat reaches desired doneness (for medium-rare, a thermometer should read 145°; medium, 160°; well-done, 170°).

3. Let stand 5 minutes before slicing. Place on a warm serving platter; cut across the grain into thick slices. Garnish with orange slices and parsley if desired.

Baked Stuffed Tomatoes

My family loves these tasty garden "containers" filled with rice and ground beef.

—**BERTILLE COOPER** CALIFORNIA, MARYLAND

YIELD: 6 SERVINGS.

- 6 **medium fresh tomatoes**
- ½ **pound ground beef**
- 1 **teaspoon chili powder**
- 1 **teaspoon sugar**
- ½ **teaspoon salt**
- ½ **teaspoon pepper**
- ¼ **teaspoon dried oregano**
- 2 **cups uncooked instant rice**
- ½ **cup dry bread crumbs**
- 2 **tablespoons butter, melted**
- 2 **tablespoons water**

1. Cut a thin slice off the top of each tomato. Leaving a ½-in.-thick shell, scoop out and reserve pulp. Invert tomatoes onto paper towels to drain.

2. Meanwhile, in a skillet, cook beef over medium heat until no longer pink; drain. Add the tomato pulp, chili powder, sugar, salt, pepper and oregano; bring to a boil. Reduce heat; simmer 45-50 minutes or until slightly thickened, stirring occasionally.

3. Add rice; mix well. Simmer 5-6 minutes longer or until rice is tender. Stuff tomatoes and place in a greased 13-in. x 9-in. baking dish. Combine bread crumbs and butter; sprinkle over tomatoes. Add water to baking dish. Bake, uncovered, at 375° for 20-25 minutes or until crumbs are lightly browned.

Vegetable Beef Casserole

This easy one-dish recipe has been a family favorite ever since my husband's aunt gave it to me more than 35 years ago. Add whatever vegetables you happen to have on hand. A simple salad goes nicely with this dish.

—**EVANGELINE REW** MANASSAS, VIRGINIA

YIELD: 6-8 SERVINGS.

- 3 medium unpeeled potatoes, sliced
- 3 carrots, sliced
- 3 celery ribs, sliced
- 2 cups cut fresh or frozen cut green beans
- 1 medium onion, chopped
- 1 pound lean ground beef (90% lean)
- 1 teaspoon dried thyme
- 1 teaspoon salt
- 1 teaspoon pepper
- 4 medium tomatoes, peeled, seeded and chopped
- 1 cup (4 ounces) shredded cheddar cheese

1. In a 3-qt. casserole, layer half of the potatoes, carrots, celery, green beans and onion. Crumble half of the uncooked beef over vegetables. Sprinkle with ½ teaspoon each of thyme, salt and pepper. Repeat layers.

2. Top with tomatoes. Cover and bake at 400° for 15 minutes. Reduce heat to 350°; bake about 1 hour longer or until the vegetables are tender and meat is no longer pink. Sprinkle with cheese; cover and let stand until cheese is melted.

Hungarian Goulash

Talk about your heirloom recipes! My grandmother made this for my mother when she was a child, and Mom made it for us to enjoy. Paprika and caraway add wonderful flavor and sour cream gives it a creamy richness. It's simply scrumptious!

—**MARCIA DOYLE** POMPANO, FLORIDA

YIELD: 12 SERVINGS.

- 3 medium onions, chopped
- 2 medium carrots, chopped
- 2 medium green peppers, chopped
- 3 pounds beef stew meat, cut into 1-inch cubes
- ½ teaspoon plus ¼ teaspoon salt, divided
- ½ teaspoon plus ¼ teaspoon pepper, divided
- 2 tablespoons olive oil
- 1½ cups reduced-sodium beef broth
- ¼ cup all-purpose flour
- 3 tablespoons paprika
- 2 tablespoons tomato paste
- 1 teaspoon caraway seeds
- 1 garlic clove, minced

Dash sugar

- 12 cups uncooked whole wheat egg noodles
- 1 cup (8 ounces) reduced-fat sour cream

1. Place the onions, carrots and green peppers in a 5-qt. slow cooker. Sprinkle meat with ½ teaspoon salt and ½ teaspoon pepper. In a large skillet, brown meat in oil in batches. Transfer to slow cooker.

2. Add broth to skillet, stirring to loosen browned bits from pan. Combine the flour, paprika, tomato paste, caraway seeds, garlic, sugar and remaining salt and pepper; stir into skillet. Bring to a boil; cook and stir for 2 minutes or until thickened. Pour over meat. Cover and cook on low for 7-9 hours or until meat is tender.

3. Meanwhile, cook noodles according to package directions. Stir the sour cream into slow cooker. Drain the noodles; serve with goulash.

Hearty Lasagna

Featuring a cute heart-shaped cutout, this eye-catching dish is perfect to share with friends and family around Valentine's Day. Best of all, you can make the lasagna ahead of time!

—**MARCY CELLA** L'ANSE, MICHIGAN

YIELD: 12 SERVINGS.

- 1½ pounds ground beef
- 1 medium onion, chopped
- 1 garlic clove, minced
- 3 tablespoons olive oil
- 1 can (28 ounces) Italian diced tomatoes, undrained
- 1 can (8 ounces) tomato sauce
- 1 can (6 ounces) tomato paste
- 1 teaspoon dried oregano
- 1 teaspoon sugar
- 1 teaspoon salt
- ¼ teaspoon pepper
- 2 carrots, halved
- 2 celery ribs, halved
- 12 ounces lasagna noodles
- 1 carton (15 ounces) ricotta cheese
- 2 cups (8 ounces) shredded part-skim mozzarella cheese
- ½ cup grated Parmesan cheese

1. In a large skillet, cook beef, onion and garlic in oil until meat is browned and onion is tender; drain. Stir in tomatoes, tomato sauce, tomato paste, oregano, sugar, salt and pepper. Place carrots and celery in sauce. Simmer, uncovered, for 1½ hours, stirring occasionally.

2. Meanwhile, cook lasagna noodles according to package directions. Drain; rinse in cold water. Remove and discard carrots and celery.

3. In a greased 13-in. x 9-in. baking dish, layer one-third of the noodles, one-third of the meat sauce, one-third of the ricotta, one-third of the mozzarella and one-third of the Parmesan. Repeat layers once. Top with remaining noodles and meat sauce.

4. Cut a heart out of aluminum foil and center on top of sauce. Dollop and spread remaining ricotta around heart. Sprinkle with remaining mozzarella and Parmesan. Bake, uncovered, at 350° for 45 minutes. Remove and discard foil heart. Let stand 10-15 minutes before cutting.

Barbecued Beef Sandwiches

You really can't taste the cabbage—which is great for non-cabbage lovers—but it makes these sandwiches hearty and moist.

—**DENISE MARSHALL** BAGLEY, WISCONSIN

YIELD: 10 SERVINGS.

- 2 pounds beef stew meat
- 2 cups water
- 4 cups shredded cabbage
- ½ cup barbecue sauce
- ½ cup ketchup
- ⅓ cup Worcestershire sauce
- 1 tablespoon prepared horseradish
- 1 tablespoon prepared mustard
- 10 hamburger or other sandwich buns, split

1. In a Dutch oven, combine the beef and water. Bring to a boil. Reduce heat; cover and simmer for 1½ hours or until tender. Drain cooking liquid, reserving ¾ cup.

2. Cool beef; shred and return to the Dutch oven. Add the cabbage, barbecue sauce, ketchup, Worcestershire sauce, horseradish, mustard and reserved cooking liquid. Cover and simmer for 1 hour. Serve warm in buns.

Round Steak Italiano

My mom's steak recipe is wonderful. She made this often while I was growing up. I've always enjoyed it and especially like the thick gravy, which is good on both the meat and the potatoes.

—DEANNE STEPHENS MCMINNVILLE, OREGON

YIELD: 8 SERVINGS.

- 2 **pounds beef top round steak**
- 1 **can (8 ounces) tomato sauce**
- 2 **tablespoons onion soup mix**
- 2 **tablespoons canola oil**
- 2 **tablespoons red wine vinegar**
- 1 **teaspoon ground oregano**
- ½ **teaspoon garlic powder**
- ¼ **teaspoon pepper**
- 8 **medium potatoes (7 to 8 ounces each)**
- 1 **tablespoon cornstarch**
- 1 **tablespoon cold water**

1. Cut steak into serving-size pieces; place in a 5-qt. slow cooker. In a large bowl, combine the tomato sauce, soup mix, oil, vinegar, oregano, garlic powder and pepper; pour over meat. Scrub and pierce potatoes; place over meat. Cover and cook on low for 7 to 7½ hours or until meat and potatoes are tender.

2. Remove meat and potatoes; keep warm. For gravy, pour cooking juices into a small saucepan; skim fat.

3. Combine cornstarch and water until smooth; gradually stir into juices. Bring to a boil; cook and stir for 2 minutes or until thickened. Serve with meat and potatoes.

Steak Potpie

When I hear "meat and potatoes," this is the recipe that comes to mind. I've made it for years and still get compliments on it. Most often, friends comment on how hearty the pie is.

—PATTIE BONNER COCOA, FLORIDA

YIELD: 4-6 SERVINGS.

- ¾ **cup sliced onions**
- 4 **tablespoons canola oil, divided**
- ¼ **cup all-purpose flour**
- 1 **teaspoon salt**
- ½ **teaspoon pepper**
- ½ **teaspoon paprika**
- **Pinch ground allspice**
- **Pinch ground ginger**
- 1 **pound beef top round steak, cut into ½-inch pieces**
- 2½ **cups boiling water**
- 3 **medium potatoes, peeled and diced**
- **Pastry for single-crust pie**

1. In a large skillet, saute the onions in 2 tablespoons oil until golden. Drain and set aside.

2. In a large resealable plastic bag, combine dry ingredients; add meat and shake to coat. Brown meat in remaining oil in the same skillet. Add water; cover and simmer until meat is tender, about 1 hour.

3. Add potatoes; simmer, uncovered, for 15-20 minutes or until the potatoes are tender. Pour into a greased 1½-qt. baking dish. Top with onion slices. Roll pastry to fit baking dish. Place over hot filling; seal to edges of dish. Make slits in the crust.

4. Bake at 450° for 25-30 minutes or until golden brown. If necessary, cover edges of crust with foil to prevent overbrowning.

Mom's Italian Beef Sandwiches

My mom made the best Italian beef. I've added to it over the years, but it's still her recipe. She made this for family reunions, and there were never leftovers. Now I make it and for convenience, freeze the beef in single-serving sizes. It makes a quick and easy meal as a sandwich or served over noodles.

—MARY MCVEY COLFAX, NORTH CAROLINA

YIELD: 16 SERVINGS.

- 1 **boneless beef rump roast or bottom round roast (2 pounds), halved**
- 1 **boneless beef chuck roast (2 pounds), halved**
- 1 **beef sirloin tip roast (1 pound)**
- 2 **tablespoons canola oil**
- 2 **cups water**
- 1 **medium onion, chopped**
- 4 **garlic cloves, minced**
- 2 **envelopes Italian salad dressing mix**
- 1 **envelope zesty Italian salad dressing mix**
- 1 **envelope (0.87 ounce) brown gravy mix**
- 2 **tablespoons crushed red pepper flakes**
- 1 **tablespoon Italian seasoning**
- 2 **teaspoons Worcestershire sauce**
- 16 **hoagie buns, split**
Sliced provolone cheese, optional
Giardiniera, optional

1. In a large skillet, brown each roast in oil on all sides. Drain. Transfer meat to a 7-qt. slow cooker. Combine the water, onion, garlic, salad dressing and gravy mixes, pepper flakes, Italian seasoning and Worcestershire sauce; pour over beef. Cover and cook on low for 8-10 hours or until meat is tender.

2. Remove beef; cool slightly. Skim fat from cooking juices. Pour juices into a large bowl. Shred beef with two forks; add to the bowl. Cool. Transfer to freezer containers. Freeze for up to 3 months.

To use frozen meat: Thaw in the refrigerator overnight. Place in a Dutch oven; heat through. Using a slotted spoon, place ½ cup on each bun. Top with cheese and giardiniera if desired.

Braciole

In our family, we served this as a special treat for birthdays and holidays. It was Grandma's specialty and the preparation was time-consuming. When the meat and sauce were fully cooked, Grandma called us into the kitchen to watch her lift the big roll from the sauce to the cutting board to slice it. The pinwheels of meat, laid side by side on the platter, topped with Grandma's delicious sauce, made a colorful picture.

—**COOKIE CURCI** SAN JOSE, CALIFORNIA

YIELD: 6 SERVINGS.

- 1 **beef flank steak (1½ pounds)**
- 4 **tablespoons olive oil, divided**
- ½ **cup soft bread crumbs**
- ½ **cup minced fresh parsley**
- ½ **cup grated Parmesan cheese**
- 2 **garlic cloves, minced**
- 1 **teaspoon dried oregano**
- ½ **teaspoon salt, divided**
- ½ **teaspoon pepper, divided**
- 1 **medium onion, chopped**
- 2 **cans (15 ounces each) tomato sauce**
- ½ **cup water**
- 1 **teaspoon Italian seasoning**
- ½ **teaspoon sugar**

Hot cooked spaghetti, optional

1. Flatten steak to ½-in. thickness. Rub with 1 tablespoon oil. Combine the bread crumbs, parsley, cheese, garlic, oregano, ¼ teaspoon salt and ¼ teaspoon pepper. Spoon over beef to within 1 in. of edges; press down. Roll up jelly-roll style, starting with a long side; tie with kitchen string.

2. In a Dutch oven, brown meat in remaining oil on all sides. Add onion and cook until tender. Stir in the tomato sauce, water, Italian seasoning, sugar and remaining salt and pepper. Bring to a boil. Reduce heat; cover and simmer for 70-80 minutes or until meat is tender.

3. Remove meat from sauce and discard string. Cut into thin slices; serve with sauce and spaghetti if desired.

Beef and Mushroom Roll

I remember watching my mom make this dish and snitching bites of the meat that were left over in the pan. I had several tastes before she realized what I was doing.

—**AMY STODDARD** UPLAND, CALIFORNIA

YIELD: 4-6 SERVINGS.

- 1 **pound ground beef**
- 1 **small onion, chopped**
- 1 **can (4 ounces) mushroom stems and pieces, drained**
- ¼ **cup dill pickle relish**
- 1 **teaspoon salt**
- ¼ **teaspoon ground mustard**
- ¼ **teaspoon pepper**
- 2 **tablespoons all-purpose flour**
- ⅓ **cup water**

PASTRY

- 2 **cups all-purpose flour**
- 2 **teaspoons baking powder**
- 1 **teaspoon salt**
- ½ **teaspoon poultry seasoning**
- ¼ **cup shortening**
- ¾ **cup plus 2 tablespoons milk, divided**

GRAVY

- 2 **tablespoons butter**
- 3 **tablespoons all-purpose flour**
- ½ **teaspoon salt**
- ¼ **teaspoon pepper**
- 2 **cups milk**

1. In a large skillet, cook beef and onion over medium heat until meat is no longer pink; drain. Add the mushrooms, relish, salt, mustard and pepper. Combine flour and water until smooth; stir into beef mixture. Bring to a boil; cook and stir for 2 minutes or until thickened. Set aside.

2. For pastry, in a large bowl, combine the flour, baking powder, salt and poultry seasoning. Cut in shortening until mixture resembles coarse crumbs. Stir in ¾ cup milk to form a soft dough. Turn onto a floured surface; pat dough into a 12-in. x 9-in. rectangle.

3. Set aside ¼ cup meat mixture. Spread remaining mixture over dough to within 1 in. of edges. Roll up, starting with a long side; pinch seam to seal. Place seam side down on a greased baking sheet; brush with remaining milk.

4. Bake at 425° for 15-20 minutes or until golden brown.

5. For gravy, melt butter in a saucepan over medium heat. Stir in the flour, salt and pepper until smooth. Gradually add milk. Bring to a boil; cook and stir for 2 minutes or until thickened. Stir in reserved meat mixture; heat through. Slice roll; serve with gravy.

Mozzarella Meat Loaf

My children were not fond of meat loaf until I dressed up this recipe with pizza flavor. Now the five children are grown and have families of their own, and they still make and serve this hearty, moist meat loaf.

—DARLIS WILFER WEST BEND, WISCONSIN

YIELD: 8-10 SERVINGS.

- 2 **pounds lean ground beef (90% lean)**
- 2 **eggs, lightly beaten**
- 1 **cup saltine cracker crumbs**
- 1 **cup milk**
- ½ **cup grated Parmesan cheese**
- ½ **cup chopped onion**
- 1½ **teaspoons salt**
- 1 **teaspoon dried oregano**
- 1 **can (8 ounce) pizza sauce**
- 3 **slices part-skim mozzarella cheese, halved**

Green pepper rings, optional
Sliced mushrooms, optional
- 2 **tablespoons butter, optional**

Chopped fresh parsley, optional

1. Mix beef, eggs, crumbs, milk, Parmesan cheese, onion, salt and oregano. Shape into a loaf and place in a greased 9-in. x 5-in. loaf pan. Bake at 350° for 1¼ hours or until no pink remains; drain.

2. Spoon the pizza sauce over loaf and top with the mozzarella cheese slices. Bake 10 minutes longer or until the cheese is melted.

3. Meanwhile, if desired, saute green pepper and mushrooms in butter; arrange on top of meat loaf. Sprinkle with parsley if desired.

Salisbury Steak Deluxe

This recipe is so good that I truly enjoy sharing it with others. I've always liked Salisbury steak, but I had to search a long time to find a recipe this tasty. It's handy, too, because it can be prepared ahead, kept in the refrigerator and warmed up later.

—DENISE BARTEET SHREVEPORT, LOUISIANA

YIELD: 6 SERVINGS.

- 1 **can (10¾ ounces) condensed cream of mushroom soup, undiluted**
- 1 **tablespoon prepared mustard**
- 2 **teaspoons Worcestershire sauce**
- 1 **teaspoon prepared horseradish**
- 1 **egg**
- ¼ **cup dry bread crumbs**
- ¼ **cup finely chopped onion**
- ½ **teaspoon salt**

Dash pepper
- 1½ **pound ground beef**
- 1 **to 2 tablespoons canola oil**
- ½ **cup water**
- 2 **tablespoons chopped fresh parsley**

1. In a small bowl, combine the soup, mustard, Worcestershire sauce and horseradish. Set aside. In another bowl, lightly beat the egg. Add the bread crumbs, onion, salt, pepper and ¼ cup of the soup mixture. Crumble beef over mixture and mix well. Shape into six patties.

2. In a large skillet, brown the patties in oil; drain. Combine remaining soup mixture with water; pour over patties. Cover and cook patties over low heat for 10-15 minutes or until meat is no longer pink and a thermometer reads 160°. Remove patties to a serving platter; serve sauce with meat. Sprinkle with parsley.

Savory Pot Roast

My old-fashioned pot roast and smooth pan gravy evoke memories of dinners at Mom's or Grandma's. My husband and I used to raise cattle, so I prepared a lot of beef, and this recipe is the best.

—**LEE LEUSCHNER** CALGARY, ALBERTA

YIELD: 14-16 SERVINGS.

- 1 **rolled boneless beef chuck roast (6 pounds)**
- 2 **tablespoons canola oil**
  Salt and coarsely ground pepper
- 1 **large onion, coarsely chopped**
- 2 **medium carrots, coarsely chopped**
- 1 **celery rib, coarsely chopped**
- 2 **cups water**
- 1 **can (14½ ounces) beef broth**
- 2 **bay leaves**
  GRAVY
- ¼ **cup butter, cubed**
- ¼ **cup all-purpose flour**
- 1 **teaspoon lemon juice**
- 4 **to 5 drops hot pepper sauce**

1. In a large skillet over medium-high heat, brown roast in oil on all sides. Transfer to a large roasting pan; season with salt and pepper. Add the onion, carrots and celery.

2. In a large saucepan, bring the water, broth and bay leaves to a boil. Pour over roast and vegetables. Cover and bake at 350° for 2½ to 3 hours or until meat is tender, turning once.

3. Remove roast to a serving platter and keep warm. For gravy, strain pan juices, reserving 2 cups. Discard vegetables and bay leaves.

4. In a large saucepan over medium heat, melt butter; stir in flour until smooth. Gradually stir in pan juices. Bring to a boil; cook and stir for 2 minutes or until thickened. Stir in lemon juice and hot pepper sauce. Serve with roast.

Editor's Note: *Ask your butcher to tie two 3-pound chuck roasts together to form a rolled chuck roast.*

Classic Beef Stew

Here's a good old-fashioned stew with rich beef gravy that lets the flavor of the potatoes and carrots come through. It's the perfect hearty dish for a blustery winter day. I make it often during the cold-weather months.

—**ALBERTA MCKAY** BARTLESVILLE, OKLAHOMA

YIELD: 6-8 SERVINGS.

- 2 **pounds beef stew meat, cut into 1-inch cubes**
- 1 **to 2 tablespoons canola oil**
- 1½ **cups chopped onion**
- 1 **can (14½ ounces) diced tomatoes, undrained**
- 1 **can (10½ ounces) condensed beef broth, undiluted**
- 3 **tablespoons quick-cooking tapioca**
- 1 **garlic clove, minced**
- 1 **tablespoon dried parsley flakes**
- 1 **teaspoon salt**
- ¼ **teaspoon pepper**
- 1 **bay leaf**
- 6 **medium carrots, cut into 2-inch pieces**
- 3 **medium potatoes, peeled and cut into 2-inch pieces**
- 1 **cup sliced celery, cut into 1-inch pieces**

1. In a Dutch oven, brown half the beef in oil. Drain. Brown remaining beef; drain. Return all meat to pan. Add onion, tomatoes, beef broth, tapioca, garlic, parsley, salt, pepper and bay leaf. Bring to a boil; remove from the heat.

2. Cover and bake at 350° for 1½ hours. Stir in carrots, potatoes and celery. Bake, covered, 1 hour longer or until meat and vegetables are tender. Discard bay leaf before serving.

Barbecued Short Ribs

This recipe for short ribs is very popular in our area. The meat is fork-tender, and the sauce is wonderfully tangy. We're retired now but raised beef for many years. We still put this recipe to good use.

—**MARGERY BRYAN** MOSES LAKE, WASHINGTON

YIELD: 4-6 SERVINGS.

  3½ to 4 pounds beef short ribs
  1½ cups water
  1 medium onion, sliced
  1 tablespoon vinegar
SAUCE
  ½ cup ketchup
  ¼ cup chopped onion
  2 tablespoons lemon juice
  2 garlic cloves, minced
  1 teaspoon sugar
  ½ teaspoon salt
  ⅛ teaspoon pepper

1. In a Dutch oven, combine ribs, water, onion and vinegar; bring to a boil. Reduce heat; cover and simmer for 1 hour, turning ribs occasionally. Drain. Place the ribs in a single layer in an ungreased 13-in. x 9-in. baking dish. Combine the sauce ingredients; spoon over the ribs. Cover and bake at 325° for 1¼ hours or until meat is tender.

Swedish Meatballs

Allspice and nutmeg—plus a hint of dill—give these tender meatballs their special Old World flavor.

—**KATHY RINGEL** SALINE, MICHIGAN

YIELD: 10-12 SERVINGS.

  2 eggs, beaten
  ½ cup milk
  1 cup dry bread crumbs
  2 teaspoons salt
  ½ teaspoon pepper
  1½ teaspoons dill weed
  ¼ teaspoon ground allspice
  ¼ teaspoon ground nutmeg
  1 cup chopped onion
  2 tablespoons butter
  2 pounds ground beef
  ½ pound ground pork
SAUCE
  ¼ cup butter
  ½ cup all-purpose flour
  2 cans (14½ ounces each) beef broth
  1 pint heavy whipping cream
  ½ teaspoon dill weed
  ½ teaspoon salt
  ¼ teaspoon pepper
Fresh dill sprigs, optional

1. In a large bowl, combine eggs, milk, bread crumbs and seasonings; set aside. In a skillet, saute onion in butter until soft; add egg to mixture. Add beef and ground pork; mix well. Cover and refrigerate for 1 hour.

2. Shape meat mixture into 1¼-in. to 1½-in. balls. Place meatballs on a greased rack in a shallow baking pan. Bake, uncovered, at 350° for 20-25 minutes or until a thermometer reads 160°. Remove from oven and place in a 3-qt. baking dish.

3. For sauce, melt butter in a saucepan; stir in flour to form a smooth paste. Gradually stir in broth; bring to a boil, stirring constantly. Reduce heat; stir in cream, dill, salt and pepper. If a thicker sauce is desired, continue cooking 10-15 minutes longer, stirring occasionally. Pour sauce over meatballs.

4. Bake, uncovered, at 350° for 40-45 minutes or until heated through and bubbly. Garnish with fresh dill if desired.

Grandma's Meat Loaf

We love Grandma's version of meat loaf so much that we have it at Thanksgiving, Christmas and Easter—the holidays wouldn't be the same without it! It's just as good the next day in a cold sandwich.

—**JOAN FREY** SPENCER, OHIO

YIELD: 8-10 SERVINGS.

  1 egg, beaten
  ¼ cup dry bread crumbs
  3 bacon strips, cut into ¼-inch pieces
  1 small onion, chopped
  2 ounces cubed cheddar cheese
  ½ teaspoon seasoned salt
  ½ teaspoon pepper
  1½ pounds lean ground beef
  ½ pound bulk pork sausage

1. In a large bowl, combine egg, bread crumbs, bacon, onion, cheese, seasoned salt and pepper. Add beef and sausage; mix well. In a shallow baking pan, shape mixture into an 8-in. x 4-in. oval.

2. Bake at 350° for 1¼ hours or until no pink remains and a thermometer reads 160°; drain.

Old-Fashioned Cabbage Rolls

An abundance of dill in my garden led me to try this. My family liked the taste so much that from then on, I always made my cabbage rolls with dill.

—FLORENCE KRANTZ BISMARCK, NORTH DAKOTA

YIELD: 6 SERVINGS.

1 **medium head cabbage (3 pounds)**
½ **pound uncooked ground beef**
½ **pound uncooked ground pork**
1 **can (15 ounces) tomato sauce,** **divided**
1 **small onion, chopped**
½ **cup uncooked long grain rice**
1 **tablespoon dried parsley flakes**
½ **teaspoon salt**
½ **teaspoon dill weed**
⅛ **teaspoon cayenne pepper**
1 **can (14½ ounces) diced tomatoes,** **undrained**
½ **teaspoon sugar**

1. In a Dutch oven, cook cabbage in boiling water just until leaves fall off head. Remove 12 large leaves for rolls; set aside remaining cabbage. Cut out the thick vein from the bottom of each reserved leaf, making a V-shaped cut to enclose filling.

2. In a small bowl, combine the beef, pork, ½ cup tomato sauce, onion, rice, parsley, salt, dill and cayenne. Place about ¼ cup meat mixture on each cabbage leaf; overlap cut ends of leaf. Fold in sides, beginning from the cut end. Roll up completely to enclose filling.

3. Slice the remaining cabbage; place in Dutch oven. Arrange the cabbage rolls seam side down over sliced cabbage. Combine the tomatoes, sugar and remaining tomato sauce; pour over the rolls.

4. Cover and bake at 350° for 1½ hours or until tender and meat thermometer reads 160°.

Baked Spaghetti

Every time that I make this cheesy dish, I get requests for the recipe. It puts a different spin on spaghetti and is great for any meal. The leftovers, if there are any, also freeze well for a quick meal later on in the week.

—RUTH KOBERNA BRECKSVILLE, OHIO

YIELD: 12 SERVINGS.

- 1 **cup chopped onion**
- 1 **cup chopped green pepper**
- 1 **tablespoon butter**
- 1 **can (28 ounces) diced tomatoes, undrained**
- 1 **can (4 ounces) mushroom stems and pieces, drained**
- 1 **can (2¼ ounces) sliced ripe olives, drained**
- 2 **teaspoons dried oregano**
- 1 **pound ground beef, browned and drained, optional**
- 12 **ounces spaghetti, cooked and drained**
- 2 **cups (8 ounces) shredded cheddar cheese**
- 1 **can (10¾ ounces) condensed cream of mushroom soup, undiluted**
- ¼ **cup water**
- ¼ **cup grated Parmesan cheese**

1. In a large skillet, saute onion and green pepper in butter until tender. Add the tomatoes, mushrooms, olives, oregano. Add ground beef if desired. Simmer, uncovered, for 10 minutes.

2. Place half of the spaghetti in a greased 13-in. x 9-in. baking dish. Layer with half of the vegetable mixture and 1 cup of the cheddar cheese. Repeat layers.

3. In a small bowl, combine soup and water until smooth; pour over the casserole. Sprinkle with Parmesan cheese. Bake, uncovered, at 350° for 30-35 minutes or until heated through.

Corned Beef and Mixed Vegetables

For St. Patrick's Day, prepare a traditional corned beef dinner and add a special twist—a colorful medley of cooked fresh vegetables. It's a festive combination to serve family or guests.

—GLORIA WARCZAK CEDARBURG, WISCONSIN

YIELD: 6-8 SERVINGS.

- 1 **corned beef brisket with spice packet (3 to 4 pounds), trimmed**
- 6 **to 8 small red potatoes**
- 3 **medium carrots, cut into 2-inch pieces**
- 3 **celery ribs, cut into 2-inch pieces**
- 2 **tablespoons chopped celery leaves**
- 2 **turnips, peeled and cut into wedges**
- 1 **medium head cabbage, cut into 6 to 8 wedges**
- ½ **pound fresh green beans**
- 3 **to 4 ears fresh corn, halved**

1. Place corned beef and enclosed seasoning packet in an 8-qt. Dutch oven. Cover with water and bring to a boil. Reduce heat; cover and simmer for 2 hours or until meat is tender.

2. Add potatoes, carrots, celery, celery leaves and turnips; return to a boil. Reduce heat; cover and simmer for 20 minutes.

3. Add cabbage, beans and corn; return to a boil. Reduce heat; cover and simmer 15-20 minutes or until vegetables are tender.

Cornish Pasties

Years ago, when bakeries in my Midwestern hometown made pasties, people scrambled to get there before they were all gone. Now I make my own. Filled with meat, potatoes and vegetables, they make a complete handheld meal.

—**GAYLE LEWIS** YUCAIPA, CALIFORNIA

YIELD: 4 SERVINGS.

FILLING
- 1 **pound beef top round steak, cut into ½-inch pieces**
- 2 **to 3 medium potatoes, peeled and cut into ½-inch cubes**
- 1 **cup chopped carrots**
- ½ **cup finely chopped onion**
- 2 **tablespoons minced fresh parsley**
- 1 **teaspoon salt**
- ½ **teaspoon pepper**
- ¼ **cup butter, melted**

PASTRY
- 3 **cups all-purpose flour**
- 1 **teaspoon salt**
- 1 **cup shortening**
- 8 **to 9 tablespoons ice water**
- 1 **egg, lightly beaten, optional**

1. In a large bowl, combine the round steak, potatoes, carrots, onion, parsley, salt and pepper. Add butter and toss to coat; set aside.

2. For pastry, combine flour and salt in a large bowl. Cut in shortening until mixture resembles coarse crumbs. Sprinkle with water, 1 tablespoon at a time. Toss lightly with a fork until dough forms a ball. Do not overmix.

3. Divide dough into fourths. Roll out one portion into a 9-in. circle; transfer to a greased baking sheet. Mound about 1¼ cups of meat filling on half of circle. Moisten edges with water; fold dough over mixture and press edges with fork to seal. Repeat with remaining pastry and filling.

4. Cut slits in top of each pasty. Brush with beaten egg if desired. Bake at 375° for 50-60 minutes or until golden brown.

All-American Barbecue Sandwiches

I came up with this delicious recipe on my own. It's my husband's favorite and is a big hit with family and friends who enjoyed it at our Fourth of July picnic.

—**SUE GRONHOLZ**
BEAVER DAM, WISCONSIN

YIELD: 18 SERVINGS.

- 4½ **pounds ground beef**
- 1½ **cups chopped onion**
- 2¼ **cups ketchup**
- 3 **tablespoons prepared mustard**
- 3 **tablespoons Worcestershire sauce**
- 2 **tablespoons vinegar**
- 2 **tablespoons sugar**
- 1 **tablespoon salt**
- 1 **tablespoon pepper**
- 18 **hamburger buns, split**

1. In a Dutch oven, cook beef and onion over medium heat until meat is no longer pink and onion is tender; drain. Combine ketchup, mustard, Worcestershire, vinegar, sugar, salt and pepper; stir into beef mixture. Heat though. Serve on buns.

> When I was in grade school, I often went to see my granny and granddad at lunchtime. Granny, who thought a cold sandwich wasn't "fitting for a growing child," always served me a hot meal with a glass of cold buttermilk from the old wooden icebox.
>
> — **DALE SMITH** WEST WORTHINGTON, OHIO

Stuffed Zucchini

An abundance of squash from my garden inspired me to make up this recipe, which is now a favorite.

—MARJORIE ROBERTS WEST CHAZY, NEW YORK

YIELD: 8-10 SERVINGS.

      1½   pounds lean ground beef (90% lean)
      1   large onion, chopped
      1   large green pepper, chopped
      1   jalapeno pepper, minced
      1¼   cups soft bread crumbs
      1   egg, beaten
      1   tablespoon dried parsley flakes
      1   teaspoon dried basil
      1   teaspoon Italian seasoning
      1   teaspoon salt
      ⅛   teaspoon pepper
      2   cans (8 ounces each) tomato sauce, divided
      2   medium tomatoes, coarsely chopped
      4   to 5 medium zucchini
      2   cups (8 ounces) shredded mozzarella cheese

1. In a large bowl, combine first 11 ingredients and one can of the tomato sauce; mix well. Stir in tomatoes. Halve zucchini lengthwise; scoop out seeds. Fill with meat mixture; place in two 13-in. x 9-in. baking dishes. Spoon remaining tomato sauce over each.

2. Bake, uncovered, at 375° for 45 minutes or until the zucchini is tender. Sprinkle with the cheese during the last few minutes of baking.

Editor's Note: *Wear disposable gloves when cutting hot peppers; the oils can burn skin. Avoid touching your face.*

Herbed Beef Stew

Packed with a variety of herbs and fresh vegetables, this hearty stew looks every bit as terrific as it tastes! Salt is optional, making this dish ideal for family members and friends who are watching their sodium intake.

—MARLENE SEVERSON EVERSON, WASHINGTON

YIELD: 10-12 SERVINGS.

      2   pounds beef stew meat, cut into 1-inch cubes
      2   tablespoons canola oil
      3   cups water
      1   large onion, chopped
      2   teaspoons pepper
      1   to 2 teaspoons salt, optional
      1½   teaspoons garlic powder
      1   teaspoon rosemary, crushed
      1   teaspoon dried oregano
      1   teaspoon dried basil
      1   teaspoon ground marjoram
      2   bay leaves
      1   can (6 ounces) tomato paste
      2   cups cubed peeled potatoes
      2   cups sliced carrots
      1   large green pepper, chopped
      1   package (9 ounces) frozen cut green beans
      1   package (10 ounces) frozen corn
      ¼   pound mushrooms, sliced
      3   medium tomatoes, chopped

1. In a Dutch oven, brown the meat in oil. Add water, onion, seasonings and tomato paste. Cover and simmer for 1½ hours or until meat is almost tender.

2. Stir in potatoes, carrots and green pepper; simmer for 30 minutes. Add additional water if necessary. Stir in remaining ingredients; cover and simmer for 20 minutes or until meat and vegetables are tender.

Perfect Pot Roast

Cooking meats, I have to confess, isn't my specialty. But everyone who tastes this main-course dish wants more! I'm a mostly at-home mom. I like to sew and read. I also enjoy gardening—we grow a good-sized patch, and it's so nice to have fresh-picked tomatoes and spinach when I make salads.

—MELODY SROUFE WICHITA, KANSAS

YIELD: 8-10 SERVINGS.

- 1 teaspoon seasoned salt
- ½ teaspoon onion powder
- ¼ teaspoon pepper
- ⅛ teaspoon garlic powder
- 1 beef chuck pot roast (3 to 4 pounds)
- 1 tablespoon olive oil
- ¾ cup water
- 1 large onion, chopped
- ¼ cup chopped green pepper
- 2 garlic cloves, minced
- 2 bay leaves
- 2 teaspoons dried parsley flakes
- ¼ teaspoon dried thyme

All-purpose flour

1. Combine first four ingredients; rub onto roast. In skillet, brown roast in oil. Place in a roasting pan. Add water, onion, green pepper and seasonings. Cover and bake at 325° for 2½ to 3 hours or until roast is tender.

2. Remove and keep warm. Discard bay leaves. Skim fat from pan juices. Measure juices and transfer to a saucepan.

3. For each cup of juices, combine 1 tablespoon flour with 2 tablespoons water; mix well. Stir flour mixture into pan. Bring to a boil; cook and stir for 2 minutes or until thickened. Serve gravy with roast.

Vegetable Beef Chili

My chili is big on fresh tomato taste. The recipe works well in a slow cooker, too.

—MARLENE MUCKENHIRN
DELANO, MINNESOTA

YIELD: 8-10 SERVINGS.

- 1 pound ground beef
- 6 medium tomatoes, cubed
- 2 medium green peppers, chopped
- 2 medium onions, chopped
- 3 garlic cloves, minced
- 1 can (16 ounces) kidney beans, rinsed and drained
- 1 can (16 ounces) chili beans, undrained
- 3 tablespoons chili powder
- 1½ teaspoons salt
- ½ teaspoon ground turmeric
- ½ teaspoon Italian seasoning
- ½ teaspoon ground cumin

1. In a 5-qt. Dutch oven, cook the beef over medium heat until no longer pink; drain. Add the tomatoes, green peppers, onions and garlic. Cook over medium-low heat for 20-30 minutes or until the vegetables are tender, stirring occasionally.

2. Add the beans and seasonings; mix well. Simmer, uncovered, for 45-50 minutes or until thickened, stirring occasionally.

Standing Rib Roast

Treat your family to tender slices of standing rib roast or use the seasoning blend on a different beef roast for a hearty, delicious main dish.

—**LUCY MEYRING** WALDEN, COLORADO

YIELD: 10 SERVINGS.

- 1 tablespoon lemon-pepper seasoning
- 1 tablespoon paprika
- 1½ teaspoons garlic salt
- 1 teaspoon dried rosemary, crushed
- ½ teaspoon cayenne pepper
- 1 bone-in beef rib roast (6 to 7 pounds)
- 2 cups water
- 1 teaspoon beef bouillon granules

1. In a small bowl, mix the first five ingredients; rub over roast. Place roast in a large roasting pan, fat side up. Roast at 325° for 2¼ to 2¾ hours or until meat reaches desired doneness (for medium-rare, a thermometer should read 145°; medium, 160°; well-done, 170°).

2. Remove roast from oven; tent with foil. Let stand for 15 minutes before slicing.

3. Meanwhile, pour drippings and loosened browned bits into a small saucepan; skim fat. Stir in water and bouillon; bring to a boil; serve with the roast.

Savory Spaghetti Sauce

My fresh-tasting spaghetti sauce is a real crowd-pleaser. With a husband and 12 kids to feed every day, I rely on this flavorful recipe often. It tastes especially good in the summer, when I can make it with fresh garden herbs.

—**ANNE HEINONEN** HOWELL, MICHIGAN

YIELD: 4-6 SERVINGS (ABOUT 1 QUART).

- 1 pound ground beef
- 1 large onion, chopped
- 2 cans (15 ounces each) tomato sauce
- 1 garlic clove, minced
- 1 bay leaf
- 1 tablespoon minced fresh basil or 1 teaspoon dried basil
- 2 teaspoons minced fresh oregano or ¾ teaspoon dried oregano
- 2 teaspoon sugar
- ½ to 1 teaspoon salt
- ½ teaspoon pepper

Hot cooked spaghetti
Fresh oregano, optional

1. In a Dutch oven, cook ground beef and onion until meat is no longer pink and onion is tender; drain. Add the next eight ingredients; bring to a boil.

2. Reduce heat; cover and simmer for 1 hour, stirring occasionally. Discard the bay leaf. Serve with spaghetti. Garnish with oregano if desired.

Barbecued Brisket

For a mouthwatering main dish to star in a summer meal, this brisket can't be beat. Baked slowly, the meat gets nice and tender and picks up the sweet and tangy flavor of the barbecue sauce.

—PAGE ALEXANDER BALDWIN CITY, KANSAS

YIELD: 6-8 SERVINGS.

    1   fresh beef brisket (3 to 4 pounds)
1¼ cups water, divided
    ½   cup chopped onion
    3   garlic cloves, minced
    1   tablespoon canola oil
    1   cup ketchup
    3   tablespoons red wine vinegar
    2   tablespoons lemon juice
    2   tablespoons brown sugar
    1   tablespoon Worcestershire sauce
    2   teaspoons cornstarch
    1   teaspoon paprika
    1   teaspoon chili powder
    ¼   teaspoon salt
    ¼   teaspoon pepper
    ¼   teaspoon Liquid Smoke, optional

1. Place brisket in a large Dutch oven. Add ½ cup water. Cover and bake at 325° for 2 hours.

2. Meanwhile, in a small saucepan, saute onion and garlic in oil until tender. Add the ketchup, vinegar, lemon juice, brown sugar, Worcestershire sauce, cornstarch, paprika, chili powder, salt, pepper and remaining water. Simmer, uncovered, for 1 hour, stirring occasionally.

3. Add Liquid Smoke; mix well. Drain drippings from Dutch oven. Pour sauce over meat. Cover and bake 1 hour longer or until meat is tender.

Editor's Note: *This is a fresh beef brisket, not corned beef.*

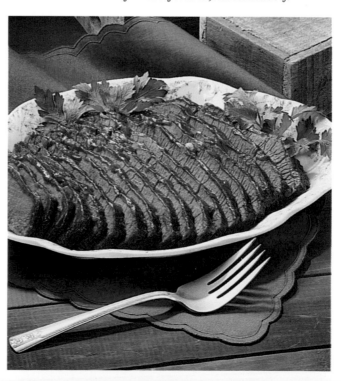

Spicy Tomato Steak

My family loves this spicy tomato dish. I came up with the recipe years ago after eating a similar dish on vacation in New Mexico. I came home and tried to duplicate it from memory. The results were delicious!

—ANNE LANDERS LOUISVILLE, KENTUCKY

YIELD: 6 SERVINGS.

    2   tablespoons cider vinegar
    1   teaspoon salt
    1   teaspoon pepper
    1   pound beef round steak, trimmed and cut into ¼-inch strips
    ¼   cup all-purpose flour
    2   tablespoons olive oil
    3   medium tomatoes, peeled, seeded and cut into wedges
    2   medium potatoes, peeled and thinly sliced
    2   cans (4 ounces each) chopped green chilies
    1   garlic clove, minced
    1   teaspoon dried basil

1. In a large resealable bag, combine the vinegar, salt and pepper. Add the beef; seal bag and turn to coat. Refrigerate for 30 minutes.

2. Drain marinade. Place flour in another large resealable bag; add beef and toss to coat. In a large skillet, cook beef in oil over medium heat for 15-20 minutes or until tender.

3. Add the remaining ingredients. Cover and simmer for 20-30 minutes or until the potatoes are tender, stirring occasionally.

Grilled Asian Flank Steak

I created this variation of the marinated ginger-sake flank steak my mother used to make. My version is lighter, but the tender meat, and the wonderful flavor and aroma, are equally as good. You'll want to try this one!
—**SHAWN SOLLEY** MORGANTOWN, WEST VIRGINIA

YIELD: 6 SERVINGS.

¼ cup Worcestershire sauce
¼ cup reduced-sodium soy sauce
3 tablespoons honey
1 tablespoon sesame oil
1 teaspoon Chinese five-spice powder
1 teaspoon minced garlic
½ teaspoon minced fresh gingerroot
1 beef flank steak (1½ pounds)
2 tablespoons hoisin sauce, warmed
3 green onions, thinly sliced
1 tablespoon sesame seeds, toasted, optional

1. In a large resealable plastic bag, combine the first seven ingredients; add steak. Seal bag and turn to coat; refrigerate overnight.

2. Drain and discard marinade. Grill steak, covered, over medium heat for 6-7 minutes on each side or until meat reaches desired doneness (for medium-rare, a thermometer should read 145°; medium, 160°; well-done, 170°). Let stand for 5 minutes.

3. Thinly slice steak across the grain. Drizzle with hoisin sauce; garnish with onions. Sprinkle with sesame seeds if desired.

Spaghetti 'n' Meatballs

One evening, we had unexpected company. Since I had some of these meatballs left over in the freezer, I warmed them up as appetizers. Everyone raved! This classic recipe makes a big batch and is perfect for entertaining.

—MARY LOU KOSKELLA PRESCOTT, ARIZONA

YIELD: 12-16 SERVINGS.

- 1½ cups chopped onion
- 2 tablespoons olive oil
- 3 garlic cloves, minced
- 3 cups water
- 1 can (29 ounces) tomato sauce
- 2 cans (12 ounces each) tomato paste
- ⅓ cup minced fresh parsley
- 1 tablespoon dried basil
- 1 tablespoon salt
- ½ teaspoon pepper

MEATBALLS
- 4 eggs, lightly beaten
- 2 cups soft bread cubes (¼-inch pieces)
- 1½ cups milk
- 1 cup grated Parmesan cheese
- 3 garlic cloves, minced
- 1 tablespoon salt
- ½ teaspoon pepper
- 3 pounds ground beef
- 2 tablespoons canola oil

Hot cooked spaghetti

1. In a Dutch oven over medium heat, saute onion in oil. Add garlic; cook 1 minute longer. Add the water, tomato sauce and paste, parsley, basil, salt and pepper; bring to a boil. Reduce heat; cover and simmer for 50 minutes.

2. In a large bowl, combine the first seven meatball ingredients. Crumble beef over mixture and mix well. Shape into 1½-in. balls.

3. In a large skillet over medium heat, brown meatballs in oil until no longer pink; drain. Add to sauce; bring to a boil. Reduce heat; cover and simmer for 1 hour or until flavors are blended, stirring occasionally. Serve with spaghetti.

Tex-Mex Beef Barbecues

I recently took this dish to a potluck and guests loved it! The recipe came from my mom and it is so easy to make.

—LYNDA ZUNIGA CRYSTAL CITY, TEXAS

YIELD: 14 SERVINGS.

- 1 fresh beef brisket (3½ pounds)
- 1 jar (18 ounces) hickory smoke-flavored barbecue sauce
- ½ cup finely chopped onion
- 1 envelope chili seasoning
- 1 tablespoon Worcestershire sauce
- 1 teaspoon minced garlic
- 1 teaspoon lemon juice
- 14 hamburger buns, split

1. Cut the brisket in half; place in a 5-qt. slow cooker.

2. In a small bowl, combine the barbecue sauce, onion, chili seasoning, Worcestershire sauce, garlic and lemon juice. Pour over the beef. Cover and cook on high for 5-6 hours or until the meat is tender.

3. Remove beef; cool slightly. Shred and return to the slow cooker; heat through. Serve on buns.

Editor's Note: *This is a fresh beef brisket, not corned beef.*

All-American Beef Stew

My mother was born and raised in Japan and wasn't familiar with many American dishes when she married my father and moved to the States. My paternal grandmother gave her this mouthwatering recipe.

—FRANCES ALDAL
ANTELOPE, CALIFORNIA

YIELD: 8 SERVINGS (2½ QUARTS).

- ¾ cup all-purpose flour, divided
- ½ teaspoon seasoned salt
- ½ teaspoon pepper, divided
- 2 pounds beef stew meat, cut into 1-inch cubes
- 1 tablespoon olive oil
- 4½ cups water, divided
- 1 large onion, halved and sliced
- 2 tablespoons Worcestershire sauce
- 1 tablespoon lemon juice
- 2 garlic cloves, minced
- 1 teaspoon sugar
- ½ teaspoon salt
- ½ teaspoon paprika
- ⅛ teaspoon ground allspice
- 1 bay leaf
- 4 medium potatoes, cubed
- 6 medium carrots, sliced

1. Place ½ cup flour, seasoned salt and ¼ teaspoon pepper in a large resealable plastic bag. Add beef, a few pieces at a time, and shake to coat.

2. In a Dutch oven, brown meat in oil in batches. Remove and set aside. Add 4 cups water to the pan, stirring to loosen browned bits. Add the onion, Worcestershire sauce, lemon juice, garlic, sugar, salt, paprika, allspice, bay leaf and remaining pepper. Return beef to the pan. Bring to a boil. Reduce heat; cover and simmer for 1 hour.

3. Stir in the potatoes and carrots. Bring to a boil. Reduce heat; cover and simmer for 30-35 minutes or until meat and vegetables are tender.

4. Combine the remaining flour and water until smooth; stir into the pan. Bring mixture to a boil; cook and stir for 2 minutes or until thickened. Discard bay leaf.

Ground Beef Macaroni Casserole

My mom often made this casserole when I was growing up, and it was one of my favorite meals. It tastes terrific with a salad and rolls.

—JUDY HLUCHY MOUNT PROSPECT, ILLINOIS

YIELD: 8 SERVINGS.

- 1 package (7 ounces) elbow macaroni
- 1 pound ground beef
- 1 medium onion, chopped
- 1 can (15 ounces) Italian tomato sauce
- 1 egg
- 1 can (10¾ ounces) condensed cream of chicken soup, undiluted
- 1½ cups 2% milk
- 2 tablespoons butter, melted
- 1 tablespoon minced fresh parsley
- 1 cup (4 ounces) shredded cheddar cheese

1. Cook macaroni according to package directions. Meanwhile, in a large skillet, cook beef and onion over medium heat until meat is no longer pink; drain. Stir in tomato sauce; heat through.

2. Drain macaroni; transfer to a greased 13-in. x 9-in. baking dish. In a small bowl, combine the egg, soup, milk, butter and parsley; pour over macaroni. Spoon beef mixture over top; sprinkle with cheese.

3. Bake, uncovered, at 350° for 25-30 minutes or until bubbly. Let stand for 10 minutes before serving.

Chipotle Beef Tenderloins

Head outside for your Sunday dinner and grill this tender steak that's kicked up with a smoky homemade picante sauce. If you have any sauce left over, it's great with tortilla chips.

—**GENE PETERS** EDWARDSVILLE, ILLINOIS

YIELD: 6 SERVINGS.

- ¾ **cup chopped sweet onion**
- ¾ **cup chopped green pepper**
- 1 **jalapeno pepper, seeded and minced**
- 1 **chipotle pepper in adobo sauce, minced**
- 2 **tablespoons olive oil**
- 3 **cups seeded chopped tomatoes**
- 1 **tablespoon chipotle hot pepper sauce**
- 2 **teaspoons sugar**
- 1 **teaspoon salt**
- 1 **teaspoon chili powder**
- ½ **teaspoon ground cumin**
- 2 **tablespoons minced fresh cilantro**
- 1 **teaspoon Liquid Smoke, optional**
- 6 **beef tenderloin steaks (1½ inches thick and 6 ounces each)**
- 2 **teaspoons steak seasoning**

1. In a Dutch oven, saute the onion, green pepper, jalapeno and chipotle pepper in oil until tender. Add the tomatoes, pepper sauce, sugar, salt, chili powder and cumin. Bring to a boil. Reduce heat; simmer, uncovered, for 30 minutes or until thickened, stirring frequently.

2. Remove from the heat; stir in the cilantro and Liquid Smoke if desired.

3. Meanwhile, sprinkle steaks with steak seasoning. Grill over medium heat for 7-8 minutes on each side or until meat reaches desired doneness (for medium-rare, a thermometer should read 145°; medium, 160°; well-done, 170°). Serve with sauce.

Blue Cheese Flank Steak

While having a house built, we lived with my parents for a few months and I plundered my mother's recipe files. The recipe for this tasty steak is one of the many treasures I collected.

—**LAURIE NUDO** THE WOODLANDS, TEXAS

YIELD: 4 SERVINGS.

- 1 **medium onion, sliced**
- 1 **garlic clove, peeled and sliced**
- ⅓ **cup water**
- ⅓ **cup white wine vinegar**
- 2 **tablespoons reduced-sodium soy sauce**
- ½ **teaspoon coarsely ground pepper**
- 1 **beef flank steak (1 pound)**
- ½ **cup crumbled blue cheese**

1. In a large resealable plastic bag, combine the first six ingredients. Add the steak; seal bag and turn to coat. Refrigerate overnight, turning occasionally.

2. Drain and discard marinade. Using long-handled tongs, moisten a paper towel with cooking oil and lightly coat the grill rack.

3. Grill beef, covered, over medium-hot heat for 5-7 minutes on each side or until meat reaches desired doneness (for medium-rare, a thermometer should read 145°; medium, 160°; well-done, 170°).

4. Let stand for 5 minutes; thinly slice across the grain. Sprinkle with blue cheese.

POULTRY

Parmesan Chicken Sandwiches

For a casual meal, turn to my fast and flavorful sandwiches. Chicken breasts are coated with seasoned bread crumbs and smothered in marinara sauce. Served on Italian rolls, they're a real treat!

—SUE BOSEK WHITTIER, CALIFORNIA

YIELD: 2 SERVINGS.

2	boneless skinless chicken breast halves (5 ounces each)
⅛	teaspoon salt
⅛	teaspoon pepper
½	cup all-purpose flour
1	egg, lightly beaten
¾	cup seasoned bread crumbs
3	tablespoons grated Parmesan cheese
2	tablespoons olive oil
2	slices provolone cheese (1 ounce each)
2	Italian rolls, split lengthwise
⅓	cup marinara sauce or meatless spaghetti sauce

1. Flatten chicken to ½-in. thickness; sprinkle both sides with salt and pepper. Place flour and egg in separate shallow bowls. In another bowl, combine bread crumbs and cheese. Dip chicken in flour, then egg; roll in crumb mixture.

2. In a large skillet, cook chicken in oil over medium heat for 4-5 minutes on each side or until no longer pink. Layer chicken and cheese on bun bottoms; spread with marinara sauce. Replace tops.

Sourdough Chicken Sandwiches: Prepare chicken as directed. Spread four slices sourdough bread with mayonnaise if desired; top two slices with a lettuce leaf, a slice of Swiss cheese, tomato slice, 1 bacon strip cooked and cut in half, and the chicken breast. Top with remaining bread.

Cornish Hens with Rice Dressing

I found this recipe in my mother's collection. It's a great main dish when you're cooking for two. I've even used these hens as a stand-in for turkey on Thanksgiving when the group was small.
—**GERALDINE GRISDALE** MOUNT PLEASANT, MICHIGAN

YIELD: 2 SERVINGS.

- 1⅓ cups chicken broth
- ½ cup uncooked long grain rice
- ½ cup sliced fresh mushrooms
- ¼ cup chopped celery
- 2 tablespoons chopped onion
- ½ teaspoon dried marjoram, divided
- ½ teaspoon salt, divided
- 2 Cornish hens (1 to 1½ pounds each)
- 1 tablespoon canola oil
- Pepper to taste

1. In an ungreased 9-in. square baking dish, combine the broth, rice, mushrooms, celery, onion, ¼ teaspoon marjoram and ¼ teaspoon salt. Place hens on rice mixture and brush with oil. Sprinkle with pepper and remaining marjoram and salt.

2. Cover and bake at 350° for 1 hour. Uncover and bake 25-35 minutes longer or until juices run clear.

Sour Cream Apple Chicken

I've found that apples and chicken go well together because they both have subtle flavors. I developed this recipe myself. I think it's not only a great-tasting main course, it also looks nice on the table.
—**CAROLYN NACE** WINTER HAVEN, FLORIDA

YIELD: 4 SERVINGS.

- 4 boneless skinless chicken breast halves
- 1 tablespoon canola oil
- 2 medium tart apples, peeled and thinly sliced
- ½ cup apple juice or cider
- ⅓ cup chopped onion
- 1 teaspoon dried basil
- ½ teaspoon salt
- 1 cup (8 ounces) sour cream
- 1 tablespoon all-purpose flour
- Cooked spinach noodles
- Paprika

1. In a large skillet, cook chicken in oil over medium heat until browned and no longer pink inside, about 6-8 minutes per side. Remove from skillet and keep warm. Add apples, juice, onion, basil and salt to the skillet; bring to a boil. Reduce heat; cover and simmer until apples are tender.

2. Combine sour cream and flour; add to skillet. Stir and cook until sauce is warm (do not boil). Arrange noodles on a serving platter. Top with chicken. Spoon apple sauce over all. Sprinkle with paprika.

Honey-Grilled Chicken Breasts

Orange juice and soy sauce make a tasty combination, and the longer this chicken marinates, the fuller the flavor! My mother-in-law shared the recipe with me.
—**JENNIFER PETERSEN** MURRAY, UTAH

YIELD: 8 SERVINGS.

- ½ cup orange juice
- ⅓ cup honey
- ¼ cup lemon juice
- ¼ cup reduced-sodium soy sauce
- 2 tablespoons minced fresh gingerroot
- 12 garlic cloves, minced
- ½ teaspoon pepper
- ¼ teaspoon salt
- 8 boneless skinless chicken breast halves (6 ounces each)

1. In a small bowl, combine the first eight ingredients. Pour ½ cup marinade into a large resealable plastic bag; add chicken. Seal bag and turn to coat; refrigerate for 8 hours or overnight. Cover and refrigerate remaining marinade.

2. Drain and discard marinade. Using long-handled tongs, moisten a paper towel with cooking oil and lightly coat the grill rack. Grill, covered, over medium heat or broil 4 in. from the heat for 5-7 minutes on each side or until a meat thermometer reads 170°, basting frequently with reserved marinade.

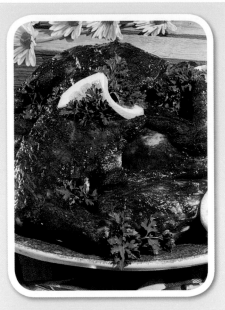

Barbecued Picnic Chicken

When we entertain friends for a picnic at our cabin, I like to serve this savory chicken. Cooked on a covered grill, the poultry stays so tender and juicy. Everyone loves the zesty, slightly sweet homemade barbecue sauce, and it's so easy to make.

—PRISCILLA WEAVER HAGERSTOWN, MARYLAND

YIELD: 8 SERVINGS.

- 2 garlic cloves, minced
- 2 teaspoons butter
- 1 cup ketchup
- ¼ cup packed brown sugar
- ¼ cup chili sauce
- 2 tablespoons Worcestershire sauce
- 1 tablespoon celery seed
- 1 tablespoon prepared mustard
- ½ teaspoon salt
- 2 dashes hot pepper sauce
- 2 broiler/fryer chickens (3½ to 4 pounds each), quartered

1. In a large saucepan, saute garlic in butter until tender. Add the next eight ingredients. Bring to a boil, stirring constantly. Remove from the heat; set aside.

2. Grill the chicken, covered, over medium heat for 30 minutes, turning occasionally. Baste with sauce. Grill 15 minutes longer or until a meat thermometer reaches 170°, basting and turning several times.

Nutty Oven-Fried Chicken

The pecans that give this dish its lovely nutty flavor are plentiful in the South, and so is chicken. I love to prepare and serve this easy dish because the chicken comes out moist, tasty and crispy.

—DIANE HIXON NICEVILLE, FLORIDA

YIELD: 6 SERVINGS.

- ½ cup evaporated milk
- 1 cup biscuit/baking mix
- ⅓ cup finely chopped pecans
- 2 teaspoons paprika
- ½ teaspoon salt
- ½ teaspoon poultry seasoning
- ½ teaspoon rubbed sage
- 1 broiler/fryer chicken (3 to 4 pounds), cut up
- ⅓ cup butter, melted

1. Place milk in a shallow bowl. In another shallow bowl, combine the baking mix, pecans and seasonings. Dip chicken pieces in milk, then coat generously with pecan mixture.

2. Place in a lightly greased 13-in. x 9-in. baking dish. Drizzle with butter. Bake, uncovered, at 350° for 1 hour or until chicken is golden brown and crispy and juices run clear.

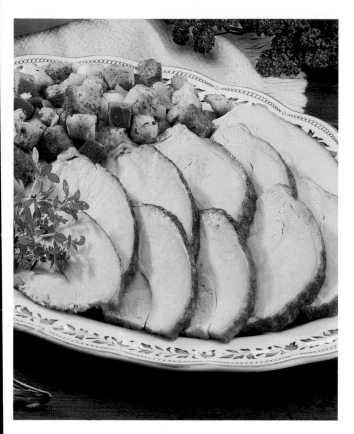

Turkey with Country Ham Stuffing

As delicious as this is right out of the oven, the bird and stuffing both taste great as leftovers, too. I am careful, though, not to overcook the turkey.

—BOBBIE LOVE KAPAA, HAWAII

YIELD: 10-12 SERVINGS.

- 3 cups cubed day-old white bread, crust removed
- 3 cups cubed day-old whole wheat bread, crust removed
- 1½ cups cubed fully cooked ham
- ½ cup butter, cubed
- 3 cups chopped onion
- 2 cups chopped celery
- 1½ teaspoons rubbed sage
- 1½ teaspoons dried thyme
- ½ teaspoon pepper
- 1 to 1½ cups chicken broth
- 1 turkey (12 to 14 pounds)

1. Place bread cubes in a single layer in a 13-in. x 9-in. baking pan. Bake at 325° for 20-25 minutes or until golden brown, stirring occasionally. Place in a large bowl; set aside.

2. In a large skillet, cook ham in butter for 5-10 minutes or until edges are crisp. Remove with a slotted spoon and place over bread cubes.

3. In the same skillet, saute the onion, celery, sage, thyme and pepper until vegetables are tender; toss with bread and ham. Stir in enough broth to moisten.

4. Just before baking, stuff the turkey. Skewer openings; tie drumsticks together. Place on a rack in a roasting pan. Bake at 325° for 4½ to 5 hours or until a thermometer reads 185°.

5. When the turkey begins to brown, cover lightly with a tent of aluminum foil and baste if needed. Cover turkey and let stand for 20 minutes before removing stuffing and carving turkey.

Cranberry Chicken

My husband loves chicken when it's nice and moist, like it is in this autumn recipe. I serve it over hot fluffy rice with a salad and warm rolls on the side. The ruby-red sauce has a tart cinnamon flavor.

—DOROTHY BATEMAN CARVER, MASSACHUSETTS

YIELD: 6 SERVINGS.

- ½ cup all-purpose flour
- ½ teaspoon salt
- ¼ teaspoon pepper
- 6 boneless skinless chicken breast halves (4 ounces each)
- 3 tablespoons butter
- 1 cup water
- 1 cup fresh or frozen cranberries
- ½ cup packed brown sugar
- Dash ground nutmeg
- 1 tablespoon red wine vinegar, optional
- Hot cooked rice, optional

1. In a shallow dish, combine flour, salt and pepper; dredge chicken. In a skillet, melt butter over medium heat. Brown the chicken on both sides. Remove and keep warm.

2. In the same skillet, add water, cranberries, brown sugar, nutmeg and vinegar if desired. Cook and stir until the berries burst, about 5 minutes. Return chicken to skillet. Cover and simmer for 20-30 minutes or until chicken is tender, basting occasionally with the sauce. Serve over rice if desired.

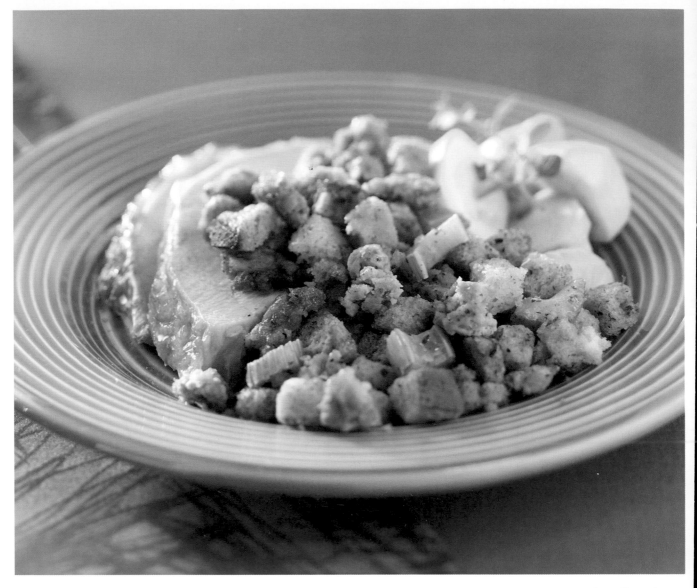

Italian Christmas Turkey

We never had stuffing without sausage, and my mom's Italian stuffing is my favorite. I rarely buy the sausage, preferring to make my own instead, the way my relatives do.

—LINDA HARRINGTON WINDHAM, NEW HAMPSHIRE

YIELD: 16 SERVINGS (12 CUPS STUFFING).

- ½ **cup butter, cubed**
- 1 **pound bulk Italian sausage**
- 2 **celery ribs, chopped**
- 1 **medium onion, chopped**
- 1 **package (14 ounces) seasoned stuffing cubes**
- ¼ **cup egg substitute**
- 2 **to 3 cups hot water**
- 1 **turkey (16 pounds)**

Salt and pepper to taste

1. In a large skillet over medium heat, melt butter. Add the sausage, celery and onion; cook and stir until meat is no longer pink. Transfer to a large bowl; stir in the stuffing cubes, egg substitute and enough water to reach desired moistness.

2. Just before baking, loosely stuff turkey with stuffing. Place remaining stuffing in a greased 2-qt. baking dish; cover and refrigerate. Remove from the refrigerator 30 minutes before baking.

3. Skewer turkey openings; tie drumsticks together. Place breast side up in a roasting pan. Rub with salt and pepper.

4. Bake, uncovered, at 325° for 3¾ to 4¼ hours or until a meat thermometer reads 180° for turkey thigh and 165° for stuffing, basting occasionally with pan drippings. (Cover loosely with foil if turkey browns too quickly.)

5. Bake additional stuffing, covered, for 25-30 minutes. Uncover; bake 10 minutes longer or until a thermometer reads 160°.

6. Cover turkey and let stand for 20 minutes before removing stuffing and carving turkey. If desired, thicken pan drippings for gravy.

Down-Home Chicken

A thick, tangy sauce coats tender chicken for a heavenly dinner. Use the sauce as a gravy over rice or mashed potatoes.

—**DONNA SASSER HINDS** MILWAUKIE, OREGON

YIELD: 6 SERVINGS.

- ½ cup all-purpose flour
- 1 teaspoon salt
- ½ teaspoon pepper
- 1 broiler/fryer chicken (3 to 4 pounds), cut up
- ¼ cup canola oil

SAUCE

- ⅔ cup lemon juice
- ⅔ cup ketchup
- ⅔ cup molasses
- ⅓ cup canola oil
- ¼ cup Worcestershire sauce
- 1 teaspoon ground cloves
- ½ teaspoon salt
- ¼ teaspoon pepper

Hot cooked rice

1. In a large resealable plastic bag, combine the flour, salt and pepper. Add chicken, a few pieces at a time, and shake to coat.

2. In a large skillet, heat oil. Brown chicken in oil on all sides; remove to paper towels. Drain drippings and return chicken to the pan.

3. In a bowl, combine the lemon juice, ketchup, molasses, oil, Worcestershire sauce, cloves, salt and pepper. Pour over chicken. Bring to a boil. Reduce heat; simmer, uncovered, for 35-40 minutes or until chicken juices run clear. Serve with rice.

Hungarian Chicken Paprikash

My mom volunteered to help prepare the dinners served at her church. As the volunteers cooked and served up a variety of dishes, she learned several new recipes, like chicken paprikash. It's my favorite main dish, and the gravy, made with paprika, sour cream and onions, is the best.

—**PAMELA EATON** MONCLOVA, OHIO

YIELD: 6 SERVINGS.

- 1 large onion, chopped
- ¼ cup butter, cubed
- 4 to 5 pounds broiler/fryer chicken pieces
- 2 tablespoons paprika
- 1 teaspoon salt
- ½ teaspoon pepper
- 1½ cups hot water
- 2 tablespoons cornstarch
- 2 tablespoons cold water
- 1 cup (8 ounces) sour cream

1. In a large skillet, saute onion in butter until tender. Sprinkle chicken with paprika, salt and pepper; place in an ungreased roasting pan. Spoon onion mixture over chicken. Add hot water. Cover and bake at 350° for 1½ hours or until chicken juices run clear.

2. Remove the chicken and keep warm. In a small bowl, combine the cornstarch and cold water until smooth. Gradually add to the pan juices with onion. Bring to a boil over medium heat; cook and stir for 2 minutes or until thickened. Remove from the heat. Stir in the sour cream. Serve with chicken.

Tropical Chicken Salad

Over the years my husband and I have moved to different areas, and I've collected recipes from all over the United States. This flavorful salad recipe comes from New York. I've served it for luncheons for many years, and it's one of my husband's very favorites.

—**LINDA WHEATLEY** GARLAND, TEXAS

YIELD: 4-6 SERVINGS.

- 2 cups cubed cooked chicken
- 1 cup chopped celery
- 1 cup mayonnaise
- ½ to 1 teaspoon curry powder
- 1 can (20 ounces) chunk pineapple, drained
- 2 large firm bananas, sliced
- 1 can (11 ounces) mandarin oranges, drained
- ½ cup flaked coconut
- Salad greens, optional
- ¾ cup salted peanuts or cashew halves

1. Place chicken and celery in a large bowl. Combine mayonnaise and curry powder; add to chicken mixture and mix well. Cover and chill for at least 30 minutes.

2. Before serving, add the pineapple, bananas, oranges and coconut; toss gently. Serve on salad greens if desired. Sprinkle with nuts.

Turkey with Corn Bread Dressing

Nothing gets family hanging around the kitchen like the aroma of a turkey stuffed with savory dressing roasting in the oven. Drizzled with hot gravy, it tastes even better than it smells!

—**NORMA POOLE** AUBURNDALE, FLORIDA

YIELD: 8-10 SERVINGS.

- 2 cups chopped celery
- 1 cup chopped onion
- ½ cup butter
- 6 cups cubed day-old corn bread
- 2 cups fresh bread crumbs
- 1 tablespoon dried sage
- 1 tablespoon poultry seasoning
- ½ cup egg substitute
- 1 cup chicken broth
- 1 turkey (10 to 12 pounds)
- Melted butter

1. In a skillet, saute celery and onion in butter until tender. Place in a large bowl with corn bread, crumbs, sage and poultry seasoning. Combine egg substitute and broth; add to corn bread mixture, stirring gently to mix.

2. Just before baking, stuff the body cavity and inside the neck with dressing. Skewer or fasten openings. Tie the drumsticks together. Place on a rack in a roasting pan. Brush with melted butter. Bake at 325° for 3½ to 4 hours or until a meat thermometer reads 180° for the turkey thigh and 165° for the stuffing. When turkey begins to brown, cover lightly with a tent of foil. When turkey is done, allow to stand for 20 minutes. Remove all dressing to a serving bowl.

Editor's Note: *Dressing may be prepared as above and baked in a greased 2-qt. baking dish. Cover and bake at 400° for 20 minutes. Uncover and bake 10 minutes longer or until lightly browned.*

Turkey Stir-Fry

Here's a tasty way to prepare turkey any time of year. My family loves the turkey strips, colorful vegetables and crunchy cashews.

—**JULIANNE JOHNSON** GROVE CITY, MINNESOTA

YIELD: 6 SERVINGS.

- 1½ pounds boneless turkey breast halves, cut into strips
- 1 tablespoon canola oil
- 1 small onion, chopped
- 1 carrot, julienned
- ½ medium green pepper, sliced
- 2 cups fresh mushrooms, sliced
- 1 cup chicken broth
- 3 tablespoons cornstarch
- 3 tablespoons reduced-sodium soy sauce
- ½ teaspoon ground ginger
- 2 cups pea pods, trimmed
- Cooked rice, optional
- ⅓ cup cashews, optional

1. In a large skillet or wok, stir-fry turkey in oil over medium-high heat until no longer pink, about 5-6 minutes. Remove turkey and keep warm. Stir-fry the onion, carrot, green pepper and mushrooms until crisp-tender, about 5 minutes.

2. In a small bowl, combine the chicken broth, cornstarch, soy sauce and ginger. Add to skillet; bring to a boil. Cook and stir for 2 minutes or until thickened.

3. Return turkey to skillet with pea pods; cook and stir until heated through. Serve with rice if desired. Top with cashews.

Artichoke Chicken

Rosemary, mushrooms and artichokes combine to give chicken a wonderful, savory flavor. I've served this dish for a large group by doubling the recipe. It's always a big hit with everyone.
—**RUTH STENSON** SANTA ANA, CALIFORNIA

YIELD: 8 SERVINGS.

  8 **boneless skinless chicken breast halves (4 ounces each)**
  2 **tablespoons butter**
  2 **jars (6 ounces each) marinated quartered artichoke hearts, drained**
  1 **jar (4½ ounces) whole mushrooms, drained**
  ½ **cup chopped onion**
  ⅓ **cup all-purpose flour**
1½ **teaspoons dried rosemary, crushed**
  1 **teaspoon salt**
  ¼ **teaspoon pepper**
  2 **cups chicken broth or 1 cup broth and 1 cup dry white wine**
Hot cooked noodles
Minced fresh parsley

1. In a large skillet, brown chicken in butter. Remove chicken to an ungreased 13-in. x 9-in. baking dish. Arrange artichokes and mushrooms on top of chicken; set aside.

2. Saute onion in pan juices until crisp-tender. Combine the flour, rosemary, salt and pepper. Stir into pan until blended. Add chicken broth. Bring to a boil; cook and stir for 2 minutes or until thickened and bubbly. Remove from the heat and spoon over chicken.

3. Cover and bake at 350° for 50 to 60 minutes or until a meat thermometer reads 170°. Arrange noodles on a serving platter; top with chicken and sauce. Sprinkle with parsley.

Chicken Cheese Lasagna

I like to make a double batch of this lasagna and freeze one for another day. The filling can also be stuffed in manicotti shells.
—**MARY ANN KOSMAS** MINNEAPOLIS, MINNESOTA

YIELD: 12 SERVINGS.

1 **medium onion, chopped**
½ **cup butter, cubed**
1 **garlic clove, minced**
½ **cup all-purpose flour**
1 **teaspoon salt**
2 **cups chicken broth**
1½ **cups 2% milk**
4 **cups (16 ounces) shredded part-skim mozzarella cheese, divided**
1 **cup grated Parmesan cheese, divided**
1 **teaspoon dried basil**
1 **teaspoon dried oregano**
½ **teaspoon white pepper**
2 **cups (15 to 16 ounces) ricotta cheese**
1 **tablespoon minced fresh parsley**
9 **lasagna noodles, cooked and drained**
2 **packages (10 ounces each) frozen spinach, thawed and well drained**
2 **cups cubed cooked chicken**

1. In a large saucepan, saute onion in butter until tender. Add garlic; cook 1 minute longer. Stir in flour and salt until blended; cook until bubbly. Gradually stir in broth and milk. Bring to a boil; cook and stir for 1 minute or until thickened. Stir in 2 cups mozzarella, ½ cup Parmesan cheese, basil, oregano and pepper; set aside.

2. In a large bowl, combine the ricotta cheese, parsley and remaining mozzarella; set aside. Spread one-quarter of the cheese sauce into a greased 13-in. x 9-in. baking dish; cover with one-third of the noodles. Layer with half of the ricotta mixture, half of the spinach and half of the chicken.

3. Cover with one-quarter of the cheese sauce and one-third of the noodles. Repeat layers of ricotta mixture, spinach, chicken and one-quarter cheese sauce. Cover with remaining noodles and cheese sauce.

4. Sprinkle with remaining Parmesan cheese. Bake at 350°, uncovered, for 35-40 minutes. Let stand 15 minutes.

Editor's Note: *For a change, substitute cooked bulk Italian sausage for the chicken. Using 1% milk and reduced-fat cheeses will help keep the calories down. You can also use no-cook lasagna noodles without making any adjustments to the liquid or cooking time.*

Honey-Glazed Chicken

My family raves over this nicely browned chicken. The rich honey glaze gives each luscious piece a spicy tang. This dish is simple enough to prepare for a family dinner and delightful enough to serve to guests.

—**RUTH ANDREWSON** LEAVENWORTH, WASHINGTON

YIELD: 4-6 SERVINGS.

- ½ cup all-purpose flour
- 1 teaspoon salt
- ½ teaspoon cayenne pepper
- 1 broiler/fryer chicken (about 3 pounds), cut up
- ½ cup butter, melted, divided
- ¼ cup packed brown sugar
- ¼ cup honey
- ¼ cup lemon juice
- 1 tablespoon reduced-sodium soy sauce
- 1½ teaspoons curry powder

1. In a large resealable plastic bag, combine the flour, salt and cayenne pepper; add the chicken pieces, a few at a time, and shake to coat. Pour 4 tablespoons butter into a 13-in. x 9-in. baking pan; place chicken in pan, turning pieces once to coat.

2. Bake, uncovered at 350° for 30 minutes. Combine brown sugar, honey, lemon juice, soy sauce, curry powder and remaining butter; pour over the chicken. Bake 45 minutes longer or until the chicken is tender, basting several times with pan drippings.

Chicken Rice Dinner

Everyone enjoys the country-style combination of chicken, rice and mushrooms. Using chicken bouillon adds to this entree's wonderful flavor.

—**JUDITH ANGLEN** RIVERTON, WYOMING

YIELD: 5 SERVINGS.

- ½ cup all-purpose flour
- 1 teaspoon salt
- ½ teaspoon pepper

- 10 bone-in chicken thighs (about 3¾ pounds)
- 3 tablespoons canola oil
- 1 cup uncooked long grain rice
- ¼ cup chopped onion
- 2 garlic cloves, minced
- 1 can (4 ounces) mushroom stems and pieces, undrained
- 2 teaspoons chicken bouillon granules
- 2 cups boiling water

Minced fresh parsley, optional

1. In a large resealable plastic bag, combine the flour, salt and pepper. Add chicken thighs, one at a time, and shake to coat. In a large skillet over medium heat, brown chicken in oil.

2. Place rice in an ungreased 13-in. x 9-in. baking dish. Sprinkle with onion and garlic; top with mushrooms. Dissolve bouillon in boiling water; pour over all. Place chicken on top.

3. Cover and bake at 350° for 1 hour or until a thermometer reads 180° and rice is tender. Sprinkle with parsley if desired.

Roasted Duck with Apple-Raisin Dressing

As a boy growing up on the farm, my husband had duck every Sunday. I tried to maintain that tradition after we married more than 50 years ago!

—**FRAN KIRCHHOFF** HARVARD, ILLINOIS

YIELD: 4 SERVINGS.

- 2 domestic ducks (4 to 5 pounds each)

Salt

DRESSING

- 1 tube (12 ounces) bulk pork sausage
- ½ cup chopped onion
- ½ cup chopped celery
- 1 cup chopped peeled apple
- 1 cup golden raisins
- ½ cup water
- 1½ teaspoons salt
- 1 teaspoon rubbed sage
- ¼ teaspoon pepper
- 2 tablespoons chopped fresh parsley
- 8 cups cubed crustless day-old white bread
- 3 eggs, lightly beaten
- ½ cup chicken broth

1. Sprinkle the inside of ducklings with salt; prick skin well all over and set aside.

2. In a large skillet, cook sausage with onion and celery until sausage is no longer pink and vegetables are tender. Add apple and simmer for 3 minutes, stirring occasionally; drain.

3. Meanwhile, simmer raisins in water for 8 minutes; do not drain. In a large bowl, combine sausage mixture, raisins, salt, sage, pepper and parsley; mix well. Add the bread cubes, eggs and broth; mix lightly. Divide and spoon into ducklings.

4. Place duck breast side up on a rack in a large shallow roasting pan. Bake, uncovered, at 375° for 1¾ to 1¼ hours or until the thermometer reads 185°. Drain fat from pan as it accumulates. Remove all dressing.

Fried Chicken with Pan Gravy

If you want your fried chicken cooked up golden brown and crispy, then this is the recipe you should be using. My mom's dish makes a satisfying meal.

—**GINNY WERKMEISTER** TILDEN, NEBRASKA

YIELD: 6 SERVINGS (1½ CUPS GRAVY).

- 1 cup all-purpose flour
- ¾ teaspoon salt
- ¼ teaspoon dried thyme
- ¼ teaspoon rubbed sage
- ¼ teaspoon pepper
- 1 broiler/fryer chicken (3½ to 4 pounds), cut up

Oil for frying

GRAVY

- 2 tablespoons all-purpose flour
- ⅛ teaspoon salt
- 1⅓ cups 2% milk

1. In a large resealable plastic bag, combine the first five ingredients. Add chicken, a few pieces at a time, and shake to coat.

2. In a large skillet over medium-high heat, heat ¼ in. of oil; fry chicken until browned on all sides. Reduce heat; cover and cook for 30-35 minutes or until juices run clear, turning occasionally. Uncover and cook 5 minutes longer. Remove chicken to paper towels and keep warm.

3. Pour off excess fat from the skillet, reserving the browned bits and 2 tablespoons drippings. Stir in flour and salt until blended; gradually add the milk. Bring to a boil; cook and stir for 1-2 minutes or until thickened. Serve with chicken.

Herbed Fried Chicken with Gravy: Omit sage. Add 1 teaspoon each dried tarragon, oregano, paprika and ground mustard, and ½ teaspoon each onion powder and garlic powder to the flour mixture. Proceed as directed.

Crescent Turkey Casserole

How did Mom make a dinner of chicken and vegetables really appealing to kids? She turned it into a pie, of course! Mom knew that everyone loves pie. This classic version is easy to do.

—**DANIELA ESSMAN** PERHAM, MINNESOTA

YIELD: 4 SERVINGS.

- ½ cup mayonnaise
- 2 tablespoons all-purpose flour
- 1 teaspoon chicken bouillon granules
- ⅛ teaspoon pepper
- ¾ cup 2% milk
- 1½ cups cubed cooked turkey breast
- 1 package (10 ounces) frozen mixed vegetables
- 1 tube (4 ounces) refrigerated crescent rolls

1. In a large saucepan, combine the mayonnaise, flour, bouillon and pepper. Gradually add milk; stir until smooth. Bring to a boil over medium heat; cook and stir for 2 minutes or until thickened. Add turkey and vegetables; cook 3-4 minutes longer, stirring occasionally. Spoon into a greased 8-in. square baking dish.

2. Unroll crescent dough and separate into two rectangles. Seal seams and perforations. Place over turkey mixture. Bake at 375° for 15-20 minutes or until golden brown.

Rolled-Up Turkey

Whenever I think of Mom's appealing rolled turkey filled with moist corn bread stuffing, I can almost smell the aroma of it baking in the oven. It's delicious!

—JUNE BLOMQUIST EUGENE, OREGON

YIELD: 8 SERVINGS.

1 turkey (12 pounds), deboned and
   giblets removed
1 cup chopped celery
1 medium onion, chopped
½ cup butter, cubed
5 cups cubed white bread
1½ cups coarsely crumbled corn bread
1 teaspoon salt, divided
½ teaspoon rubbed sage
¾ to 1 cup chicken broth
3 tablespoons canola oil
¼ teaspoon pepper

1. Unroll turkey on a large cutting board. With a sharp knife, remove the wings (save for another use). Flatten turkey to ¾-in. thickness. Cut between the turkey breast and thighs to separate into three sections.

2. In a large skillet, saute celery and onion in butter until tender. In a large bowl, combine bread and corn bread; add celery mixture, ½ teaspoon salt and sage. Stir in enough broth to moisten.

3. Spoon 2 cups stuffing over turkey breast to within 1 in. of edges. Roll up jelly-roll style, starting with a long side. Tie with kitchen string at 1½-in. intervals. Place on a rack in a large shallow roasting pan.

4. Spoon 1 cup stuffing over each thigh section to within 1 in. of edges. Roll up jelly-roll style, starting with a short side. Tie with kitchen string; place on a rack in another shallow roasting pan.

Brush turkey with oil; sprinkle with pepper and remaining salt. Bake turkey breast at 325° for 2 to 2½ hours or until a meat thermometer reads 170°; bake thighs for 1½ to 1¾ hours or until a meat thermometer reads 180° for turkey and 165° for stuffing. Let turkey stand for 15 minutes before slicing.

Editor's Note: *Ask the butcher to debone the turkey for you.*

Prosciutto Chicken Cacciatore

I like to free up my time but still serve a welcoming meal for dinner, so I took one my mother's recipes and adapted it for the slow cooker. The hearty result is perfect for busy weekday nights.

—SANDRA PUTNAM
CORVALLIS, MONTANA

YIELD: 6-8 SERVINGS.

- 2 pounds boneless skinless chicken thighs
- 1½ pounds boneless skinless chicken breast halves
- ½ cup all-purpose flour
- 1 teaspoon salt
- ¼ teaspoon pepper
- 3 tablespoons olive oil
- 1 can (14½ ounces) chicken broth
- 1 can (14½ ounces) diced tomatoes, undrained
- 1 cup sliced fresh mushrooms
- 1 medium onion, chopped
- 1 package (3 ounces) thinly sliced prosciutto or deli ham, coarsely chopped
- 1 tablespoon diced pimientos
- 2 garlic cloves, minced
- ½ teaspoon Italian seasoning
- Hot cooked linguine
- Grated Parmesan cheese

1. Cut chicken into serving-size pieces. In a large resealable plastic bag, combine the flour, salt and pepper. Add chicken, a few pieces at a time, and shake to coat.

2. In a large skillet, brown chicken in oil in batches. Transfer to a 5-qt. slow cooker.

3. Stir in the broth, tomatoes, mushrooms, onion, prosciutto, pimientos, garlic and Italian seasoning. Cover and cook on low for 4 to 4½ hours or until chicken juices run clear. Serve with a slotted spoon over linguine; sprinkle with cheese.

Mom's Chicken 'n' Buttermilk Dumplings

I serve this with a tossed or cucumber salad to friends dining with us, or when our two sons and their families visit.

—ELLEN PROEFROCK BRODHEAD, WISCONSIN

YIELD: 6-8 SERVINGS.

- 1 stewing chicken (about 5 pounds), cut up
- 10 cups water
- 1 large onion, chopped
- 2 medium carrots, sliced
- 3 celery ribs, chopped
- 4 garlic cloves, minced
- 1 teaspoon salt
- ¼ cup butter
- 6 tablespoons all-purpose flour
- ⅛ teaspoon paprika
- ⅛ teaspoon pepper
- ½ cup half-and-half cream

DUMPLINGS
- 2 cups all-purpose flour
- 4 teaspoons baking powder
- 4 teaspoons sugar
- 1 teaspoon salt
- 2 eggs
- ½ cup buttermilk
- ¼ cup butter, melted

1. In a stockpot or Dutch oven, combine the first seven ingredients. Bring to a boil; skim foam from broth. Reduce heat; cover and simmer for 1½ hours or until chicken is tender. Remove chicken; when cool enough to handle, debone and dice. Strain broth, reserving broth and vegetables.

2. In the same pot, melt butter. Stir in the flour, paprika and pepper until smooth. Gradually stir in 6 cups reserved broth (save remaining broth for another use). Bring to a boil; cook and stir for 2 minutes or until thickened. Reduce heat; stir in the cream, reserved vegetables and chicken. Cover and bring to a boil; reduce the heat to simmer.

3. For dumplings, combine flour, baking powder, sugar and salt in a bowl. Combine eggs, buttermilk and butter; stir into dry ingredients to form a stiff batter.

4. Drop by tablespoonfuls onto simmering mixture. Cover and simmer for 20 minutes or until a toothpick inserted in a dumpling comes out clean (do not lift cover while simmering). Serve immediately.

Making egg noodles with my grandmother is one of my most mouthwatering memories.

I dumped each ingredient into a bowl; then her experienced hands worked them into bright yellow dough. We'd roll the dough, cut it into circles, and then she'd drop them into bubbling chicken broth.

— DONNA LAUERMANN CHILLICOTHE, OHIO

Turkey with Herbed Rice Dressing

My husband is a devoted fan of my cooking, and my three daughters have all become wonderful cooks in their own right! This is one of our favorite recipes.

—MELANIE HABENER LOMPOC, CALIFORNIA

YIELD: 8-10 SERVINGS.

- ½ pound bulk pork sausage
- ½ pound ground beef
- ½ cup chopped onion
- ½ cup egg substitute
- 1 tablespoon poultry seasoning
- 2 tablespoons chopped fresh parsley
- 2 tablespoons chopped celery leaves
- 2 teaspoons salt, divided
- 2 teaspoons pepper, divided
- ¾ teaspoon garlic powder, divided
- 4 cups cooked white rice, cooled
- 1 turkey (10 to 12 pounds)
- 3 garlic cloves, minced
- 1 teaspoon each dried thyme, tarragon and marjoram
- 2 cans (14½ ounces each) chicken broth
- 3 tablespoons butter

1. In a large skillet, cook the pork, beef and onion over medium heat until meat is no longer pink; drain. In a large bowl, combine egg substitute, poultry seasoning, parsley, celery leaves, 1 teaspoon salt, 1 teaspoon pepper and ½ teaspoon garlic powder. Add meat mixture and rice.

2. Just before baking, stuff turkey. Skewer openings; tie drumsticks together. Place breast side up on a rack in roasting pan. Combine the garlic, thyme, tarragon, marjoram and remaining salt, pepper and garlic powder; rub over turkey. Add broth and butter to pan.

3. Bake at 325° for 4 to 4½ hours or until a meat thermometer reads 180° for the turkey thigh and 165° for the stuffing, basting frequently. When turkey begins to brown, cover lightly with a tent of foil. Remove all dressing.

Editor's Note: *Dressing may be baked in a greased 2½-qt. covered baking dish at 325° for 70 minutes (uncover during the last 10 minutes). Dressing yields about 8 cups.*

Teriyaki Chicken

These drumsticks get their great flavor and golden color from the tasty, easy-to-prepare marinade. During hurried workweeks, it's convenient to marinate the chicken overnight and then bake it the next day.

—JEAN CLARK ALBION, MAINE

YIELD: 6 SERVINGS.

- ¾ cup soy sauce
- ¼ cup canola oil
- 3 tablespoons brown sugar
- 2 tablespoons sherry, optional
- ½ teaspoon ground ginger
- ½ teaspoon garlic powder
- 12 chicken drumsticks (4 ounces each)

1. In a large resealable plastic bag, combine the soy sauce, oil, brown sugar, sherry if desired, ginger and garlic powder; add drumsticks. Seal bag and turn to coat; cover and refrigerate 1 hour or overnight, turning occasionally.

2. Drain and discard marinade. Place chicken in a single layer on a foil-lined baking sheet. Bake, uncovered, at 375° for 35-45 minutes or until a meat thermometer reads 180° and juices run clear.

Three-Cheese Chicken Bake

This is a hearty, comforting casserole that's always a crowd-pleaser. The combination of flavors and interesting colors ensures I come home with an empty dish!

—**VICKI RAATZ** WATERLOO, WISCONSIN

YIELD: 12-15 SERVINGS.

- ½ cup chopped onion
- ½ cup chopped green pepper
- 3 tablespoons butter
- 1 can (10¾ ounces) condensed cream of chicken soup, undiluted
- 1 jar (8 ounces) sliced mushrooms, drained
- 1 jar (2 ounces) diced pimientos, drained
- ½ teaspoon dried basil
- 1 package (8 ounces) noodles, cooked and drained
- 3 cups diced cooked chicken
- 2 cups ricotta cheese
- 2 cups (8 ounces) shredded cheddar cheese
- ½ cup grated Parmesan cheese
- ¼ cup buttered bread crumbs

1. In a large skillet, saute the onion and green pepper in butter until tender. Remove from the heat. Stir in the soup, mushrooms, pimientos and basil; set aside.

2. In a large bowl, combine the noodles, chicken and cheeses; add mushroom sauce and mix well. Transfer to a greased 13-in. x 9-in. baking dish.

3. Bake, uncovered, at 350° for 40-45 minutes or until bubbly. Sprinkle with crumbs. Bake 15 minutes longer or until browned.

Smoked Turkey and Apple Salad

An eye-catching dish, this refreshing salad is a great main course for a summer lunch or light dinner. The dressing's Dijon flavor goes nicely with the turkey, and the apples add crunch.

—**CAROLYN NACE** WINTER HAVEN, FLORIDA

YIELD: 8 SERVINGS.

DRESSING
- 5 tablespoons olive oil
- 2 tablespoons cider vinegar
- 1 tablespoon Dijon mustard
- 1 teaspoon lemon-pepper seasoning
- ½ teaspoon salt, optional

SALAD
- 1 bunch watercress or romaine, torn into bite-size pieces
- 1 medium carrot, julienned
- 10 cherry tomatoes, halved
- 8 ounces smoked turkey, julienned
- 4 unpeeled apples, sliced
- ⅓ cup chopped walnuts, toasted

1. Whisk together dressing ingredients; set aside.

2. Just before serving, arrange salad greens on a platter or individual plates. Top with carrot, tomatoes, turkey and apples. Drizzle dressing over salad; toss to coat. Sprinkle with walnuts.

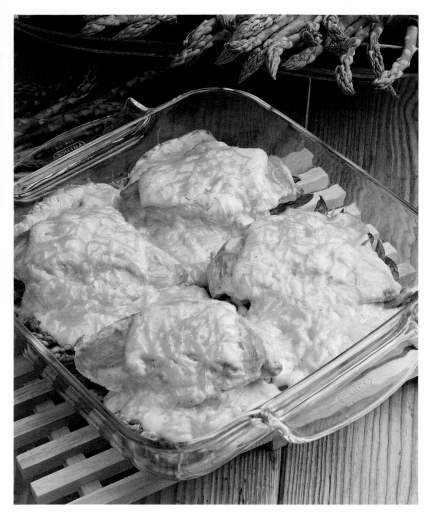

Saucy Chicken and Asparagus

You won't believe how delicious yet how easy this dish is. We tasted it for the first time when our son's godparents made it for us. Even my grandmother—who's 95 years old—likes to serve this creamy dish for luncheons with friends!
—VICKI SCHLECHTER DAVIS, CALIFORNIA

YIELD: 4 SERVINGS.

- 1½ pounds fresh asparagus spears, halved
- 4 boneless skinless chicken breast halves
- 2 tablespoons canola oil
- ½ teaspoon salt
- ¼ teaspoon pepper
- 1 can (10¾ ounces) condensed cream of chicken soup, undiluted
- ½ cup mayonnaise
- 1 teaspoon lemon juice
- ½ teaspoon curry powder
- 1 cup (4 ounces) shredded cheddar cheese

1. If desired, partially cook asparagus; drain. Place the asparagus in a greased 9-in. square baking dish. In a skillet over medium heat, brown the chicken in oil on both sides. Season with salt and pepper. Arrange chicken over asparagus.

2. In a bowl, mix soup, mayonnaise, lemon juice and curry powder; pour over chicken. Cover and bake at 375° for 40 minutes or until the chicken is tender and juices run clear. Sprinkle with cheese. Let stand 5 minutes before serving.

Marinated Turkey

When I first fixed this, we were living on a ranch along a river with lots of game. Wild turkey can be dry, but not prepared this way! Of course, it's just as tasty with store-bought turkey. And the gravy it makes is out of this world.
—WILMA LOVEJOY HASTINGS, NEBRASKA

YIELD: 8-10 SERVINGS.

- 1 cup soy sauce
- 1 cup canola oil
- ¼ cup honey
- 4 teaspoons Worcestershire sauce
- 2 teaspoons ground ginger
- 2 teaspoons ground mustard
- 2 teaspoons lemon juice
- 4 garlic cloves, minced
- 6 to 7 pounds fresh turkey parts
- ¼ cup all-purpose flour, optional
- Salt and pepper, optional

1. In a small bowl, combine the first eight ingredients. Place the turkey in a large heavy-duty plastic bag; add half of the marinade. Close the bag; refrigerate overnight, turning bag occasionally. Cover and refrigerate remaining marinade.

2. Drain and discard marinade from turkey; arrange turkey in a single layer in large shallow roasting pan. Pour reserved marinade over turkey. Bake, uncovered, at 325° for 1½ to 2 hours or until tender, basting occasionally if desired. Remove turkey to serving platter and keep warm.

3. If desired, make gravy: Strain pan juices into a large measuring cup. Skim fat and pour ¼ cup in a medium saucepan; discard remaining fat. Blend flour into saucepan. Add water to pan juices to make 2 cups. Add to saucepan; bring to a boil over medium heat. Cook and stir for 1-2 minutes or until thickened. Season with salt and pepper. Serve with turkey.

Wild Goose with Giblet Stuffing

This recipe is one of our favorite ways to prepare goose, and it's especially nice for the holidays. My husband does a lot of hunting, so I'm always looking for new ways to fix game.

—LOUISE LAGINESS
EAST JORDAN, MICHIGAN

YIELD: 6-8 SERVINGS.

  1 **wild goose (6 to 8 pounds)**
Lemon wedges
Salt
STUFFING
Goose giblets
  2 **cups water**
10 **cups crumbled corn bread**
  2 **large Granny Smith apples, chopped**
  1 **large onion, chopped**
⅓ **cup minced fresh parsley**
  1 **to 2 tablespoons rubbed sage**
  1 **teaspoon salt**
¼ **teaspoon pepper**
¼ **teaspoon garlic powder**
Butter, softened

1. Rub inside goose cavity with lemon and salt; set aside. In a saucepan, cook giblets in water until tender, about 20-30 minutes.

2. Remove giblets with a slotted spoon and reserve liquid. Chop giblets and place in a large bowl with the corn bread, apples, onion, parsley, sage, salt, pepper and garlic powder. Add enough of the reserved cooking liquid to make a moist stuffing; toss gently. Stuff the body and neck cavity; truss openings. Place goose, breast side up, on a rack in a shallow roasting pan. Spread with softened butter.

3. Bake, uncovered, at 325° for 25 minutes per pound or until fully cooked and tender. If goose is an older bird, add 1 cup of water to pan and cover for the last hour of baking.

Oven Barbecued Chicken

Chicken and Sunday dinner go together in my mind. During my 20 years of married life on a dairy farm, I'd often brown the chicken and mix up the sauce while my husband milked, then pop it in the oven when we left for church.

—ESTHER SHANK HARRISONBURG, VIRGINIA

YIELD: 6-8 SERVINGS.

  1 **broiler/fryer chicken, cut up (3 to 4 pounds)**
  2 **tablespoons canola oil**
⅓ **cup chopped onion**
  3 **tablespoons butter**
¾ **cup ketchup**
½ **cup hot water**
⅓ **cup cider vinegar**
  3 **tablespoons brown sugar**
  1 **tablespoon Worcestershire sauce**
  2 **teaspoons prepared mustard**
¼ **teaspoon salt**
⅛ **teaspoon pepper**

1. In a large skillet, brown chicken in oil in batches. Drain chicken on paper towels.

2. Meanwhile, in a small saucepan, saute onion in butter until tender; stir in the remaining ingredients. Simmer, uncovered, for 15 minutes.

3. Place chicken in an ungreased 13-in. x 9-in. baking dish. Pour barbecue sauce over chicken. Bake, uncovered, at 350° for 45-60 minutes or until chicken juices run clear, basting occasionally.

Roasted Chicken with Rosemary

Herbs, garlic and butter give this hearty meal-in-one a classic flavor. It's a lot like pot roast, only it uses chicken instead of beef.
—**ISABEL ZIENKOSKY** SALT LAKE CITY, UTAH

YIELD: 9 SERVINGS.

½ cup butter, cubed
4 tablespoons minced fresh rosemary or 2 tablespoons dried rosemary, crushed
2 tablespoons minced fresh parsley
3 garlic cloves, minced
1 teaspoon salt
½ teaspoon pepper
1 whole roasting chicken (5 to 6 pounds)
6 small red potatoes, halved
6 medium carrots, halved lengthwise and cut into 2-inch pieces
2 medium onions, quartered

1. In a small saucepan, melt butter; stir in the seasonings. Place chicken breast side up on a rack in a shallow roasting pan; tie drumsticks together with kitchen string. Spoon half of the butter mixture over chicken. Place the potatoes, carrots and onions around chicken. Drizzle remaining butter mixture over vegetables.

2. Cover and bake at 350° for 1½ hours, basting every 30 minutes. Uncover; bake 30-60 minutes longer or until a thermometer reads 180° in chicken thigh, basting occasionally.

3. Cover chicken with foil and let stand for 10-15 minutes before carving. Serve with the vegetables.

Chicken and Dumpling Casserole

Basil adds just the right touch of flavor and makes the whole house smell so good while this dish cooks. My husband loves the fluffy dumplings with plenty of gravy poured over them.
—**SUE MACKEY** JACKSON, WISCONSIN

YIELD: 6-8 SERVINGS.

- ½ cup chopped onion
- ½ cup chopped celery
- ¼ cup butter, cubed
- 2 garlic cloves, minced
- ½ cup all-purpose flour
- 2 teaspoons sugar
- 1 teaspoon salt
- 1 teaspoon dried basil
- ½ teaspoon pepper
- 4 cups chicken broth
- 1 package (10 ounces) frozen green peas
- 4 cups cubed cooked chicken

DUMPLINGS
- 2 cups biscuit/baking mix
- 2 teaspoons dried basil
- ⅔ cup 2% milk

1. In a large saucepan, saute onion and celery in butter until tender. Add garlic; cook 1 minute longer. Stir in the flour, sugar, salt, basil and pepper until blended. Gradually add broth; bring to a boil. Cook and stir for 1 minute or until thickened; reduce heat. Add peas and cook for 5 minutes, stirring constantly. Stir in chicken. Pour into a greased 13-in. x 9-in. baking dish.

2. For dumplings, in a small bowl, combine baking mix and basil. Stir in the milk with a fork until moistened. Drop by tablespoonfuls into 12 mounds over chicken mixture.

3. Bake, uncovered, at 350° for 30 minutes. Cover and bake 10 minutes longer or until a toothpick inserted in a dumpling comes out clean.

Parmesan Chicken

The savory coating on this chicken has the satisfying flavor of Parmesan cheese. It's easy enough to be a family weekday meal yet impressive enough to serve to guests. When I make this chicken for dinner, we never have leftovers.
—**SCHELBY THOMPSON** CAMDEN WYOMING, DELAWARE

YIELD: 6-8 SERVINGS.

- ½ cup butter, melted
- 2 teaspoons Dijon mustard
- 1 teaspoon Worcestershire sauce
- ½ teaspoon salt
- 1 cup dry bread crumbs
- ½ cup grated Parmesan cheese
- 6 to 8 boneless skinless chicken breast halves

1. In a pie plate or shallow bowl, combine butter, mustard, Worcestershire sauce and salt. In a plastic bag, combine crumbs and cheese. Dip chicken in butter mixture, then shake in crumb mixture, a few pieces at a time.

2. Place in an ungreased 13-in. x 9-in. baking pan. Drizzle with any remaining butter mixture. Bake at 350° for 40-45 minutes or until a meat thermometer reads 170°.

Cheddary Chicken Potpie

This is a comforting chicken dish that features a medley of flavorful cheeses. Some days I make it in the morning so I can just pop it in the oven for dinner or have my husband start baking it if I'm not home.

—VICKI RAATZ WATERLOO, WISCONSIN

YIELD: 6 SERVINGS.

- 1 can (10¾ ounces) condensed cream of chicken soup, undiluted
- 1 cup milk, divided
- ½ cup chopped onion
- 1 package (3 ounces) cream cheese, softened
- ¼ cup chopped celery
- ¼ cup shredded carrots
- ¼ cup grated Parmesan cheese
- ½ teaspoon salt
- 3 cups cubed cooked chicken
- 3 cups frozen chopped broccoli, cooked and drained
- 1 egg
- 1 tablespoon canola oil
- 1 cup buttermilk complete pancake mix
- 1 cup (4 ounces) shredded sharp cheddar cheese
- ¼ cup sliced almonds, optional

1. In a large saucepan, combine soup, ½ cup of milk, onion, cream cheese, celery, carrots, Parmesan cheese and salt. cook and stir until the mixture is hot and cream cheese is melted. Stir in the chicken and broccoli; heat through. Pour into an ungreased 2-qt. baking dish.

2. In a bowl, combine the egg, oil and remaining milk. Add the pancake mix and cheddar cheese; blend well. Spoon over hot chicken mixture. Sprinkle with almonds if desired. Bake, uncovered, at 375° for 20-25 minutes or until golden brown.

Turkey with Sausage Stuffing

Here's a super way to savor roast turkey and stuffing without having to cook the big holiday bird. The stuffing is hearty, and the meat is juicy and tender.

—AURA LEE JOHNSON VERMILION, OHIO

YIELD: 15-20 SERVINGS.

- 1 whole bone-in turkey breast (5 to 7 pounds)
- ¼ cup butter, melted
- 2 packages (12 ounces each) bulk pork sausage
- 2 cups sliced celery
- 2 medium onions, chopped
- 4 cups dry bread cubes
- 2 cups pecan halves
- 1 cup raisins
- ⅔ cup chicken broth
- ½ cup egg substitute
- 1 teaspoon salt
- ½ teaspoon rubbed sage
- ¼ teaspoon pepper

1. Place turkey breast side up in a shallow roasting pan. Brush with butter. Bake, uncovered, at 325° for 2 to 2½ hours or until a meat thermometer reads 170° (cover loosely with foil if needed to prevent overbrowning).

2. Meanwhile, in a skillet, cook the sausage, celery and onions over medium heat until meat is no longer pink and vegetables are tender; drain. Transfer to a bowl; stir in the bread cubes, pecans, raisins, broth, eggs, salt, sage and pepper.

3. Spoon into a greased 3-qt. baking dish. Cover and bake at 325° for 1 hour. Serve with sliced turkey.

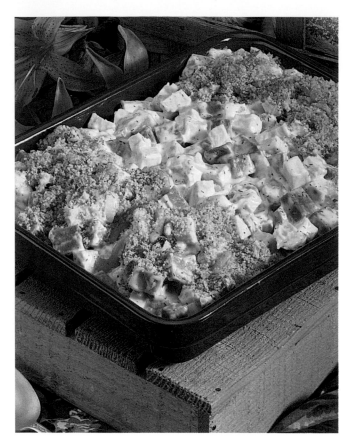

Cordon Bleu Casserole

When I'm invited to a potluck, people often ask me to bring this tempting casserole. The turkey, ham and cheese are delectable combined with the crunchy topping. When I bake a turkey, I prepare the leftovers for this dish, knowing I'll be making it again soon.

—**JOYCE PAUL** MOOSE JAW, SASKATCHEWAN

YIELD: 10 SERVINGS.

- 4 cups cubed cooked turkey
- 3 cups cubed fully cooked ham
- 1 cup (4 ounces) shredded cheddar cheese
- 1 cup chopped onion
- ¼ cup butter, cubed
- ⅓ cup all-purpose flour
- 2 cups half-and-half cream
- 1 teaspoon dill weed
- ⅛ teaspoon ground mustard
- ⅛ teaspoon ground nutmeg

TOPPING

- 1 cup dry bread crumbs
- 2 tablespoons butter, melted
- ¼ teaspoon dill weed
- ¼ cup shredded cheddar cheese
- ¼ cup chopped walnuts

1. In a large bowl, combine the turkey, ham and cheese; set aside. In a large saucepan, saute onion in butter until tender. Add flour; stir until blended. Gradually add cream, stirring constantly. Bring to a boil; cook and stir for 1-2 minutes or until thickened. Stir in the dill, mustard and nutmeg. Remove from the heat and pour over meat mixture.

2. Spoon into a greased 13-in. x 9-in. baking dish. In a small bowl, combine the bread crumbs, butter and dill. Stir in cheese and walnuts. Sprinkle over casserole.

3. Bake, uncovered, at 350° for 30 minutes or until heated through.

Turkey Tetrazzini

This recipe comes from a cookbook our church compiled. It's convenient because it can be made ahead and frozen. After the holidays, we use leftover turkey to prepare a meal for university students. They clean their plates!

—**GLADYS WALDROP** CALVERT CITY, KENTUCKY

YIELD: 6-8 SERVINGS.

- 1 package (7 ounces) spaghetti, broken into 2-inch pieces
- 2 cups cubed cooked turkey
- 1 cup (4 ounces) shredded cheddar cheese
- 1 can (10¾ ounces) condensed cream of mushroom soup, undiluted
- 1 medium onion, chopped
- 2 cans (4 ounces each) sliced mushrooms, drained
- ⅓ cup 2% milk
- ¼ cup chopped green pepper
- 1 jar (2 ounces) chopped pimientos, drained
- ¼ teaspoon salt
- ⅛ teaspoon pepper

Additional shredded cheddar cheese, optional

1. Cook spaghetti according to package directions; drain. Transfer to a large bowl; add the next 10 ingredients.

2. Spoon into a greased 2½-qt. casserole; sprinkle with cheese if desired. Bake, uncovered, at 375° for 40-45 minutes or until heated through.

Chicken 'n' Hash Brown Bake

The first time I served this dish for company was to a family with five children. The kids and the adults loved it! This is one recipe I often make for potlucks—it goes a long way, and all ages enjoy it.

—RUTH ANDREWSON LEAVENWORTH, WASHINGTON

YIELD: 8-10 SERVINGS.

- 1 package (32 ounces) frozen cubed hash brown potatoes, thawed
- 1 teaspoon salt
- ¼ teaspoon pepper
- 4 cups diced cooked chicken
- 1 can (4 ounces) mushroom stems and pieces, drained
- 1 cup (8 ounces) sour cream
- 2 cups chicken broth or stock
- 1 can (10¾ ounces) condensed cream of chicken soup, undiluted
- 2 teaspoons chicken bouillon granules
- 2 tablespoons finely chopped onion
- 2 tablespoons finely chopped sweet red pepper
- 1 garlic clove, minced

Paprika

- ¼ cup sliced almonds

1. Spread potatoes in an ungreased 13-in. x 9-in. baking dish. Sprinkle with salt and pepper. Sprinkle chicken and mushrooms over the top. Combine the sour cream, broth, soup, bouillon, onion, red pepper and garlic; pour over mushrooms.

2. Sprinkle with paprika and almonds. Bake, uncovered, at 350° for 50-60 minutes or until heated through.

Chicken Provençal

When I serve this entree at a dinner party, people always comment on the tender chicken and flavorfully seasoned beans. I sometimes fix it a day ahead— it's as good as it is the first day it's made.

—BARBARA ZEILINGER
COLUMBUS, INDIANA

YIELD: 4 SERVINGS.

- 1 broiler/fryer chicken (3 to 4 pounds), cut up
- 1 tablespoon canola oil
- 1½ cup chopped onion
- 3 garlic cloves, minced
- 2 cans (15½ ounces each) great northern beans, rinsed and drained
- 1 can (29 ounces) diced tomatoes, undrained
- 3 medium carrots, sliced ¼ inch thick
- 1 tablespoon chicken bouillon granules
- 1 teaspoon dried thyme
- ½ teaspoon dried oregano
- ½ teaspoon pepper

1. In a large skillet, brown chicken in oil; remove and set aside.

2. Saute onion and garlic in drippings until tender. Stir in remaining ingredients.

3. Spoon into a 3-qt. baking dish; arrange chicken pieces on top. Cover and bake at 350° for 65-75 minutes or until chicken juices run clear.

Savory Lemonade Chicken

I don't know where it originally came from, but my mother used to prepare this chicken for our family when I was little. Now I love to make it! A sweet and tangy sauce nicely glazes the chicken.

—**JENNY COOK** EAU CLAIRE, WISCONSIN

YIELD: 6 SERVINGS.

- 6 **boneless skinless chicken breast halves (4 ounces each)**
- ¾ **cup thawed lemonade concentrate**
- 3 **tablespoons ketchup**
- 2 **tablespoons brown sugar**
- 1 **tablespoon cider vinegar**
- 2 **tablespoons cornstarch**
- 2 **tablespoons cold water**

1. Place chicken in a 5-qt. slow cooker. In a small bowl, combine the lemonade concentrate, ketchup, brown sugar and vinegar; pour over chicken. Cover and cook on low for 2½ hours or until chicken is tender.

2. Remove chicken and keep warm. For gravy, combine the cornstarch and water until smooth; gradually stir into the cooking juices. Cover and cook on high for 30 minutes or until thickened. Return chicken to the slow cooker; heat through.

Turkey Mushroom Casserole

My mother first cooked up her fabulous casserole years ago. The flavor, cheese and splash of sherry make it elegant enough to serve at a dinner party.

—**PEGGY KROUPA** LEAWOOD, KANSAS

YIELD: 2 CASSEROLES (4 SERVINGS EACH).

- 1 **pound uncooked spaghetti**
- ½ **pound sliced fresh mushrooms**
- 1 **cup chopped onion**
- 2 **tablespoons olive oil**
- ½ **teaspoon minced garlic**
- 3 **cans (10¾ ounces each) condensed cream of mushroom soup, undiluted**
- 3 **cups cubed cooked turkey**
- 1 **cup chicken broth**
- ⅓ **cup sherry or additional chicken broth**
- 1 **teaspoon Italian seasoning**
- ¾ **teaspoon pepper**
- 2 **cups grated Parmesan cheese, divided**

1. Cook spaghetti according to package directions.

2. Meanwhile, in a Dutch oven, saute the mushrooms and onion in oil until tender. Add the garlic; cook 1 minute longer. Stir in the soup, turkey, broth, sherry, Italian seasoning, pepper and 1 cup cheese. Drain spaghetti; stir into turkey mixture.

3. Transfer to two greased 8-in. square baking dishes. Sprinkle with remaining cheese. Cover and freeze one casserole for up to 3 months. Cover and bake the remaining casserole at 350° for 30-40 minutes or until heated through.

To use frozen casserole: Thaw in the refrigerator overnight. Remove from the refrigerator 30 minutes before baking. Cover and bake at 350° for 45 minutes. Uncover; bake 5-10 minutes longer or until bubbly.

Fried Chicken Strips

I recently made this recipe of Mom's for my in-laws and they said it was the best fried chicken ever. Slicing the chicken breasts into strips cuts down on cooking time and ensures that every piece is crunchy and evenly coated.

—**GENNY MONCHAMP** REDDING, CALIFORNIA

YIELD: 6 SERVINGS.

2⅔ cups crushed saltines (about 80 crackers)
  1 teaspoon garlic salt
  ½ teaspoon dried basil
  ½ teaspoon paprika
  ⅛ teaspoon pepper
  1 egg
  1 cup milk
1½ pounds boneless skinless chicken breasts, cut into ½-inch strips
Oil for frying

1. In a shallow bowl, combine the first five ingredients. In another shallow bowl, beat egg and milk. Dip chicken into egg mixture, then cracker mixture.

2. In an electric skillet or deep-fat fryer, heat oil to 375°. Fry chicken, a few strips at a time, for 2-3 minutes on each side or until golden brown. Drain on paper towels.

Duck with Cherry Sauce

My mom prepared this tender roast duck often for Sunday dinner when I was growing up. It was one of my dad's favorite meals. The cherry sauce stirs up easily and makes this duck simply delightful.

—**SANDY JENKINS** ELKHORN, WISCONSIN

YIELD: 4-5 SERVINGS.

  1 domestic duckling (4 to 5 pounds)
  1 jar (12 ounces) cherry preserves
  1 to 2 tablespoons red wine vinegar
Bing cherries, star fruit and kale, optional

1. Prick skin of duckling well and place breast side up on a rack in a shallow roasting pan. Tie drumsticks together. Bake, uncovered, at 350° for 2 to 2½ hours or until juices run clear and a thermometer reads 180°. (Drain fat from pan as it accumulates.) Cover and let stand 20 minutes before carving.

2. Meanwhile, for sauce, combine preserves and vinegar in a small saucepan. Cook and stir over medium heat until heated through. Serve with duck. Garnish platter with fruit and kale if desired.

PORK, HAM & SAUSAGE

Oktoberfest Pork Roast

My favorite fall flavors, such as apples, pork roast, sauerkraut and potatoes, are combined in one sensational dish. I took my mom's dish and changed it for the slow cooker. I often coat the slow cooker insert with cooking spray to prevent the potatoes and meat from sticking.

—TONYA SWAIN SEVILLE, OHIO

YIELD: 8 SERVINGS.

16 small red potatoes

1 can (14 ounces) sauerkraut, rinsed and well drained

2 large tart apples, peeled and cut into wedges

1 pound smoked kielbasa or Polish sausage, cut into 16 slices

2 tablespoons brown sugar

1 teaspoon caraway seeds

1 teaspoon salt, divided

1 teaspoon pepper, divided

1 boneless pork loin roast (3 pounds)

3 tablespoons canola oil

1. Place potatoes in a greased 6-qt. slow cooker. Top with sauerkraut, apples and kielbasa. Sprinkle with brown sugar, caraway seeds, ½ teaspoon salt and ½ teaspoon pepper.

2. Cut roast in half. Combine remaining salt and pepper; rub over meat. In a large skillet, brown meat in oil on all sides. Transfer to slow cooker. Cover and cook on low for 8-10 hours or until a thermometer reads 160° and vegetables are tender. Skim fat and thicken pan juices if desired.

Smoked Sausage Potato Bake

This delicious bake came from my mom's recipes files. I often fix it for company because it's pleasing to the eye as well as the appetite. I rarely have leftovers, as second helpings are a given.

—**JOANNE WERNER** LA PORTE, INDIANA

YIELD: 4-6 SERVINGS.

- 1¾ cups water
- ⅔ cup milk
- 5 tablespoons butter, divided
- ½ teaspoon salt
- 2⅔ cups mashed potato flakes
- 1 cup (8 ounces) sour cream
- 1 cup (4 ounces) shredded cheddar cheese
- 1 pound smoked sausage links, halved lengthwise and cut into ½-inch slices
- 1 cup (4 ounces) shredded Monterey Jack cheese
- 2 tablespoons dry bread crumbs

1. In a large saucepan, bring the water, milk, 4 tablespoons butter and salt to a boil. Remove from the heat; stir in potato flakes. Let stand for 30 seconds or until liquid is absorbed. Whip with a fork until fluffy. Stir in the sour cream and cheddar cheese.

2. Spoon half into a greased 2-qt. baking dish. Top with sausage and remaining potatoes. Sprinkle with Monterey Jack cheese.

3. Melt the remaining butter and toss with bread crumbs; sprinkle over the top. Bake, uncovered, at 350° for 30-35 minutes or until heated through and edges are golden brown.

Grandma Edna's Cajun Pork

My grandma used to make this every year as part of our Christmas dinner. She's been gone for a few years, but we still carry on the delicious tradition of serving Grandma's Cajun pork.

—**TONYA CLINE** GREENVILLE, OHIO

YIELD: 12 SERVINGS (2¼ CUPS SAUCE).

- 1 small onion
- 1 celery rib
- 1 small green pepper
- 3 tablespoons butter
- 3 garlic cloves, minced
- 2 teaspoons dried thyme
- 1 teaspoon paprika
- ½ teaspoon each salt, white pepper and pepper
- ½ teaspoon ground mustard
- ½ teaspoon hot pepper sauce
- 1 boneless whole pork loin roast (4 pounds)
- 2 tablespoons cornstarch
- 2 tablespoons cold water

1. Finely chop vegetables. In a large skillet, saute vegetables in butter until tender. Add garlic; cook 1 minute longer. Stir in seasonings and pepper sauce.

2. Cut roast in half. Cut several slits in roast to within ½ in. of bottom. Place in a 4-qt. slow cooker. Spoon onion mixture between slits and over the top of meat. Cover and cook on low for 6-8 hours or until pork is tender.

3. Transfer the roast to a serving platter; keep warm. Let stand for 10 minutes before slicing. Pour cooking juices into a small saucepan. Combine cornstarch and water until smooth; stir into the pan. Bring to a boil; cook and stir for 2 minutes or until thickened. Serve with roast.

Apricot Baked Ham

Ham is a super choice for a holiday meal because once you put it in the oven, it practically takes care of itself until dinnertime. I serve it because everyone in my family loves it! The sugary crust makes the ham loook beautiful.

—MARGE CLARK WEST LEBANON, INDIANA

YIELD: 10-14 SERVINGS.

- 1 **fully cooked bone-in ham (5 to 7 pounds)**
- 20 **whole cloves**
- ½ **cup apricot preserves**
- 3 **tablespoons ground mustard**
- ½ **cup packed light brown sugar**

1. Place ham on a rack in a shallow roasting pan. Score the surface of the ham, making diamond shapes ½ in. deep; insert a clove in each diamond. Combine preserves and mustard; spread over ham. Pat brown sugar into apricot mixture.

2. Bake at 325° for 1¾ to 2¼ hours or until a thermometer reads 140°.

Garlic Pork Roast

Mom cooked for 11 children, so her menus usually featured basic, simple foods. But on New Year's Day, she always treated us to this special pork roast.

—RUBY WILLIAMS BOGALUSA, LOUISIANA

YIELD: 6-8 SERVINGS.

- 1 **bone-in pork loin roast (5 pounds), backbone loosened**
- ½ **medium green pepper, finely chopped**
- ½ **cup thinly sliced green onions**
- ½ **cup chopped celery**
- 8 **garlic cloves, minced**
- 1 **teaspoon salt**
- ¼ **teaspoon cayenne pepper**

1. With a sharp knife, cut a deep pocket between each rib on meaty side of roast. In a large bowl, combine the green pepper, green onions, celery and garlic; stuff vegetable mixture into pockets. Sprinkle roast with salt and cayenne pepper.

2. Place the roast, rib side down, in a shallow roasting pan. Bake, uncovered, at 350° for 1 hour 40 minutes or until a thermometer in the pork reads 145°-160°. Let stand for 15 minutes before carving.

Herbed Pork and Apples

Whenever I make this dish for friends and family, I'm reminded of the wonderful scent of the Maine orchards where we picked our own apples every fall until we moved to Missouri. The aroma of the pork and apples certainly takes the chill out of crisp autumn air.

—LOUISE KEITHLEY COLUMBIA, MISSOURI

YIELD: ABOUT 12 SERVINGS.

- 1 **teaspoon each dried sage, thyme, rosemary and marjoram, crushed**
- 1 **teaspoon salt**
- 1 **teaspoon pepper**
- 1 **bone-in pork loin roast (about 6 pounds)**
- 4 **medium tart apples, cut into 1-inch chunks**
- 1 **large red onion, cut into 1-inch chunks**
- 3 **tablespoons brown sugar**
- 1 **cup apple juice**
- ⅔ **cup maple syrup**

1. Combine herbs, salt and pepper; rub over roast. Cover and refrigerate for several hours or overnight.

2. Bake, uncovered, at 325° for 1½ hours. Drain fat. Mix apples and onion with brown sugar; spoon around roast. Continue to roast 1 hour or until a thermometer reads 145°-160°. Transfer the roast, apples and onion to a serving platter and keep warm.

3. Skim excess fat from meat juices; pour into a heavy skillet (or leave in the roasting pan if it can be heated on stovetop). Add apple juice and syrup. Cook and stir over medium-high heat until liquid has been reduced by half, about 1 cup. Slice roast and serve with gravy.

Country Pork 'n' Sauerkraut

The "secret ingredient" in this recipe is the applesauce. When everything's cooked up, you wouldn't know it's in there...yet the taste's just a bit sweeter. My mother and grandmother once ran a beanery for a train crew. That inspired a lot of my cooking. In fact, I adapted this recipe from one of theirs. Luckily for me, my husband likes to eat what I fix as much as I like to cook it! He and I have three children, all now grown, and six grandchildren.

—DONNA HELLENDRUNG
MINNEAPOLIS, MINNESOTA

YIELD: 4 SERVINGS.

- 2 pounds bone-in country-style pork ribs
- 1 medium onion, chopped
- 1 tablespoon canola oil
- 1 can (14 ounces) sauerkraut, undrained
- 1 cup unsweetened applesauce
- 2 tablespoons brown sugar
- 2 teaspoons caraway seeds
- 1 teaspoon garlic powder
- ½ teaspoon pepper

1. In a Dutch oven, cook the ribs and onion in oil until ribs are browned and onion is tender. Remove from the heat. Combine remaining ingredients and pour over ribs.

2. Cover and bake at 350° for 1½ to 2 hours or until ribs are tender.

Barbecue Ham Sandwiches

My mother used to buy ham and make a batch of sauce on Saturday. Then after church on Sunday, our hungry family would be able to quickly sit down and have a fast, hearty meal.

—MOLLIE FRY RALEIGH, NORTH CAROLINA

YIELD: 6 SERVINGS.

- 1 cup plus 2 tablespoons chili sauce
- ¾ cup packed brown sugar
- ½ cup plus 1 tablespoon water
- ¾ teaspoon prepared mustard
- ¼ to ½ teaspoon chili powder
- ⅛ teaspoon ground cloves
- 1½ pounds shaved fully cooked ham
- 6 hamburger buns, split and toasted

1. In a large saucepan, combine the first six ingredients. Cook, uncovered, over low heat for 15 minutes. Stir in ham; heat through. Using a slotted spoon, serve ham on the buns.

Sausage over Rice

Come in from the cold and warm up with this satisfying, no-fuss dish. I remember my mother fixing this when I was a little girl, and now I cook it for my family.

—SARAH LEE GREENBERG COOPERSTOWN, PENNSYLVANIA

YIELD: 3 SERVINGS.

- ½ pound bulk pork sausage
- ⅓ cup chopped onion
- ⅓ cup chopped green pepper
- 1 celery rib, sliced
- 1 garlic clove, minced
- 1 can (8 ounces) tomato sauce
- ¾ cup canned kidney beans, rinsed and drained
- ½ cup water
- ½ teaspoon garlic powder
- ½ teaspoon chili powder
- ½ teaspoon Worcestershire sauce
- ¼ teaspoon pepper
- ⅛ teaspoon hot pepper sauce
- 2 cups hot cooked rice

1. In a large skillet, cook the sausage, onion, green pepper, celery and garlic over medium heat until sausage is no longer pink; drain.

2. Add the tomato sauce, beans, water, garlic powder, chili powder, Worcestershire sauce, pepper and pepper sauce; bring to a boil. Reduce heat; cover and simmer for 30 minutes or until flavors are blended. Serve with rice.

Creamy Cabbage-Pork Stew

Savory flavors blend beautifully in this hearty recipe. The stew can also be made in a slow cooker. In a pinch, I use a ring of garlic bologna cut into chunks in place of the pork shoulder.

—RUTH ANN STELFOX RAYMOND, ALBERTA

YIELD: 6 SERVINGS.

- 1 boneless pork shoulder butt roast (1 pound), cut into ¾-inch cubes
- 1 tablespoon canola oil
- 2 cans (10¾ ounces each) condensed cream of celery soup, undiluted
- 1½ cups apple juice
- 2 medium red potatoes, cut into 1-inch chunks
- 3 medium carrots, sliced
- ¼ teaspoon caraway seeds
- ¼ teaspoon pepper
- 3 cups coarsely chopped cabbage
- ½ cup 2% milk

1. In a large skillet over medium-high heat, brown pork in oil on all sides; drain.

2. Transfer to a 3-qt. slow cooker; stir in the soup, apple juice, potatoes, carrots, caraway and pepper. Cover and cook on high for 3-4 hours.

3. Add the cabbage and milk. Cover and cook 2 hours longer or until meat and vegetables are tender.

Spiral Stromboli

I'm sure your family will love this sandwich. One bite and you'll know why. Gooey cheese, warm bread and savory deli meats—what's not to like? My mom gave me this quick and simple recipe.

—**BETH BRUHN** WILLMAR, MINNESOTA

YIELD: 6 SERVINGS.

- 1 tube (11 ounces) refrigerated crusty French loaf
- ¾ cup shredded part-skim mozzarella cheese
- ¾ cup shredded cheddar cheese
- ¼ pound thinly sliced hard salami
- ¼ pound thinly sliced deli ham
- 1 jar (2 ounces) diced pimientos, drained
- 1 tablespoon butter, melted
- 3 tablespoons shredded Parmesan cheese

1. Unroll dough on a lightly floured surface. Pat into a 14-in. x 12-in. rectangle; sprinkle mozzarella and cheddar cheeses to within ½ in. of edges. Layer with salami, ham and pimientos.

2. Roll up tightly jelly-roll style, starting from a short side; pinch seam to seal. Place the stromboli seam side down on an ungreased baking sheet. Brush with butter; sprinkle with Parmesan cheese.

3. Bake at 375° for 20-25 minutes or until golden brown. Cool on a wire rack for 5 minutes. Cut with a serrated knife. Serve warm. Refrigerate leftovers.

Sauerkraut 'n' Sausage

I've fixed this satisfying stovetop supper for dozens of group gatherings, and everyone seems to enjoy the wonderful blend of flavors. Sweet and tart ingredients balance nicely, complemented with bacon and spices.

—EDNA HOFFMAN HEBRON, INDIANA

YIELD: 10-12 SERVINGS.

- 1 small onion, chopped
- 1 tablespoon butter
- 1 jar (32 ounces) sauerkraut, rinsed and drained
- 1 pound fully cooked Polish sausage, cut into ½-inch chunks
- 3½ cups diced cooked peeled potatoes
- 1 cup apple juice
- 2 medium unpeeled apple, diced
- 2 tablespoons brown sugar
- 2 tablespoons all-purpose flour
- 1 tablespoon caraway seeds
- 3 bacon strips, cooked and crumbled

1. In a large saucepan, saute the onion in butter until tender. Add the sauerkraut, sausage, potatoes, apple juice and apple. In a small bowl, combine the brown sugar, flour and caraway; stir into saucepan. Simmer for 35 minutes, stirring occasionally. Garnish with bacon.

Kielbasa Skillet Stew

I grew up on a Montana ranch, and this dish reminds me of the type of stew we used to prepare for the hay and harvest crews. The bacon and sausage provide rich flavor in this comforting meal.

—MACHELLE LEWIS HENDERSON, NEVADA

YIELD: 6-8 SERVINGS.

- 5 bacon strips
- 1 to 1½ pounds smoked kielbasa or Polish sausage, thinly sliced
- 1 medium onion, chopped
- 2 cans (15½ ounces each) great northern beans, undrained
- 2 cans (8 ounces each) tomato sauce
- 1 can (4 ounces) chopped green chilies
- 2 medium carrots, thinly sliced
- ½ medium green pepper, chopped
- ½ teaspoon Italian seasoning
- ½ teaspoon dried thyme
- ⅛ teaspoon pepper

1. In a 12-in. skillet, cook bacon until crisp; remove to paper towel to drain. Cook sausage and onions in drippings over medium heat until onion is tender; drain.

2. Stir in remaining ingredients; bring to a boil. Reduce heat; cover and simmer for 45 minutes or until vegetables are tender, stirring occasionally. Crumble bacon; sprinkle over stew.

Sweet-and-Sour Pork

My children asked for this tangy pork dish whenever they came home from school for the weekend. Today, they still appreciate the stir-fry's comforting flavor.

—**DORIS SOKOLOTOSKY** SMOKY LAKE, ALBERTA

YIELD: 4 SERVINGS.

- 1 can (20 ounces) pineapple chunks
- 2 tablespoons cornstarch
- ¼ cup soy sauce
- 1 tablespoon honey
- ½ teaspoon chicken bouillon granules
- 1 garlic clove, minced
- ⅛ teaspoon pepper
- 2 tablespoons canola oil
- ¾ pound pork tenderloin, cut into bite-size pieces
- 1 medium green pepper, thinly sliced

Hot cooked rice

1. Drain pineapple, reserving the juice; set pineapple aside. Add enough water to juice to measure ¾ cup. Combine the cornstarch, soy sauce, honey, bouillon, garlic, pepper and pineapple juice mixture until smooth; set aside.

2. Heat oil in a large skillet; cook and stir pork and green pepper for 6-8 minutes or until pork is no longer pink and green pepper is crisp-tender.

3. Stir the pineapple juice mixture; add to the skillet with pineapple. Bring to a boil. Cook and stir for 1-2 minutes or until thickened and bubbly. Serve with rice.

Ham-Stuffed Manicotti

Here's a fun and different use for ham. It's unexpected combined with the manicotti, yet delicious. The creamy cheese sauce makes this casserole perfect for chilly days. I'm always asked for the recipe whenever I serve it.

—**DOROTHY ANDERSON** OTTAWA, KANSAS

YIELD: 8 SERVINGS.

- 8 manicotti shells
- ½ cup chopped onion
- 1 tablespoon canola oil
- 3 cups (1 pound) ground fully cooked ham
- 1 can (4 ounces) sliced mushrooms, drained
- 1 cup (4 ounces) shredded Swiss cheese, divided
- 3 tablespoons grated Parmesan cheese
- ¼ to ½ cup chopped green pepper
- 3 tablespoons butter
- 3 tablespoons all-purpose flour
- 2 cups 2% milk

Paprika
Chopped fresh parsley

1. Cook manicotti according to package directions; set aside. In a large skillet, saute onion in oil until tender. Remove from the heat. Add the ham, mushrooms, half of Swiss and Parmesan cheeses; set aside.

2. In a small saucepan, saute green pepper in butter until tender. Stir in flour until combined. Add milk; cook and stir for 2 minutes or until thickened. Stir a quarter of the sauce into ham mixture.

3. Stuff each shell with about ⅓ cup of filling. Place in a greased 11-in. x 7-in. baking dish. Top with remaining sauce; sprinkle with paprika.

4. Cover and bake at 350° for 30 minutes or until heated through. Sprinkle with parsley and remaining Swiss cheese before serving.

Editor's Note: *Recipe can easily be doubled for a larger group.*

Once in a while we traveled to Kansas to visit my grandparents. One thing I especially remember is going down the steps into the dark, damp cellar. After my eyes adjusted to the darkness, I could distinguish the rows of canned fruit on the shelves and the bins of potatoes and other vegetables. My grandmother would uncover a wooden barrel and dig out a ham that had been placed in there to cure. It smelled so good—and tasted even better.

— **MRS. ZANE FRASIER** CORTEZ, COLORADO

Grilled Ham Steak

Here's a quick and impressive ham dish to prepare. It tastes great with the smoky grill flavor and tangy sauce.

—**SHARON MENSING** GREENFIELD, IOWA

YIELD: 6 SERVINGS.

- ¼ **cup apricot or plum preserves**
- 1 **tablespoon prepared mustard**
- 1 **teaspoon lemon juice**
- ⅛ **teaspoon ground cinnamon**
- 1 **ham steak (about 2 pound and 1 inch thick)**

1. In a small saucepan, combine the preserves, mustard, lemon juice and cinnamon. Cook and stir over low heat for 2-3 minutes. Set glaze aside. Score edges of ham.

2. Grill, uncovered, over medium heat for 8-10 minutes on each side, brushing with glaze during the last few minutes of grilling.

Asparagus Ham Rolls

I love this delicious recipe because it includes three of my favorite locally produced foods—ham, asparagus and cheese. It's a great way to use leftover ham—and to make the most of fresh asparagus.

—**LAURIE TIMM** MINNEISKA, MINNESOTA

YIELD: 8 SERVINGS.

- 2 **tablespoons butter**
- ¼ **cup all-purpose flour**
- 2 **cups milk**
- ½ **cup shredded cheddar cheese**
- ¼ **teaspoon salt**
- ¼ **teaspoon white pepper**
- 24 **fresh or frozen asparagus spears**
- 8 **thin slices fully cooked ham (about ½ pound)**
- ¼ **cup dry bread crumbs**

1. In a saucepan, melt the butter; stir in flour until smooth. Gradually stir in the milk. Bring to a boil. Cook and stir for 2 minutes or until thickened.

2. Stir in cheese, salt and pepper. Remove from the heat. Place three asparagus spears on each ham slice. Roll up; secure with toothpicks if necessary.

3. Place in 13-in. x 9-in. baking dish; top with cheese sauce. Sprinkle with crumbs. Bake, uncovered, at 375° for 20 minutes or until heated through.

Scalloped Potatoes and Pork Chops

I truly enjoy trying new recipes and baking hearty casseroles like this one for my family. This dish is easy to prepare, and baking the chops with the potatoes gives the whole meal great flavor.

—SUSAN CHAVEZ VANCOUVER, WASHINGTON

YIELD: 6 SERVINGS.

    5   cups thinly sliced peeled potatoes
    1   cup chopped onion
Salt and pepper to taste
    1   can (10¾ ounces) condensed cream of mushroom soup, undiluted
    ½   cup sour cream
    6   pork loin chops (1 inch thick)
Chopped fresh parsley

1. In a greased 13-in. x 9-in. baking dish, layer half of the potatoes and onion; sprinkle with salt and pepper. Repeat layers. Combine the soup and sour cream; pour over potato mixture. Cover and bake at 375° for 30 minutes.

2. Meanwhile in a nonstick skillet, brown pork chops on both sides. Place chops on top of casserole. Cover and bake for 30 minutes. Uncover and bake 15 minutes longer or until chops are tender. Sprinkle with parsley.

Ham Loaves

This is a great recipe if your family enjoys meat loaf. The brown sugar mixture makes it so tasty.

—CAROL VAN SICKLE
VERSAILLES, KENTUCKY

YIELD: 12 SERVINGS.

    4   cups dry bread crumbs
    4   eggs, lightly beaten
    1   cup 2% milk
    2   pounds ground pork
    2   pounds ground fully cooked ham
 1½   cups packed brown sugar
    ¾   cup water
    ½   cup white vinegar
    1   teaspoon ground mustard

1. In a large bowl, combine the bread crumbs, eggs and milk. Crumble pork and ham over mixture and mix well. Shape into 12 ovals, using 1 cup of mixture for each.

2. Place in an ungreased 15-in. x 10-in. x 1-in. baking pan. Combine the brown sugar, water, vinegar and mustard; pour over loaves.

3. Bake, uncovered, at 350° for 1¼ hours or until a thermometer reads 160°, basting every 15-20 minutes. Place loaves on a serving platter; drizzle with pan juices.

Pork Chops with Caraway Cabbage

Pork and cabbage naturally bring out the best flavors in each other. Each fall, my family requests this hearty skillet supper.

—DAVID FRAME WAXAHACHIE, TEXAS

YIELD: 4 SERVINGS.

- 4 pork loin chops (¾ inch thick)
- 2 tablespoons canola oil
- ½ teaspoon pepper
- 1½ cups finely chopped onion
- 3 tablespoons butter
- 6 cups shredded cabbage
- 2 garlic cloves, minced
- 3 tablespoons red wine vinegar
- 1 teaspoon caraway seeds
- ½ teaspoon salt

1. In a large skillet over medium heat, brown the pork chops in oil; drain. Sprinkle with pepper; remove and keep warm.

2. In same skillet, saute onion in butter for 1-2 minutes or until tender. Add the cabbage, garlic, vinegar, caraway and salt; cook, stirring occasionally, until the cabbage wilts. Add chops to the skillet. Cover and simmer for 15-17 minutes or until meat is tender. Serve immediately.

Broccoli-Ham Hot Dish

One of my best friends shared this recipe with me. My family loves it because it includes one of our favorite vegetables—broccoli. It's a delicious and colorful way to use up leftover ham.

—MARGARET ALLEN ABINGDON, VIRGINIA

YIELD: 8 SERVINGS.

- 2 packages (10 ounces each) frozen cut broccoli
- 2 cups cooked rice
- 6 tablespoons butter, cubed
- 2 cups fresh bread crumbs (about 2½ slices)
- 1 medium onion, chopped
- 3 tablespoons all-purpose flour
- 1 teaspoon salt
- ¼ teaspoon pepper
- 3 cups milk
- 1½ pounds fully cooked ham, cubed
- Shredded cheddar or Swiss cheese

1. Cook broccoli according to package directions; drain. Spoon rice into a 13-in. x 9-in. baking pan. Place broccoli over rice.

2. Melt butter in a large skillet. Sprinkle 2 tablespoons of melted butter over the bread crumbs and set aside. In remaining butter, saute the onion until soft. Add the flour, salt and pepper, stirring constantly until blended; stir in milk. Bring to a boil; cook and stir for 2 minutes or until thickened. Add the ham.

3. Pour over rice and broccoli. Sprinkle with the crumbs. Bake at 350° for 30 minutes or until heated through. Sprinkle with the cheese; let stand for 5 minutes before serving.

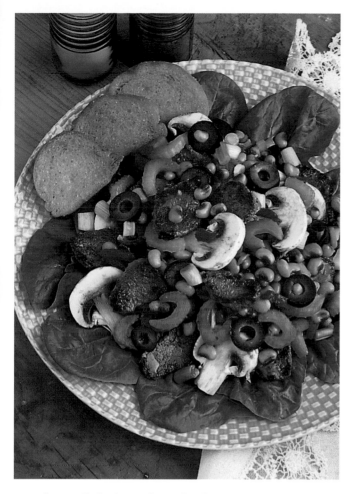

Cranberry-Glazed Pork Roast

My family loves this festive treatment for pork. I think you'll be just as proud as we are to serve this succulent roast with its ruby glaze at the holidays year after year.

—THERESA PEARSON OGILVIE, MINNESOTA

YIELD: 12-14 SERVINGS.

 1 boneless pork shoulder butt roast (3½ to 4 pounds)
 12 small whole onions
 2 teaspoons cornstarch
 ¼ cup orange juice
 1 can (14 ounces) whole-berry cranberry sauce
 ½ to 1 teaspoon grated orange peel
 ¼ teaspoon ground cinnamon
 ⅛ teaspoon salt

1. Place the roast, fat side up, in a greased roasting pan. Bake, uncovered, at 325° for 45 minutes. Place onions around roast, cover and bake for 30 minutes.

2. Meanwhile, in a saucepan, combine cornstarch and orange juice until smooth. Stir in the cranberry sauce, orange peel, cinnamon and salt. Bring to a boil over medium heat; cook and stir for 2 minutes or until thickened. Spoon ¾ cup over roast and onions; set remaining sauce aside.

3. Bake, basting occasionally, 30-45 minutes longer or until a thermometer reads 145°-160° and onions are tender. Let stand for 15 minutes before slicing. Heat reserved sauce; serve with roast and onions.

Pork and Spinach Salad

I serve this hearty main dish salad at family gatherings throughout the year. You just can't beat a salad that tastes great and is good for you, too.

—MARIAN PRATT SEQUIM, WASHINGTON

YIELD: 4 SERVINGS.

 1 package (10 ounces) fresh spinach, torn
 1 can (15½ ounces) black-eyed peas, rinsed and drained
 ½ cup sliced fresh mushrooms
 ⅓ cup Italian or low-fat Italian dressing
 2 green onions, thinly sliced
 ¼ cup sliced celery
 1 jar (2 ounces) sliced pimientos, drained
 2 to 3 tablespoons sliced ripe olives
 ½ pound pork tenderloin, cut into thin strips
 1 tablespoon olive oil
 2 garlic cloves, minced

1. Line four plates with spinach leaves; set aside. In a large bowl, combine the black-eyed peas, mushrooms, dressing, onions, celery, pimientos and olives; set aside.

2. In a small skillet, saute the pork in oil for 1 minute. Add the garlic; saute 1-2 minutes longer or until no longer pink. Remove from the heat; add to black-eyed pea mixture and mix well.

3. Spoon mixture onto spinach-lined plates. Serve immediately.

Skillet Pork Chops with Zucchini

My husband and I live on a small farm with our two young sons. We're always blessed with plenty of zucchini from our garden in summer, so I try lots of different zucchini recipes. This is one of my family's favorites.

—DIANE BANASZAK WEST BEND, WISCONSIN

YIELD: 6 SERVINGS.

  6 tablespoons all-purpose flour
  ⅔ cup grated Parmesan cheese, divided
  3 teaspoons salt
  1 teaspoon dill weed
  ½ teaspoon pepper
  6 boneless pork loin chops (¾ inches thick and 4 ounces each)
  1 tablespoon canola oil
  2 medium onions, sliced
  ⅓ cup warm water
  3 medium zucchini (about 1 pound), sliced
  ½ teaspoon paprika

1. In a small bowl, combine the flour, ⅓ cup cheese, salt, dill weed and pepper. Pour half into a large resealable plastic bag; Add pork, a few pieces at a time, and shake to coat; shake off excess flour. Set aside remaining flour mixture.

2. In a large skillet, brown pork chops on both sides over medium-high heat. Top with onion slices; add water. Bring to a boil. Reduce heat; cover and simmer for 15 minutes.

3. Place zucchini over the onion. Combine remaining cheese with reserved flour mixture; sprinkle over zucchini. Sprinkle with paprika. Cover and simmer for 25 minutes or until a thermometer reads 160°.

Maple Country Ribs

I brought this recipe with me from Quebec after my husband and I were married. The rich maple flavor impressed my in-laws the first time I made dinner for them.

—ANNE-MARIE FORTIN SWANTON, VERMONT

YIELD: 4 SERVINGS.

  3 pounds bone-in country-style pork ribs
  1 cup maple syrup
  ½ cup applesauce
  ¼ cup ketchup
  3 tablespoons lemon juice
  ¼ teaspoon each salt, pepper, paprika, garlic powder and ground cinnamon

1. Place ribs in a Dutch oven. Cover with water; bring to a boil. Reduce heat and simmer for 10 minutes. Drain.

2. Place ribs in a greased 13-in. x 9-in. baking dish. In a small bowl, combine the remaining ingredients; pour half over ribs.

3. Bake, uncovered, at 325° for 1½ hours or until tender, basting often with remaining sauce.

Potato Pork Pie

A true comfort food that's impossible to resist, this main dish is hearty and saucy with flavors that blend so nicely together. Many shepherd's pie recipes call for beef, so a pork version is a tasty change of pace.

—MICHELLE ROSS STANWOOD, WASHINGTON

YIELD: 6 SERVINGS.

2	pounds potatoes, peeled and cubed
⅓	cup heavy whipping cream
4	tablespoons butter, divided
¾	teaspoon salt
⅛	teaspoon pepper
1	medium onion, chopped
1	garlic clove, minced
¼	cup all-purpose flour
1	can (14½ ounces) beef broth
1	tablespoon Dijon mustard
1	teaspoon dried thyme
4	tablespoons minced fresh parsley, divided
2½	cups cubed cooked pork

1. Place potatoes in a large saucepan and cover with water; bring to a boil. Cover and cook for 20-25 minutes or until very tender. Drain well. Mash the potatoes with the cream, 2 tablespoons butter, salt and pepper. Spread 1½ cups of mashed potatoes into a greased shallow 1½-qt. baking dish.

2. In a large skillet, saute onion in remaining butter until tender. Add garlic; cook 1 minute longer. Stir in the flour until blended. Gradually stir in the broth, mustard, thyme and 2 tablespoons parsley. Bring to a boil; cook and stir for 2 minutes or until thickened. Stir in pork; heat through. Pour over potato crust.

3. Pipe or spoon remaining mashed potatoes over top. Bake, uncovered, at 375° for 35-40 minutes or until the potatoes are lightly browned. Sprinkle with remaining parsley.

Sugar-Glazed Ham

An old-fashioned sugar glaze gives ham a pretty, golden-brown coating just like Grandma used to make. The mustard and vinegar complement the brown sugar and add fantastic flavor. Be prepared to serve seconds!

—CAROL STRONG BATTLE HEATHSVILLE, VIRGINIA

YIELD: 10-14 SERVINGS.

1	fully cooked bone-in ham (5 to 7 pounds)
1	cup packed brown sugar
2	teaspoons prepared mustard
1	to 2 tablespoons cider vinegar

1. Score the surface of the ham, making diamond shapes ½ in. deep with a sharp knife. Place ham on a rack in a shallow baking pan. Bake at 325° for 1¾ to 2¼ hours or until a thermometer reads 140°.

2. In a small bowl, combine brown sugar, mustard and enough vinegar to make a thick paste. During the last hour of baking, brush glaze on the ham every 15 minutes.

Ham a la King

My mom and I used to have a catering business, and this dish was a popular choice from our menu. It looks elegant on the plate and people always enjoy it. Being able to make the sauce a day ahead is a big plus.

—JEAN GRUBB BASTROP, TEXAS

YIELD: 6 SERVINGS.

- 1 package (10 ounces) frozen puff pastry shells
- ¼ cup butter, cubed
- ¼ cup all-purpose flour
- 1 teaspoon chicken bouillon granules
- ½ cup hot water
- 1½ cups milk
- 3 slices process American cheese
- 1 teaspoon Worcestershire sauce
- 1 teaspoon prepared mustard
- 2 cups cubed fully cooked ham
- ½ cup frozen peas, thawed, optional
- 1 can (2¼ ounces) sliced ripe olives, drained
- 2 tablespoons diced pimientos
- 2 tablespoons minced fresh parsley

1. Bake pastry shells according to the package directions. Meanwhile, in a large saucepan, melt butter; stir in flour until smooth. Dissolve bouillon in water. Gradually add the milk and bouillon to the saucepan. Bring to a boil; cook and stir for 2 minutes or until thickened.

2. Reduce heat; add the cheese, Worcestershire sauce and mustard. Stir until cheese is melted. Add the ham, peas if desired, olives, pimientos and parsley; heat through. Serve in pastry shells.

Ham 'n' Cheese Pasta

Whenever we had leftover ham, we could look forward to my mother preparing her yummy, comforting pasta. Horseradish gives it a nice zip. I quickened the preparation by using process cheese instead of making a cheese sauce from scratch. Now my kids love it.

—KAREN KOPP INDIANAPOLIS, INDIANA

YIELD: 4 SERVINGS.

- 8 ounces uncooked medium pasta shells
- 1 pound process cheese (Velveeta), cubed
- ½ cup milk
- 2 tablespoons ketchup
- 1 tablespoon prepared horseradish
- 2 cups cubed fully cooked ham
- 1 package (8 ounces) frozen peas, thawed

1. Cook pasta according to package directions. Meanwhile, in a microwave-safe bowl, combine cheese and milk. Cover and microwave on high for 2 minutes; stir. Heat 1-2 minutes longer or until smooth, stirring twice. Stir in ketchup and horseradish until blended.

2. Drain pasta and place in a large bowl. Stir in the ham, peas and cheese sauce.

3. Transfer to a greased 2-qt. baking dish. Cover and bake at 350° for 30-35 minutes or until heated through.

Sweet-Sour Franks

When I married my husband more than 30 years ago, I asked my mother-in-law for some of his favorite dishes. Knowing money was tight, she sent a budget-friendly hot dog dish along. It's so good that I still make it today.

—DIANE HENDRIXSON WAPAKONETA, OHIO

YIELD: 3 SERVINGS.

1 **can (20 ounces) pineapple tidbits**
1 **teaspoon beef bouillon granules**
⅓ **cup boiling water**
1 **tablespoon cornstarch**
1 **tablespoon brown sugar**
2 **tablespoons cider vinegar**
1 **tablespoon reduced-sodium soy sauce**
1 **medium onion, chopped**
1 **medium green pepper, julienned**
2 **tablespoons butter**
5 **hot dogs, halved lengthwise and cut into ½-inch slices**
3 **cups hot cooked rice**

1. Drain pineapple, reserving juice. Set aside 1 cup pineapple and 6 tablespoons juice; refrigerate remaining pineapple and juice for another use. Dissolve bouillon in water. In a small bowl, combine the cornstarch, brown sugar, vinegar, soy sauce, bouillon and reserved juice until smooth; set aside.

2. In a large skillet, saute the onion and green pepper in butter. Stir cornstarch mixture; stir into skillet. Bring to a boil; cook and stir for 2 minutes or until thickened. Add the hot dogs and reserved pineapple; cook until heated through. Serve over rice.

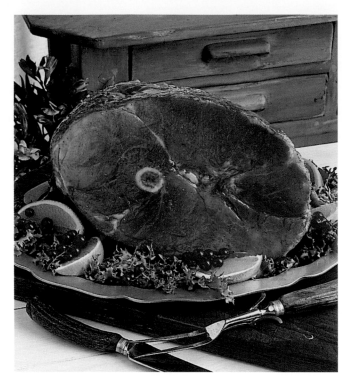

Festive Ham Glaze

As long as I can remember, my favorite room's been the kitchen. My glaze dates back to shortly after my husband and I were married. My parents were visiting, I cooked a Sunday ham with this glaze—and I've done it that same way ever since. Since my husband made his career in the Air Force, we spent years in the city or living in close quarters. When he retired, we decided to plant roots here where we could experience the daily rise and set of the sun.

—**BECKY MAGEE** CHANDLER, ARIZONA

YIELD: 10-16 SERVINGS.

    1   bone-in fully cooked ham (5 to 8 pounds)
    1½ cups orange juice
    1¼ cups packed brown sugar
    1   tablespoon grated orange peel
    1   teaspoon ground mustard
    ¼   teaspoon ground cloves

1. Score surface of ham, making diamond shapes ½ in. deep. Place in a large baking dish.

2. In a bowl, combine remaining ingredients; pour over ham. Cover and refrigerate overnight, turning ham occasionally.

3. Reserving glaze, remove the ham to a rack in a shallow roasting pan. Insert thermometer. Bake, uncovered, at 325° until thermometer registers 140° about 1¾ to 2½ hours, brushing occasionally with glaze during the first hour of cooking.

Pork Chow Mein

I give all the credit for my love of cooking and baking to my mother, grandmother and mother-in-law. That trio inspired delicious dishes like this hearty skillet dinner. When we get a taste for stir-fry, this dish really hits the spot.

—**HELEN CARPENTER** ALBUQUERQUE, NEW MEXICO

YIELD: 6 SERVINGS.

    1   pound boneless pork loin
    2   garlic cloves, minced
    4   tablespoons soy sauce, divided
    2   tablespoons cornstarch
    ½   to 1 teaspoon ground ginger
    1   cup chicken broth
    1   tablespoon canola oil
    1   cup thinly sliced carrots
    1   cup thinly sliced celery
    1   cup chopped onion
    1   cup coarsely chopped cabbage
    1   cup coarsely chopped fresh spinach
Hot cooked rice, optional

1. Cut pork into 4-in. x ¼-in. strips; place in a bowl. Add garlic and 2 tablespoons soy sauce. Cover and refrigerate for 2-4 hours.

2. Meanwhile, combine the cornstarch, ginger, broth and remaining soy sauce until smooth; set aside. Heat oil in a large skillet or wok on high; stir-fry pork until no longer pink.

3. Remove and keep warm. Add carrots and celery; stir-fry for 3-4 minutes. Add the onion, cabbage and spinach; stir-fry for 2-3 minutes. Stir broth mixture; stir into skillet along with pork. Bring to a boil; cook and stir for 3-4 minutes or until thickened. Serve immediately over rice if desired.

Barbecued Spareribs

My husband is a meat cutter at a supermarket and likes to find new ways to smoke or barbecue meat. Several years ago, he discovered this recipe for pork ribs covered in a rich, tangy sauce. It was an instant success with our family and friends.

—BETTE BROTZEL BILLINGS, MONTANA

YIELD: 4 SERVINGS.

- 4 **pounds pork spareribs, cut into serving-size pieces**
- 1 **medium onion, quartered**
- 2 **teaspoons salt**
- ¼ **teaspoon pepper**

SAUCE

- ½ **cup packed brown sugar**
- ½ **cup cider vinegar**
- ½ **cup ketchup**
- ¼ **cup Worcestershire sauce**
- ¼ **cup chili sauce**
- 2 **tablespoons chopped onion**
- 1 **tablespoon lemon juice**
- ½ **teaspoon ground mustard**
- 1 **garlic clove, minced**

Dash cayenne pepper

1. In a Dutch oven, place ribs and onion; sprinkle with salt and pepper. Add enough water to cover ribs; bring to a boil. Reduce heat; cover and simmer for 1½ hours or until meat is tender; drain.

2. Meanwhile, in a small saucepan, combine sauce ingredients. Simmer, uncovered, for 1 hour or until slightly thickened, stirring occasionally.

3. Arrange ribs on a rack in a broiler pan. Brush with sauce. Broil 5 in. from the heat for 5 minutes on each side, brushing frequently with sauce.

Ham Buns

My tasty sandwiches are a great way to use leftover ham. Friends with whom I've shared the recipe tell me these yummy bites tend to disappear fast at potlucks and parties.

—ESTHER SHANK
HARRISONBURG, VIRGINIA

YIELD: 6-8 MAIN DISH OR 16-20 APPETIZER SERVINGS.

- ½ **cup butter, softened**
- 1 **small onion, grated**
- 1 **tablespoon poppy seed**
- 2 **teaspoons Worcestershire sauce**
- 2 **teaspoons prepared mustard**
- 1¼ **cups finely chopped fully cooked ham (about 8 ounces)**
- 1 **cup (4 ounces) shredded Swiss cheese**
- 6 **to 8 hamburger buns, split or 16 to 20 mini buns**

1. In a large bowl, combine the butter, onion, poppy seed, Worcestershire sauce and mustard until well blended. Add ham and cheese; mix well.

2. Divide evenly among buns. Place in a shallow baking pan and cover with foil. Bake at 350° for 15-20 minutes or until heated through.

Sausage and Mushroom Stew

The perfect dish for a hungry, hardworking bunch, this savory stew has a hearty sausage flavor and a delicious creamy sauce. Lots of vegetables add color and interest to each ladleful.

—**ANN NACE** PERKASIE, PENNSYLVANIA

YIELD: 6-8 SERVINGS.

- 2 cans (10¾ ounces each) condensed cream of mushroom soup, undiluted
- 1½ pounds smoked kielbasa, cut into 1-inch slices
- 5 medium potatoes, peeled and cut into 1-inch chunks
- 4 medium carrots, peeled and cut into 1-inch pieces
- 3 medium onions, coarsely chopped
- 1 cup fresh green beans, halved
- ¾ pound fresh mushrooms, halved
- ½ medium head cabbage, coarsely chopped

1. In an ovenproof 5-qt. Dutch oven or baking dish, combine the first seven ingredients. Cover and bake at 350° for 1¼ hours.

2. Uncover and stir. Add the cabbage. Cover and bake 30 minutes longer or until vegetables are tender. Stir before serving.

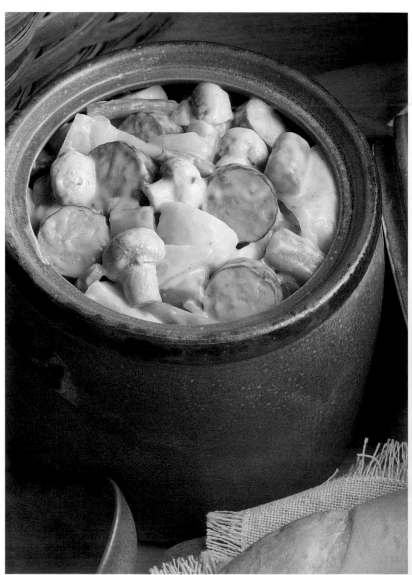

Tuscan Pork Roast

Everyone's eager to eat after the wonderful aroma of this roast tempts us all afternoon. This is a great Sunday dinner with little fuss.

—**ELINOR STABILE** CANMORE, ALBERTA

YIELD: 10 SERVINGS.

- 5 to 8 garlic cloves, peeled
- 1 tablespoon dried rosemary, crushed
- 1 tablespoon olive oil
- ½ teaspoon salt
- 1 boneless pork loin roast (3 to 4 pounds)

1. In a food processor, combine the garlic, rosemary, oil and salt; cover and process until mixture becomes a paste. Rub over the roast; cover and let stand for 30 minutes.

2. Place roast fat side up on a greased baking rack in a shallow roasting pan. Bake, uncovered, at 350° for 1 to 1¼ hours or until a thermometer reads 145°-160°. Let meat stand for 10 minutes before slicing.

One-Dish Pork Chop Dinner

This is a meaty main dish for any affair, but it's great for St. Pat's. Apple juice gives the chops a wonderful flavor, and the cabbage isn't particularly strong so it appeals to a wide variety of tastes.
—PAT WAYMIRE YELLOW SPRINGS, OHIO

YIELD: 8 SERVINGS.

- ⅓ cup all-purpose flour, divided
- **Salt and pepper to taste**
- 8 boneless pork loin chops (½ inch thick and 4 ounces each)
- ¼ cup butter, cubed
- 2 cups apple juice
- 2 pounds small red potatoes
- 1 pound or 1 jar (16 ounces) small whole onions, drained
- 1 pound carrots, cut into 3-inch pieces
- 6 to 8 cups shredded cabbage

1. In a large resealable plastic bag, place ¼ cup flour, salt and pepper; add pork chops. Seal bag; toss to coat. In a Dutch oven over medium-high heat, brown chops in butter on both sides. Remove pork chops; set aside and keep warm.

2. Stir the remaining flour into pan drippings until blended. Gradually whisk in apple juice. Bring to a boil. Cook and stir for 2 minutes or until thickened.

3. Return chops to pan; add the potatoes, onions and carrots. Cover and bake at 350° for 30 minutes.

4. Top with cabbage; cover and bake for 50-60 minutes longer or until a thermometer reads 145°-160° and vegetables are tender, basting occasionally with juices.

Dandy Ham Sandwiches

Caraway gives these special sandwiches a different taste. They are lovely to serve for a luncheon when you are expecting guests.
—MRS. WALLACE CARLSON TWO HARBORS, MINNESOTA

YIELD: 10 SANDWICHES.

- 2 cups (8 ounces) shredded cheddar cheese
- 1½ cups ground fully cooked ham
- ½ cup finely chopped onion
- ⅓ cup French salad dressing
- 2 tablespoons prepared mustard
- 4 teaspoons caraway seeds
- 5 hamburger buns, split

1. In a small bowl, combine the first six ingredients. Spread over cut sides of buns. Place on a greased baking sheet. Bake at 350° for 15-20 minutes or until cheese is melted.

Grilled Pizza Sandwiches

My father-in-law loves pizza toppings and grilled cheese sandwiches, so my mother-in-law and I came up with this recipe that combines the two. These are great with ranch dresssing.
—STACIE SIMPSON FLORENCE, TEXAS

YIELD: 2 SERVINGS.

- ¼ cup pizza sauce
- 2 tablespoons chopped pepperoni
- 2 tablespoons chopped smoked kielbasa or Polish sausage
- ⅛ teaspoon garlic powder
- ⅛ teaspoon onion powder
- **Dash salt and pepper**
- 4 slices white bread
- ⅓ cup shredded part-skim mozzarella cheese
- 1 tablespoon butter, softened

1. In a small microwave-safe bowl, combine the first seven ingredients. Cover and microwave on high until heated through. Spread two slices of bread with meat mixture; sprinkle with cheese. Top with remaining bread. Butter outsides of sandwiches.

2. Cook in a preheated sandwich maker according to the manufacturer's directions until golden brown and cheese is melted.

SEAFOOD & MEATLESS MAIN DISHES

Broiled Fish

Mother's secret in preparing this recipe was to butter the fish before dusting it with flour. That seals in the moisture, making it succulent and absolutely delicious.
—**ANN BERG** CHESAPEAKE, VIRGINIA

YIELD: 4 SERVINGS.

- 4 orange roughy, red snapper, catfish or trout fillets (1½ to 2 pounds)
- 6 tablespoons butter, melted, divided
- 1 tablespoon all-purpose flour
- Paprika
- Juice of 1 lemon
- 1 tablespoon minced fresh parsley
- 2 teaspoons Worcestershire sauce

1. Place fish on a broiler rack that has been coated with cooking spray. Drizzle 3 tablespoons butter over fillets; dust with flour and sprinkle with paprika.

2. Broil 5-6 in. from the heat for 5 minutes or until the fish just begins to brown. Combine the lemon juice, parsley, Worcestershire sauce and remaining butter; pour over fish. Broil 5 minutes longer or until fish flakes easily with a fork.

Budget Macaroni and Cheese

You can't beat this comforting recipe for pleasing the family and going easy on the budget. It's a classic, satisfying meatless entree.
—**DEBBIE CARLSON** SAN DIEGO, CALIFORNIA

YIELD: 4 SERVINGS.

- 1 package (7 ounces) elbow macaroni
- 3 tablespoons butter
- 3 tablespoons all-purpose flour
- ¼ teaspoon salt
- Dash pepper
- 1 cup milk
- 1 cup (4 ounces) shredded cheddar cheese

1. Cook the macaroni according to the package directions. Meanwhile, in a large saucepan, melt butter over medium-low heat. Add the flour, salt and pepper; stir until smooth; gradually add milk. Bring to a boil; cook and stir for 2 minutes or until thickened. Remove from the heat; stir in cheese until melted.

2. Drain macaroni. Add to the cheese mixture; toss to coat.

Red Beans and Rice

This recipe originated with my sister-in-law, but I changed it around a bit to suit the tastes of my family.
—**MARCIA SALISBURY** WAUKESHA, WISCONSIN

YIELD: 12 SERVINGS.

- ½ pound dried kidney beans, rinsed
- ½ pound dried pinto beans, rinsed
- 4 cups water
- 4 cups chicken broth
- 2 garlic cloves, minced
- 2 bay leaves
- 1 can (14½ ounces) diced tomatoes, undrained
- 1 jar (4 ounces) chopped pimientos, drained
- 1 large green pepper, chopped
- 1 large sweet red pepper, chopped
- 1 large onion, chopped
- 1 cup chopped celery
- 1 can (4 ounces) diced green chilies
- ¼ cup snipped fresh parsley
- 1 tablespoon vinegar
- 1 teaspoon salt
- 1 teaspoon paprika
- ¼ to ½ teaspoon ground cumin
- ¼ to ½ teaspoon crushed red pepper flakes
- ¼ to ½ teaspoon hot pepper sauce
- Hot cooked rice

1. Place beans in a Dutch oven with water. Bring to a boil; boil for 2 minutes. Remove from the heat; cover and let soak for 1-4 hours or until softened. Drain and rinse beans; discard liquid.

2. Return beans to Dutch oven; add the broth, garlic and bay leaves. Bring to a boil. Reduce heat; cover and simmer for 1¼ hours. Stir in remaining ingredients except rice. Cover and simmer 1 hour longer or until beans and vegetables are tender andsauce is thickened. Remove bay leaves. Serve over rice.

Lime Broiled Catfish

To serve a reduced-calorie dish that is ready in about 15 minutes, I came up with this fast recipe. I think the lime juice adds fresh flavor to the mild taste of the fish.

—**NICK NICHOLSON** CLARKSDALE, MISSISSIPPI

YIELD: 2 SERVINGS.

1	**tablespoon butter**
2	**tablespoons lime juice**
½	**teaspoon salt, optional**
¼	**teaspoon pepper**
¼	**teaspoon garlic powder**
2	**catfish fillets (6 ounces each)**

Lime slices or wedges, optional
Fresh parsley, optional

1. Melt butter in a small saucepan. Stir in the lime juice, salt if desired, pepper and garlic powder. Remove from the heat and set aside.

2. Place fillets in a shallow baking pan. Brush each fillet generously with lime-butter sauce. Broil for 5-8 minutes or until fish flakes easily with a fork.

3. Remove to a warm serving dish; spoon pan juices over each fillet. Garnish with lime slices and parsley if desired.

Mushroom Crab Melts

I received this recipe from my grandmother. The rich open-faced treats are great with a green salad, but I've also cut them into quarters to serve as hors d'oeuvres. To save time, make the crab-mushroom topping early in the day and store it in the refrigerator.

—JEAN BEVILACQUA RHODODENDRON, OREGON

YIELD: 6 SERVINGS.

3   **bacon strips, diced**
1   **cup sliced fresh mushrooms**
¼   **cup chopped onion**
1   **can (6 ounces) crabmeat, drained, flaked and cartilage removed or 1 cup chopped imitation crabmeat**
1   **cup (4 ounces) shredded Swiss cheese**
½   **cup mayonnaise**
⅓   **cup grated Parmesan cheese**
2   **tablespoons butter, softened**
6   **English muffins, split**
Dash each cayenne pepper and paprika

1. In a large skillet, cook bacon over medium heat until crisp; remove to paper towels. Drain, reserving 2 tablespoons drippings. Saute mushrooms and onion in drippings until tender.

2. In a large bowl, combine the crab, Swiss cheese, mayonnaise, mushroom mixture, Parmesan cheese and bacon.

3. Spread butter over muffin halves. Top with crab mixture; sprinkle with cayenne and paprika. Place on an ungreased baking sheet.

4. Bake at 400° for 10-15 minutes or until lightly browned.

Eggplant Parmigiana

This delicious eggplant casserole—from my mom—makes a wonderful meatless meal. It's a resourceful way to use up the eggplant in your garden, and the homemade marinara sauce tastes really good.

—VALERIE BELLEY ST. LOUIS, MISSOURI

YIELD: 10-12 SERVINGS.

- 2 medium eggplant, peeled and cut into ½-inch slices
- 2 teaspoons salt
- 2 large onions, chopped
- 2 tablespoons minced fresh basil or 2 teaspoons dried basil
- 2 bay leaves
- 1 tablespoon minced fresh oregano or 1 teaspoon dried oregano
- 1 tablespoon minced fresh thyme or 1 teaspoon dried thyme
- 3 tablespoons olive oil
- 1 can (14½ ounces) diced tomatoes, undrained
- 1 can (12 ounces) tomato paste
- 1 tablespoon honey
- 1½ teaspoons lemon pepper seasoning
- 4 garlic cloves, minced
- 2 eggs, lightly beaten
- ½ teaspoon pepper
- 1½ cups dry bread crumbs
- ¼ cup butter, divided
- 8 cups (32 ounces) shredded part-skim mozzarella cheese
- 1 cup grated Parmesan cheese

1. Place the eggplant in a colander; sprinkle with salt. Let stand for 30 minutes. Meanwhile, in a large skillet, saute the onions, basil, bay leaves, oregano and thyme in oil until the onions are tender.

2. Add the tomatoes, tomato paste, honey and lemon-pepper. Bring to a boil. Reduce heat; cover and simmer for 30 minutes. Add garlic; simmer 10 minutes longer. Discard bay leaves.

3. Rinse eggplant slices; pat dry with paper towels. In a shallow bowl, combine eggs and pepper; place bread crumbs in another shallow bowl. Dip eggplant into eggs, then coat with crumbs. Let stand for 5 minutes.

4. In a large skillet, cook half of the eggplant in 2 tablespoons butter for 3 minutes on each side or until lightly browned. Repeat with remaining eggplant and butter.

5. In each of two greased 11-in. x 7-in. baking dishes, layer a fourth of each of the eggplant, tomato sauce and mozzarella cheese. Repeat layers. Sprinkle with the Parmesan cheese. Bake, uncovered, at 375° for 35 minutes or until a thermometer reads 160°.

Grandma's French Tuna Salad Wraps

My French-Canadian grandmother always made tuna salad with chopped egg in it. I tried a version of it, added veggies for complete nutrition and turned it into a wrap. It's fun to eat, and we are reminded of my grandmother with each bite.

—JENNIFER MAGREY STERLING, CONNECTICUT

YIELD: 2 SERVINGS.

- 1 can (5 ounces) light water-packed tuna, drained and flaked
- 1 celery rib, finely chopped
- ¼ cup fat-free mayonnaise
- ¼ teaspoon pepper
- 2 whole wheat tortillas (8 inches), room temperature
- ½ cup shredded lettuce
- 1 small carrot, shredded
- 4 slices tomato
- 2 slices red onion, separated into rings
- 1 hard-cooked egg, sliced

1. In a small bowl, combine the tuna, celery, mayonnaise and pepper. Spoon tuna mixture down the center of each tortilla. Top with lettuce, carrot, tomato, onion and egg. Roll up tightly; secure with toothpicks.

Lemon Herbed Salmon

We sometimes send our delicious Washington salmon all the way to Michigan for my sister to use in this family-favorite dish! The tasty topping can be used on other types of fish, too. Fresh thyme from your garden will really spark the flavor.

—**PERLENE HOEKEMA** LYNDEN, WASHINGTON

YIELD: 8 SERVINGS.

2½ cups fresh bread crumbs
 4 garlic cloves, minced
½ cup chopped fresh parsley
 6 tablespoons grated Parmesan cheese
¼ cup chopped fresh thyme or 1 tablespoon dried thyme
 2 teaspoons grated lemon peel
½ teaspoon salt
 6 tablespoons butter, melted, divided
 1 salmon fillet (3 to 4 pounds)

1. In a shallow bowl, combine bread crumbs, garlic, parsley, Parmesan cheese, thyme, lemon peel and salt; mix well. Add 4 tablespoons butter and toss lightly to coat; set aside.

2. Pat salmon dry. Place skin side down in a greased baking dish. Brush with the remaining butter; cover with crumb mixture. Bake at 350° for 20 to 25 minutes or until salmon flakes easily with a fork.

Honey Walleye

Our state is known as the Land of 10,000 Lakes, so fishing is a big recreational activity here. This recipe is a quick way to prepare all the fresh walleye our family's anglers bring home.

—**KITTY MCCUE** ST. LOUIS PARK, MINNESOTA

YIELD: 4-6 SERVINGS.

 1 egg
 2 teaspoons honey

 2 cups crushed butter-flavored crackers (about 45 to 50)
½ teaspoon salt
 4 to 6 walleye fillets (1½ to 2 pounds)
⅓ to ½ cup canola oil
Lemon wedges, optional

1. In a shallow bowl, beat the egg; add honey. In a plastic bag, combine crackers and salt. Dip fish in egg mixture, then shake in bag until coated.

2. In a skillet, cook the fillets in oil for 3-5 minutes per side or until golden and fish flakes easily with a fork. Serve with lemon wedges if desired.

Clam Stuffing Bake

It seemed like Mom was always standing at her old black stove, coming up with new recipes. This was one of the old-time favorites. I loved eating stuffed clams, and still do. I buy clams fresh when in season and use canned clams the rest of the year.

—**LILLIAN BUTLER** STRATFORD, CONNECTICUT

YIELD: 2 SERVINGS.

 2 tablespoons each chopped celery, green pepper and sweet red pepper
4½ teaspoons chopped onion
 2 tablespoons butter, divided
½ cup chicken broth
¼ cup shredded carrot
 1 cup seasoned stuffing mix
 1 can (6½ ounces) minced clams, drained
¼ teaspoon lemon juice

1. In a small saucepan, saute the celery, peppers and onion in 1 tablespoon butter until almost tender. Stir in broth and carrot. Bring to a boil. Stir in stuffing mix. Remove from the heat; cover and let stand for 5 minutes. Stir in clams.

2. Transfer to two 6-oz. ramekins or custard cups coated with cooking spray. Melt remaining butter; stir in lemon juice. Drizzle over the stuffing mix. Bake, uncovered, at 350° for 15-20 minutes or until heated through and golden brown.

Florida Seafood Casserole

We have lots of friends from up north who come down to Florida each winter to be out of the snow and in the sun. They love to be served fresh seafood, a green salad, and pie made with just-ripened strawberries. So I always try to accommodate them. And they usually compliment the chef!

—LUCILLE PENNINGTON ORMOND BEACH, FLORIDA

YIELD: 6 SERVINGS.

- ⅓ cup finely chopped onion
- ¼ cup butter, cubed
- ¼ cup all-purpose flour
- ½ teaspoon salt
- ½ teaspoon pepper
- 1 cup milk
- 1 cup half-and-half cream
- 2 cups cooked long grain rice
- 1 cup chopped cooked peeled shrimp
- 1 cup crabmeat, drained, flaked and cartilage removed
- 1 can (8 ounces) sliced water chestnuts, drained
- 2 tablespoons lemon juice
- 1 tablespoon chopped pimientos
- 1 tablespoon minced fresh parsley
- 1 cup (4 ounces) shredded cheddar cheese, divided

1. In a small saucepan, saute onion in butter. Stir in the flour, salt and pepper until blended. Gradually whisk in milk and cream. Bring to a boil. Cook and stir for 2 minutes or until thickened. Remove from the heat; stir in the rice, shrimp, crab, water chestnuts, lemon juice, pimientos, parsley and ½ cup cheese.

2. Transfer to a greased 2½-qt. baking dish. Bake at 350° for 25-30 minutes or until heated through. Sprinkle with remaining cheese.

Tomato Quiche

I first tried this recipe at a family gathering and loved it! Serve hot or cold for a great meatless brunch dish. This is my most requested dish for parties, and a fairly simple one to make. Enjoy!

—HEIDI ANNE QUINN
WEST KINGSTON, RHODE ISLAND

YIELD: 6-8 SERVINGS.

- 1 cup chopped onion
- 2 tablespoons butter
- 4 large tomatoes, peeled, seeded, chopped and drained
- 1 teaspoon salt
- ¼ teaspoon pepper
- ¼ teaspoon dried thyme
- 2 cups (8 ounces) Monterey Jack cheese, divided
- 1 unbaked pastry shell (10 inches)
- 4 eggs
- 1½ cups half-and-half cream

1. In a large skillet, saute onion in butter until tender. Add the tomatoes, salt, pepper and thyme. Cook over medium-high heat until liquid is almost evaporated, about 10 to 15 minutes. Remove from the heat.

2. Sprinkle 1 cup of the cheese into bottom of the pie shell. Cover with the tomato mixture; sprinkle with the remaining cheese.

3. In a small bowl, beat eggs until foamy. Beat in the cream. Pour into pie shell.

4. Bake quiche at 425° for 10 minutes. Reduce heat to 325°; bake 40 minutes longer or until top begins to brown and a knife inserted near the center comes out clean. Let stand for 10 minutes before cutting.

Three-Cheese Spinach Calzones

My Italian mother used to whip up these yummy dough pockets when I came home from school for lunch. They're easy to pick up and dip in sauce.

—MARIE RIZZIO INTERLOCHEN, MICHIGAN

YIELD: 4 SERVINGS.

- 1 **package (10 ounces) frozen chopped spinach, thawed and squeezed dry**
- 1 **cup (4 ounces) shredded fontina cheese**
- ½ **cup part-skim ricotta cheese**
- ½ **cup crumbled Gorgonzola cheese**
- 3 **green onions, chopped**
- ¼ **teaspoon salt**
- ⅛ **teaspoon pepper**
- 1 **tube (13.8 ounces) refrigerated pizza crust**
- 1 **egg, lightly beaten**
- 1 **teaspoon water**
- 1 **cup spaghetti sauce, warmed**

1. In a large bowl, combine the first seven ingredients. On a lightly floured surface, unroll the pizza crust into an 11-in. square. Cut into four squares. Transfer to a greased baking sheet. Spoon the spinach mixture over half of each square to within ½ in. of edges.

2. For each calzone, fold one corner over filling to the opposite corner, forming a triangle; press edges with a fork to seal. Cut slits in top. Combine egg and water; brush over calzones.

3. Bake at 375° for 12-15 minutes or until golden brown. Serve with the spaghetti sauce.

Stuffed Trout

Fish is perfect for a busy cook like me, since it's so quick and easy to prepare. This recipe enhances trout's naturally pleasant taste.

—SHIRLEY COLEMAN MONKTON, VERMONT

YIELD: 4 SERVINGS.

- 2 **bacon strips, cooked and crumbled**
- ½ **cup fresh coarse bread crumbs**
- ¼ **cup chopped onion**
- 2 **tablespoons chopped fresh parsley**
- ⅛ **teaspoon salt**
- ⅛ **teaspoon pepper**
- 4 **dressed trout (½ pound each)**

1. In a medium bowl, combine the first six ingredients; mix well. Stuff ¼ cup into cavity of each trout. Place on a lightly greased rack in a shallow roasting pan. Bake at 350° for 35-40 minutes or until fish flakes easily with a fork.

Tuna Mushroom Casserole

The first time I made this dish, my uncle asked for seconds even though tuna casseroles are not usually his favorite. The green beans add nice texture, color and flavor.

—JONE FURLONG SANTA ROSA, CALIFORNIA

YIELD: 4-6 SERVINGS.

- ½ cup water
- 1 teaspoon chicken bouillon granules
- 1 package (9 ounces) frozen cut green beans
- 1 cup chopped onion
- 1 cup sliced fresh mushrooms
- ¼ cup chopped celery
- 1 garlic clove, minced
- ½ teaspoon dill weed
- ½ teaspoon salt
- ⅛ teaspoon pepper
- 4 teaspoons cornstarch
- 1½ cups cold milk
- ½ cup shredded Swiss cheese
- ¼ cup mayonnaise
- 2½ cups egg noodles, cooked and drained
- 1 can (12 ounces) light tuna in water, drained and flaked
- ⅓ cup dry bread crumbs
- 1 tablespoon butter

1. In a large saucepan, bring water and bouillon to a boil; stir until bouillon is dissolved. Add the next eight ingredients; bring to a boil. Reduce heat; cover and simmer for 5 minutes or until vegetables are tender.

2. In a small bowl, combine cornstarch and milk until smooth; gradually add to vegetable mixture. Bring to a boil; cook and stir for 2 minutes or until thickened. Remove from the heat; stir in the cheese and mayonnaise until cheese is melted. Fold in the noodles and tuna.

3. Pour into a greased 2½-qt. baking dish. In a small skillet, brown bread crumbs in butter; sprinkle over casserole. Bake, uncovered, at 350° for 25-30 minutes or until heated through.

Tuna Burgers

My family was hesitant to try these burgers when I first prepared them, because they were so accustomed to the typical beef burger. But any skepticism disappeared after one bite.

—KIM STOLLER SMITHVILLE, OHIO

YIELD: 4 SERVINGS.

- 1 can (6 to 7 ounces) tuna, drained and flaked
- ½ cup dry bread crumbs
- ½ cup finely chopped celery
- ⅓ cup mayonnaise
- ¼ cup finely chopped onion
- 2 tablespoons chili sauce
- 1 egg, beaten
- 2 tablespoons butter
- 4 hamburger buns, split and toasted
- Lettuce, optional
- Sliced tomatoes, optional

1. In a bowl, combine the tuna, bread crumbs, celery, mayonnaise, onion, chili sauce and egg. Shape into four patties.

2. Melt butter in a skillet; cook patties for 4-5 minutes on each side or until lightly browned. Serve on buns with lettuce and tomatoes if desired.

North Carolina Shrimp Saute

Seafood is very popular in my state. I found this recipe years ago and improved it several times. It is truly a family favorite.

—TERESA HILDRETH STONEVILLE, NORTH CAROLINA

YIELD: 4 SERVINGS.

- ¼ cup butter, cubed
- 1 pound raw shrimp, peeled and deveined
- ½ pound fresh mushrooms, sliced
- 1 small green pepper, chopped
- 3 garlic cloves, minced
- 8 ounces linguine or spaghetti
- ½ cup grated Romano cheese
- ½ teaspoon salt
- ¼ teaspoon pepper
- Chopped fresh parsley
- Lemon slices

1. In a skillet, melt butter over medium heat. Add shrimp, mushrooms and green pepper. Saute until the shrimp turn pink, about 3-5 minutes. Add garlic; cook 1 minute longer.

2. Meanwhile, cook pasta according to package directions; drain and place on a large serving platter. Top with shrimp mixture. Sprinkle with the cheese, salt, pepper and parsley. Toss well; garnish with lemon. Serve immediately.

Stuffed Sole

Seafood was a staple for my large family when I was growing up. Inspired by my mother's delicious meals, I developed this recipe. The fish is moist and flavorful, and the sauce is so good over rice. I predict you'll get many compliments and recipe requests when you serve this dish, just as I do.

—WINNIE HIGGINS SALISBURY, MARYLAND

YIELD: 8 SERVINGS.

- 1 cup chopped onion
- 2 cans (6 ounces each) small shrimp, rinsed and drained
- 1 jar (4½ ounces) sliced mushrooms, drained
- 2 tablespoons butter
- ½ pound fresh cooked or canned crabmeat, drained and cartilage removed
- 8 sole or flounder fillets (2 to 2½ pounds)
- ½ teaspoon salt
- ¼ teaspoon pepper
- ¼ teaspoon paprika
- 2 cans (10¾ ounces each) condensed cream of mushroom soup, undiluted
- ⅓ cup chicken broth
- 2 tablespoons water
- ⅔ cup shredded cheddar cheese
- 2 tablespoons minced fresh parsley

Cooked wild, brown or white rice or a mixture, optional

1. In a large saucepan, saute onion, shrimp and mushrooms in butter until onion is tender. Add the crabmeat; heat through. Sprinkle fillets with salt, pepper and paprika. Spoon crabmeat mixture on fillets; roll up and fasten with a toothpick.

2. Place in a greased 13-in. x 9-in. baking dish. Combine the soup, broth and water; blend until smooth. Pour over fillets. Sprinkle with cheese.

3. Cover and bake at 400° for 30 minutes. Sprinkle with parsley; return to the oven, uncovered, for 5 minutes or until the fish flakes easily with a fork. Serve with rice if desired.

Tomato Pizza

My children liked to eat pizza with a lot of toppings, so I came up with this recipe for them. With fresh tomatoes available year-round here, we still make it often, even though the kids are now grown. It's a delightful change from the usual meat-topped pizza.

—LOIS MCATEE OCEANSIDE, CALIFORNIA

YIELD: 8 SERVINGS.

- 6 medium firm tomatoes, thinly sliced
- 1 prebaked 12-inch pizza crust
- 2 tablespoons olive oil
- 1 teaspoon salt
- 1 teaspoon pepper
- 1 can (2¼ ounces) sliced ripe olives, drained, optional
- ½ cup diced green pepper
- ½ cup diced onion
- 1 tablespoon minced fresh basil
- 1 cup (4 ounces) shredded mozzarella cheese
- 1 cup (4 ounces) shredded cheddar cheese

1. Place tomato slices in a circle on crust, overlapping slightly until crust is completely covered. Drizzle with olive oil. Season with salt and pepper. Cover with olives if desired, green pepper and onion. Sprinkle with basil.

2. Cover with mozzarella and cheddar cheeses. Bake at 400° for 15 minutes or until cheese is melted. Serve immediately.

Homemade Pasta Sauce

When my tomatoes ripen, the first things I make are BLT's and this from-scratch spaghetti sauce.

—**SONDRA BERGY** LOWELL, MICHIGAN

YIELD: 2 QUARTS.

- 4 medium onions, chopped
- ½ cup canola oil
- 12 cups chopped peeled fresh tomatoes
- 4 garlic cloves, minced
- 3 bay leaves
- 4 teaspoons salt
- 2 teaspoons dried oregano
- 1¼ teaspoons pepper
- ½ teaspoon dried basil
- 2 cans (6 ounces each) tomato paste
- ⅓ cup packed brown sugar
Hot cooked spaghetti

1. In a Dutch oven, saute onions in oil until tender. Add the tomatoes, garlic, bay leaves, salt, oregano, pepper and basil. Bring to a boil. Reduce heat; cover and simmer for 2 hours, stirring occasionally.

2. Add tomato paste and brown sugar; simmer, uncovered, for 1 hour. Discard bay leaves. Serve with spaghetti.

Editor's Note: *Browned ground beef or Italian sausage can be added to the cooked sauce if desired. The sauce also freezes well.*

Mock Lobster

When I want a quick fish dinner, this is the mouthwatering recipe I turn to. My husband and I like the flavor so much that I serve it a couple of times a month.

—**GLORIA JARRETT** LOVELAND, OHIO

YIELD: 4-6 SERVINGS.

- 1½ to 2 pounds cod or haddock
- 1½ teaspoons salt
- 2 teaspoons seafood seasoning or paprika
- 3 tablespoons white vinegar
Melted butter
Lemon wedges

1. Cut fillets into 2-in. x 2-in. pieces; place in a large skillet. Cover with water. Add salt and seafood seasoning; bring to a boil. Reduce heat; simmer, uncovered, for 10 minutes. Drain.

2. Cover with cold water. Add vinegar and bring to a boil. Reduce heat; simmer, uncovered, for 10 minutes or until fish flakes easily with a fork. Drain. Serve with melted butter and lemon.

Vegetarian Stuffed Peppers

These filling and flavorful peppers are an updated version of the stuffed peppers I had as a child. Whenever I make them, I'm reminded of home.

—MELISSA MCCABE LONG BEACH, CALIFORNIA

YIELD: 6 SERVINGS.

6	**large sweet peppers**
2	**cups cooked brown rice**
3	**small tomatoes, chopped**
1	**cup frozen corn, thawed**
1	**small sweet onion, chopped**
⅓	**cup canned red beans, rinsed and drained**
⅓	**cup canned black beans, rinsed and drained**
¾	**cup cubed Monterey Jack cheese**
1	**can (4¼ ounces) chopped ripe olives**
4	**fresh basil leaves, thinly sliced**
3	**garlic cloves, minced**
1	**teaspoon salt**
½	**teaspoon pepper**

¾	**cup meatless spaghetti sauce**
½	**cup water**
4	**tablespoons grated Parmesan cheese, divided**

1. Cut tops off peppers and remove seeds; set aside. In a large bowl, combine the rice, tomatoes, corn, onion and beans. Stir in the Monterey Jack cheese, olives, basil, garlic, salt and pepper. Spoon into peppers.

2. Combine spaghetti sauce and water; pour half into an oval 5-qt. slow cooker. Add the stuffed peppers. Top with remaining sauce. Sprinkle with 2 tablespoons Parmesan cheese.

3. Cover and cook on low for 3½ to 4 hours or until peppers are tender and filling is heated through. Sprinkle with remaining Parmesan cheese.

Baked Vegetarian Stuffed Peppers: Fill the peppers as directed. Spoon half of the sauce mixture into an ungreased 3-qt. baking dish. Add the peppers; top with remaining sauce mixture. Sprinkle with cheese as directed. Cover and bake at 350° for 30-35 minutes or until peppers are tender and filling is heated through.

Garden Vegetable Bake

With every spoonful of this vegetable bake, I drift back to a simpler time in my mom's garden. We weren't allowed in it unless she was with us, filling her basket with ripe tomatoes, pea pods, carrots, green onions and herbs.

—PAULA MARCHESI LENHARTSVILLE, PENNSYLVANIA

YIELD: 6 SERVINGS.

- 2 cups chopped carrots
- ½ cup fresh or frozen lima beans
- ½ cup cut fresh green beans
- 2 cups chopped cauliflower
- 2 cups chopped fresh broccoli
- ½ cup fresh or frozen whole kernel corn
- ½ cup fresh or frozen peas
- 1 large sweet onion, chopped
- ¼ cup butter, cubed
- 3 tablespoons all-purpose flour
- 1 cup half-and-half cream
- 1 cup 2% milk
- 1 package (8 ounces) spreadable garlic and herb cream cheese
- 1 cup (4 ounces) shredded sharp cheddar cheese
- ½ cup shredded part-skim mozzarella cheese
- ½ cup minced fresh parsley
- ¼ teaspoon each salt and pepper

Dash each white pepper and ground nutmeg
- 1 cup panko (Japanese) bread crumbs
- ½ cup each shredded Parmesan and Romano cheeses

1. Place the carrots, lima beans and green beans in a steamer basket; place in a large saucepan over 1 in. of water. Bring to a boil; cover and steam for 4-5 minutes or until crisp-tender, adding the cauliflower, broccoli, corn and peas during the last 2 minutes. Transfer to a large bowl; stir in onion.

2. Meanwhile, in a large saucepan, melt butter. Stir in flour until smooth; gradually add the cream and milk. Bring to a boil; cook and stir for 1 minute or until thickened. Stir in the cream cheese, cheddar cheese, mozzarella cheese, parsley and seasonings; cook and stir until blended.

3. Pour sauce over the vegetables; gently toss to coat. Transfer to a greased 13-in. x 9-in. baking dish. Combine bread crumbs, Parmesan and Romano cheeses; sprinkle over the vegetable mixture. Bake, uncovered, at 350° for 25-30 minutes or until bubbly.

Shrimp Shell Salad

My mother came up with this lovely salad when she lived in Anchorage, Alaska, and I modified it to make it lower in fat. Instead of buying small shrimp and chopping them, I often use salad shrimp.

—ADRIENNE BARBE LITCHFIELD, CONNECTICUT

YIELD: 5 SERVINGS.

- 1 cup fat-free mayonnaise
- ½ cup seafood cocktail sauce
- 1 teaspoon prepared horseradish
- ½ teaspoon dried tarragon
- ½ teaspoon dried basil
- ¼ teaspoon celery seed
- ⅛ teaspoon pepper
- 2 hard-cooked eggs
- 2 cups cooked small shrimp, divided
- 2 cups cooked small pasta shells
- 3 celery ribs with leaves, chopped
- 3 green onions, thinly sliced
- 5 lettuce leaves

1. For dressing, in a bowl, whisk the first seven ingredients. Cover and refrigerate until chilled. Cut eggs in half; discard yolks or save for another use. Chop egg whites. Set aside 10 shrimp for garnish; chop remaining shrimp.

2. In a bowl, combine the chopped shrimp, pasta, celery, egg whites and green onions. Add dressing and toss to coat. Serve on lettuce. Garnish with reserved shrimp.

Catfish with Lemon-Butter Sauce

I created this recipe for a catfish cooking contest by modifying a recipe for shrimp and spaghetti that I'd also developed.
—**RITA FUTRAL** STARKVILLE, MISSISSIPPI

YIELD: 6-8 SERVINGS.

- ¾ cup butter
- 8 ounces fresh mushrooms, sliced
- 1 garlic clove, minced
- ½ cup chicken broth or dry white wine
- 2 tablespoons lemon juice
- ¼ to ⅓ cup chopped fresh parsley
- 1 teaspoon salt
- ½ teaspoon pepper
- 1½ pounds catfish fillets, cut into bite-size pieces
- 16 ounces spaghetti, cooked and drained
- ½ cup grated Parmesan cheese
- Lemon slices or wedges, optional
- Additional parsley, optional

1. In a large skillet, melt butter over medium heat. Cook the mushrooms and garlic, for 5 minutes, stirring occasionally. Add the broth or wine, lemon juice, parsley, salt and pepper; cook 3 minutes, stirring occasionally.

2. Add the catfish, simmer, uncovered, for 6 to 8 minutes or until fish flakes easily with a fork. (Butter sauce will be thin.) Serve over spaghetti. Sprinkle with Parmesan cheese. Garnish with lemon and parsley if desired.

Tuna Dill Spread

We like to slather crackers with this easy, tasty tuna spread.
—**GERALDINE GRISDALE** MOUNT PLEASANT, MICHIGAN

YIELD: 5 SERVINGS.

- 1 can (6 ounces) tuna, drained and flaked
- 1 package (3 ounces) cream cheese, softened
- ⅓ cup finely chopped seeded cucumber
- 2 tablespoons lemon juice
- 1 to 2 tablespoons minced fresh dill
- ½ teaspoon salt
- ¼ teaspoon pepper

1. In a bowl, combine all the ingredients; mix well. Use as a sandwich filling or spread on crackers.

Simple Pan-Fried Trout

When my husband and I were enjoying our first getaway in years, we found ourselves stranded in our cabin cruiser with a dead battery. When hunger set in, my husband rigged up a fishing line, and soon there were two trout sizzling on the portable grill. We eventually made it home all right—and kept the recipe we'd devised.
—**FELICIA CUMMINGS** RAYMOND, MAINE

YIELD: 4 SERVINGS.

- 4 lake trout fillets (about 8 ounces each)
- ½ cup grated Parmesan cheese
- ½ cup bacon-flavored crackers, crushed
- ½ cup cornmeal
- ¼ to ½ teaspoon garlic salt
- Dash pepper
- 2 eggs
- ½ cup milk
- ½ cup canola oil
- Lemon wedges and/or minced chives or parsley, optional

1. Rinse fish in cold water; pat dry. In a shallow bowl, combine the cheese, cracker crumbs, cornmeal, garlic salt and pepper. In another bowl, beat the eggs and milk. Dip fish in the egg mixture, then gently roll in the crumb mixture.

2. In a large skillet, fry fish in oil for 3-4 minutes on each side or until it flakes easily with a fork. Garnish with lemon, chives and/or parsley if desired.

Puff Pastry Salmon Bundles

The combination of tender salmon, fresh cucumber sauce and a crisp, flaky crust makes this impressive dish perfect for special occasions. Mom likes to decorate the pastry with a star or leaf design for holidays.

—KIMBERLY LAABS HARTFORD, WISCONSIN

YIELD: 8 SERVINGS.

- 2 **packages (17.3 ounces each) frozen puff pastry, thawed**
- 8 **salmon fillets (6 ounces each), skin removed**
- 1 **egg**
- 1 **tablespoon water**
- 2 **cups shredded cucumber**
- 1 **cup (8 ounces) sour cream**
- 1 **cup mayonnaise**
- 1 **teaspoon dill weed**
- ½ **teaspoon salt**

1. On a lightly floured surface, roll each pastry sheet into a 12-in. x 10-in. rectangle. Cut each into two 10-in. x 6-in. rectangles. Place a salmon fillet in the center of each rectangle.

2. Beat egg and water; lightly brush over pastry edges. Bring opposite corners of pastry over each fillet; pinch seams to seal tightly. Place seam side down in a greased 15-in. x 10-in. x 1-in. baking pan; brush with remaining egg mixture.

3. Bake at 400° for 25-30 minutes or until pastry is golden brown. In a small bowl, combine the cucumber, sour cream, mayonnaise, dill and salt. Serve with the bundles.

Curried Egg Salad

Curry and ginger add an interesting flavor twist to egg salad. I prefer to serve mine as an open-faced sandwich for a pretty presentation.

—JOYCE MCDOWELL
WEST UNION, OHIO

YIELD: 6 SERVINGS.

- ½ **cup mayonnaise**
- ½ **teaspoon honey**
- ½ **teaspoon ground curry**
- **Dash ground ginger**
- 6 **hard-cooked eggs, coarsely chopped**
- 3 **green onions, sliced**
- 6 **slices whole wheat bread**
- **Sliced tomato, optional**

1. In a large bowl, combine the mayonnaise, honey, curry and ginger. Stir in eggs and green onions. Divide among bread slices. Top with a tomato slice if desired.

> Grandmothers cook like artists paint, using what looks or feels right, instead of following exact directions. Learning to cook the "old way" is more than just passing family recipes from one generation to the next. It's like solder in a link of chain, connecting each new link to the last.
>
> **—LORETTA BAUGHAN**
> COMSTOCK PARK, MICHIGAN

Catch-of-the-Day Casserole

My dear mother-in-law is one of the best cooks I know and one of the best mothers—a real gem. This casserole was one of her recipes.

—CATHY CLUGSTON
CLOVERDALE, INDIANA

YIELD: 4 SERVINGS.

- 4 ounces uncooked small shell pasta
- 1 can (10¾ ounces) condensed cream of celery soup, undiluted
- ½ cup mayonnaise
- ¼ cup milk
- ¼ cup shredded cheddar cheese
- 1 package (10 ounces) frozen peas, thawed
- 1 can (7½ ounces) salmon, drained, bones and skin removed
- 1 tablespoon finely chopped onion

1. Cook pasta according to package directions. Meanwhile, in a large bowl, combine the soup, mayonnaise, milk and cheese until blended. Stir in peas, salmon and onion.

2. Drain pasta; add to salmon mixture. Transfer to a greased 2-qt. baking dish. Bake, uncovered, at 350° for 30-35 minutes or until bubbly.

Catfish Cakes

These cakes are crispy on the outside and moist and flavorful on the inside—a real treat! I like to serve them with hush puppies and coleslaw. I use this recipe to make the most of all the catfish we catch at our lake cabin.

—JAN CAMPBELL HATTIESBURG, MISSISSIPPI

YIELD: 8 SERVINGS.

- 1½ pounds catfish fillets
- 2 eggs, lightly beaten
- 1 large potato, peeled, cooked and mashed
- 1 large onion, finely chopped
- 1 to 2 tablespoons minced fresh parsley
- 2 to 3 drops hot pepper sauce
- 1 garlic clove, minced
- 1 teaspoon salt
- ½ teaspoon pepper
- ½ teaspoon dried basil
- 2 cups finely crushed butter-flavored crackers

Canola oil

Tartar sauce, optional

1. Poach or bake catfish fillets until fish flakes easily with a fork. Drain and refrigerate. Flake cooled fish into a large bowl. Add the eggs, potato, onion, parsley, pepper sauce, garlic, salt, pepper and basil; mix well. Shape into eight patties.

2. Place cracker crumbs in a shallow bowl. Coat patties in cracker crumbs. In a large skillet over medium heat, cook catfish cakes in oil in batches on each side or until golden brown. Serve with tartar sauce if desired.

Grilled Salmon

We love to cook on the grill at our house. I've used this flavorful salmon recipe several times and we always enjoy it. The parsley, rosemary and green onions help make the tender fillets a tempting main dish that looks impressive.

—**MONELL NUCKOLS** CARPINTERIA, CALIFORNIA

YIELD: 4 SERVINGS.

- 2 salmon fillets (about 1 pound each)
- ½ cup canola oil
- ½ cup lemon juice
- 4 green onions, thinly sliced
- 3 tablespoons minced fresh parsley
- 1½ teaspoons minced fresh rosemary or ½ teaspoon dried rosemary, crushed
- ½ teaspoon salt
- ⅛ teaspoon pepper

1. Place salmon in shallow dish. Combine the remaining ingredients. Set aside ¼ cup for basting; pour the remaining marinade over salmon. Cover and refrigerate for 30 minutes.

2. Drain, discarding marinade. Grill salmon over medium heat, skin side down, for 15-20 minutes or until fish flakes easily with a fork. Baste occasionally with reserved marinade.

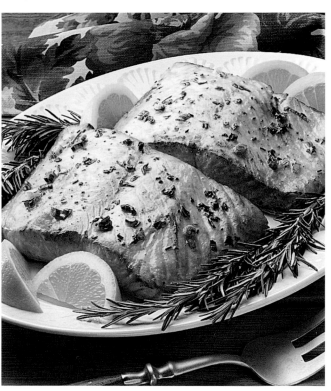

Baked Lemon Haddock

Fish products are abundant here on the East Coast, so I'm always in search of new and fun ways to prepare it. Our family never tires of this simple but superb baked fish. As a matter of fact, it's my husband's favorite.

—**JEAN ANN PERKINS** NEWBURYPORT, MARYLAND

YIELD: 6 SERVINGS.

- 2 pounds haddock fillets
- 1 cup seasoned dry bread crumbs
- ¼ cup butter, melted
- 2 tablespoons dried parsley flakes
- 2 teaspoons grated lemon peel
- ½ teaspoon garlic powder

1. Cut the fish into serving-size pieces. Place in a greased 11-in. x 7-in. baking dish. Combine remaining ingredients; sprinkle over fish. Bake at 350° for 25 minutes or until fish flakes easily with a fork.

To me, nothing tasted as good as the cool water that came from the well on my grandparents' farm. We lowered a wooden bucket with a rope on a pulley, and when we pulled that bucket back up, we'd drink from a tin dipper.

— **DOROTHY ELLIOTT** ORANGE, TEXAS

Shrimp Scampi

Served over pasta, this main dish is pretty enough for company, yet is a snap to prepare. You'll love the fresh flavor the lemon and herbs add to the dish.

—LORI PACKER OMAHA, NEBRASKA

YIELD: 4 SERVINGS.

    3 to 4 garlic cloves, minced
    ¼ cup butter, cubed
    ¼ cup olive oil
    1 pound uncooked medium shrimp, peeled and deveined
    ¼ cup lemon juice
    ½ teaspoon pepper
    ¼ teaspoon dried oregano
    ½ cup grated Parmesan cheese
    ¼ cup dry bread crumbs
    ¼ cup minced fresh parsley
Hot cooked angel hair pasta

1. In a 10-in. ovenproof skillet, saute garlic in butter and oil for 1 minute or until tender. Stir in the shrimp, lemon juice, pepper and oregano; cook and stir for 2-3 minutes or until shrimp turn pink. Sprinkle with the cheese, bread crumbs and parsley.

2. Broil 6 in. from the heat for 2-3 minutes or until topping is golden brown. Serve with pasta.

Crispy Cajun Panfish

My mother was happiest with a fishing rod in her hands, and her method of frying her catch was always a hit. Whenever someone gives us fresh fish or if I buy some, I use this wonderful recipe of hers.

—GAYLE COOK MINOT, NORTH DAKOTA

YIELD: 8 SERVINGS.

- 2 **cups all-purpose flour**
- 2 **teaspoons salt**
- 2 **teaspoons Cajun seasoning**
- 1½ **teaspoons pepper**
- ⅛ **teaspoon ground cinnamon**
- 2 **pounds bass or perch fillets**
- 2 **eggs**
- ¼ **cup water**
- 2 **cups mashed potato flakes**
- 6 **tablespoons canola oil**

1. In a large resealable plastic bag, combine the first five ingredients. Add fish, one piece at a time; shake to coat. Whisk eggs and water in a shallow dish. Place potato flakes in another shallow dish. Dip each fillet in eggs, then coat with potato flakes. Dip fish again in eggs and potato flakes.

2. In a large skillet, heat 3 tablespoons oil over medium-high heat. Cook fish in batches for 3-4 minutes on each side or until fish flakes easily with a fork, adding oil as needed.

Sole in Herbed Butter

I often rely on seafood recipes for quick meals. This flavorful fish is easy to make and is ready in just a few minutes. I know your family will request this often throughout the year!

—MARILYN PARADIS
WOODBURN, OREGON

YIELD: 6 SERVINGS.

- 4 **tablespoons butter, softened**
- 1 **teaspoon dill weed**
- ½ **teaspoon onion powder**
- ½ **teaspoon garlic powder**
- ½ **teaspoon salt, optional**
- ¼ **teaspoon white pepper**
- 2 **pounds sole fillets**

Fresh dill and lemon wedges, optional

1. In a small bowl, combine the butter, dill, onion powder, garlic powder, salt if desired and pepper.

2. Transfer to a large skillet; heat on medium heat until melted. Add the sole and saute several minutes on each side or until fish flakes easily with a fork. Garnish with dill and lemon if desired.

CAKES & CHEESECAKES

Butter Pecan Cheesecake

Fall always makes me yearn for this pecan cheesecake, but it's delicious any time of year. You'll want to put it on your list of favorite holiday desserts.

—**LAURA SYLVESTER** MECHANICSVILLE, VIRGINIA

YIELD: 16 SERVINGS.

1½ cups graham cracker crumbs
½ cup finely chopped pecans
⅓ cup sugar
⅓ cup butter, melted

FILLING

3 packages (8 ounces each) cream cheese, softened
1½ cups sugar
2 cups (16 ounces) sour cream
1 teaspoon vanilla extract
½ teaspoon butter flavoring
3 eggs, lightly beaten
1 cup finely chopped pecans

1. In a large bowl, combine the cracker crumbs, pecans, sugar and butter; set aside ⅓ cup for topping. Press remaining crumb mixture onto the bottom and 1 in. up the sides of a greased 9-in. springform pan.

2. Place springform pan on a double thickness of heavy-duty foil (about 18 in. square). Securely wrap foil around pan.

3. In a large bowl, beat cream cheese and sugar until smooth. Beat in the sour cream, vanilla and butter flavoring. Add eggs; beat on low speed just until combined. Fold in pecans. Pour into crust; sprinkle with reserved crumb mixture. Place springform pan in a large baking pan; add 1 in. of hot water to larger pan.

4. Bake at 325° for 70-80 minutes or until center is almost set. Remove springform pan from water bath. Cool on a wire rack for 10 minutes. Carefully run a knife around the edge of pan to loosen; cool 1 hour longer. Refrigerate overnight. Remove the sides of pan.

Banana Cupcakes

I've been making these scrumptious cupcakes for more than 40 years. My husband's mother passed along the recipe for them. They taste as good today as they did back then!

—ARLOIA LUTZ SEBEWAING, MICHIGAN

YIELD: 1 DOZEN.

- ⅓ cup shortening
- ⅔ cup sugar
- 1 egg
- 1 teaspoon vanilla extract
- ¾ cup mashed ripe bananas (about 2 small bananas)
- 1⅓ cups cake flour
- 1 teaspoon baking powder
- ½ teaspoon salt
- ½ teaspoon baking soda
- ½ teaspoon ground cinnamon
- ½ teaspoon ground cloves
- ¼ teaspoon ground nutmeg
- 1 tablespoon confectioners' sugar

1. In a large bowl, cream shortening and sugar until light and fluffy. Beat in the egg, vanilla and bananas. Combine the flour, baking powder, salt, baking soda, cinnamon, cloves and nutmeg; add to the creamed mixture just until combined.

2. Fill paper-lined muffin cups two-thirds full. Bake at 375° for 18-20 minutes or until a toothpick comes out clean. Cool for 10 minutes before removing from pan to a wire rack to cool completely. Dust with confectioners' sugar.

Toffee Poke Cake

My family and friends have declared my poke cake one of their favorite treats. I enjoy making it because it is so simple. The oozing caramel tastes wonderful with the smooth chocolate cake.

—JEANETTE HOFFMAN
OSHKOSH, WISCONSIN

YIELD: 15 SERVINGS.

- 1 package (18¼ ounces) chocolate cake mix
- 1 jar (17 ounces) butterscotch-caramel ice cream topping
- 1 carton (12 ounces) frozen whipped topping, thawed
- 3 Heath candy bars (1.4 ounces each), chopped

1. Prepare and bake cake according to package directions, using a greased 13-in. x 9-in. baking pan. Cool on a wire rack.

2. Using the handle of a wooden spoon, poke holes in the cake. Pour ¾ cup caramel topping into holes. Spoon remaining caramel over cake. Top with whipped topping. Sprinkle with the candy. Refrigerate for at least 2 hours before serving.

Apple Walnut Cake

This moist cake gets its appeal from big chunks of sweet apples.

—**RENAE MONCUR** BURLEY, IDAHO

YIELD: 16-20 SERVINGS.

- 1²⁄₃ cups sugar
- 2 eggs
- ½ cup canola oil
- 2 teaspoons vanilla extract
- 2 cups all-purpose flour
- 2 teaspoons baking soda
- 1½ teaspoons ground cinnamon
- 1 teaspoon salt
- ½ teaspoon ground nutmeg
- 4 cups chopped unpeeled apples
- 1 cup chopped walnuts

FROSTING
- 2 packages (3 ounce each) cream cheese, softened
- 3 tablespoons butter, softened
- 1 teaspoon vanilla extract
- 1½ cups confectioners' sugar

1. In a large bowl, beat sugar and eggs. Add oil and vanilla; mix well. Combine flour, baking soda, cinnamon, salt and nutmeg. Gradually add to sugar mixture; mix well. Stir in apples and nuts.

2. Pour into a greased and floured 13-in. x 9-in. baking pan. Bake at 350° for 50-55 minutes or until a toothpick inserted near the center comes out clean. Cool on a wire rack.

3. For frosting, beat the cream cheese, butter and vanilla in a bowl. Gradually add confectioners' sugar until the frosting has reached desired spreading consistency. Frost cooled cake.

Pumpkin Raisin Cake

I say this nutty golden cake is one of my mom's best!

—**RUBY WILLIAMS** BOGALUSA, LOUISIANA

YIELD: 12-16 SERVINGS.

- 2 cups all-purpose flour
- 2 cups sugar
- 2 teaspoons pumpkin pie spice

- 2 teaspoons baking powder
- 1 teaspoon baking soda
- ½ teaspoon salt
- 4 eggs
- 1 can (15 ounces) solid-pack pumpkin
- ¾ cup canola oil
- 2 cups uncooked oat bran cereal
- 1 cup chopped pecans
- 1 cup raisins

Confectioners' sugar, optional

1. In a large bowl, combine the flour, sugar, pumpkin pie spice, baking powder, baking soda and salt. In a large bowl, whisk eggs, pumpkin and oil; stir in cereal just until moistened. Stir into dry ingredients just until moistened. Fold in nuts and raisins.

2. Pour into a greased 10-in. tube pan. Bake at 350° for 60-65 minutes or until a toothpick inserted near the center comes out clean. Cool for 10 minutes; remove from pan to a wire rack to cool. Dust with confectioners' sugar before serving if desired.

New York-Style Cheesecake

An Italian friend of my mother-in-law shared this recipe with her many years ago. I added the chocolate-nut crust.

—**GLORIA WARCZAK** CEDARBURG, WISCONSIN

YIELD: 12 SERVINGS.

- 1¼ cups crushed chocolate wafers
- ½ cup chopped walnuts
- ⅓ cup sugar
- ½ cup butter, melted

FILLING
- 2 packages (8 ounces each) cream cheese, softened
- 3 tablespoons sour cream
- ⅓ cup sugar
- 2 eggs, lightly beaten
- ½ cup evaporated milk
- 1 teaspoon lemon juice

TOPPING
- 2 cups (16 ounces each) sour cream
- 5 tablespoons sugar
- 1 teaspoon vanilla extract

Cherry pie filling

1. In a small bowl, combine wafer crumbs, walnuts and sugar; stir in butter. Press onto the bottom and halfway up the sides of an ungreased 10-in. springform pan. Freeze for 15 minutes.

2. In a large bowl, beat the cream cheese, sour cream and sugar until smooth. Add eggs; beat on low speed just until combined. Combine milk and lemon juice; add to cream cheese mixture just until blended. Pour into crust. Place pan on a baking sheet. Bake at 350° for 35-40 minutes or until center is almost set.

3. Combine sour cream, sugar and vanilla; carefully spread over cheesecake. Bake 10 minutes longer. Cool on a wire rack for 10 minutes. Carefully run a knife around edge of pan to loosen; cool 1 hour longer. Refrigerate overnight. Top with the cherry pie filling. Refrigerate leftovers.

Sandy's Chocolate Cake

I held this velvety, rich cake on my lap during the 4½-hour drive to the Greatest Cocoa Cake Contest at the Pennsylvania Farm Show one year. By the time we got to the judges' table, I was almost too tired to care if I won. But win I did—topping 59 other entries!
—**SANDRA JOHNSON** TIOGA, PENNSYLVANIA

YIELD: 12-14 SERVINGS.

3 cups packed brown sugar
1 cup butter, softened
4 eggs
2 teaspoons vanilla extract
2⅔ cups all-purpose flour
¾ cup baking cocoa
1 tablespoon baking soda
½ teaspoon salt
1⅓ cups sour cream
1⅓ cups boiling water

FROSTING
½ cup butter, cubed
3 ounces unsweetened chocolate, chopped
3 ounces semisweet chocolate, chopped

5 cups confectioners' sugar
1 cup (8 ounces) sour cream
2 teaspoons vanilla extract

1. In a bowl, cream brown sugar and butter until light and fluffy. Add eggs, one at a time, beating well after each addition. Beat in vanilla. Combine the flour, cocoa, baking soda and salt; add alternately with sour cream to creamed mixture. Mix on low just until combined. Stir in water until blended.

2. Pour into three greased and floured 9-in. round baking pans. Bake at 350° for 35 minutes. Cool in pans 10 minutes; remove to wire racks to cool completely.

3. For frosting, in a small saucepan, melt butter and chocolates over low heat. Cool for several minutes.

4. In a bowl, combine the confectioners' sugar, sour cream and vanilla. Add chocolate mixture and beat until smooth. Spread frosting between layers and over top and sides of cake. Store in the refrigerator.

Luscious Almond Cheesecake

Almonds and almond extract give a traditional sour cream-topped cheesecake a tasty twist.

—**BRENDA CLIFFORD** OVERLAND PARK, KANSAS

YIELD: 14-16 SERVINGS.

1¼ cups crushed vanilla wafers (about 40 wafers)
¾ cup finely chopped almonds
¼ cup sugar
⅓ cup butter, melted
FILLING
4 packages (8 ounces each) cream cheese, softened
1¼ cups sugar
4 eggs, lightly beaten
1½ teaspoons almond extract
1 teaspoon vanilla extract
TOPPING
2 cups (16 ounces) sour cream
¼ cup sugar
1 teaspoon vanilla extract
⅛ cup toasted sliced almonds

1. In a bowl, combine the wafer crumbs, almonds and sugar; stir in the butter and mix well. Press into the bottom of a greased 10-in. springform pan; set aside.

2. In a large bowl, beat cream cheese and sugar until smooth. Add eggs; beat on low speed just until combined. Stir in extracts. Pour into crust. Place on a baking sheet.

3. Bake at 350° for 50-55 minutes or until center is almost set. Remove from the oven; let stand for 5 minutes (leave oven on). Combine the sour cream, sugar and vanilla. Spoon topping around the edge of cheesecake; carefully spread over filling. Bake 5 minutes longer. Cool on a wire rack for 10 minutes. Carefully run a knife around edge of pan to loosen; cool 1 hour longer. Refrigerate overnight.

4. Just before serving, sprinkle with almonds and remove sides of pan. Refrigerate leftovers.

Pineapple Bundt Cake

I write a recipe column for my local newspaper, so I try lots of new recipes. This one's a keeper. Fruity and firm-textured, this beautiful cake makes a delicious dessert or a nice afternoon treat.

—**FAYNE LUTZ** TAOS, NEW MEXICO

YIELD: 12-16 SERVINGS.

1 cup butter, softened
1½ cups sugar

2 eggs, lightly beaten
2 egg whites
2 teaspoons lemon extract
2⅔ cups all-purpose flour
1 teaspoon baking powder
1 can (8 ounces) crushed pineapple, undrained

GLAZE
1 cup confectioners' sugar
1 to 2 tablespoons milk
½ teaspoon lemon extract

1. In a large bowl, cream butter and sugar until light and fluffy. Beat in the eggs, egg whites and extract until well blended. Combine flour and baking powder; gradually add to creamed mixture, beating well after each addition. Stir in pineapple.

2. Pour into a greased 10-in. fluted tube pan. Bake at 350° for 55-60 minutes. Cool for 10 minutes before removing from pan to a wire rack to cool completely. In a small bowl, combine glaze ingredients. Drizzle over cake.

White Texas Sheet Cake

This cake gets better the longer it sits, so make it a day ahead.
—**JOANIE WARD** BROWNSBURG, INDIANA

YIELD: 20 SERVINGS.

1 cup butter, cubed
1 cup water
2 cups all-purpose flour
2 cups sugar
2 eggs, beaten
½ cup sour cream
1 teaspoon salt
1 teaspoon baking powder
1 teaspoon almond extract
¼ teaspoon baking soda

FROSTING
½ cup butter, cubed
¼ cup milk
4½ cups confectioners' sugar
½ teaspoon almond extract
1 cup chopped walnuts

1. In a large saucepan, bring the butter and water just to a boil. Immediately remove from the heat; stir in the flour, sugar, eggs, sour cream, salt, baking powder, extract and baking soda until smooth.

2. Pour into a greased 15-in. x 10-in. x 1-in. baking pan. Bake at 375° for 18-22 minutes or until golden brown and a toothpick inserted near the center comes out clean. Cool on a wire rack for 20 minutes.

3. For frosting, in a large saucepan, bring the butter and milk just to a boil. Immediately remove from the heat; stir in the confectioners' sugar and extract. Stir in walnuts; spread over warm cake. Cool completely.

Great-Grandma's Ginger Cake

I received this recipe from my great-grandmother and it remains one of my favorite cakes to make during the holidays. It is so tasty.
—**TERESA PELKEY** CHERRY VALLEY, MASSACHUSETTS

YIELD: 9 SERVINGS.

½ cup shortening
½ cup sugar
⅔ cup molasses
1 egg
2¼ cups all-purpose flour
1 teaspoon baking soda
1 teaspoon ground ginger
1 teaspoon ground cinnamon
½ teaspoon salt
Dash ground cloves
¾ cup water
Whipped topping

1. In a small bowl, cream shortening and sugar until light and fluffy. Add molasses and egg; mix well. Combine the flour, baking soda, ginger, cinnamon, salt and cloves. Add to the creamed mixture alternately with water, beating well after each addition.

2. Pour into a greased 9-in. square baking pan. Bake at 350° for 35-40 minutes or until a toothpick inserted near the center comes out clean. Cool on a wire rack. Garnish with the whipped topping.

Saucy Apple Cake

I found this recipe in a Midwestern cookbook. My friends and family consider it one of their favorite desserts. I like it because it's so easy to make. One delectable slice calls for another!

—**DE ETTA TWEDT** MESA, ARIZONA

YIELD: 9 SERVINGS.

- 1 cup sugar
- ¼ cup shortening
- 1 egg, beaten
- 1 cup all-purpose flour
- 1 teaspoon baking soda
- ½ teaspoon ground cinnamon
- ¼ teaspoon salt
- 2 cups shredded peeled tart apples
- ¼ cup chopped walnuts

VANILLA SAUCE

- 1 cup sugar
- 2 tablespoons cornstarch
- ½ cup half-and-half cream
- ½ cup butter
- 1½ teaspoons vanilla extract

1. In a bowl, cream sugar and shortening. Add egg and mix well. Add the dry ingredients; mix well. Fold in apples and nuts.

2. Spread in a greased 8-in. square baking pan. Bake at 350° for 35-40 minutes or until a toothpick inserted near the center comes out clean.

3. For sauce, combine sugar, cornstarch and cream in a saucepan. Bring to a boil over medium heat; cook and stir for 2 minutes. Remove from the heat. Add butter and vanilla; stir until butter is melted. Serve warm over warm cake.

Chocolate Potato Cake

Potatoes are the secret ingredient in this moist, rich chocolate cake with a firm texture. It's wonderful for a special occasion. The fluffy white frosting is perfect with the dark chocolate cake.

—**JILL KINDER** RICHLANDS, VIRGINIA

YIELD: 16-20 SERVINGS.

- ¾ cup butter, softened
- 1½ cups sugar, divided
- 4 eggs, separated
- 1 cup hot mashed potatoes (without milk or butter)
- 1½ cups all-purpose flour
- ½ cup baking cocoa
- 2 teaspoons baking powder
- 1 teaspoon ground cinnamon
- ½ teaspoon salt
- ½ teaspoon ground nutmeg
- ¼ teaspoon ground cloves
- 1 cup milk
- 1 teaspoon vanilla extract
- 1 cup chopped nuts

FLUFFY WHITE FROSTING

- 1½ cups sugar
- 2 egg whites
- ⅓ cup water
- 2 teaspoons light corn syrup
- ⅛ teaspoon salt
- 1 teaspoon vanilla extract

1. In a bowl, cream butter and 1 cup sugar. Add egg yolks; beat well. Add potatoes and mix thoroughly. Combine flour, cocoa, baking powder, cinnamon, salt, nutmeg and cloves; add to creamed mixture alternately with milk, beating until smooth. Stir in vanilla and nuts.

2. In a bowl, with clean beaters, beat egg whites until foamy. Gradually add remaining sugar; beat until stiff peaks form. Fold into batter. Pour into a greased and floured 13-in. x 9-in. baking pan. Bake at 350° for 40-45 minutes or until a toothpick comes out clean. Cool.

3. In a small heavy saucepan, combine the sugar, egg whites, water, corn syrup and salt. Beat on low speed for 1 minute. Place pan over low heat; continue beating on low until a thermometer reads 160°.

4. Transfer to a bowl. Add vanilla; beat on high until stiff glossy peaks form, about 7 minutes. Frost cake.

> I loved to help Grandma bake cakes. I delighted in sifting a "mountain" of flour, then poking the mountain with my fingertip to watch it fall.
>
> — **CAROLYN HUTCHESON** COCOA, FLORIDA

Orange-Date Nut Cake

One of my fondest childhood memories is the aroma of this cake cooling on my mom's dining room table. For those who like dates, nuts and oranges, it is heavenly.

—TERESA SWITZER FAYETTEVILLE, GEORGIA

YIELD: 12 SERVINGS.

- 1 cup chopped dates
- 2½ cups all-purpose flour, divided
- 1 cup butter, softened
- 1 cup sugar
- 2 eggs
- ¼ cup grated orange peel
- 1 teaspoon baking powder
- ½ teaspoon baking soda
- ½ teaspoon salt
- 1 cup buttermilk
- 1 cup chopped walnuts or pecans

ORANGE GLAZE
- 1 cup orange juice
- 1 cup confectioners' sugar
- 1 teaspoon vanilla extract

1. Toss dates with ¼ cup flour; set aside. In a large bowl, cream butter and sugar until light and fluffy. Add eggs, one at a time, beating well after each addition. Stir in orange peel. Combine the baking powder, baking soda, salt and remaining flour; add to creamed mixture alternately with buttermilk, beating well after each addition. Stir in dates and nuts.

2. Transfer to a greased and floured 10-in. fluted tube pan. Bake at 350° for 50-55 minutes or until a toothpick inserted near the center comes out clean.

3. For glaze, combine the orange juice and confectioners' sugar in a small saucepan. Bring to a boil. Remove from the heat; stir in vanilla. Cool for 30 minutes.

4. Cool cake on a wire rack for 10 minutes before inverting onto a serving plate. Poke holes in cake top with a long-handle fork. Drizzle glaze over top and sides of cake; cool completely before serving.

Pumpkin Sheet Cake

The pastor at our church usually cuts his message short on carry-in dinner days when he knows this sheet cake is waiting in the fellowship hall. (I think he prays for leftovers, since he gets to take them home!) This moist cake travels well and is also easy to prepare.

—NANCY BAKER BOONVILLE, MISSOURI

YIELD: 20-24 SERVINGS.

- 1 can (15 ounces) solid-pack pumpkin
- 2 cups sugar
- 1 cup canola oil
- 4 eggs, lightly beaten
- 2 cups all-purpose flour
- 2 teaspoons baking soda
- 1 teaspoon ground cinnamon
- ½ teaspoon salt

FROSTING
- 1 package (3 ounces) cream cheese, softened
- 5 tablespoons butter, softened
- 1 teaspoon vanilla extract
- 1¾ cups confectioners' sugar
- 3 to 4 teaspoons milk

Chopped nuts

1. In a large bowl, beat pumpkin, sugar and oil until blended. Beat in eggs. Combine flour, baking soda, cinnamon and salt; gradually add to pumpkin mixture, beating until well blended.

2. Pour into a greased 15-in. x 10-in. x 1-in. baking pan. Bake at 350° for 25-30 minutes or until a toothpick inserted near the center comes out clean. Cool on a wire rack.

3. For frosting, in a small bowl, beat the cream cheese, butter and vanilla until fluffy. Gradually beat in the sugar until smooth. Add milk until frosting reaches desired spreading consistency. Frost cake. Sprinkle with the nuts.

Fresh Citrus Cheesecake

Here's the perfect cheesecake for spring. The rich cookie-like crust and creamy filling make the zesty citrus taste a wonderful surprise.

—**MARCY CELLA** L'ANSE, MICHIGAN

YIELD: 12-14 SERVINGS.

½ cup butter, softened
⅓ cup sugar
1 egg yolk
½ teaspoon vanilla extract
1¼ cups all-purpose flour
1 teaspoon grated lemon peel
FILLING
5 packages (8 ounces each) cream cheese, softened
1¾ cups sugar
3 tablespoons all-purpose flour
1½ teaspoons grated lemon peel
1½ teaspoons grated orange peel
¼ teaspoon vanilla extract
5 eggs, lightly beaten
2 egg yolks, lightly beaten
¼ cup heavy whipping cream
TOPPING
1½ cups (about 12 ounces) sour cream
3 tablespoons sugar
1 teaspoon vanilla extract

1. In a large bowl, cream butter and sugar until light and fluffy. Beat in egg yolk and vanilla. Combine flour and lemon peel; gradually add to creamed mixture. Mix until dough forms a ball and pulls away from the sides of the bowl. Divide dough in half; cover and refrigerate for 1 hour or until easy to handle.

2. Remove sides of a 9-in. springform pan. Grease bottom. Between waxed paper, roll half the dough to fit bottom of pan. Peel off top paper; invert dough onto bottom of pan. Remove paper; trim dough to fit pan.

3. Place on a baking sheet. Bake at 400° for 6-8 minutes or until light browned. Cool completely on a wire rack.

4. Attach sides of the pan and grease sides. Pat remaining dough 1½ in. up sides of pan, pressing dough to bottom crust to seal.

5. For filling, in another large bowl, beat the cream cheese, sugar, flour, peels and vanilla until smooth. Add eggs and yolks; beat on low speed just until combined. Stir in cream just until combined. Pour into crust. Return pan to baking sheet.

6. Bake at 400° for 10 minutes. Reduce heat to 325°; bake 55-65 minutes or until center is almost set. Cool on a wire rack for 10 minutes.

7. Carefully run a knife around edge of pan to loosen; cool 1 hour longer. Combine topping ingredients; spread over cheesecake. Refrigerate overnight.

Heavenly Surprise Mini Cupcakes

My grandmother was an accomplished baker, and this was one of the many special treats she liked to make. It's fun to bite into these dense chocolate cupcakes and discover a surprise inside.

—**JORUN MEIERDING** MANKATO, MINNESOTA

YIELD: 6 DOZEN.

FILLING
- 1 package (8 ounces) cream cheese, softened
- ⅓ cup sugar
- 1 egg
- ⅛ teaspoon salt
- 1 cup flaked coconut
- 1 cup finely chopped walnuts
- 1 cup (6 ounces) miniature semisweet chocolate chips

BATTER
- 2 cups sugar
- 1½ cups water
- ¾ cup canola oil
- 2 eggs
- 2 teaspoons vanilla extract
- 1 teaspoon white vinegar
- 3 cups all-purpose flour
- ½ cup baking cocoa
- 1 teaspoon baking soda
- 1 teaspoon salt

FROSTING
- 1⅓ cups semisweet chocolate chips
- ½ cup heavy whipping cream

1. For filling, in a small bowl, beat cream cheese and sugar until light and fluffy. Add egg and salt; mix well. Stir in the coconut, walnuts and chocolate chips. Set aside.

2. For batter, in a large bowl, beat the sugar, water, oil, eggs, vanilla and vinegar until well blended. Combine the flour, cocoa, baking soda and salt; gradually beat into oil mixture until blended.

3. Fill paper-lined miniature muffin cups one-third full with batter. Drop filling by teaspoonfuls into center of each. Top with additional batter, filling muffin cups three-fourths full.

4. Bake at 350° for 12-15 minutes or until a toothpick inserted in the cake portion of a cupcake comes out clean. Cool in pans for 10 minutes before removing to wire racks to cool completely.

5. For frosting, in a small saucepan, melt chocolate with cream over low heat; stir until blended. Remove from the heat. Cool to room temperature. Frost cupcakes. Refrigerate leftovers.

Editor's Note: *Cupcakes may also be baked in 30 paper-lined standard-size muffin cups for 20-25 minutes.*

Ladyfinger Cheesecake

My mom's friend made this cheesecake. After one taste, we knew we had to have the recipe. It's so good that we've promised to never make cheesecake any other way.

—**MARCIA SAVERY** NEW BEDFORD, MASSACHUSETTS

YIELD: 14 SERVINGS.

- 4½ cups sliced fresh strawberries (about 2 pounds)
- 2 tablespoons plus 2 cups sugar, divided
- 3 packages (3 ounces each) ladyfingers, split
- 4 packages (8 ounces each) cream cheese, softened
- 2 cups heavy whipping cream

1. In a large bowl, combine strawberries and 2 tablespoons sugar. Cover; refrigerate for at least 1 hour. Meanwhile, arrange 25 split ladyfingers around the edges of a lightly greased 10-in. springform pan. Place 25 more on the bottom; set aside.

2. In a large bowl, beat cream cheese and remaining sugar until smooth. In another large bowl, beat cream until stiff peaks form. Gradually fold into cream cheese mixture.

3. Spoon half of the cream cheese mixture into prepared pan. Spread with half of strawberry mixture to within 1 in. of edges. Cover; refrigerate remaining strawberry mixture.

4. Arrange remaining ladyfingers over top. Spoon remaining cream cheese mixture over ladyfingers. Cover and refrigerate overnight. Serve with reserved strawberry mixture.

Chocolate Almond Bundt

Folks will be pleasantly surprised to see a rich chocolate cake beneath the white frosting. Sliced toasted almonds on top add a little crunch.

—**SHERRI GENTRY** DALLAS, OREGON

YIELD: 12-16 SERVINGS.

- ¾ cup butter, softened
- 1⅔ cups sugar
- 2 eggs
- ¾ cup sour cream
- 1 teaspoon vanilla extract
- 1 teaspoon almond extract
- 2 cups all-purpose flour
- ⅔ cup baking cocoa
- 2 teaspoons baking soda
- ½ teaspoon salt
- 1 cup buttermilk

FROSTING

- 5 tablespoons butter, softened
- 2½ cups confectioners' sugar
- 1 teaspoon vanilla extract
- ½ teaspoon almond extract
- 3 to 4 tablespoons milk
- Sliced almonds, toasted

1. In a large bowl, cream butter and sugar. Add eggs, one at a time, beating well after each addition. Add sour cream and extracts; mix well. Combine flour, cocoa, baking soda and salt; add to the creamed mixture alternately with buttermilk, beating well after each addition.

2. Pour into a greased 10-in. fluted tube pan. Bake at 350° for 50-55 minutes or until a toothpick inserted near the center comes out clean. Cool for 10 minutes before removing from pan to a wire rack to cool completely.

3. For frosting, cream butter, sugar and extracts in a small bowl until smooth. Add milk until the frosting achieves desired spreading consistency. Spread over cake. Sprinkle with almonds.

Spiced Pudding Cake

I came across this recipe years ago and made a few changes. It's very popular. My mom's church group serves it for dessert regularly.

—**KELLY KIRBY** WESTVILLE, NOVA SCOTIA

YIELD: 15 SERVINGS.

- ½ cup butter, softened
- ½ cup sugar
- 1 egg
- 1 cup molasses
- 2½ cups all-purpose flour
- 1½ teaspoons baking soda
- 1½ teaspoons ground cinnamon
- 1¼ teaspoons ground ginger
- ½ teaspoon ground allspice
- ¼ teaspoon ground nutmeg
- ¼ teaspoon salt
- 1 cup water
- ⅔ cup packed brown sugar
- 1½ cups water
- ¼ cup butter, cubed
- Whipped cream and ground cinnamon, optional

1. In a large bowl, cream butter and sugar until light and fluffy. Add egg; beat well. Beat in molasses. Combine the flour, baking soda, spices and salt; add to the creamed mixture alternately with water, beating well after each addition.

2. Transfer to an ungreased 13-in. x 9-in. baking pan; sprinkle with brown sugar. In a microwave, heat water and butter until butter is melted; carefully pour mixture over batter.

3. Bake at 350° for 35-40 minutes or until a toothpick inserted near the center comes out clean. Serve warm. Garnish with whipped cream and cinnamon if desired.

Grandma's Red Velvet Cake

No one thinks it's Christmas in our family without this cake. I baked the first one for Christmas in 1963 when I found the recipe in the newspaper. It's different than other versions I've tasted over the years, since it has a mild chocolate taste, and the icing is as light as snow.

—**KATHRYN DAVISON** CHARLOTTE, NORTH CAROLINA

YIELD: 14 SERVINGS.

- ½ cup butter, softened
- 1½ cups sugar
- 2 eggs
- 2 bottles (1 ounce each) red food coloring
- 1 tablespoon white vinegar
- 1 teaspoon vanilla extract
- 2¼ cups cake flour
- 2 tablespoons baking cocoa
- 1 teaspoon baking soda
- 1 teaspoon salt
- 1 cup buttermilk

FROSTING

- 1 tablespoon cornstarch
- ½ cup water
- 2 cups butter, softened
- 2 teaspoons vanilla extract
- 3½ cups confectioners' sugar

1. In a large bowl, cream butter and sugar until light and fluffy. Add eggs, one at a time, beating well after each addition. Beat in the food coloring, vinegar and vanilla. Combine the flour, cocoa, baking soda and salt; add to creamed mixture alternately with buttermilk, beating well after each addition.

2. Pour into two greased and floured 9-in. round baking pans. Bake at 350° for 20-25 minutes or until a toothpick inserted near the center comes out clean. Cool for 10 minutes before removing from pans to wire racks to cool completely.

3. For frosting, in a small saucepan, combine cornstarch and water until smooth. Cook and stir over medium heat for 2-3 minutes or until thickened and opaque. Cool to room temperature.

4. In a large bowl, beat butter and vanilla until light and fluffy. Beat in cornstarch mixture. Gradually add confectioners' sugar; beat until frosting is light and fluffy. Spread frosting between layers and over top and sides of cake.

Chocolate Caramel Cheesecake

Our guests love this rich, delicious dessert, and I like being able to make it the day before. I garnish it just before serving.

—**JO GROTH** PLAINFIELD, IOWA

YIELD: 16 SERVINGS.

- 2 cups vanilla wafer crumbs
- ½ cup butter, melted
- 1 package (14 ounces) caramels
- 1 can (5 ounces) evaporated milk
- 2 cups chopped pecans, toasted, divided
- 4 packages (8 ounces each) cream cheese, softened
- 1 cup sugar
- 2 teaspoons vanilla extract
- 4 eggs, lightly beaten
- 1 cup (6 ounces) semisweet chocolate chips, melted and slightly cooled

Whipped cream, optional

1. In a bowl, combine the wafer crumbs and butter. Press into the bottom and 2 in. up the sides of a 10-in. springform pan. Place pan on a baking sheet. Bake at 350° for 8-10 minutes or until set. Cool on a wire rack.

2. In a microwave melt caramels with milk; stir until smooth. Cool for 5 minutes. Pour into crust; top with 1½ cups of pecans.

3. In a bowl, beat cream cheese until smooth. Add sugar and vanilla; mix well. Add eggs; beat on low speed just until combined. Add chocolate; mix just until blended. Carefully spread over pecans. Return to baking sheet.

4. Bake at 350° for 55-65 minutes or until center is almost set. Cool on a wire rack for 10 minutes. Carefully run a knife around the edge of pan to loosen; cool 1 hour longer. Refrigerate overnight.

5. Remove sides of pan. Garnish with remaining pecans and whipped cream if desired. Refrigerate leftovers.

Texas Chocolate Cupcakes

My husband remembers his mother making "little black cupcakes with caramel icing," so she passed down this recipe to me. I never thought about putting caramel icing on chocolate cupcakes, but boy, was I wrong. It's to die for!

—CATHY BODKINS DAYTON, VIRGINIA

YIELD: 2 DOZEN.

- 2 cups all-purpose flour
- 2 cups sugar
- 1 teaspoon salt
- ½ teaspoon baking soda
- ¼ cup baking cocoa
- 1 cup water
- 1 cup canola oil
- ½ cup butter, cubed
- 2 eggs
- ⅓ cup buttermilk
- 1 teaspoon vanilla extract

CARAMEL ICING

- 1 cup packed brown sugar
- ½ cup butter, cubed
- ¼ cup milk
- 2 to 2¼ cups confectioners' sugar

1. In a large bowl, combine the flour, sugar, salt and baking soda. In a large saucepan over medium heat, bring the cocoa, water, oil and butter to a boil. Gradually add to dry ingredients and mix well. Combine the eggs, buttermilk and vanilla; gradually add to batter and mix well (batter will be very thin).

2. Fill paper-lined muffin cups three-fourths full. Bake at 350° for 15-20 minutes or until a toothpick inserted near the center comes out clean. Cool for 10 minutes before removing from pans to wire racks to cool completely.

3. For icing, in a heavy saucepan, combine the brown sugar, butter and milk. Cook and stir over low heat until sugar is dissolved. Increase heat to medium. Do not stir. Cook mixture for 3-6 minutes or until bubbles form in the center and syrup turns amber. Remove from the heat; transfer to a small bowl. Cool to room temperature. Gradually beat in confectioners' sugar until smooth. Frost cupcakes.

Cupcake Cones

I experimented with these cupcakes when my girls were young. Now I'm a grandmother of nine, and these are still our favorites. They're a great treat for kids to take to school.

—BETTY ANDERSON STURGEON BAY, WISCONSIN

YIELD: ABOUT 3 DOZEN.

- 1 package (18¼ ounces) chocolate cake mix
- 1 package (8 ounces) cream cheese, softened
- ⅓ cup sugar
- 1 egg
- ½ teaspoon vanilla extract
- 1 cup miniature semisweet chocolate chips
- 36 ice-cream cake cones (about 3 inches tall)

FROSTING

- ½ cup shortening
- 3¾ cups confectioners' sugar
- 1 teaspoon vanilla extract
- 4 to 5 tablespoons milk

Sprinkles

1. Prepare cake mix according to package directions; set aside. In a large bowl, beat the cream cheese, sugar, egg and vanilla until smooth; stir in chocolate chips.

2. Place ice cream cones in muffin cups. Spoon about 1 tablespoon of cake batter into each cone; top with a rounded teaspoon of cream cheese mixture. Fill with remaining batter to within ¾ in. of top.

3. Bake at 350° for 25-30 minutes or until a toothpick inserted near the center comes out clean.

4. In a small bowl, beat the shortening, confectioners' sugar and vanilla until smooth. Add enough milk to achieve spreading consistency. Frost tops of cooled cones and top with sprinkles.

Editor's Note: *These cupcakes are best served the day they are made.*

Brittle Torte

For special occasions, my mom wanted no treat but this torte. When I was in high school, she often asked me to make it for her. The brittle gives it a satisfying crunch.

—PHYLLIS MURPHEY LOWER LAKE, CALIFORNIA

YIELD: 12 SERVINGS.

    8 eggs, separated
 1½ cups all-purpose flour
 1½ cups sugar
    1 teaspoon salt
  ¼ cup water
    1 teaspoon lemon juice
    1 teaspoon vanilla extract
    1 teaspoon cream of tartar

TOPPING

 1½ cups sugar
  ¼ cup light corn syrup
  ¼ cup water
  ¼ teaspoon instant coffee granules
    1 teaspoon baking soda

WHIPPED CREAM

    2 cups heavy whipping cream
    2 tablespoons sugar
    2 teaspoons vanilla extract

1. Let eggs stand at room temperature 30 minutes. Combine flour, sugar and salt. Whisk egg yolks, water, lemon juice and vanilla; add to flour mixture. Beat until blended.

2. Beat egg whites and cream of tartar until soft peaks form; fold into batter. Spoon into an ungreased 10-in. tube pan. Cut through batter with a knife to remove air pockets. Bake on lowest oven rack at 325° for 50-60 minutes or until top springs back when touched. Immediately invert pan; cool completely.

3. For topping, grease a 15-in. x 10-in. x 1-in. pan. In a heavy saucepan, combine the sugar, corn syrup, water and coffee granules. Bring to a boil; stir constantly. Cook, without stirring, until a candy thermometer reads 300° (hard-crack stage).

4. Remove from heat; stir in baking soda. Immediately pour into prepared pan. Stretch brittle in pan with two forks; cool. Break into pieces. In a large bowl, beat cream until it begins to thicken. Add sugar and vanilla; beat until stiff peaks form.

5. Unmold cake; cut horizontally into four layers. Place bottom layer on a serving plate; top with ½ cup whipped cream. Repeat layers twice; top with remaining layer. Frost top and sides of cake with remaining cream. Sprinkle with brittle.

Editor's Note: *We recommend testing your candy thermometer before using by placing it in boiling water; it should read 212°. Adjust recipe temperature up or down based on this test.*

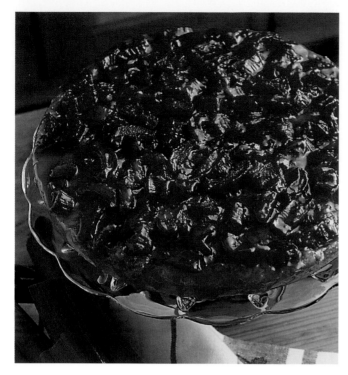

Rhubarb Upside-Down Cake

I've baked this cake every spring for many years, and my family loves it! At potluck dinners it disappears quickly, drawing compliments even from those who normally don't care for rhubarb. Use your own rhubarb or find a neighbor who'll trade stalks for the recipe!

—**HELEN BREMAN** MATTYDALE, NEW YORK

YIELD: 8-10 SERVINGS.

TOPPING

3 cups sliced fresh or frozen rhubarb
1 cup sugar
2 tablespoons all-purpose flour
¼ teaspoon ground nutmeg
¼ cup butter, melted

BATTER

¼ cup butter, melted
¾ cup sugar
1 egg
1½ cups all-purpose flour
2 teaspoons baking powder
½ teaspoon ground nutmeg
¼ teaspoon salt
⅔ cup milk
Sweetened whipped cream, optional

1. Place rhubarb in a greased 10-in. heavy ovenproof skillet. Combine sugar, flour and nutmeg; sprinkle over rhubarb. Drizzle with butter; set aside. For batter, in a large bowl, beat the butter and sugar until blended. Beat in the egg. Combine the flour, baking powder, nutmeg and salt. Gradually add to egg mixture alternately with milk, beating well after each addition.

2. Spread over rhubarb mixture. Bake at 350° for 35 minutes or until a toothpick inserted near the center comes out clean. Loosen edges immediately and invert onto a serving dish. Serve warm. Serve with whipped cream if desired.

Snowflake Cake

This beautiful dessert with coconut frosting is an elegant ending for any special meal.

—**LYNNE PETERSON** SALT LAKE CITY, UTAH

YIELD: 12-16 SERVINGS.

2 eggs plus 4 egg yolks
1½ cups sugar
1 cup milk
½ cup butter, cubed
2½ cups all-purpose flour
1 tablespoon baking powder
1 teaspoon vanilla extract
½ cup chopped nuts, optional

FROSTING

1¾ cups sugar
½ cup water
4 egg whites
½ teaspoon cream of tartar
1 teaspoon vanilla extract
2 cups flaked coconut

1. In a bowl, beat eggs, egg yolks and sugar until light and fluffy, about 5 minutes. In a saucepan, heat the milk and butter until butter melts. Combine flour and baking powder; add to the egg mixture alternately with milk mixture. Beat until well mixed. Add vanilla. Fold in nuts if desired. Pour into three greased 9-in. round baking pans. Bake at 350° for 15-18 minutes or until toothpick inserted in center comes out clean. Cool in pans 10 minutes before removing to wire racks to cool completely.

2. For frosting, in a saucepan, combine sugar and water. Bring to a boil; cook over medium-high heat until a thermometer reads 244° (firm-ball stage). Meanwhile, beat egg whites and cream of tartar in a bowl on high speed until foamy. Slowly pour the hot sugar syrup over the egg whites while beating continuously. Continue beating on high until stiff glossy peaks form, about 7 minutes. Add vanilla; beat until frosting cools slightly and reaches desired consistency.

3. Place one cake layer on a serving plate; spread with ½ cup frosting. Sprinkle with ¼ cup coconut. Repeat layers. Top with remaining cake layer. Frost top and sides of cakes; sprinkle with remaining coconut. Refrigerate until serving.

Editor's Note: *We recommend testing your candy thermometer before using it. In boiling water, it should read 212°. Adjust recipe temperature up or down based on this test.*

Decadent Fudge Cake

Everyone I serve this to seems to love the rich flavor. Four types of chocolate make it so wonderfully decadent

—**ANNA HOGGE** YORKTOWN, VIRGINIA

YIELD: 16-20 SERVINGS.

    1   **cup butter, softened**
    1½ **cups sugar**
    4   **eggs**
    2½ **cups all-purpose flour**
    ½   **teaspoon baking soda**
    1   **cup buttermilk**
    8   **ounces German sweet chocolate, melted**
    1   **cup chocolate syrup**
    2   **teaspoons vanilla extract**
    1¼ **cups miniature semisweet chocolate chips, divided**
    4   **ounces white baking chocolate, chopped**
    2   **tablespoons plus 1 teaspoon shortening, divided**

1. In a large bowl, cream butter and sugar until light and fluffy. Add eggs, one at a time, beating well after each addition. Combine flour and baking soda; add to creamed mixture alternately with buttermilk, beginning and ending with flour. Add melted chocolate, chocolate syrup and vanilla. Stir in 1 cup miniature chocolate chips. Pour into a greased and floured 10-in. fluted tube pan. Bake at 325° for 1¼ hours or until a toothpick inserted near the center comes out clean. Immediately invert cake onto a serving plate; cool completely.

2. Meanwhile, in a microwave, melt white chocolate and 2 tablespoons shortening; stir until smooth. Cool slightly; drizzle over cake. Melt remaining chips and shortening in a small saucepan over low heat, stirring until smooth. Remove from the heat; cool slightly. Drizzle over white chocolate.

Golden Chocolate Cake

At our Wisconsin farm, dessert was just as important as the main course. This idea has followed us to California, where I'm still on the lookout for good dessert recipes. This moist cake is a favorite since it's full of fun ingredients like chocolate candy bar pieces, coconut and pecans.

—**KAY HANSEN** ESCONDIDO, CALIFORNIA

YIELD: 12 SERVINGS.

    1   **package (18¼ ounces) yellow
        cake mix**
    1   **package (3.4 ounces) instant
        vanilla pudding mix**
    4   **eggs**
    1   **cup (8 ounces) sour cream**
    ½   **cup canola oil**
    ½   **cup water**
    3   **milk chocolate candy bars
        (1.55 ounces each), chopped**
    1   **cup (6 ounces) semisweet
        chocolate chips**
    1   **cup chopped pecans**
    1   **cup flaked coconut**
Confectioners' sugar, optional

1. In a large bowl, combine the cake mix, pudding mix, eggs, sour cream, oil and water; beat on low speed for 30 seconds. Beat on medium for 2 minutes. Stir in candy bars, chocolate chips, nuts and coconut.

2. Pour into a greased and floured 10-in. fluted tube pan. Bake at 350° for 60-65 minutes or until a toothpick inserted near the center comes out clean.

3. Cool in pan 15 minutes before removing to a wire rack to cool completely. Chill before slicing. Dust with confectioners' sugar if desired.

Viennese Plum Cake

This is one of my husband's all-time favorite desserts. His mother gave me the recipe. She was usually pretty hesitant to share recipes, but knew how much he loved this one.
—**LORRAINE DYDA** RANCHO PALOS VERDES, CALIFORNIA

YIELD: 9 SERVINGS.

- ½ cup butter, softened
- ½ cup plus 1 tablespoon sugar, divided
- 2 eggs
- 1 teaspoon vanilla extract
- 1 cup all-purpose flour
- 1 teaspoon baking powder
- ¼ teaspoon salt
- 3 cups sliced fresh plums (about 1¾ pounds)
- ¼ teaspoon ground cinnamon

TOPPING
- ½ cup all-purpose flour
- ¼ cup sugar
- ¼ cup cold butter, cubed
- 3 tablespoons chopped walnuts, optional

1. In a large bowl, cream butter and ½ cup sugar until light and fluffy. Add eggs, one at a time, beating well after each addition. Beat in vanilla. Combine the flour, baking powder and salt; add to creamed mixture and mix well.

2. Transfer to a greased 9-in. square baking dish. Top with plums. Combine cinnamon and remaining sugar; sprinkle over plums.

3. For topping, in a small bowl, combine flour and sugar; cut in butter until mixture resembles coarse crumbs. Stir in walnuts if desired. Sprinkle over top.

4. Bake at 350° for 50-55 minutes or until topping is golden brown and plums are tender. Cool on a wire rack.

Banana Nut Layer Cake

On family birthdays, the "birthday child" always wants this cake!
—**PATSY HOWARD** BAKERSFIELD, CALIFORNIA

YIELD: 10-12 SERVINGS.

- ½ cup shortening
- 2 cups sugar
- 1 egg plus 1 egg white
- 1 cup buttermilk
- 1 cup mashed ripe bananas
- 1 teaspoon vanilla extract
- 2 cups all-purpose flour
- 1 teaspoon baking soda
- 1 teaspoon salt
- ½ cup chopped walnuts

FILLING
- ¼ cup butter, cubed
- ½ cup packed brown sugar
- ¼ cup all-purpose flour
- Pinch salt
- ¾ cup milk

1 egg yolk
1 teaspoon vanilla extract
½ cup chopped walnuts
Confectioners' sugar

1. In a large bowl, cream shortening and sugar until light and fluffy. Beat in egg and egg white. Add the buttermilk, bananas and vanilla. Combine flour, baking soda and salt; stir into the creamed mixture. Stir in walnuts.

2. Pour into two greased and floured 9-in. round baking pans. Bake at 350° for 35 minutes or until a toothpick inserted near the center comes out clean. Cool in pans 10 minutes before removing to a wire rack.

3. For filling, in a small saucepan, melt butter and brown sugar over medium heat. In a small bowl, combine flour and salt with a small amount of milk until smooth. Gradually add the remaining milk. Stir in egg yolk. Add to brown sugar mixture. Cook and stir mixture over medium heat for about 10 minutes or until thickened.

4. Remove from the heat; add vanilla and nuts. Cool. Spread between cake layers. Dust with confectioners' sugar. Chill. Store in refrigerator.

Mocha Cupcakes

A bit of instant coffee adds depth of flavor to this luscious cake's chocolate frosting.

—LORNA SMITH NEW HAZELTON, BRITISH COLUMBIA

YIELD: ABOUT 1½ DOZEN.

1 cup boiling water
1 cup mayonnaise
1 teaspoon vanilla extract
2 cups all-purpose flour
1 cup sugar
½ cup baking cocoa

2 teaspoons baking soda
MOCHA FROSTING
¾ cup confectioners' sugar
¼ cup baking cocoa
½ to 1 teaspoon instant coffee granules
Pinch salt
1½ cups heavy whipping cream

1. In a large bowl, combine the water, mayonnaise and vanilla. Combine the flour, sugar, cocoa and baking soda; add to the mayonnaise mixture and beat until well mixed.

2. Fill greased or paper-lined muffins cups two-thirds full. Bake at 350° for 20-25 minutes or until a toothpick comes out clean. Cool for 10 minutes before removing to wire racks to cool completely.

3. For frosting, combine the, confectioners' sugar, cocoa, coffee granules and salt in a large bowl. Stir in cream. Place mixer beaters in bowl; cover and chill for 30 minutes. Beat frosting until stiff peaks form. Frost the cupcakes. Refrigerate leftovers.

Carrot Cake

You'll love the texture this pretty, moist cake gets from pineapple, coconut and, of course, carrots. Its traditional cream cheese frosting adds just the right amount of sweetness.

—DEBBIE JONES CALIFORNIA, MARYLAND

YIELD: 12-16 SERVINGS.

2 cups all-purpose flour
2 cups sugar
2 teaspoons ground cinnamon
1 teaspoon baking soda
½ teaspoon salt
3 eggs
1½ cups canola oil
2 cups finely grated carrots
1 teaspoon vanilla extract
1 cup well-drained crushed pineapple
1 cup flaked coconut
1 cup chopped nuts
CREAM CHEESE FROSTING
2 packages (3 ounces each) cream cheese, softened
6 tablespoons butter, softened
3 cups confectioners' sugar
1 teaspoon vanilla extract
Additional nuts

1. In a large bowl, combine the flour, sugar, cinnamon, baking soda and salt. Add the eggs, oil, carrots and vanilla; beat until combined. Stir in pineapple, coconut and nuts.

2. Pour into a greased 13-in. x 9-in. baking pan. Bake at 350° for 50-60 minutes or until a toothpick inserted near the center comes out clean. Cool on a wire rack.

3. For frosting, beat the cream cheese and butter in a small bowl until fluffy. Add the confectioners' sugar and vanilla; beat until smooth. Frost cake. Sprinkle with remaining nuts. Store in the refrigerator.

Orange Chiffon Cake

The delicate orange flavor of this simply delicious cake is perfect for rounding out a rich meal. If you don't have time to bake, just use the orange glaze to dress up a store-bought angel food cake.

—**MARJORIE EBERT** CONEWANGO VALLEY, NEW YORK

YIELD: 16 SERVINGS.

- 6 **eggs, separated**
- 2 **cups all-purpose flour**
- 1½ **cups sugar**
- 1 **teaspoon salt**
- ½ **teaspoon baking soda**
- ¾ **cup fresh orange juice**
- ½ **cup canola oil**
- 2 **tablespoons grated orange peel**
- ½ **teaspoon cream of tartar**

ORANGE GLAZE

- ½ **cup butter**
- 2 **cups confectioners' sugar**
- 2 **to 4 tablespoons fresh orange juice**
- ½ **teaspoon grated orange peel**

1. Let eggs stand at room temperature for 30 minutes. In a large bowl, combine the flour, sugar, salt and baking soda. In a bowl, whisk the egg yolks, orange juice, oil and orange peel; add to dry ingredients. Beat until well blended.

2. In another large bowl and with clean beaters, beat egg whites and cream of tartar on high speed until stiff peaks form. Fold into orange mixture.

3. Gently spoon batter into an ungreased 10-in. tube pan. Cut through the batter with a knife to remove air pockets. Bake on the lowest rack at 350° for 45-50 minutes or until top springs back when lightly touched. Immediately invert pan; cool completely. Run a knife around sides and center tube of pan. Invert cake onto a serving plate.

4. For glaze, melt butter in a small saucepan; add remaining glaze ingredients. Stir until smooth. Pour over top of cake, allowing it to drizzle down sides.

Cherry Spice Cake

At least four generations of women in my family have baked this cake. It's always my mom's pick for her birthday. I like to use cream cheese frosting, but when my mother was growing up, my grandma frosted the cake with buttercream.

—**LAURIE SANDERS** MANCHESTER, MICHIGAN

YIELD: 16 SERVINGS.

- ½ **cup butter, softened**
- 1½ **cups sugar**
- 2 **eggs**
- 2 **cups all-purpose flour**
- 1 **teaspoon ground cinnamon**
- 1 **teaspoon ground cloves**
- ½ **teaspoon baking soda**
- ¼ **teaspoon baking powder**
- ¼ **teaspoon salt**
- 1 **cup buttermilk**
- 1 **can (14½ ounces) pitted tart cherries, drained**
- ½ **cup chopped pecans or walnuts**

FROSTING

- 1 **package (8 ounces) cream cheese, softened**
- 3¾ **cups confectioners' sugar**
- 1 **to 2 teaspoons water**
- 2 **to 3 drops red food coloring, optional**

Additional chopped pecans, optional

1. Line two 9-in. round baking pans with waxed paper. Grease and flour the pans and paper; set aside.

2. In a large bowl, cream butter and sugar until light and fluffy. Add eggs, one at a time, beating well after each addition. Combine the flour, cinnamon, cloves, baking soda, baking powder and salt. Add to the creamed mixture alternately with buttermilk, beating well after each addition. Fold in cherries and pecans.

3. Pour the batter into prepared pans. Bake at 350° for 25-30 minutes or until a toothpick inserted near the center comes out clean. Cool for 10 minutes before removing from pans to wire racks to cool completely.

4. For frosting, in a large bowl, beat the cream cheese until fluffy. Add the confectioners' sugar and enough water to achieve spreading consistency. Tint with food coloring if desired. Spread frosting between layers and over top and sides of cake. Garnish with additional pecans. Store in the refrigerator.

Streusel-Topped Apple Cheesecake

I just love cheesecake and apple pie so what could be better than to combine the two! It has everything that makes an apple pie delicious—apples, cinnamon, and a nice crumble topping plus the creamy goodness of a cheesecake.

—SARAH GILBERT BEAVERTON, OREGON

YIELD: 16 SERVINGS.

1¼ cups crushed gingersnap cookies (about 25 cookies)
3 tablespoons butter, melted

FILLING

2 packages (8 ounces each) reduced-fat cream cheese
1 package (8 ounces) fat-free cream cheese
1 cup sugar
¼ cup fat-free milk
2 tablespoons all-purpose flour
1 teaspoon vanilla extract
3 eggs, lightly beaten
2 medium tart apples, peeled and thinly sliced
2 tablespoons brown sugar
1 teaspoon ground cinnamon

TOPPING

¼ cup all-purpose flour
¼ cup packed brown sugar
2 tablespoons butter, melted

1. In a small bowl, combine crushed cookies and butter. Press onto the bottom of a 9-in. springform pan coated with cooking spray. Place pan on a baking sheet. Bake at 325° for 10 minutes. Cool on a wire rack.

2. In a large bowl, beat cream cheeses and sugar until smooth. Beat in the milk, flour and vanilla. Add eggs; beat on low speed just until combined. Pour 2 cups filling over crust. In a large bowl, toss the apples, brown sugar and cinnamon until well coated; arrange over filling to within 1 in. of edges. Pour remaining filling over apple mixture. Bake at 325° for 30 minutes.

3. In a small bowl, combine topping ingredients. Sprinkle over cheesecake. Bake 15-20 minutes longer or until center is almost set. Cool on a wire rack for 10 minutes.

4. Carefully run a knife around edge of pan to loosen; cool 1 hour longer. Refrigerate overnight. Remove sides of pan.

Spicy Applesauce Cake

My moist cake cake travels and slices exceptionally well, making it perfect to pack and take along for a picnic or other outing.

—MARIAN PLATT SEQUIM, WASHINGTON

YIELD: 20-24 SERVINGS.

2 cups applesauce
1½ cups sugar
½ cup shortening
2 eggs, lightly beaten
2 cups all-purpose flour
1 tablespoon baking cocoa
1½ teaspoons baking soda
1 teaspoon salt
1 teaspoon each ground cinnamon, nutmeg, allspice and cloves
1 cup raisins
½ cup semisweet chocolate chips
½ cup chopped walnuts

TOPPING

½ cup semisweet chocolate chips
½ cup chopped walnuts
2 tablespoons brown sugar

1. In a large bowl, beat the applesauce, sugar, shortening and eggs. Combine the flour, cocoa, baking soda, salt, cinnamon, nutmeg, allspice and cloves; gradually beat into applesauce mixture until blended. Stir in the raisins, chocolate chips and walnuts.

2. Pour into a greased 13-in. x 9-in. baking pan. Combine topping ingredients and sprinkle over batter. Bake at 350° for 35-40 minutes or until a toothpick inserted near the center comes out clean. Cool on a wire rack.

Cherry Cheesecake Dessert

My grown sons consider this my signature dessert, but it really is my mother's creation. Sometimes I bake and freeze the cheesecake ahead. On the day I serve it, I thaw it, then add the fruit.

—CHRISTINE EILERTS TULSA, OKLAHOMA

YIELD: 9 SERVINGS.

- 1¼ cups graham cracker crumbs
- 2 tablespoons sugar
- ⅓ cup butter, melted

FILLING
- 2 packages (one 8 ounces, one 3 ounces) cream cheese, softened
- ½ cup sugar
- 1 teaspoon vanilla extract
- 2 eggs, lightly beaten
- 1 can (21 ounces) cherry pie filling

1. In small bowl, combine the cracker crumbs and sugar; stir in the butter. Press into a greased 8-in. square baking dish; set aside.

2. In a large bowl, beat cream cheese, sugar and vanilla until smooth. Add the eggs; beat on low speed just until combined. Pour into crust.

3. Bake at 350° for 15-20 minutes or until almost set. Cool for 1 hour on a wire rack. Refrigerate for 8 hours or overnight. Spoon pie filling over top.

Almond Pear Torte

We had fruit trees in our garden when I was growing up. My mother spiced up the pears in her torte with nutmeg, so I do, too. I serve this in the fall, when pears are abundant at the farmers market and crisp evenings call for a traditional dessert.

—TRISHA KRUSE EAGLE, IDAHO

YIELD: 14 SERVINGS.

- 1⅓ cups all-purpose flour
- ¾ cup butter, softened
- ½ cup sugar
- ½ cup ground almonds, toasted
- ¼ teaspoon ground nutmeg

FILLING
- 2 packages (8 ounces each) cream cheese, softened
- ¼ cup packed brown sugar
- ¼ teaspoon almond extract
- 2 eggs, lightly beaten

TOPPING
- ½ cup packed brown sugar
- ¼ teaspoon ground nutmeg
- 3 cups thinly sliced peeled fresh pears
- ½ cup slivered almonds

1. In a small bowl, combine the flour, butter, sugar, almonds and nutmeg. Press onto the bottom of a greased 9-in. springform pan; set aside.

2. In a large bowl, beat the cream cheese, brown sugar and extract until smooth. Add eggs; beat on low speed just until combined. Pour over crust.

3. For topping, combine brown sugar and nutmeg. Add pears; toss to coat. Arrange over top. Sprinkle with almonds.

4. Bake at 350° for 50-60 minutes or until center is almost set. Cool on a wire rack for 10 minutes. Carefully run a knife around edge of pan to loosen; cool 1 hour longer. Refrigerate leftovers.

Lemon Chiffon Cake

This moist, airy cake was my dad's favorite. Mom revamped the original recipe to include lemons. I'm not much of a baker, so I don't make it very often. But when I do, my family is thrilled!

—TRISHA KAMMERS CLARKSTON, WASHINGTON

YIELD: 12-16 SERVINGS.

7 eggs, separated
2 cups all-purpose flour
1½ cups sugar
3 teaspoons baking powder
1 teaspoon salt
¾ cup water
½ cup canola oil
4 teaspoons grated lemon peel
2 teaspoons vanilla extract
½ teaspoon cream of tartar

LEMON FROSTING
⅓ cup butter, softened
3 cups confectioners' sugar
¼ cup lemon juice
4½ teaspoons grated lemon peel
Dash salt

1. Place egg whites in a large bowl; let stand at room temperature for 30 minutes.

2. In a large bowl, combine the flour, sugar, baking powder and salt. In another bowl, whisk the egg yolks, water, oil, lemon peel and vanilla; add to dry ingredients and beat until well blended. Add cream of tartar to egg whites; with clean beaters, beat on medium speed until soft peaks form. Fold into batter.

3. Gently spoon into an ungreased 10-in. tube pan. Cut through batter with a knife to remove air pockets. Bake on the lowest oven rack at 325° for 50-55 minutes or until cake springs back when lightly touched. Immediately invert pan; cool completely, about 1 hour.

4. Run a knife around sides and center tube of pan. Remove cake to a serving plate. In a small bowl, combine frosting ingredients; beat until smooth. Frost top of cake.

PIES

Club Pie

During the '30s, my mother made this pie for the ladies in her club. I'd hurry home from school so I could help her and then try a piece myself! It became such a family favorite that Mother made it part of our Christmas meals.

—**MELVIN WELSHHAUS**
BARBERTON, OHIO

YIELD: 6-8 SERVINGS.

- ⅓ cup butter, softened
- 1 cup sugar
- 2 eggs, separated
- ¼ cup milk
- ½ cup chopped walnuts
- 1 cup raisins
- 1 unbaked pie pastry (9 inches)

Whipped cream, optional

1. In a bowl, cream butter and sugar. Add the egg yolks; beat well. Blend in milk. Stir in nuts and raisins; set aside. Using clean beaters, beat egg whites until stiff peaks form; fold into the raisin mixture. Pour into pie shell.

2. Bake the pie at 350° for 15 minutes. Reduce the temperature to 300°; bake 40 minutes longer or until lightly browned. Cool. Refrigerate. Serve pie chilled with whipped cream if desired.

Peanut Butter Pie

Who can resist a tempting chocolate crumb crust and a creamy filling with big peanut butter taste? Be prepared to take an empty plate home when you serve this pie at your next potluck.

—**DORIS DOHERTY** ALBANY, OREGON

YIELD: 8-10 SERVINGS.

- 1¼ cup chocolate cookie crumbs (20 cookies)
- ¼ cup sugar
- ¼ cup butter, melted

FILLING

- 1 package (8 ounces) cream cheese, softened
- 1 cup creamy peanut butter
- 1 cup sugar
- 1 tablespoon butter, softened
- 1 teaspoon vanilla extract
- 1 cup heavy whipping cream, whipped

Grated chocolate or chocolate cookie crumbs, optional

1. In a small bowl, combine cookie crumbs and sugar; stir in butter. Press onto the bottom and up the sides of a 9-in. pie plate. Bake at 375° for 10 minutes. Cool on a wire rack.

2. For filling, in a large bowl, beat the cream cheese, peanut butter, sugar, butter and vanilla until smooth. Fold in whipped cream. Gently spoon into crust. Garnish with chocolate or cookie crumbs if desired. Store in refrigerator.

Grandma's Berry Tart

With seven children and 12 grandchildren, our household is always busy. But everyone makes time for a slice of this fruity pie from my grandma.

—LORRAINE NUZZO STATEN ISLAND, NEW YORK

YIELD: 6-8 SERVINGS.

1¼ cups all-purpose flour
¼ teaspoon salt
¼ cup cold butter, cubed
¼ cup shortening
5 to 6 tablespoons cold water

FILLING
1 cup each fresh blueberries, raspberries, blackberries and sliced strawberries
½ cup sugar
2 tablespoons cornstarch
2 teaspoons grated lemon peel
1 teaspoon vanilla extract
½ teaspoon ground ginger
¼ teaspoon ground allspice
Milk
Additional sugar

TOPPING
¼ cup sugar
3 tablespoons all-purpose flour
2 tablespoons cold butter

1. In a small bowl, combine flour and salt; cut in butter and shortening until crumbly. Gradually add water, tossing with a fork until dough forms a ball. On a lightly floured surface, roll out dough into a 13-in. circle. Transfer to a 9-in. deep-dish pie plate.

2. Place the berries in a large bowl. Combine the sugar, cornstarch, lemon peel, vanilla, ginger and allspice; add to berries and toss gently to coat. Pour into crust. Fold edges of pastry over filling. Brush folded pastry with milk; sprinkle with sugar.

3. For topping, combine the sugar and flour in a small bowl; cut in butter until crumbly. Sprinkle over filling.

4. Bake at 400° for 50-55 minutes or until pastry is golden brown. Cool on a wire rack.

Mom's Peach Pie

A delightful summertime pie, this dessert is overflowing with fresh peach flavor. Each sweet slice is pack with old-fashioned appeal. The streusel topping makes it a little different than the ordinary fruit pie and adds homemade flair.

—SALLY HOLBROOK PASADENA, CALIFORNIA

YIELD: 6-8 SERVINGS.

- 1 refrigerated pie pastry
- 1 egg white, lightly beaten
- ¾ cup all-purpose flour
- ½ cup packed brown sugar
- ⅓ cup sugar
- ¼ cup cold butter, cubed
- 6 cups sliced peeled fresh peaches

1. Unroll pastry into a 9-in. pie plate; flute edges. Brush egg white over the bottom and sides of the pastry.

2. In a small bowl, combine flour and sugars; cut in butter until mixture resembles fine crumbs. Sprinkle two-thirds into pastry; top with peaches. Sprinkle with remaining crumb mixture.

3. Bake at 375° for 40-45 minutes or until filling is bubbly and peaches are tender.

Freezer Pumpkin Pie

Here's a cool twist on tradition with this wonderful do-ahead dessert. Gingersnaps and pecans form the delicious baked crust for this pie's pumpkin and ice cream filling.

—VERA REID LARAMIE, WYOMING

YIELD: 6-8 SERVINGS.

- 1 cup ground pecans
- ½ cup finely crushed gingersnaps

- ¼ cup sugar
- ¼ cup butter, softened

FILLING
- 1 cup canned pumpkin
- ½ cup packed brown sugar
- ½ teaspoon salt
- ½ teaspoon ground cinnamon
- ½ teaspoon ground ginger
- ¼ teaspoon ground nutmeg
- 1 quart vanilla ice cream, slightly softened

1. In a bowl, combine pecans, gingersnaps, sugar and butter; mix well. Press into a 9-in. pie pan; bake at 450° for 5 minutes. Cool completely.

2. In a bowl, beat first six filling ingredients. Stir in ice cream and mix until well blended. Spoon into crust. Freeze until firm, at least 2-3 hours. Store in freezer.

Citrus Cranberry Pie

This lattice-topped pie showcases abundant fall cranberries. A dollop of orange cream complements the slightly tart flavor.

—TASTE OF HOME TEST KITCHEN

YIELD: 6-8 SERVINGS.

Pastry for double-crust pie (9 inches)
- 3½ cups fresh or frozen cranberries
- 1 small navel orange, peeled, sectioned and chopped
- 1 cup sugar
- 2 tablespoons butter, melted
- 4½ teaspoons all-purpose flour
- 2 teaspoons grated lemon peel
- 1 teaspoon grated orange peel

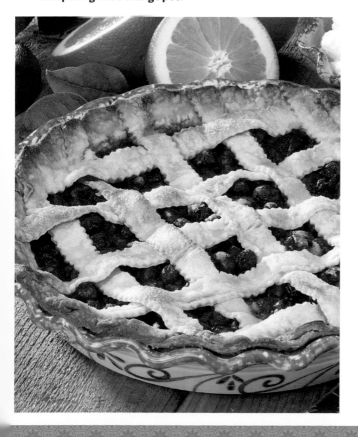

- ¼ teaspoon salt
- 1 egg, lightly beaten

Additional sugar

ORANGE CREAM
- 1 cup heavy whipping cream
- 1 tablespoon sugar
- 2 teaspoons grated orange peel
- 1 teaspoon orange extract

1. Line a 9-in. pie plate with bottom pastry; trim pastry even with edge of plate. In a large bowl, combine the cranberries, orange, sugar, butter, flour, lemon and orange peel and salt. Pour into pastry shell.

2. Roll out remaining pastry; make a lattice crust. Trim, seal and flute edges. Brush lattice crust with egg. Sprinkle with additional sugar. Cover edges loosely with foil.

3. Bake at 450° for 10 minutes. Reduce heat to 350° and remove foil. Bake 40-45 minutes longer or until golden brown.

4. Meanwhile, in a large bowl, beat cream until it begins to thicken. Add the sugar, orange peel and extract; beat until stiff peaks form. Cover and refrigerate. Serve with warm pie.

Cookie Sheet Apple Pie

This dessert is a real time-saver when you have a large crowd to feed. It serves more than a traditional pie with about the same amount of effort.

—BERTHA JEFFRIES GREAT FALLS, MONTANA

YIELD: 16-20 SERVINGS.

- 6 cups all-purpose flour
- 1½ teaspoons salt
- 1½ teaspoons baking powder
- 1½ cups shortening
- 6 egg yolks
- ¾ cup plus 4½ teaspoons water
- 3 tablespoons lemon juice
- 8 cups sliced peeled tart apples
- 1½ cups sugar
- 1 cup crushed cornflakes
- 1 teaspoon ground cinnamon
- ½ teaspoon ground nutmeg
- 1 egg white, lightly beaten

1. In a large bowl, combine the flour, salt and baking powder. Cut in shortening until mixture resembles coarse crumbs. Whisk the egg yolks, water and lemon juice; gradually add to flour mixture, tossing with a fork until dough forms a ball. Cover and refrigerate for 30 minutes.

2. Divide dough in half so that one portion is slightly larger than the other. On a lightly floured surface, roll out larger portion to fit the bottom and sides of a greased 15-in. x 10-in. x 1-in. baking pan. Arrange apples over crust. Combine the sugar, cornflakes, cinnamon and nutmeg; sprinkle over apples.

3. Roll out remaining dough to fit top of pie; place over apples. Seal edges; cut slits in top. Brush with egg white. Bake at 400° for 15 minutes. Reduce heat to 350°; bake 20-25 minutes longer or until golden brown.

Lemon Blueberry Pie

When blueberries are ripe, I find every way possible to enjoy them. My tart, delicious pie proves the point!

—PATRICIA KILE
ELIZABETHTOWN, PENNSYLVANIA

YIELD: 8 SERVINGS.

- 6 eggs, lightly beaten
- 1 cup sugar
- ½ cup butter, cubed
- ⅓ cup lemon juice
- 2 teaspoons grated lemon peel
- 1 pastry shell (9 inches), baked
- 3 cups fresh blueberries
- ⅓ cup sugar
- 1 tablespoon cornstarch
- ¼ cup orange juice

1. In a saucepan, combine the eggs, sugar, butter, lemon juice and peel; cook over medium-low heat,, stirring constantly, until mixture is thickened, about 20 minutes. Cool the mixture for 20 minutes, stirring occasionally. Pour into pie shell.

2. In a saucepan, toss blueberries and sugar. Combine the cornstarch and orange juice until smooth; add to blueberries. Cook over medium heat until mixture comes to a boil, about 8 minutes, stirring gently. Cook and stir for 2 minutes or until thickened. Cool for 15 minutes, stirring occasionally. Spoon over lemon layer. Refrigerate for 4-6 hours.

Grandma's Sour Cream Raisin Pie

The aroma of this pie baking in my farm kitchen oven reminds me of my dear grandma, who made this pretty dessert for special occasions.

—BEVERLY MEDALEN WILLOW CITY, NORTH DAKOTA

YIELD: 8 SERVINGS.

- 1 cup raisins
- ⅔ cup sugar
- 3 tablespoons cornstarch
- ⅛ teaspoon salt
- ⅛ teaspoon ground cloves
- ½ teaspoon ground cinnamon
- 1 cup (8 ounces) sour cream
- ½ cup milk
- 3 egg yolks
- ½ cup chopped nuts, optional
- 1 pie shell (9 inches), baked

MERINGUE

- 3 egg whites
- ¼ teaspoon salt
- 5 tablespoons sugar

1. In a small saucepan, place raisins and enough water to cover; bring to a boil. Remove from the heat; set aside.

2. In a large saucepan, combine the sugar, cornstarch, salt, cloves and cinnamon. Stir in sour cream and milk until smooth. Cook and stir over medium-high heat until thickened and bubbly. Reduce heat to low; cook and stir for 2 minutes longer. Remove from the heat. Stir a small amount of hot filling into egg yolks; return all to the pan, stirring constantly. Bring to a gentle boil; cook and stir for 2 minutes. Remove from the heat.

3. Drain raisins, reserving ½ cup liquid. Gently stir liquid into filling. Add raisins, and nuts if desired. Pour into pie shell.

4. For meringue, in a small bowl, beat egg whites and salt on medium speed until soft peaks form. Gradually beat in sugar, 1 tablespoon at a time, on high until stiff peaks form. Spread over hot filling, sealing edges to crust.

5. Bake at 350° for 15 minutes or until golden brown. Cool on a wire rack for 1 hour; refrigerate for 1-2 hours before serving. Refrigerate leftovers.

Lattice-Topped Apple Pie

You can't beat my mom's yummy apple pie. Pretty as a picture, the golden crust is flaky and the filling has just the right amount of spices.
—**ANNE HALFHILL** SUNBURY, OHIO

YIELD: 6-8 SERVINGS.

    5½ cups thinly sliced peeled apples (about 6 medium)
      1 cup sugar
      2 tablespoons water
    4½ teaspoons quick-cooking tapioca
      ½ teaspoon ground cinnamon
      ¼ teaspoon ground nutmeg
PASTRY
      2 cups all-purpose flour
      ½ teaspoon baking powder
      ½ teaspoon salt
      ⅔ cup shortening
      5 to 6 tablespoons cold water
      3 tablespoons butter
      2 tablespoons milk
      1 tablespoon sugar

1. In a large bowl, combine the apples, sugar, water, tapioca, cinnamon and nutmeg; toss to coat. Let stand for 15 minutes.

2. In a large bowl, combine the flour, baking powder and salt; cut in shortening until crumbly. Gradually add water, tossing with a fork until dough forms a ball. Divide in half, making one half slightly larger.

3. On a lightly floured surface, roll out larger portion of pastry to fit a 9-in. pie plate. Transfer pastry to plate; trim even with edge of plate. Add filling; dot with butter. Roll out remaining pastry; make a lattice crust.

4. Trim, seal and flute edges. Brush with milk; sprinkle with sugar. Cover edges loosely with foil.

5. Bake at 400° for 15 minutes. Reduce heat to 350°; bake 40-50 minutes longer or until crust is golden brown and filling is bubbly. Cool on a wire rack.

Fluffy Cranberry Cheese Pie

This pie has a light texture and zippy flavor that's very festive. And even though it looks fancy, it's easy to make.
—**MARY PARKONEN** W. WAREHAM, MASSACHUSETTS

YIELD: 6-8 SERVINGS.

CRANBERRY TOPPING
      1 package (3 ounces) raspberry gelatin
      ⅓ cup sugar
    1¼ cups cranberry juice
      1 can (8 ounces) jellied cranberry sauce
FILLING
      1 package (3 ounces) cream cheese, softened
      ¼ cup sugar
      1 tablespoon milk
      1 teaspoon vanilla extract
      ½ cup whipped topping
      1 pastry shell (9 inches), baked

1. In a bowl, combine the gelatin and sugar; set aside. In a saucepan, bring cranberry juice to a boil. Remove from the heat and pour over gelatin mixture, stirring to dissolve. Stir in the cranberry sauce. Chill until slightly thickened.

2. Meanwhile, in another bowl, beat cream cheese, sugar, milk and vanilla until fluffy. Fold in the whipped topping. Spread evenly into pie shell. Beat cranberry topping until frothy; pour over filling. Chill overnight.

Vanilla Custard Pie

My grandmother passed down this recipe to my mother, who in turn passed it down to me. Now my daughter is making it for her family. With a graham cracker crust, custard filling and meringue topping, this pie was one of my favorites when I was growing up and it still is today.

—BERNARD PARYS IXONIA, WISCONSIN

YIELD: 8 SERVINGS.

1¼ cups graham cracker crumbs
3 tablespoons brown sugar
⅓ cup butter, melted
FILLING
½ cup sugar
¼ cup all-purpose flour
½ teaspoon salt
2 cups milk
2 egg yolks, lightly beaten
2 teaspoons vanilla extract
MERINGUE
2 egg whites
¼ teaspoon vanilla extract
⅛ teaspoon cream of tartar
¼ cup sugar
¼ cup graham cracker crumbs

1. Combine the graham cracker crumbs, brown sugar and butter; press onto the bottom and up the sides of an ungreased 9-in. pie plate. Bake at 350° for 8-10 minutes or until lightly browned. Cool on a wire rack.

2. In a small saucepan, combine the sugar, flour and salt. Stir in milk until smooth. Cook and stir over medium-high heat until thickened and bubbly. Reduce heat; cook and stir 2 minutes longer. Remove from the heat. Stir a small amount of hot filling into egg yolks; return all to the pan. Bring to a gentle boil, stirring constantly; cook and stir 2 minutes longer. Remove from the heat. Gently stir in vanilla. Pour into crust.

3. In a small bowl, beat the egg whites, vanilla and cream of tartar on medium speed until soft peaks form. Gradually beat in sugar, 1 tablespoon at a time, on high until stiff peaks form. Spread over hot filling, sealing edges to crust. Sprinkle with graham cracker crumbs.

4. Bake at 350° for 15 minutes or until golden brown. Cool the pie on a wire rack for 1 hour. Refrigerate for at least 3 hours before serving.

Cherry-Berry Peach Pie

I had an overabundant supply of cherries one year, so I adapted several recipes to use them up. I knew this one was a keeper when I received phone calls from my mother and grandmother complimenting me on it.

—AMY HARTKE ELGIN, ILLINOIS

YIELD: 6-8 SERVINGS.

2½ cups all-purpose flour
2 tablespoons sugar
½ teaspoon salt
1 cup cold butter, cubed
4 to 6 tablespoons cold water
FILLING
2 cups fresh or frozen sliced peaches, thawed
1¾ cups pitted fresh dark sweet cherries or 1 can (15 ounces) pitted dark sweet cherries, drained
1 cup fresh or frozen blueberries, thawed
1 teaspoon almond extract
1 teaspoon vanilla extract
1½ cups sugar
¼ cup all-purpose flour
¼ cup quick-cooking tapioca
½ teaspoon salt
½ teaspoon ground nutmeg
1 tablespoon butter

1. In a large bowl, combine the flour, sugar and salt; cut in butter until crumbly. Gradually add water, tossing with a fork until dough forms a ball. Divide dough in half. Roll out one portion to fit a 9-in. deep-dish pie plate; transfer to pie plate. Trim pastry even with edge of plate; set aside.

2. In a large bowl, combine the peaches, cherries, blueberries and extracts. Combine the sugar, flour, tapioca, salt and nutmeg; sprinkle over fruit and gently toss to coat. Let stand for 15 minutes.

3. Spoon filling into crust. Dot with butter. Roll out remaining pastry; make a lattice crust. Seal and flute edges.

4. Bake at 375° for 50-55 minutes or until the crust is golden brown and filling is bubbly. Cover the edges with foil during the last 15 minutes to prevent overbrowning if necessary. Cool on a wire rack.

Toffee Almond Tart

My aunt passed this recipe on to my mother, who later shared it with me. Both of them are excellent cooks, so I knew it had to be a winner. I wasn't disappointed! The rich tart is wonderful as a holiday dessert.

—SHARLYN NICHOLS LIVINGSTON, CALIFORNIA

YIELD: 14 SERVINGS.

　2　**cups all-purpose flour**
　3　**tablespoons plus 1½ cups sugar, divided**
　¾　**cup cold butter, cubed**
　3　**egg yolks**
　1½　**cups heavy whipping cream**
　¼　**teaspoon salt**
　2　**cups sliced almonds**
　1　**teaspoon vanilla extract**

1. In a large bowl, combine the flour and 3 tablespoons sugar; cut in butter until mixture resembles fine crumbs. Add the egg yolks, tossing with a fork until combined.

2. Press dough onto the bottom and up the sides of an ungreased 11-in. fluted tart pan with removable bottom. Place pan on a baking sheet. Bake at 375° for 10 minutes or until golden brown.

3. Meanwhile, in a large saucepan, combine the cream, salt and remaining sugar. Bring to a boil over medium heat, stirring constantly. Remove from the heat; stir in almonds and vanilla. Pour into crust.

4. Bake for 30-35 minutes or until golden brown. Cool on a wire rack. Store in the refrigerator.

Creamy Pineapple Pie

Pineapple is so sweet and makes for a lovely dessert. This pie is no exception. It is so easy to whip up, yet it's fancy enough to serve to guests.

—BONNIE SANDLIN LAKELAND, FLORIDA

YIELD: 6-8 SERVINGS.

　¼　**cup sugar**
　3　**tablespoons cornstarch**
　1⅓　**cups pineapple juice**
　1　**egg yolk**
　2　**cups fresh pineapple chunks**
　　　(½-inch pieces)
　1　**pastry shell (9 inches), baked**
　¼　**cup flaked coconut, toasted**

1. In a saucepan, combine sugar and cornstarch. Add pineapple juice; bring to a boil, stirring occasionally. Boil for 2 minutes.

2. In a small bowl, beat egg yolk; stir in ¼ cup of hot mixture. Return all to pan; cook and stir for 1 minute. Remove from the heat; stir in pineapple.

3. Pour into the crust. Refrigerate for 2 hours or until firm. Store in the refrigerator. Sprinkle with coconut just before serving.

Editor's Note: *Canned pineapple can be substituted for fresh. Use one 20-ounce can and one 8-ounce can of pineapple tidbits. Drain, reserving juice. Add additional pineapple juice if necessary to measure 1⅓ cups. Prepare recipe as directed.*

Four-Fruit Pie

Buy the rhubarb, blueberries and raspberries when they are in season and freeze. That way you can make this fruit-filled pie any time of the year.

—JOAN ROSE LANGLEY, BRITISH COLUMBIA

YIELD: 6-8 SERVINGS.

- 1 **cup sliced rhubarb (1-inch pieces)**
- 1 **cup chopped peeled apple**
- 1 **cup blueberries**
- 1 **cup raspberries**
- 1 **teaspoon lemon juice**
- ¾ **cup sugar**
- ¼ **cup all-purpose flour**

Pastry for double-crust pie (9 inches)

- 2 **tablespoons butter**

Additional sugar, optional

1. In a large bowl, gently toss rhubarb, apple, berries and lemon juice. Combine sugar and flour; stir into the fruit and let stand for 30 minutes.

2. Line a pie plate with bottom crust. Add filling; dot with butter. Roll out remaining pastry to fit top of pie. Place over filling. Trim, seal and flute edges. Cut slits in pastry. Bake at 400° for 50-60 minutes or until crust is golden brown. Sprinkle with sugar if desired. Cool on a wire rack. Store in the refrigerator.

Pecan Fudge Pie

Everyone will swoon over this chocolaty twist on traditional pecan pie. Top each slice with a dollop of whipped cream, and you'll be basking in compliments as soon as people dig in!

—JACQUELYN SMITH SOPERTON, GEORGIA

YIELD: 6-8 SERVINGS.

- 1¼ **cups light corn syrup**
- ½ **cup sugar**
- ⅓ **cup baking cocoa**
- ⅓ **cup all-purpose flour**
- ¼ **teaspoon salt**

3 eggs
3 tablespoons butter, softened
1½ teaspoons vanilla extract
1 cup chopped pecans
1 unbaked pastry shell (9 inches)
Whipped cream, optional

1. In a large bowl, beat the first eight ingredients until smooth. Stir in nuts; pour into pie shell. Bake at 350° for 55-60 minutes or until set. Cool pie completely. Garnish with whipped cream if desired.

Grandma's Chocolate Meringue Pie

My grandmother served chocolate meringue pie after Sunday dinner each week, usually with an apology, saying it was "too runny" or had something else wrong with it. Of course, it was never less than perfect!

—**DONNA VEST TILLEY** CHESTERFIELD, VIRGINIA

YIELD: 8 SERVINGS.

¾ cup sugar
5 tablespoons baking cocoa
3 tablespoons cornstarch
¼ teaspoon salt
2 cups milk
3 egg yolks, beaten
1 teaspoon vanilla extract
1 pie shell (9 inches), baked
MERINGUE
3 egg whites
¼ teaspoon cream of tartar
6 tablespoons sugar

1. In a saucepan, mix sugar, cocoa, cornstarch and salt; gradually add milk. Cook and stir over medium-high heat until thickened and bubbly. Reduce heat; cook and stir 2 minutes more. Remove from heat. Stir about 1 cup of the hot filling into the egg yolks. Return to saucepan and bring to a gentle boil. Cook and stir 2 minutes. Remove from the heat and stir in vanilla. Pour hot filling into pie crust.

2. For meringue, beat egg whites with cream of tartar until soft peaks form. Gradually add sugar and continue to beat until stiff and glossy. Spread evenly over hot filling, sealing meringue to pie crust. Bake at 350° for 12-15 minutes or until golden.

Sour Cream Apple Pie

A cool, creamy version of the original, this delicious dessert is the perfect finish to a satisfying summer meal. Its crumbly topping and smooth apple filling are delightful!

—**SHARON BICKETT** CHESTER, SOUTH CAROLINA

YIELD: 8 SERVINGS.

2 eggs
1 cup (8 ounces) sour cream
1 cup sugar
6 tablespoons all-purpose flour, divided
1 teaspoon vanilla extract
¼ teaspoon salt
3 cups chopped peeled tart apples
1 unbaked pie shell (9 inches)
¼ cup packed brown sugar
3 tablespoons cold butter

1. In a large bowl, beat eggs. Add sour cream. Stir in sugar, 2 tablespoons flour, vanilla and salt; mix well. Gently stir in apples. Pour into pie shell. Bake at 375° for 15 minutes.

2. Meanwhile, combine brown sugar and remaining flour; cut in butter until mixture is crumbly. Sprinkle over top of pie. Bake 20 to 25 minutes longer or until filling is set. Cool completely on a wire rack. Serve or cover and refrigerate.

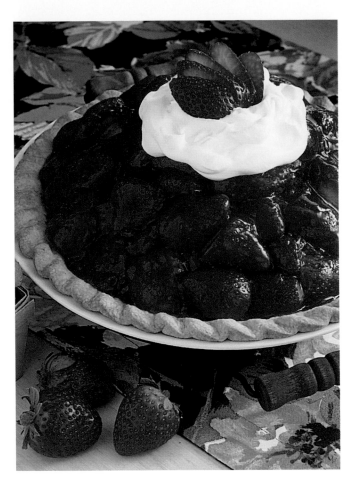

Sky-High Strawberry Pie

This pie is my specialty. It's fairly simple to make but so dramatic to serve. The ultimate taste of spring, this luscious pie has a big, fresh berry taste. I'm often asked to bring it to gatherings.

—JANET MOOBERRY PEORIA, ILLINOIS

YIELD: 8-10 SERVINGS.

```
  3  quarts fresh strawberries, divided
1½  cups sugar
  6  tablespoons cornstarch
⅔   cup water
Red food coloring, optional
  1  deep-dish pastry shell (10 inches), baked
  1  cup heavy whipping cream
4½  teaspoons instant vanilla pudding mix
```

1. In a large bowl, mash enough berries to equal 3 cups. In a large saucepan, combine sugar and cornstarch. Stir in mashed berries and water. Bring to a boil over medium heat, stirring constantly. Cook and stir for 2 minutes or until thickened.

2. Remove from the heat; add food coloring if desired. Pour into a large bowl. Chill for 20 minutes, stirring occasionally, until mixture is just slightly warm. Fold in the remaining berries. Pile into pastry shell. Chill for 2-3 hours.

3. In a small bowl, beat cream until soft peaks form. Sprinkle dry pudding mix over cream and beat until stiff. Pipe around edge of pie or dollop on individual slices.

Rustic Autumn Fruit Tart

Your guests are sure to love this impressive dessert featuring rich, buttery pastry with apple and pear. It's surprisingly easy.
—JENNIFER WICKES PINE BEACH, NEW JERSEY

YIELD: 6 SERVINGS.

```
½   cup butter, softened
  4  ounces cream cheese, softened
1½  cups all-purpose flour
  2  large apples, peeled and thinly sliced
  1  medium pear, peeled and thinly sliced
4½  teaspoons cornstarch
½   teaspoon ground cinnamon
¼   teaspoon ground cardamom
¼   teaspoon ground nutmeg
¼   cup orange juice
⅓   cup packed brown sugar
½   cup apricot jam, warmed
```

1. In a small bowl, beat butter and cream cheese until smooth. Gradually add the flour, beating just until mixture forms a ball. Cover and refrigerate for 1 hour.

2. In a large bowl, combine apples and pear. In a small bowl, combine cornstarch and spices; stir in orange juice until smooth. Stir in brown sugar until blended. Add to apple mixture and stir gently to coat.

3. On a lightly floured surface, roll out dough into a 14-in. circle. Transfer to a parchment paper-lined baking sheet. Spoon filling over the pastry to within 2 in. of edges. Fold up edges of pastry over filling, leaving center uncovered.

4. Bake at 375° for 40-45 minutes or until crust is golden and filling is bubbly. Spread with apricot jam. Using parchment paper, slide tart onto a wire rack to cool.

Coconut-Pecan Pie

I grew up on a farm with pecan trees, so we always had plenty of nuts for baking. Here's one of my favorites uses for them.

—BARBARA ANN MCKENZIE
KEYTESVILLE, MISSOURI

YIELD: 6-8 SERVINGS.

  3 **eggs**
1½ **cups sugar**
  ½ **cup butter, melted**
  2 **teaspoons lemon juice**
  1 **teaspoon vanilla extract**
1¼ **cups flaked coconut**
  ½ **cup coarsely chopped pecans**
  1 **unbaked pastry shell (9 inches)**

1. In a bowl, beat eggs. Add sugar, butter, lemon juice and vanilla; mix well. Stir in coconut and pecans; pour into pie shell.

2. Bake at 350° for 45-50 minutes or until set. Cool completely. Store in the refrigerator.

Cran-Raspberry Pie

Jewel-toned fruits team up to pack this lattice-topped pie. It's a lovely addition to holiday meals.

—VERONA KOEHLMOOS PILGER, NEBRASKA

YIELD: 6-8 SERVINGS.

  2 **cups chopped fresh or frozen cranberries**
  5 **cups fresh or frozen unsweetened raspberries, thawed**
  ½ **teaspoon almond extract**
  1 **to 1¼ cups sugar**
  ¼ **cup quick-cooking tapioca**
  ¼ **teaspoon salt**
Pastry for double-crust pie (9 inches)

1. In a large bowl, combine the cranberries, raspberries and extract. Combine the sugar, tapioca and salt. Add to fruit mixture; toss gently to coat. Let stand for 15-20 minutes.

2. Line pie plate with bottom pastry; trim to 1 in. beyond edge of plate. Add filling. Roll out remaining pastry; make a lattice crust. Trim, seal and flute edges. Cover edges loosely with foil.

3. Bake at 375° for 40-45 minutes or until crust is golden brown and filling is bubbly. Cool on a wire rack.

Fall Pear Pie

A wide slice of this festive, fruity pie is a great way to end a delicious meal. The mellow flavor of pears is a refreshing alternative to the more traditional pies prepared for the holidays. It's nice to serve a dessert that's a little unexpected.

—KEN CHURCHES KAILUA-KONA, HAWAII

YIELD: 8 SERVINGS.

    8 cups thinly sliced peeled pears
    ¾ cup sugar
    ¼ cup quick-cooking tapioca
    ¼ teaspoon ground nutmeg
Pastry for double-crust pie (9 inches)
    1 egg, lightly beaten
    ¼ cup heavy whipping cream, optional

1. In a large bowl, combine the pears, sugar, tapioca and nutmeg; let stand for 15 minutes.

2. Line a pie plate with bottom crust; add pear mixture. Roll out remaining pastry to fit top of pie; cut large slits in top. Place over filling; seal and flute edges. Brush with egg.

> Granny would roll out her pie crusts into thin layers, and she'd always poke a hole in the middle of one of the smaller crusts. Then she'd bake them until they were light brown and crisp. When they cooled, she'd spread jelly on the crust with the hole. I stood in her kitchen with my chin on the counter and my mouth watering—I could hardly wait for that special treat she made just for me!
>
> **— SHERRIE CALLISON** CABOT, ARKANSAS

3. Bake at 375° for 55-60 minutes or until pears are tender. Remove to a wire rack. Pour the cream through slits if desired. Cool.

Strawberry-Pecan Pie

I stock up on locally grown berries for treats like this pie, which pairs them with pecans. I received a ribbon for this at the strawberry festival in nearby Poteet.

—BECKY DUNCAN LEMING, TEXAS

YIELD: 6-8 SERVINGS.

    1½ cups sugar
    ¼ cup all-purpose flour
    1 teaspoon ground nutmeg
    1 teaspoon ground cinnamon
    2 cups chopped fresh strawberries
    1 cup chopped pecans
Pastry for double-crust pie (9 inches)
    1 to 2 tablespoons butter

1. In a large bowl, combine the sugar, flour, nutmeg and cinnamon. Add strawberries and pecans; toss gently.

2. Line pie plate with bottom crust. Add filling; dot with butter. Make lattice top. Bake at 375° for 50-55 minutes or until crust is golden brown. Cool on a wire rack.

Raspberry Ribbon Pie

As a boy, my husband considered this his favorite Christmas dessert. When we married, his mother gave me the recipe. I take it to family gatherings during the holidays and have yet to bring any leftovers home! It's a cool recipe for summer as well.
—**VICTORIA NEWMAN** ANTELOPE, CALIFORNIA

YIELD: 6-8 SERVINGS.

2 packages (3 ounces each) cream cheese, softened
½ cup confectioners' sugar
Dash salt
1 cup heavy whipping cream, whipped
Pastry for deep-dish single-crust pie (9 inches), baked
1 package (3 ounces) raspberry gelatin

1¼ cups boiling water
1 tablespoon lemon juice
1 package (10 ounces) frozen raspberries in syrup, thawed

1. In a large bowl, beat the cream cheese, sugar and salt until smooth. Fold in cream. Spread half into pie shell. Chill 30 minutes.

2. Meanwhile, dissolve gelatin in water; add lemon juice and raspberries. Carefully spoon half over cream cheese layer. Chill until set, about 30 minutes.

3. Set aside the remaining gelatin mixture at room temperature. Carefully spread remaining cream cheese mixture over top of pie. Chill for 30 minutes. Top with remaining gelatin. Chill until firm.

Peach Cream Pie

The sour cream filling and cinnamon crumb topping complement the fruit flavor in this yummy pie.

—DENISE GOEDEKEN
PLATTE CENTER, NEBRASKA

YIELD: 6-8 SERVINGS.

1½ cups all-purpose flour
½ teaspoon salt
½ cup cold butter, cubed

FILLING

4 cups unsweetened sliced peaches (about 6 medium)
1 cup sugar, divided
2 tablespoons all-purpose flour
1 egg
½ teaspoon vanilla extract
¼ teaspoon salt
1 cup (8 ounces) sour cream

TOPPING

⅓ cup sugar
⅓ cup all-purpose flour
1 teaspoon ground cinnamon
¼ cup cold butter, cubed

1. In a small bowl, combine flour and salt; cut in butter until crumbly. Press into a 9-in. pie plate.

2. For filling, place peaches in a large bowl; sprinkle with ¼ cup sugar and toss gently to coat. In another small bowl, combine the flour, egg, vanilla, salt and remaining sugar; fold in sour cream. Stir into peaches.

3. Pour into crust. Bake at 400° for 15 minutes. Reduce heat to 350°; bake for 20 minutes.

4. Meanwhile, prepare topping. In a small bowl, combine the sugar, flour and cinnamon. Cut in butter until crumbly. Sprinkle topping over top of pie. Bake at 450° for 15 minutes or until topping is browned. Cool on a wire rack. Store in the refrigerator.

Creamy Banana Pie

When I read that *Taste of Home* was having a banana recipe contest, I knew instantly the recipe I should share. This delectable pie is from a recipe I found years ago, and everyone who tastes it enjoys its delicious old-fashioned flavor.

—RITA PRIBYL WAUKESHA, WISCONSIN

YIELD: 8 SERVINGS.

1 envelope unflavored gelatin
¼ cup cold water
¾ cup sugar
¼ cup cornstarch
½ teaspoon salt
2¾ cups milk
4 egg yolks, beaten
2 tablespoons butter
1 tablespoon vanilla extract
4 medium firm bananas, divided
1 cup heavy whipping cream, whipped
1 pastry shell (10 inches), baked
Juice and grated peel of 1 lemon
½ cup apple jelly

1. Soften gelatin in cold water; set aside. In a saucepan, combine the sugar, cornstarch and salt. Whisk in the milk until smooth. Cook and stir over medium-high heat until thickened and bubbly. Reduce heat; cook and stir 2 minutes longer. Remove from the heat.

2. Stir a small amount of hot filling into yolks. Return all to the pan, stirring constantly. Bring to a gentle boil. Cook and stir 2 minutes longer. Remove from the heat; stir in softened gelatin until dissolved. Stir in butter and vanilla. Cover the surface of custard with plastic wrap and chill until no longer warm.

3. Slice 3 bananas; fold into custard along with whipped cream. Spoon into pie shell. Cover and refrigerate until set, about 4-5 hours.

4. Just before serving, place the lemon juice in a small bowl and slice the remaining banana into it. Melt jelly in a saucepan over low heat. Drain banana; pat dry and arrange over filling. Brush banana with the jelly. Sprinkle with grated lemon peel. Serve immediately. Refrigerate leftovers.

Editor's Note: *The filling is very light in color. It is not topped with additional whipped cream.*

Cherry Pie

For a traditional delicious treat, serve this pretty cherry pie.

—FRANCES POSTE WALL, SOUTH DAKOTA

YIELD: 6-8 SERVINGS.

PASTRY
- 1½ cups all-purpose flour
- ½ teaspoon salt
- ½ cup shortening
- ¼ cup ice water

FILLING
- 2 cans (16 ounces each) tart cherries
- 1 cup sugar
- 3 tablespoons quick-cooking tapioca
- ¼ teaspoon almond extract
- ¼ teaspoon salt
- Red food coloring, optional
- 1 tablespoon butter

1. In a large bowl, combine flour and salt; cut in shortening until crumbly. Gradually add water, tossing with a fork until dough forms a ball. Divide dough in half. Roll out one portion. Line a 9-in. pie plate with the bottom crust; trim pastry even with edge.

2. Drain cherries, reserving ¼ cup juice. In a large bowl, combine the sugar, tapioca, extract, salt, food coloring if desired and reserved juice. Gently stir in the cherries; let stand for 15 minutes.

3. Pour into the crust. Dot with butter. Roll out remaining pastry; make a lattice crust. Seal and flute edges. Bake at 375° for 55-60 minutes. Cool on a wire rack.

Golden Apricot Pie

Our pie has wonderful apricot flavor. The fruit's golden-orange color shows through the lattice top beautifully.

—JO AND JOE MARTIN PATTERSON, CALIFORNIA

YIELD: 8 SERVINGS.

- 2 packages (6 ounces each) dried apricots
- 2¾ cups water
- Pastry for double-crust pie (9 inches)
- 1 cup sugar
- 3 tablespoons cornstarch
- ⅛ teaspoon nutmeg
- 1 tablespoon butter

1. In a small saucepan, combine apricots and water; bring to a boil. Reduce heat and simmer for 20-22 minutes. Remove from the heat; cool.

2. Place bottom pastry in a 9-in. pie plate. Drain the apricots, reserving ¾ cup liquid. Arrange apricots in pie shell. Combine the sugar, cornstarch, nutmeg and reserved apricot liquid.

3. Pour over apricots; dot with butter. Top with a lattice crust. Bake at 400° for 50-55 minutes or until crust is golden brown and filling is bubbly.

Praline Pumpkin Pie

This makes a sweet ending to winter meals. The sweet pecans are a delightful contrast to the smooth pumpkin filling.

—SANDRA HAASE BALTIMORE, MARYLAND

YIELD: 10 SERVINGS.

- ⅓ cup finely chopped pecans
- ⅓ cup packed brown sugar
- 3 tablespoons butter, softened
- 1 unbaked pastry shell (10 inches)

FILLING
- 3 eggs, lightly beaten
- ½ cup sugar
- ½ cup packed brown sugar
- 2 tablespoons all-purpose flour
- ¾ teaspoon ground cinnamon
- ½ teaspoon salt
- ½ teaspoon ground ginger
- ¼ teaspoon ground cloves
- 1 can (15 ounces) solid-pack pumpkin
- 1½ cups half-and-half cream
- Additional chopped pecans, optional

1. In a small bowl, combine the pecans, sugar and butter; press onto the bottom of pie shell. Prick sides of pastry with a fork. Bake at 450° for 10 minutes. Cool on a wire rack for 5 minutes. Reduce heat to 350°.

2. For filling, combine the eggs, sugars, flour and spices in a large bowl; stir in pumpkin. Gradually add cream. Pour into pastry shell. If desired, sprinkle chopped pecans on top.

3. Bake at 350° for 45-50 minutes or until a knife inserted near the center comes out clean. Cool on a wire rack for 1 hour. Refrigerate for at least 3 hours before serving. Store in the refrigerator.

Blueberry Pie with Lemon Crust

I just had to share this recipe. Mom and I have fun making it together, and I hope to one day be a great baker like she is.

—SARA WEST BROKEN ARROW, OKLAHOMA

YIELD: 6-8 SERVINGS.

     2   **cups all-purpose flour**
     1   **teaspoon salt**
    ½   **teaspoon grated lemon peel**
    ⅔   **cup shortening**
     1   **tablespoon lemon juice**
     4   **to 6 tablespoons cold water**
FILLING
     4   **cups fresh blueberries**
    ¾   **cup sugar**
     3   **tablespoons all-purpose flour**
    ½   **teaspoon grated lemon peel**
Dash salt
     1   **to 2 teaspoons lemon juice**
     1   **tablespoon butter**

1. In a large bowl, combine the flour, salt and lemon peel. Cut in the shortening until crumbly. Add lemon juice. Gradually add water, tossing with a fork until a ball forms. Cover and refrigerate for 1 hour.

2. Divide dough in half. On a lightly floured surface, roll out one portion to fit a 9-in. pie plate. Transfer pastry to pie plate; trim to 1 in. beyond edge of plate.

3. In a large bowl, combine the blueberries, sugar, flour, lemon peel and salt; spoon into crust. Drizzle with lemon juice; dot with butter. Roll out remaining pastry; place over filling. Seal and flute edges. Cut slits in top crust.

4. Bake at 400° for 40-45 minutes or until the crust is golden brown and filling is bubbly. Cool pie on a wire rack. Store in the refrigerator.

Rhubarb Meringue Pie

My husband's grandmother was a great cook and didn't always share her secrets, so we are fortunate to have her recipe for rhubarb cream pie. I added one of my favorite crusts and a never-fail meringue.

—ELAINE SAMPSON COLESBURG, IOWA

YIELD: 6-8 SERVINGS.

    ¾   **cup all-purpose flour**
    ¼   **teaspoon salt**
    ¼   **teaspoon sugar**
    ¼   **cup shortening**

1 tablespoon beaten egg
¼ teaspoon white vinegar
3 to 4½ teaspoons cold water

FILLING

3 cups chopped fresh or frozen rhubarb
1 cup sugar
2 tablespoons all-purpose flour
Dash salt
3 egg yolks
1 cup heavy whipping cream

MERINGUE

4 teaspoons plus ⅓ cup sugar, divided
2 teaspoons cornstarch
⅓ cup water
3 egg whites
⅛ teaspoon cream of tartar

1. In a small bowl, combine flour, salt and sugar; cut in shortening until crumbly. Combine egg and vinegar; sprinkle over crumb mixture. Gradually add water, tossing with a fork until a ball forms. Cover and chill for 1 hour or until easy to handle.

2. On a lightly floured surface, roll out pastry to fit a 9-in. pie plate. Trim to ½ in. beyond edge of plate; flute edges.

3. Place rhubarb in crust. Whisk the sugar, flour, salt, egg yolks and cream; pour over rhubarb. Bake at 350° for 50-60 minutes or until a knife comes out clean.

4. In a small saucepan, combine 4 teaspoons sugar and cornstarch. Gradually stir in water. Bring to a boil, stirring constantly; cook for 1-2 minutes or until thickened. Cool to room temperature.

5. In a small bowl, beat egg whites and cream of tartar until frothy. Add cornstarch mixture; beat on high until soft peaks form. Gradually beat in remaining sugar, 1 tablespoon at a time, on high until stiff glossy peaks form and sugar is dissolved.

6. Spread evenly over hot filling, sealing edges to crust. Bake for 15 minutes or until meringue is golden brown. Cool on a wire rack for 1 hour. Store in the refrigerator.

Editor's Note: *If using frozen rhubarb, measure rhubarb while still frozen, then thaw completely. Drain in a colander, but do not press liquid out.*

Irish Coffee Pie

Even though we aren't Irish, my Mom made this pie for my dad every St. Patrick's Day.

—HOLLY NAUROTH FRUITA, COLORADO

YIELD: 4 SERVINGS.

⅔ cup graham cracker crumbs
2 tablespoons sugar
2 tablespoons butter, melted
4 ounces cream cheese, softened
¼ cup sugar
¼ cup water
1 tablespoon whiskey, optional
2 teaspoons instant coffee granules
1 carton (8 ounces) frozen whipped topping, thawed

1. Combine the cracker crumbs, sugar and butter; press onto the bottom and up the sides of a greased 7-in. pie plate. Bake at 375° for 8-10 minutes or until lightly browned. Cool on a wire rack.

2. In a small bowl, beat the cream cheese and sugar until smooth. Combine the water, whiskey if desired and coffee granules; beat into cream cheese mixture until smooth. Fold in whipped topping.

3. Spoon into the crust. Cover and refrigerate for at least 2 hours before serving. Refrigerate leftovers.

COOKIES
& BARS

Spiced Oatmeal Cookies

I'm the fourth generation of cooks in my family to bake these cookies. When my grandmother sent me a batch for my birthday one year, I asked her for the recipe—not knowing I already had it in a booklet of handwritten recipes she'd given me. Embarrassed, I looked—and sure enough, there it was. That's when I learned it was originally my great-grandmother's recipe. I'll be certain to pass it down to the next generation!

—LORETTA PAKULSKI INDIAN RIVER, MICHIGAN

YIELD: 4 DOZEN.

1 cup shortening
2 cups packed brown sugar
2 eggs
2 tablespoons milk
2½ cups all-purpose flour
2 cups old-fashioned oats
1 teaspoon baking soda
1 teaspoon salt
1 teaspoon ground cinnamon

1. In a bowl, cream shortening and brown sugar. Add eggs and milk; mix well. Combine flour, oats, baking soda, salt and cinnamon; add to the creamed mixture.

2. Drop by rounded teaspoonfuls 2 in. apart onto lightly greased baking sheets. Bake at 350° for 12-15 minutes or until done. Remove to wire racks.

Fudge Brownies

There's no brownie recipe or mix I've ever tried that's better than this! It's so easy—you can mix it in just a few minutes. My husband's grandmother passed the recipe down to us and now our son makes these brownies for after-school snacks.

—**BECKY ALBRIGHT** NORWALK, OHIO

YIELD: ABOUT 24 BROWNIES.

- 1⅓ cups all-purpose flour
- 2 cups sugar
- ¾ cup baking cocoa
- 1 teaspoon baking powder
- ½ teaspoon salt
- ½ cup chopped nuts
- ⅔ cup vegetable oil
- 4 eggs, lightly beaten
- 2 teaspoons vanilla extract
- 1 cup chopped nuts, optional

1. In a bowl, combine first six ingredients. In another bowl, combine oil, eggs and vanilla; add to dry ingredients. Do not overmix ingredients.

2. Spread in a 13-in. x 9-in. baking pan. Sprinkle with nuts if desired. Bake at 350° for 20-25 minutes or until toothpick inserted in center comes out clean.

Pizzelle

My Italian-born mother and grandmother used old irons on a gas stove when they made their pizzelle. I modified their original and make them in the convenient electric pizzelle irons. The cookies are so delectable and beautiful, they're worth it!

—**ELIZABETH SCHWARTZ** TREVORTON, PENNSYLVANIA

YIELD: 7 DOZEN.

- 18 eggs
- 3½ cups sugar
- 1¼ cups canola oil

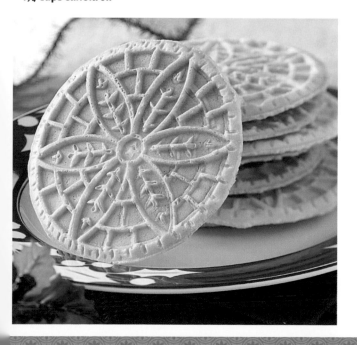

- 1 tablespoon anise oil
- 6½ cups all-purpose flour

1. In a large bowl, beat the eggs, sugar and oils until smooth. Gradually add flour and mix well.

2. Bake in a preheated pizzelle iron according to the manufacturer's directions until golden brown. Remove to wire racks to cool. Store in an airtight container.

Soft Buttermilk Sugar Cookies

Gatherings are very important to my family and we have lots of recipes we like to share. My grandma introduced these cookies into the family a long time ago. They always remind me of her.

—**TRACI ROWLETT** OLDENBURG, INDIANA

YIELD: ABOUT 2½ DOZEN.

- ½ cup shortening
- 1¼ cups sugar, divided
- 2 eggs
- 2 teaspoons vanilla extract
- 2 cups all-purpose flour
- 2 teaspoons baking powder
- 1 teaspoon salt
- ½ teaspoon baking soda
- ½ cup buttermilk
- ¼ teaspoon ground cinnamon

1. In a large bowl, cream shortening and 1 cup sugar until light and fluffy. Beat in eggs and vanilla. Combine the flour, baking powder, salt and baking soda; add to creamed mixture alternately with buttermilk, beating well after each addition (batter will be moist).

2. Combine cinnamon and remaining sugar. Drop dough by tablespoonfuls onto greased baking sheets. Sprinkle with cinnamon-sugar.

3. Bake at 375° for 8-10 minutes or until edges begin to brown. Remove to wire racks. Store in an airtight container.

Cookie Jar Gingersnaps

My grandma kept two cookie jars in her pantry. One of the jars, which I now have, always had these crisp and chewy gingersnaps in it.

—**DEB HANDY** POMONA, KANSAS

YIELD: 3-4 DOZEN.

- ¾ cup shortening
- 1 cup sugar
- 1 egg
- ¼ cup molasses
- 2 cups all-purpose flour
- 2 teaspoons baking soda
- 1½ teaspoons ground ginger
- 1 teaspoon ground cinnamon
- ½ teaspoon salt
- Additional sugar

1. In a large bowl, cream shortening and sugar until light and fluffy. Beat in the egg and molasses. Combine the flour, baking soda, ginger, cinnamon and salt; gradually add to creamed mixture and mix well.

2. Shape rounded teaspoonfuls of dough into balls. Dip one side into sugar; place sugar side up 2 in. apart on greased baking sheets. Bake at 350° for 12-15 minutes or until lightly browned and crinkly. Remove to wire racks to cool.

Apricot-Coconut Bars

My family likes snacking on these beautiful rich-tasting bars. This recipe's one I've used and shared for over 30 years.

—**HELEN CLUTS** EDEN PRAIRIE, MINNESOTA

YIELD: 2 TO 2½ DOZEN.

- 1 cup all-purpose flour
- 1 teaspoon baking powder
- ½ cup cold butter
- 1 egg
- 1 tablespoon milk
- 1 cup apricot preserves
- **TOPPING**
- 1 egg, lightly beaten
- ⅔ cup sugar
- ¼ cup butter, melted
- 1 teaspoon vanilla extract
- 2 cups flaked coconut

1. In a large bowl, combine flour and baking powder. Cut in butter until the mixture resembles coarse crumbs. In a small bowl, beat egg and milk; stir into flour mixture.

2. Spread in a greased 9-in. square baking pan. Spread preserves over crust. Combine topping ingredients; carefully drop by tablespoonfuls over apricot layer. Bake at 350° for 25-30 minutes or until golden brown. Cool on a wire rack; cut into small bars.

Chocolaty Double Crunchers

I first tried these fun crispy cookies at a family picnic when I was a child. Packed with oats, cornflakes and coconut, they quickly became a regular treat at our house. Years later, I still make them for my own family.

—**CHERYL JOHNSON** UPPER MARLBORO, MARYLAND

YIELD: 2 DOZEN.

- ½ cup butter, softened
- ½ cup sugar
- ½ cup packed brown sugar
- 1 egg
- ½ teaspoon vanilla extract
- 1 cup all-purpose flour
- ½ teaspoon baking soda
- ¼ teaspoon salt
- 1 cup quick-cooking oats
- 1 cup crushed cornflakes
- ½ cup flaked coconut
- **FILLING**
- 2 packages (3 ounces each) cream cheese, softened
- 1½ cups confectioners' sugar
- 2 cups (12 ounces) semisweet chocolate chips, melted

1. In a large bowl, cream butter and sugars until light and fluffy. Beat in egg and vanilla. Combine the flour, baking soda and salt; gradually add to creamed mixture and mix well. Stir in the oats, cornflakes and coconut.

2. Shape into 1-in. balls and place 2 in. apart on greased baking sheets. Flatten with a glass dipped lightly in flour. Bake at 350° for 8-10 minutes or until lightly browned. Remove to wire racks to cool.

3. For filling, beat cream cheese and sugar until smooth. Beat in chocolate. Spread about 1 tablespoon on half of the cookies and top each with another cookie. Store in refrigerator.

Peanut Butter Cookies

This treasured recipe is the only one my grandmother ever put in writing! When my mother got married, she asked Grandma to write down just one recipe for her. That required some real effort, because Grandma was a pioneer-type cook who used a little of this or that until it felt right.

—JANET HALL CLINTON, WISCONSIN

YIELD: 3 DOZEN.

1	**cup shortening**
1	**cup peanut butter**
1	**cup sugar**
1	**cup packed brown sugar**
3	**eggs**
3	**cups all-purpose flour**
2	**teaspoons baking soda**
¼	**teaspoon salt**

1. In a large bowl, cream shortening, peanut butter and sugars until light and fluffy. Add eggs, one at a time, beating well after each addition. Combine the flour, baking soda and salt; add to creamed mixture and mix well.

2. Roll into 1½-in. balls. Place 3 in. apart on ungreased baking sheets. Flatten with a fork or meat mallet if desired. Bake at 375° for 10-15 minutes. Remove to wire racks.

Chocolate Date Squares

My mother-in-law used to send these moist bars to my husband when he was in the Army.

—PAT WALTER PINE ISLAND, MINNESOTA

YIELD: 24 SERVINGS.

- 2 **cups chopped dates**
- 1 **cup hot water**
- 1 **cup sugar**
- ⅔ **cup shortening**
- 2 **eggs**
- 1½ **cups all-purpose flour**
- 1 **teaspoon baking soda**
- ½ **teaspoon salt**

TOPPING
- 1 **cup (6 ounces) semisweet chocolate chips**
- ½ **cup packed brown sugar**
- ½ **cup chopped nuts**

1. In a small bowl, combine dates and water; set aside to cool (do not drain). In a large bowl, cream sugar and shortening until light and fluffy. Beat in eggs. Combine the flour, baking soda and salt; gradually added to creamed mixture. Stir in dates.

2. Pour into a greased and floured 13-in. x 9-in. baking pan. Combine the topping ingredients; sprinkle over batter. Bake at 350° for 40 minutes or until a toothpick inserted near the center comes out clean. Cool on a wire rack.

Scotch Shortbread Cookies

This simple three-ingredient recipe makes wonderfully rich, tender cookies. Serve them with fresh berries of the season for a nice, light dessert. You'll get miles of smiles when you provide these for afternoon tea or at a bridal shower.

—MARLENE HELLICKSON BIG BEAR CITY, CALIFORNIA

YIELD: 4 DOZEN.

- 4 **cups all-purpose flour**
- 1 **cup sugar**
- 1 **pound cold butter, cubed**

1. In a large bowl, combine flour and sugar. Cut in butter until mixture resembles fine crumbs. Knead dough until smooth, about 6-10 times. Pat dough into an ungreased 15-in. x 10-in. x 1-in. baking pan. Pierce with a fork.

2. Bake at 325° for 25-30 minutes or until lightly browned. Cut into squares while warm. Cool on a wire rack.

Editor's Note: *This recipe makes a dense, crisp bar, so it does not call for baking powder or soda.*

Mom's Soft Raisin Cookies

With four sons in service during World War II, my mother sent these favorite cookies as a taste from home to "her boys" in different parts of the world. These days, my grandchildren are enjoying them as we did, along with my stories of long ago.

—PEARL COCHENOUR WILLIAMSPORT, OHIO

YIELD: 6 DOZEN.

- 1 cup water
- 2 cups raisins
- 1 cup shortening
- 1¾ cups sugar
- 2 eggs, lightly beaten
- 1 teaspoon vanilla extract
- 3½ cups all-purpose flour
- 1 teaspoon baking powder
- 1 teaspoon baking soda
- 1 teaspoon salt
- ½ teaspoon ground cinnamon
- ½ teaspoon ground nutmeg
- ½ cup chopped walnuts

1. Combine raisins and water in a small saucepan; bring to a boil. Cook for 3 minutes; remove from the heat and let cool (do not drain).

2. In a large bowl, cream shortening and sugar until light and fluffy. Beat in eggs and vanilla. Combine dry ingredients; gradually add to creamed mixture and mix well. Stir in nuts and raisins.

3. Drop by teaspoonfuls 2 in. apart on greased baking sheets. Bake at 350° for 12-14 minutes.

Coconut Washboards

This simple yet satisfying coconut cookie recipe has been around for generations. Pressing a fork into the top gives the look of an old-fashioned washboard.

—TOMMIE SUE SHAW
MCALESTER, OKLAHOMA

YIELD: 9 DOZEN.

- ½ cup butter, softened
- ½ cup shortening
- 2 cups packed brown sugar
- 2 eggs
- ¼ cup water
- 1 teaspoon vanilla extract
- 4 cups all-purpose flour
- 1½ teaspoons baking powder
- ½ teaspoon baking soda
- ¼ teaspoon salt
- 1 cup flaked coconut

1. In a large bowl, cream the butter, shortening and sugar until light and fluffy. Beat in eggs. Gradually add water and vanilla; mix well. Combine the flour, baking powder, baking soda and salt; add to the creamed mixture and mix well. Fold in coconut. Cover and refrigerate for 2-4 hours.

2. Shape into 1-in. balls. Place 2 in. apart on greased baking sheets; flatten with fingers into 2½-in. x 1-in. rectangles. Press lengthwise with a floured fork. Bake at 400° for 8-10 minutes or until lightly browned. Cool 2 minutes before removing to a wire rack to cool completely.

Frosted Cookie Brownies

Years ago, my children and I came up with these bars by combining two of their favorite treats. With a crisp cookie crust and a fluffy frosting, these brownies are now the most requested treats at our house.

—**ALICIA FRENCH** COLTON, CALIFORNIA

YIELD: 15 SERVINGS.

- 1 tube (18 ounces) refrigerated chocolate chip cookie dough
- 3 cups miniature marshmallows
- 2 cups (12 ounces) semisweet chocolate chips
- 1 cup butter, cubed
- 4 eggs
- 2 teaspoons vanilla extract
- 1 cup all-purpose flour
- ½ teaspoon baking powder
- ¼ teaspoon salt
- 1 cup chopped walnuts

FROSTING

- 2 cups miniature marshmallows
- 6 tablespoons milk
- ¼ cup butter, softened
- 2 ounces unsweetened chocolate
- 3 cups confectioners' sugar

1. Press cookie dough into a greased 13-in. x 9-in. baking pan. Bake at 350° for 10 minutes.

2. Meanwhile, in a large saucepan, combine marshmallows, chips and butter; cook and stir over low heat until melted and smooth. Transfer to a large bowl; cool. Beat in eggs and vanilla. Combine the flour, baking powder and salt; gradually stir into marshmallow mixture. Stir in nuts.

3. Spread over cookie crust. Bake for 30-35 minutes or until a toothpick inserted near the center comes out clean. Cool on a wire rack.

4. For frosting, in a small saucepan, combine marshmallows, milk, butter and chocolate. Cook and stir over low heat until smooth. Remove from the heat; beat in confectioners' sugar until smooth. Frost brownies. Cut into bars.

Old-Fashioned Whoopie Pies

Who can resist soft chocolate sandwich cookies filled with a layer of fluffy white frosting? Mom has made these for years. They never lasted very long with me and my two brothers around.

—**MARIA COSTELLO** MONROE, NORTH CAROLINA

YIELD: 2 DOZEN.

- ½ cup baking cocoa
- ½ cup hot water
- ½ cup shortening
- 1½ cups sugar
- 2 eggs
- 1 teaspoon vanilla extract
- 2⅔ cups all-purpose flour
- 1 teaspoon baking powder
- 1 teaspoon baking soda
- ¼ teaspoon salt
- ½ cup buttermilk

FILLING

- 3 tablespoons all-purpose flour

Dash salt

- 1 cup 2% milk
- ¾ cup shortening
- 1½ cups confectioners' sugar
- 2 teaspoons vanilla extract

1. In a small bowl, combine the cocoa and water. Cool for 5 minutes. In a large bowl, cream shortening and sugar until light and fluffy. Beat in the eggs, vanilla and cocoa mixture. Combine dry ingredients; gradually add to creamed mixture alternately with buttermilk, beating well after each addition

2. Drop by rounded tablespoonfuls 2 in. apart onto greased baking sheets. Flatten slightly with a spoon. Bake at 350° for 10-12 minutes or until firm to the touch. Remove to wire racks to cool.

3. In a small saucepan, combine flour and salt. Gradually whisk in the milk until smooth; cook and stir over medium-high heat until thick, 5-7 minutes. Remove from the heat. Cover and refrigerate until completely cool.

4. In a small bowl, cream the shortening, sugar and vanilla until light and fluffy. Add milk mixture; beat for 7 minutes or until fluffy. Spread filling on half of the cookies; top with remaining cookies. Store in the refrigerator.

Lemon Bars

I've been serving these fantastic bars for many years. The original recipe came from my mother's file. The bars have a wonderful tangy flavor, and they're always a hit.

—**ETTA SOUCY** MESA, ARIZONA

YIELD: 9 SERVINGS.

- 1   cup all-purpose flour
- ½   cup butter, softened
- ¼   cup confectioners' sugar

FILLING

- 2   eggs
- 1   cup sugar
- 2   tablespoons all-purpose flour
- ½   teaspoon baking powder
- 2   tablespoons lemon juice
- 1   teaspoon grated lemon peel

Additional confectioners' sugar

1. In a bowl, combine the flour, butter and confectioners' sugar. Pat into an ungreased 8-in. square baking pan. Bake at 350° for 20 minutes.

2. For filling, in a small bowl, beat eggs. Add the sugar, flour, baking powder, lemon juice and peel; beat until frothy. Pour over the crust. Bake 25 minutes longer or until light golden brown. Cool on a wire rack. Dust with confectioners' sugar. Cut into bars.

Chocolate-Peanut Butter Cookies

Kids will love making these easy cookies with mom, dad or the grandparents. They are dense and rich cookies—delicious with a cup of coffee.

—**ELAINE STEPHENS** CARMEL, INDIANA

YIELD: 3½ DOZEN.

- 2   cans (16 ounces each) chocolate fudge frosting, divided
- 1   egg
- 1   cup chunky peanut butter
- 1½ cups all-purpose flour

Granulated sugar

1. Set aside one can plus ⅓ cup frosting. In a large bowl, combine the egg, peanut butter and remaining frosting. Stir in flour just until moistened.

2. Drop by rounded tablespoonfuls 2 in. apart on baking sheets coated with cooking spray. Flatten cookies with a fork dipped in sugar.

3. Bake at 375° for 8-11 minutes or until set. Remove to wire racks. Cool completely; spread with reserved frosting.

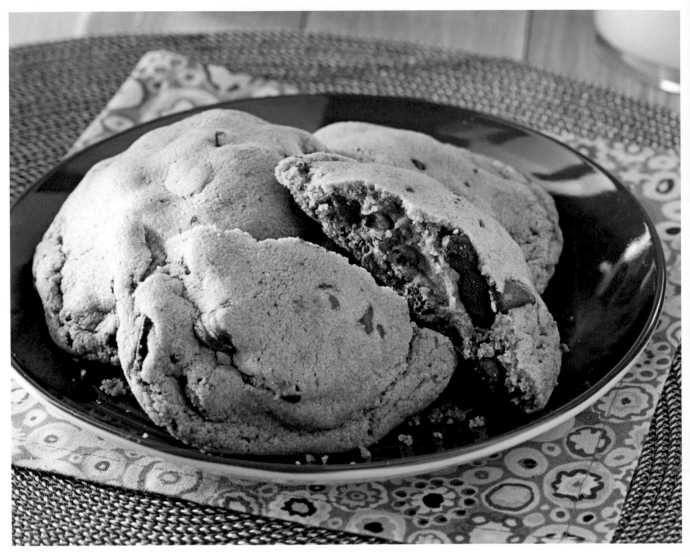

Chocolate Malted Cookies

Like good old-fashioned malted milk? Here's the next best thing! Malted milk powder, chocolate syrup, and chocolate chips and chunks make these the yummiest cookies I've ever tasted. With six kids, I've made a lot of them over the years.

—**TERI RASEY** CADILLAC, MICHIGAN

YIELD: ABOUT 1½ DOZEN.

- 1   **cup butter-flavored shortening**
- 1¼ **cups packed brown sugar**
- ½   **cup malted milk powder**
- 2   **tablespoons chocolate syrup**
- 1   **tablespoon vanilla extract**
- 1   **egg**
- 2   **cups all-purpose flour**
- 1   **teaspoon baking soda**
- ½   **teaspoon salt**
- 1½ **cups semisweet chocolate chunks**
- 1   **cup milk chocolate chips**

1. In a large bowl, beat the shortening, brown sugar, malted milk powder, chocolate syrup and vanilla for 2 minutes. Add egg.

2. Combine the flour, baking soda and salt; gradually add to creamed mixture, mixing well after each addition. Stir in chocolate chunks and chips.

3. Shape into 2-in. balls; place 3 in. apart on ungreased baking sheets. Bake at 375° for 12-14 minutes or until golden brown. Cool for 2 minutes before removing to a wire rack.

Chocolate Marshmallow Bars

I've been asked to share this chocolaty layered recipe more than any other in my collection. It's a longtime favorite of our three daughters and I can't even begin to count how many times I have made them!

—**ESTHER SHANK** HARRISONBURG, VIRGINIA

YIELD: ABOUT 3 DOZEN.

- ¾   **cup butter, softened**
- 1½ **cups sugar**
- 3   **eggs**
- 1   **teaspoon vanilla extract**
- 1⅓ **cups all-purpose flour**
- 3   **tablespoons baking cocoa**

- ½ teaspoon baking powder
- ½ teaspoon salt
- ½ cup chopped nuts, optional
- 4 cups miniature marshmallows

TOPPING
- 1⅓ cups semisweet chocolate chips
- 1 cup peanut butter
- 3 tablespoons butter
- 2 cups Rice Krispies

1. In a small bowl, cream the butter and sugar until light and fluffy. Add eggs, one at a time, beating well after each addition. Beat in vanilla.

2. Combine the flour, cocoa, baking powder and salt; gradually add to creamed mixture. Stir in nuts if desired. Spread in a greased 15-in. x 10-in. x 1-in. baking pan.

3. Bake at 350° for 15-18 minutes or until set. Sprinkle with marshmallows; bake 2-3 minutes longer or until melted. Place pan on a wire rack. Using a knife dipped in water, spread marshmallows evenly over the top. Cool completely.

4. For topping, combine the chocolate chips, peanut butter and butter in a small saucepan. Cook and stir over low heat until blended. Remove from the heat; stir in cereal. Spread over bars immediately. Chill.

Turtle Bars

This recipe of my mother's is a must for the holidays. I always have good intentions of taking some to Christmas parties, but my family finishes them too soon!

—**FAYE HINTZ** SPRINGFIELD, MISSOURI

YIELD: ABOUT 8 DOZEN.

- ½ cup butter, softened
- 1 cup packed brown sugar

- 2 cups all-purpose flour
- 1 cup pecan halves

TOPPING
- ⅔ cup butter, cubed
- ½ cup packed brown sugar
- 1 cup (6 ounces) semisweet chocolate chips

1. In a large bowl, beat the butter and sugar until smooth. Gradually add flour; beat until crumbly. Press firmly into an ungreased 13-in. x 9-in. baking pan. Arrange pecans over crust.

2. In a small heavy saucepan, combine the butter and brown sugar. Bring to a boil; boil for 1 minute or until smooth, stirring constantly. Pour over pecans.

3. Bake at 350° for 18-22 minutes or until bubbly. Sprinkle the chocolate chips on top. Cool in pan on a wire rack for 3 minutes. Spread chocolate but allow some chips to remain whole. Cool completely; cut into small squares.

Hazelnut Shortbread

Traditional shortbread only contains flour, sugar and butter, resulting in a rich, crumbly cookie. This delectable version gets added flavor from chopped hazelnuts, some maple syrup and a touch of chocolate.

—**KAREN MORRELL** CANBY, OREGON

YIELD: 6 DOZEN.

- 1 cup butter, softened
- ½ cup sugar
- 2 tablespoons maple syrup or honey
- 2 teaspoons vanilla extract
- 2 cups all-purpose flour
- 1¼ cups finely chopped hazelnuts
- ½ cup each white, red, green, yellow and dark chocolate candy coating disks

1. In a large bowl, cream butter and sugar until light and fluffy. Add syrup and vanilla. Beat in flour just until combined; fold in nuts. Shape into two 1½-in. rolls; wrap tightly in waxed paper. Chill for 2 hours or until firm.

2. Cut into ¼-in. slices and place 2 in. apart on ungreased baking sheets. Bake at 325° for 14-16 minutes or until edges begin to brown. Remove to wire racks to cool.

3. In separate microwave-safe bowls, melt candy coating disks; stir until smooth. Drizzle over cookies. Let stand until set.

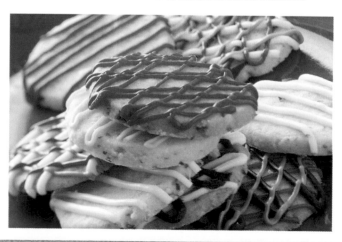

Icebox Cookies

This cookie recipe from my grandmother was my grandfather's favorite. I keep the dough in the freezer because I love to make a fresh batch when company drops in.

—**CHRIS PAULSEN** GLENDALE, ARIZONA

YIELD: ABOUT 7 DOZEN.

- ½ cup butter, softened
- 1 cup packed brown sugar
- 1 egg, beaten
- ½ teaspoon vanilla extract
- 2 cups all-purpose flour
- ½ teaspoon baking soda
- ½ teaspoon cream of tartar
- ½ teaspoon salt
- 1 cup chopped walnuts, optional

1. In a bowl, cream the butter and brown sugar. Add egg and vanilla; beat well. Combine dry ingredients; add to the creamed mixture. Stir in the nuts if desired.

2. On a lightly floured surface, shape the dough into three 10-in. x 1-in. rolls. Tightly wrap each roll in waxed paper. Freeze for at least 12 hours.

3. Cut into ⅜-in. slices and place 2 in. apart on greased baking sheets. Bake at 350° for 6-8 minutes. Remove to a wire rack to cool.

> Coffee breaks at Grandma's were a local ritual at 10 and 3 o'clock. With a fresh pot of coffee, homemade cookies, open-faced sandwiches or fresh bread with preserves, it was an event. Husbands and wives, children, field workers, neighbors, the postman, the parson... everyone gathered for food and fellowship.
>
> — **SUSAN HUPPERT**
> PALMETTO, FLORIDA

Chewy Brownie Cookies

Bite into one of these chocolaty cookies, and you'll discover they're like chewy brownies inside. Yum!

—**JONIE ADAMS** ALBION, MICHIGAN

YIELD: 3 DOZEN.

- ⅔ cup shortening
- 1½ cups packed brown sugar
- 2 eggs
- 1 tablespoon water
- 3 teaspoons vanilla extract
- 1½ cups all-purpose flour
- ⅓ cup baking cocoa
- ½ teaspoon salt
- ¼ teaspoon baking soda
- 2 cups (12 ounces) semisweet chocolate chips
- ½ cup chopped walnuts or pecans, optional

1. In a large bowl, cream shortening and sugar until light and fluffy. Beat in the eggs, water and vanilla. Combine the flour, cocoa, salt and baking soda; gradually add to creamed mixture and beat just until blended. Stir in chocolate chips and nuts if desired.

2. Drop by rounded teaspoonfuls 2 in. apart on ungreased baking sheets. Bake at 375° for 7-9 minutes; do not overbake. Cool 2 minutes before removing to wire racks to cool.

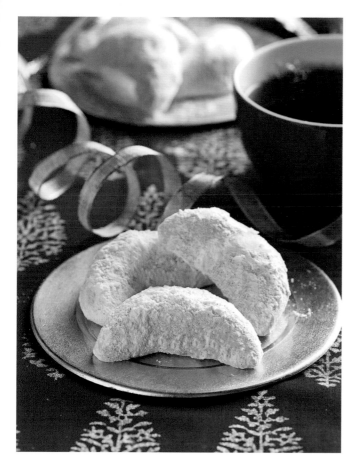

Pecan Squares

These bars are good for snacking when you're on the road or for taking to gatherings. If you love pecan pie, you will surely find them irresistible!

—**SYLVIA FORD** KENNETT, MISSOURI

YIELD: 4 DOZEN.

CRUST
- 2 **cups all-purpose flour**
- ⅓ **cup sugar**
- ¼ **teaspoon salt**
- ¾ **cup cold butter**

FILLING
- 4 **eggs**
- 1½ **cups corn syrup**
- 1½ **cups sugar**
- 3 **tablespoons butter, melted**
- 1½ **teaspoons vanilla extract**
- 2½ **cups chopped pecans**

1. In a large bowl, combine the flour, sugar and salt; cut in butter until mixture resembles coarse crumbs. Press firmly and evenly into a greased 15-in. x 10-in. x 1-in. baking pan. Bake at 350° for 20 minutes.

2. For filling, in a bowl, combine the eggs, corn syrup, sugar, butter and vanilla. Stir in pecans. Spread evenly over hot crust. Bake 25-30 minutes longer or until set. Cool on a wire rack. Cut into squares.

Vanilla Crescent Cookies

This recipe originated in Croatia and has been in my husband's family for generations. I was thrilled when my mother-in-law shared it with me.

—**BEVERLY WILLIAMS** RHINELANDER, WISCONSIN

YIELD: 4 DOZEN.

- 1 **cup butter, softened**
- 1 **cup confectioners' sugar, divided**
- 1 **teaspoon vanilla extract**
- ½ **teaspoon grated lemon peel**
- 2½ **cups all-purpose flour**
- ¼ **teaspoon salt**
- ½ **cup finely chopped walnuts**
- 2 **tablespoons sugar**
- 1 **vanilla bean**

1. In a large bowl, cream butter and ½ cup confectioners' sugar until light and fluffy. Beat in vanilla and lemon peel. Combine flour and salt; gradually add to creamed mixture and mix well. Stir in walnuts.

2. Shape tablespoonfuls of dough into crescent shapes. Place 2 in. apart on ungreased baking sheets. Bake at 375° for 10-12 minutes or until edges are lightly browned.

3. Place sugar in a food processor. Split vanilla bean and scrape seeds into food processor. Discard vanilla bean. Pulse mixture until combined. Transfer to a small bowl; stir in remaining confectioners' sugar. Coat warm cookies with sugar mixture. Cool completely on wire racks. Store in an airtight container.

Caramel-Pecan Dream Bars

These ooey-gooey cake bars pull ever so gently from the pan and hold a firm cut. They're a baker's dream come true.
—**CAY KEPPERS** NISSWA, MINNESOTA

YIELD: 2 DOZEN.

- 1 **package (18¼ ounces) yellow cake mix**
- ½ **cup butter, softened**
- 1 **egg**

FILLING
- 1 **can (14 ounces) sweetened condensed milk**
- 1 **egg**
- 1 **teaspoon vanilla extract**
- 1 **cup chopped pecans**
- ½ **cup brickle toffee bits**

1. In a large bowl, beat the cake mix, butter and egg until crumbly. Press onto the bottom of a greased 13-in. x 9-in. baking pan.

2. In a small bowl, beat the milk, egg and vanilla until combined. Stir in pecans and toffee bits. Pour over crust.

3. Bake at 350° for 20-25 minutes or until golden brown. Cool on a wire rack. Cut into bars.

Peanut Butter Squares

I grew up in Lancaster County, Pennsylvania, and spent a lot of time with my mom and grandmother in the kitchen, making Pennsylvania Dutch classics. This scrumptious recipe, which combines two of our favorite flavors, is one I adapted.
—**RACHEL GREENAWALT KELLER** ROANOKE, VIRGINIA

YIELD: 4 DOZEN.

- ¾ **cup cold butter, cubed**
- 2 **ounces semisweet chocolate**
- 1½ **cups graham cracker crumbs (about 24 squares)**
- 1 **cup flaked coconut**
- ½ **cup chopped salted peanuts**
- ¼ **cup toasted wheat germ**

FILLING
- 2 **packages (8 ounces each) cream cheese, softened**

¾ cup sugar
⅔ cup chunky peanut butter
1 teaspoon vanilla extract
TOPPING
4 ounces semisweet chocolate, chopped
¼ cup butter, cubed

1. In a microwave-safe bowl, melt butter and chocolate; stir until smooth. Stir in the cracker crumbs, coconut, peanuts and wheat germ. Press into a greased 13-in. x 9-in. pan. Cover and refrigerate for at least 30 minutes.

2. In a small bowl, combine filling ingredients. Spread over crust. Cover and refrigerate for at least 30 minutes.

3. In a microwave, melt chocolate and butter; stir until smooth. Pour over filling. Cover and refrigerate for at least 30 minutes or until topping is set. Cut into squares. Refrigerate leftovers.

Orange Cocoa Sandies

When I was growing up, I loved to help my mom cut out the appealing dessert recipes from newspapers and magazines. Then we would paste them all into a big book. This recipe is one of our favorites from the collection.

—**NELLA PARKER** HERSEY, MICHIGAN

YIELD: ABOUT 2 DOZEN.

½ cup butter, softened
½ cup plus 2 tablespoons confectioners' sugar, divided
½ teaspoon orange extract
1 cup all-purpose flour
2 tablespoons baking cocoa
½ cup finely chopped pecans

1. In a large bowl, cream butter and ½ cup confectioners' sugar until light and fluffy; beat in extract. Combine flour and cocoa; gradually add to creamed mixture. Stir in pecans.

2. Roll into 1-in. balls. Place 1 in. apart on ungreased baking sheets. Bake at 350° for 12-14 minutes or until set. Cool for 1-2 minutes before removing to wire racks. Dust with remaining confectioner's sugar.

Grandma's Date Bars

These bars are not only delicious, they're good for those trying to make healthier food choices, as they use no shortening, butter or oil. My great-grandmother, who was born in 1868, made these bars, and the recipe has come down through the generations. Now my children are making them.

—**MARILYN REID**
CHERRY CREEK, NEW YORK

YIELD: 16 SERVINGS.

1 cup sugar
1 cup all-purpose flour
1 teaspoon baking powder
½ teaspoon salt
1 cup chopped dates
1 cup chopped walnuts
3 eggs, beaten
Confectioners' sugar

1. In a large bowl, combine the first seven ingredients. Transfer to a greased 8-in. square baking pan.

2. Bake at 350° for 25 minutes or until a toothpick inserted near the center comes out clean. Cool on a wire rack. Dust with confectioners' sugar. Cut into squares.

Gingerbread Cutouts

For the young and young at heart, Christmas isn't complete without these gingerbread cutouts adorning a holiday table. You can make them like a pro with this wonderful recipe.

—LAJUNTA MALONE CAMDEN, ALABAMA

YIELD: ABOUT 6 DOZEN.

- 1 **cup butter, softened**
- 1 **cup sugar**
- ½ **cup dark corn syrup**
- 1 **teaspoon each ground cinnamon, nutmeg, cloves and ginger**
- 2 **eggs, beaten**
- 1 **teaspoon cider vinegar**
- 5 **cups all-purpose flour**
- 1 **teaspoon baking soda**

Red Hots candies

1. In a large saucepan, combine the butter, sugar, corn syrup and spices; bring to a boil, stirring constantly. Remove from the heat and cool until lukewarm. Stir in eggs and vinegar. Combine the flour and baking soda; stir into sugar mixture to form a soft dough. Cover and refrigerate for several hours or until easy to handle.

2. On a lightly floured surface, roll dough to ¼-in. thickness. Cut with a floured 2½-in. gingerbread man cookie cutter. Place on greased baking sheets. Use Red Hots for eyes and buttons. Bake at 350° for 8-10 minutes. Remove to wire racks to cool.

Lemon Butter Cookies

These tender cookies have a slight lemon flavor that makes them stand out from the other cutouts. They're very easy to roll out compared to other sugar cookie doughs I've worked with. I know you'll enjoy them as much as we do.

—JUDY MCCREIGHT SPRINGFIELD, ILLINOIS

YIELD: ABOUT 13 DOZEN.

- 1 **cup butter, softened**
- 2 **cups sugar**
- 2 **eggs, lightly beaten**
- ¼ **cup milk**
- 2 **teaspoons lemon extract**
- ½ **teaspoon salt**
- 4½ **cups all-purpose flour**
- 2 **teaspoons baking powder**
- ¼ **teaspoon baking soda**

Colored sugar, optional

1. In a large bowl, cream butter and sugar until light and fluffy. Beat in the eggs, milk and extract. Combine dry ingredients; gradually add to creamed mixture and mix well. Cover and chill for 2 hours.

2. Roll out on a lightly floured surface to ⅛-in. thickness. Cut with a 2-in. cookie cutter dipped in flour. Place 2 in. apart on ungreased baking sheets. Sprinkle with colored sugar if desired.

3. Bake at 350° for 8-9 minutes or until the edges just begin to brown. Remove to wire racks to cool.

> No trip to Grandma's would be complete without enjoying a batch of her snickerdoodle cookies. How we loved the spicy scent of cinnamon and the sweet taste of those sugar-coated treats!
>
> **— JADA O'TOOLE** WAPPINGERS FALLS, NEW YORK

3. Bake at 300° for 20-25 minutes or until bottom edges are golden brown. Cool on a wire rack. When cool, dust with confectioners' sugar.

Chocolate Chip Brownies

People love these very rich brownies so much that I never take them anywhere without bringing along several copies of the recipe to hand out. These treats are wonderful to take on a picnic because you don't have to worry about frosting melting.

—BRENDA KELLY ASHBURN, VIRGINIA

YIELD: 3-4 DOZEN.

1	**cup butter, softened**
3	**cups sugar**
6	**eggs**
1	**tablespoon vanilla extract**
2¼	**cups all-purpose flour**
½	**cup baking cocoa**
1	**teaspoon baking powder**
½	**teaspoon salt**
1	**cup (6 ounces) semisweet chocolate chips**
1	**cup vanilla or white chips**
1	**cup chopped walnuts**

1. In a large bowl, cream butter and sugar until light and fluffy. Add eggs and vanilla; mix well. Combine the flour, cocoa, baking powder and salt; gradually add to creamed mixture just until blended (do not overmix).

2. Pour into two greased 9-in. square baking pans. Sprinkle with chips and nuts. Bake at 350° for 30-35 minutes or until toothpick inserted near the center comes out clean. Cool.

Pecan Sandies Cookies

Whenever Mother made these cookies, there never seemed to be enough! Even now when I make them, they disappear quickly. These melt-in-your mouth treats are great with a cold glass of milk or a steaming mug of hot chocolate.

—DEBBIE CARLSON SAN DIEGO, CALIFORNIA

YIELD: ABOUT 5 DOZEN.

2	**cups butter, softened**
1	**cup confectioners' sugar**
2	**tablespoons water**
4	**teaspoons vanilla extract**
4	**cups all-purpose flour**
2	**cups chopped pecans**

Additional confectioners' sugar

1. In a large bowl, cream butter and sugar. Add water and vanilla; mix well. Gradually add flour; fold in pecans.

2. Roll dough into 1-in. balls. Place on ungreased baking sheets and flatten with fingers.

Grandma's Polish Cookies

Our family's traditional khruchiki recipe came down through my mother's side from my great-grandmother. As a child, it was my job to loop the end of each cookie through its hole.

—SHERINE ELISE GILMOUR BROOKLYN, NEW YORK

YIELD: 40 COOKIES.

- 4 **cups all-purpose flour**
- 1 **teaspoon salt**
- 1 **cup cold butter**
- 4 **egg yolks**
- 1 **cup evaporated milk**
- 2 **teaspoons vanilla extract**

Oil for deep-fat frying
Confectioners' sugar

1. In a large bowl, combine flour and salt. Cut in butter until mixture resembles coarse crumbs. In another bowl, beat egg yolks until foamy; add milk and vanilla. Stir into crumb mixture until dough is stiff enough to knead.

2. Turn onto a lightly floured surface; knead 8-10 times. Divide dough into four pieces. Roll each portion into a ¼-in.-thick rectangle; cut into 4-in. x 1½-in. strips. Cut a 2-in. lengthwise slit down the middle of each strip; pull one of the ends through the slit like a bow.

3. In an electric skillet or deep-fat fryer, heat oil to 375°. Fry dough strips, a few at a time, until golden brown on both sides. Drain on paper towels. Dust with confectioners' sugar

Macaroon Brownies

These three-layer brownies make for a pretty presentation on any dessert table. I was first introduced to these coconut-filled brownies when my mother-in-law made them for my bridal shower and wedding reception. After the first bite, I understood why my husband loved them!

—CHRISTINE FOUST STONEBORO, PENNSYLVANIA

YIELD: 4 DOZEN.

- 1 **cup butter, softened**
- 2 **cups sugar**
- 4 **eggs**
- 1 **teaspoon vanilla extract**
- 2 **cups all-purpose flour**
- ½ **cup baking cocoa**
- ½ **teaspoon cream of tartar**
- ½ **cup chopped walnuts**

MACAROON FILLING
- 1 **package (14 ounces) flaked coconut**
- 1 **can (14 ounces) sweetened condensed milk**
- 2 **teaspoons vanilla extract**

FROSTING
- ¾ **cup sugar**
- ¼ **cup milk**
- 2 **tablespoons butter**
- 1 **cup miniature marshmallows**
- 1 **cup (6 ounces) semisweet chocolate chips**
- 1 **teaspoon vanilla extract**

1. In a large bowl, cream butter and sugar until light and fluffy. Add eggs and vanilla; mix well. Combine the flour, cocoa and cream of tartar; gradually add to creamed mixture. Stir in nuts. Spread half into a greased 13-in. x 9-in. baking pan.

2. For filling, combine the coconut, condensed milk and vanilla; carefully spread over batter in pan. Top with the remaining batter. Bake at 350° for 40-45 minutes or until a toothpick inserted near the center comes out clean. Cool on a wire rack.

3. For frosting, combine the sugar, milk and butter in a saucepan; cook and stir until sugar is dissolved. Add the marshmallows and chocolate chips; cook and stir until melted. Remove from the heat; stir in vanilla. Cool until frosting reaches spreading consistency, about 25 minutes. Spread over the cooled brownies. Cut into bars.

Swedish Raspberry Almond Bars

When I was a single mom with a young daughter and little money, my Swedish neighbor brought me a batch of these cookies at Christmas. My daughter's 36 now, and I still make these wonderful cookies.

—MARINA CASTLE LA CRESCENTA, CALIFORNIA

YIELD: 2 DOZEN.

- ¾ **cup butter, softened**
- ¾ **cup confectioners' sugar**
- 1½ **cups all-purpose flour**
- ¾ **cup seedless raspberry jam**
- 3 **egg whites**
- 6 **tablespoons sugar**
- ½ **cup flaked coconut**
- 1 **cup sliced almonds, divided**
- **Additional confectioners' sugar**

1. In a large bowl, cream butter and confectioners' sugar until light and fluffy. Gradually add flour and mix well. Press onto the bottom of a greased 13-in. x 9-in. baking pan. Bake at 350° for 18-20 minutes or until lightly browned.

2. Spread jam over crust. In a large bowl, beat egg whites until soft peaks form. Gradually beat in sugar, 1 tablespoon at a time, on high until stiff peaks form. Fold in coconut and ½ cup almonds. Spread over jam. Sprinkle with remaining almonds. Bake at 350° for 18-22 minutes or until golden brown. Cool completely on a wire rack. Dust with confectioners' sugar.

Caramel Heavenlies

My mom made these dressy, sweet cookies for cookie exchanges when I was a little girl, letting me sprinkle on the almonds and coconut. They're so easy to fix that sometimes I can't wait until Christmas to make a batch.

—DAWN BURNS LAKE ST. LOUIS, MISSOURI

YIELD: ABOUT 6 DOZEN.

12	whole graham crackers
2	cups miniature marshmallows
¾	cup butter
¾	cup packed brown sugar
1	teaspoon ground cinnamon
1	teaspoon vanilla extract
1	cup sliced almonds
1	cup flaked coconut

1. Line a 15-in. x 10-in. x 1-in. baking pan with foil. Place graham crackers in pan; cover with marshmallows. In a saucepan over medium heat, cook and stir butter, brown sugar and cinnamon until the butter is melted and sugar is dissolved. Remove from the heat; stir in vanilla.

2. Spoon over the marshmallows. Sprinkle with almonds and coconut. Bake at 350° for 14-16 minutes or until browned. Cool completely. Cut into 2-in. squares, then cut each square in half to form triangles.

Iced Anise Cookies

On Thanksgiving, Christmas and Easter we could always expect to see a plate of these scrumptious cookies. My grandmother always kept some on hand for her hungry grandchildren.

—LINDA HARRINGTON WINDHAM, NEW HAMPSHIRE

YIELD: 6 DOZEN.

2⅔ cups all-purpose flour
½ cup sugar
3 teaspoons baking powder
3 eggs
½ cup butter, melted
¼ cup 2% milk
2 teaspoons anise extract

ICING

¼ cup butter, softened
2 cups confectioners' sugar
3 tablespoons 2% milk
½ teaspoon lemon extract
Coarse and colored sugars, optional

1. In a large bowl, combine 2 cups flour, sugar and baking powder. In a small bowl, whisk the eggs, butter, milk and extract. Stir into dry ingredients until blended. Stir in remaining flour until dough forms a ball. Turn onto a floured surface; knead until smooth.

2. Shape dough by rounded teaspoonfuls into thin 6-in. ropes; twist each rope into a "Q" shape. Place on ungreased baking sheets. Bake at 350° for 8-10 minutes or until set. Remove from pans to wire racks to cool completely.

3. For icing, in a small bowl, beat butter until fluffy. Add the confectioners' sugar, milk and extract; beat until smooth. Spread over tops of cookies; decorate with sugars if desired.

Raspberry Coconut Cookies

My mother gave me the recipe for these rich, buttery cookies. Raspberry preserves and a cream filling make them doubly delicious.

—JUNE BROWN VENETA, OREGON

YIELD: 2½ DOZEN.

¾ cup butter, softened
½ cup sugar
1 egg
1 teaspoon vanilla extract
2 cups all-purpose flour
½ cup flaked coconut
1½ teaspoons baking powder
¼ teaspoon salt

FILLING

¼ cup butter, softened
¾ cup confectioners' sugar
2 teaspoons 2% milk
½ teaspoon vanilla extract
½ cup raspberry preserves

1. In a large bowl, cream butter and sugar until light and fluffy. Beat in egg and vanilla. Combine the flour, coconut, baking powder and salt; gradually add to creamed mixture and mix well.

2. Shape into 1-in. balls. Place 1½ in. apart on ungreased baking sheets; flatten with a glass dipped in flour.

3. Bake at 350° for 12-14 minutes or until edges begin to brown. Cool on wire racks.

4. In a small bowl, beat the butter, confectioners' sugar, milk and vanilla until smooth. Place ½ teaspoon preserves and a scant teaspoon of filling on the bottom of half of the cookies; top with remaining cookies. Store in an airtight container in the refrigerator.

DESSERTS

Chocolate Sauce

I make different toppings so we can enjoy our favorite snack—ice cream sundaes. This smooth chocolate sauce is always a big hit.
—**NANCY MCDONALD** BURNS, WYOMING

YIELD: ABOUT 3⅓ CUPS.

- ½ cup butter
- 2 ounces unsweetened chocolate
- 2 cups sugar
- 1 cup half-and-half cream or evaporated milk
- ½ cup light corn syrup
- 1 teaspoon vanilla extract

1. In a large heavy saucepan, melt butter and chocolate; stir until smooth. Add the sugar, cream and corn syrup. Bring to a boil, stirring constantly. Boil for 1½ minutes. Remove from the heat.

2. Stir in vanilla. Serve warm or cold over ice cream or pound cake. Refrigerate leftovers.

Frozen Chocolate Torte

In summer, this cool make-ahead dessert is one of my favorites.
—**TAMMY NEUBAUER** IDA GROVE, IOWA

YIELD: 12 SERVINGS.

- 1 package (10½ ounces) miniature marshmallows
- 1 cup (6 ounces) semisweet chocolate chips
- 1 can (12 ounces) evaporated milk
- 1 cup flaked coconut
- ½ cup butter, cubed
- 2 cups graham cracker crumbs
- ½ gallon vanilla ice cream, softened

1. In a saucepan over low heat, melt marshmallows and chocolate chips with milk. Remove from heat; cool.

2. In a skillet, stir coconut in butter until browned. Remove from the heat; stir in the crumbs. Pat three-fourths into a 13-in. x 9-in. dish; cool. Spoon half of the ice cream onto crust.

3. Top with half of the chocolate mixture. Layer with the remaining ice cream and chocolate. Sprinkle with the remaining crumbs. Cover and freeze for at least 2 hours.

1-2-3 Blackberry Sherbet

My mom gave me this recipe, which was a special favorite when I was young. Now when I make it, my mouth is watering before I'm finished!

—LISA EREMIA IRWIN, PENNSYLVANIA

YIELD: 1 QUART.

- 4 **cups fresh or frozen blackberries, thawed**
- 2 **cups sugar**
- 2 **cups buttermilk**

1. In a food processor, combine blackberries and sugar; cover and process until smooth. Strain and discard seeds and pulp. Stir in buttermilk.

2. Transfer the puree to a 13-in. x 9-in. dish. Freeze for 1 hour or until edges begin to firm. Stir and return to freezer. Freeze 2 hours longer or until firm.

3. Just before serving, transfer to a food processor; cover and process for 2-3 minutes or until smooth.

Seven-Minute Pudding

If you've never made pudding from scratch, you'll find this rich, smooth version satisfying and easy. It couldn't be quicker to make, and it has unbeatable homemade flavor.

—RENEE SCHWEBACH DUMONT, MINNESOTA

YIELD: 3-4 SERVINGS.

- ⅓ **cup sugar**
- 2 **tablespoons cornstarch**
- 2 **cups milk**
- 2 **egg yolks**
- 2 **tablespoons butter**
- 1 **teaspoon vanilla extract**

1. In a microwave-safe bowl, combine sugar and cornstarch. With a hand mixer, beat in milk and egg yolks until smooth. Microwave on medium for 5 minutes. Beat well with mixer. Microwave on high for 2 minutes; stir. Blend in butter and vanilla. Pour into serving dishes; cool.

Editor's Note: *This recipe was tested in a 1,100-watt microwave.*

Apple Turnovers with Custard

I'm almost finished writing my own cookbook. When I was working on the apple section, I knew I had to submit this recipe for an apple contest. With the flaky turnovers and rich sauce, it outshines every other apple recipe I make!

—LEORA MUELLERLEILE TURTLE LAKE, WISCONSIN

YIELD: 8 SERVINGS.

CUSTARD
- ⅓ **cup sugar**
- 2 **tablespoons cornstarch**
- 2 **cups milk or half-and-half cream**
- 3 **egg yolks, lightly beaten**
- 1 **tablespoon vanilla extract**

TURNOVERS
- 4 **medium baking apples, peeled and cut into ¼-in slices**
- 1 **tablespoon lemon juice**
- 2 **tablespoons butter, diced**
- ⅓ **cup sugar**
- ¾ **teaspoon ground cinnamon**
- 1 **tablespoon cornstarch**
Pastry for double-crust pie
Milk

1. Combine sugar and cornstarch in a saucepan. Stir in milk until smooth. Cook and stir over medium-high heat until thickened and bubbly. Reduce heat; cook and stir for 2 minutes. Remove from heat; stir 1 cup into yolks. Return all to pan. Bring to a gentle boil; cook and stir for 2 minutes. Remove from heat; stir in vanilla. Cool slightly. Cover surface of custard with waxed paper; chill.

2. Place apples in a bowl; sprinkle with lemon juice. Add butter. Combine sugar, cinnamon and cornstarch; mix with apples and set aside.

3. Divide pastry into eight portions; roll each into a 5-in. square. Spoon filling off-center on each. Brush edges with milk. Fold over to form a triangle; seal. Crimp with tines of fork. Make steam vents on top.

4. Place on greased baking sheets. Chill 15 minutes. Brush with milk. Bake at 400° for 35 minutes. Serve warm with custard.

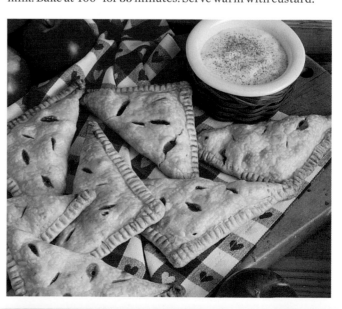

Layered Banana Pudding

My mother gave me this recipe, which an old friend had shared with her. When my children were still at home, we enjoyed this satisfying pudding often, and now I make it for company. There's no comparison between this recipe and the instant pudding mixes from the grocery store!

—ESTHER MATTESON SOUTH BEND, INDIANA

YIELD: 8 SERVINGS.

½ cup all-purpose flour
⅔ cup packed brown sugar
2 cups milk
2 egg yolks, beaten
2 tablespoons butter
1 teaspoon vanilla extract
1 cup heavy whipping cream, whipped
4 to 6 medium firm bananas, sliced
Chopped walnuts, optional

1. In a large saucepan, combine the flour and brown sugar. Stir in milk until smooth. Cook and stir over medium-high heat until thickened and bubbly. Reduce heat; cook and stir 2 minutes longer. Remove from the heat.

2. Stir a small amount of hot filling into egg yolks; return all to pan, stirring constantly. Bring to a gentle boil; cook and stir 2 minutes longer. Remove from the heat; stir in the butter and vanilla. Cool to room temperature without stirring. Fold in the whipped cream.

3. Layer a third of the pudding in a 2-qt. glass bowl; top with half of the bananas. Repeat layers. Top with the remaining pudding. Sprinkle with nuts if desired. Cover and refrigerate for at least 1 hour before serving.

Pineapple Cheese Torte

This light and yummy pineapple dessert looks prettiest when it's garnished with fresh strawberries. I serve it at summer picnics or family get-togethers. It's a hit any time of year!

—DIANE BRADLEY SPARTA, MICHIGAN

YIELD: 12-16 SERVINGS.

PAT-IN-THE-PAN CRUST
1 cup all-purpose flour
¼ cup confectioners' sugar
¼ cup finely chopped almonds
⅓ cup butter, softened

FILLING
2 packages (8 ounces each) cream cheese, softened
½ cup sugar
2 eggs
⅔ cup unsweetened pineapple juice

PINEAPPLE TOPPING
1 can (20 ounces) crushed pineapple
¼ cup all-purpose flour
¼ cup sugar
½ cup heavy whipping cream
Fresh strawberries, optional

1. In a bowl, combine crust ingredients until blended; pat into a greased 11-in. x 7-in. baking dish. Bake at 350° for 20 minutes. In a small bowl, beat cream cheese and sugar until light and fluffy. Beat in eggs. Stir in juice. Pour over hot crust. Bake for 25 minutes or until center is set. Cool on a wire rack.

2. For topping, drain pineapple, reserving 1 cup juice. Set pineapple aside. In a small saucepan, combine flour, sugar and reserved pineapple juice until smooth. Bring to a boil. Cook and stir for 1 minute or until thickened and bubbly. Remove from the heat; fold in pineapple. Cool.

3. In a small bowl, beat cream until soft peaks form; fold into topping. Carefully spread over top. Refrigerate for 6 hours or overnight. Garnish with strawberries if desired.

Cherry Cobbler

I've made this recipe for years, adapting it to suit our taste. It's a delicious way to use lots of cherries. I hope you enjoy this tart treat!

—PEGGY BURDICK BURLINGTON, MICHIGAN

YIELD: 6-8 SERVINGS.

- 5 cups pitted canned tart red cherries
- ⅓ cup sugar
- ⅓ cup packed brown sugar
- 2 tablespoons plus 1½ teaspoons cornstarch
- 1 teaspoon ground cinnamon
- ¼ teaspoon ground nutmeg
- 2 tablespoons plus 1½ teaspoons lemon juice

TOPPING
- 1 cup all-purpose flour
- 1 tablespoon sugar
- 1 teaspoon baking powder
- ¼ teaspoon salt
- 2 tablespoons cold butter
- ⅓ to ½ cup milk

1. Drain cherries, reserving 1¼ cups juice; set aside. Discard remaining juice. In a large saucepan, combine the sugars, cornstarch, cinnamon and nutmeg; stir in lemon juice and reserved cherry juice until smooth. Bring to a boil. Cook and stir for 2 minutes or until thickened and bubbly.

2. Add cherries; pour into an ungreased 9-in. square baking pan. For topping, combine the flour, sugar, baking powder and salt; cut in butter until crumbly. Stir in enough milk to moisten. Drop by tablespoonfuls over cherries. Bake at 450° for 10-13 minutes or until golden brown.

Blueberry Grunt

The name may make you smile—and the flavor of this stovetop treat is guaranteed to have the same effect. Make this traditional dessert in a skillet with a tight-fitting lid, and you'll hear it "grunt" as it cooks!

—IOLA EGLE BELLA VISTA, ARKANSAS

YIELD: 6-8 SERVINGS.

- 4 cups fresh blueberries
- 1 cup sugar
- 1 cup water
- 1½ cups all-purpose flour
- 2 teaspoons baking powder
- 2 tablespoons grated orange peel
- ½ teaspoon ground cinnamon
- ¼ teaspoon ground nutmeg
- ¼ teaspoon salt
- ¾ cup milk
- Heavy whipping cream, optional

1. In a skillet, combine blueberries, sugar and water; bring to a boil. Simmer, uncovered, for 20 minutes.

2. In a bowl, combine the next six ingredients; stir in milk just until moistened (dough will be stiff). Drop by tablespoonfuls over blueberries.

3. Cover and cook 10-15 minutes or until the dumplings are puffed and a toothpick inserted near the center comes out clean. Serve warm with cream if desired.

Making ice cream was the highlight of summer picnics at my great-grandparents' farm. The excitement rose when the cranking became labored, because that meant the dasher would soon be lifted out. For me, no ice cream has ever tasted as good as that sweet treat clinging to the cold metal!

— BETTE HILLEGASS BLACK MOUNTAIN, NORTH CAROLINA

Mocha Pudding Cakes

Mouthwatering mini cakes are the perfect treat for a twosome. My mom used to make these when I was a little girl. Now I whip them up for a speedy dessert.

—DEBORA SIMMONS EGLON, WEST VIRGINIA

YIELD: 2 SERVINGS.

- ¼ **cup all-purpose flour**
- 3 **tablespoons sugar**
- 1½ **teaspoons baking cocoa**
- ½ **teaspoon baking powder**
- ⅛ **teaspoon salt**
- 3 **tablespoons 2% milk**
- 1½ **teaspoons butter, melted**
- ¼ **teaspoon vanilla extract**

TOPPING

- 2 **tablespoons brown sugar**
- 1½ **teaspoons baking cocoa**
- 3 **tablespoons hot brewed coffee**
- 1 **tablespoon hot water**

Whipped topping, optional

1. In a small bowl, combine the flour, sugar, cocoa, baking powder and salt. Stir in the milk, butter and vanilla until smooth. Spoon into two 4-oz. ramekins coated with cooking spray.

2. Combine brown sugar and cocoa; sprinkle over batter. Combine coffee and water; pour over topping. Bake at 350° for 15-20 minutes or until a knife inserted near the center comes out clean. Serve warm or at room temperature with whipped topping if desired.

Ice Cream Cookie Dessert

Our family loves dessert, and this tempting treat with chocolaty layers is one of Mom's most requested recipes. It looks fancy but is so easy to prepare.

—KIMBERLY LAABS
HARTFORD, WISCONSIN

YIELD: 12 SERVINGS.

- 1 **package (15½ ounces) Oreo cookies**
- ¼ **cup butter, melted**
- ½ **gallon vanilla ice cream, softened**
- 1 **jar (16 ounces) hot fudge ice cream topping, warmed**
- 1 **carton (8 ounces) frozen whipped topping, thawed**

1. In a large bowl, combine 3¾ cups cookie crumbs and butter. Press into a greased 13-in. x 9-in. dish. Spread with ice cream; cover and freeze until set.

2. Drizzle fudge topping over ice cream; cover and freeze until set. Spread with whipped topping; sprinkle with remaining cookie crumbs. Cover and freeze for 2 hours or until firm. Remove from the freezer 10 minutes before serving.

Chocolate-Filled Cream Puffs

I make this every year to take to school for a co-worker's birthday. He adores them, along with everyone else. It's my mother's recipe; I grew up eating cream puffs. I have to make a triple batch when I take them to school.

—DIANA VOLAND MARTINSVILLE, INDIANA

YIELD: 3 DOZEN.

1 cup water
½ cup butter, cubed
1 cup all-purpose flour
4 eggs

CHOCOLATE CREAM FILLING
¾ cup sugar
5 tablespoons baking cocoa
3 tablespoons cornstarch
½ teaspoon salt
2 cups 2% milk
2 egg yolks, lightly beaten
1 tablespoon butter
1 teaspoon vanilla extract

Hot fudge ice cream topping and citrus sugar, white chocolate shavings or confectioners' sugar, optional

1. In a large saucepan, bring water and butter to a boil. Add flour all at once and stir until a smooth ball forms. Remove from the heat; let stand for 5 minutes. Add eggs, one at a time, beating well after each addition. Continue beating until mixture is smooth and shiny.

2. Drop by rounded tablespoonfuls 3 in. apart onto greased baking sheets. Bake at 400° for 20-25 minutes or until golden brown. Remove to wire racks. Immediately split puffs open; remove tops and set aside. Discard soft dough from inside. Cool puffs. Freeze in airtight containers for up to 2 months.

To use frozen cream puffs: Thaw at room temperature for 10 minutes. Place cream puffs on a baking sheet. Bake at 375° for 3-4 minutes or until crisp.

3. For filling, in a large heavy saucepan, combine the sugar, cocoa, cornstarch and salt. Stir in milk until smooth. Cook and stir over medium-high heat until thickened and bubbly. Reduce heat to low; cook and stir 2 minutes longer.

4. Remove from the heat. Stir a small amount of hot mixture into egg yolks; return all to the pan, stirring constantly. Bring to a gentle boil; cook and stir 2 minutes longer. Remove from the heat. Gently stir in butter and vanilla. Cover with waxed paper or plastic wrap. Cool for 15 minutes without stirring.

5. To serve, spoon chocolate cream filling into cream puffs; replace tops. Top with warmed hot fudge sauce and citrus sugar, white chocolate shavings or confectioners' sugar if desired.

Editor's Note: *To make citrus sugar, press grated citrus peels into sugar to release their oils. Store citrus sugar in an airtight container at room temperature for 2-3 weeks or until the flavor diminishes.*

Old-Fashioned Ice Cream Roll

When I think of my grandmother, I think of this wonderful dessert. The warm caramel sauce melts the ice cream slightly. Oh, it is so good!

—**DARLENE BRENDEN** SALEM, OREGON

YIELD: 8-10 SERVINGS (2 CUPS SAUCE).

  4 **eggs**
  ¾ **cup sugar**
  1 **teaspoon vanilla extract**
  ¾ **cup all-purpose flour**
  ¾ **teaspoon baking powder**
  ¼ **teaspoon salt**
  ½ **gallon vanilla ice cream, slightly softened**

CARAMEL SAUCE

  1 **cup packed brown sugar**
  ½ **cup sugar**
  ¼ **teaspoon salt**
  ½ **cup light corn syrup**
  1 **cup heavy whipping cream**
    Chopped pecans, optional

1. Line a greased 15-in. x 10-in. x 1-in. baking pan with waxed paper. Grease the paper; set aside. In a large bowl, beat eggs for 3 minutes. Gradually add sugar; beat for 2 minutes or until mixture becomes thick and lemon-colored. Beat in vanilla. Combine dry ingredients; fold into egg mixture.

2. Spread batter evenly into prepared pan. Bake at 375° for 10-12 minutes or until cake springs back when lightly touched. Cool for 5 minutes. Invert onto a kitchen towel dusted with confectioners' sugar. Gently peel off waxed paper. Roll up cake in the towel jelly-roll style, starting with a short side. Cool completely on a wire rack.

3. Spread cooled cake with ice cream; roll up again. Freeze until firm.

4. For sauce, in a small saucepan, combine the sugars, salt and corn syrup. Cook and stir until mixture comes to a boil. Remove from the heat; cool slightly. Stir in cream. Serve with ice cream roll. Sprinkle with pecans if desired.

Variation: Use strawberry ice cream instead of vanilla and eliminate caramel sauce. Garnish with fresh strawberries and whipped cream.

Homemade Butterscotch Pudding

Homemade pudding stirs memories of grandmothers and their secret knowledge of how to change milk and eggs into creamy concoctions they poured into dessert glasses. The essence of butterscotch adds a caramel-sweet touch.

—TERESA WILKES PEMBROKE, GEORGIA

YIELD: 6 SERVINGS.

- ½ cup sugar
- ½ cup packed dark brown sugar
- 3 tablespoons cornstarch
- ¼ teaspoon salt
- ⅛ teaspoon ground nutmeg
- 3 cups 2% milk
- 3 egg yolks
- 2 tablespoons butter, cubed
- 2 teaspoons vanilla extract
- **Whipped cream, optional**

1. In a large heavy saucepan, combine the first five ingredients. Stir in the milk until smooth. Cook and stir over medium-high heat until thickened and bubbly. Reduce heat to low; cook and stir 2 minutes longer. Remove from the heat.

2. Stir a small amount of hot mixture into the egg yolks; return all to the pan. Bring to a gentle boil, stirring constantly; cook 2 minutes or until mixture is thickened and coats the back of a spoon. Remove from the heat.

3. Stir in butter and vanilla. Cool for 15 minutes, stirring occasionally. Transfer to six dessert dishes. Cover and refrigerate until chilled. Garnish with whipped cream if desired.

Butterfinger Delight

I got the recipe for this wonderful no-bake treat from my mother-in-law because it's my husband's favorite. I'm frequently asked to bring this yummy dessert to get-togethers. Everyone loves it.

—LINDA WINTER ENID, OKLAHOMA

YIELD: 12-15 SERVINGS.

- 1 cup crushed butter-flavored crackers (about 30 crackers)
- 1 cup graham cracker crumbs
- 4 Butterfinger candy bars (2.1 ounces each), crushed
- ¾ cup butter, melted
- 1½ cups cold milk
- 2 packages (3.4 ounces each) instant vanilla pudding mix
- 1 quart reduced-fat chocolate frozen yogurt, softened
- 1 carton (12 ounces) frozen whipped topping, thawed, divided

1. In a large bowl, combine the first four ingredients; set aside ½ cup for topping. Press remaining crumb mixture into an ungreased 13-in. x 9-in. dish. Chill for 5 minutes.

2. Meanwhile, in a large bowl, whisk milk and pudding mixes for 2 minutes. Let stand for 2 minutes or until set (mixture will be thick). Stir in frozen yogurt and 1 cup whipped topping until smooth. Spread over crust.

3. Top with remaining whipped topping. Sprinkle with reserved crumb mixture. Refrigerate for 8 hours or overnight.

Banana Split Cream Puffs

These cream puffs cleverly sandwich banana split ingredients, but you can use whatever ice cream and toppings your family prefers.

—SANDY MCKENZIE
BRAHAM, MINNESOTA

YIELD: 1 DOZEN.

- 1 **cup water**
- ½ **cup butter**
- 1 **cup all-purpose flour**
- ¼ **teaspoon salt**
- 4 **eggs**
- 12 **scoops vanilla ice cream**
- 1 **cup sliced fresh strawberries**
- 1 **large or 2 medium bananas, thinly sliced**
- ¾ **cup pineapple tidbits, drained**
- ½ **cup hot fudge sauce**

1. In a large saucepan over medium heat, bring water and butter to a boil. Add flour and salt all at once; stir until a smooth ball forms. Remove from the heat; let stand 5 minutes. Add eggs, one at a time, beating well after each addition. Beat until mixture is smooth and shiny.

2. Drop by rounded tablespoonfuls onto a greased baking sheet. Bake at 400° for 30-35 minutes or until cream puffs are golden brown. Remove to a wire rack. Immediately split puffs open; remove tops and set aside. Discard soft dough from inside.

3. Fill each puff with a scoop of ice cream and top with fruit. Drizzle with hot fudge sauce. Replace tops and serve immediately.

Chocolate Caramels

When I was growing up, my mom made these delicious candies every Christmas. They were my favorite then and still are today. Whenever I make them, they bring back a flood of happy childhood memories.

—SUE GRONHOLZ BEAVER DAM, WISCONSIN

YIELD: 1¼ POUNDS.

- 1 **teaspoon butter, softened**
- 1 **cup sugar**
- ¾ **cup light corn syrup**
- 2 **ounces unsweetened chocolate, chopped**
- 1½ **cups heavy whipping cream, divided**

1. Line a 9-in. x 5-in. loaf pan with foil and grease the foil with butter; set aside.

2. In a large heavy saucepan, bring the sugar, corn syrup and chocolate to a boil over medium heat; stir until smooth. Add ½ cup cream; cook, stirring constantly, until a candy thermometer reads 234° (soft-ball stage). Add another ½ cup cream; return mixture to 234° (soft-ball stage). Add the remaining cream; cook to 248° (firm-ball stage).

3. Immediately pour into prepared pan (do not scrape saucepan). Let stand until firm, about 5 hours or overnight. Using foil, lift candy out of pan. Discard foil; cut candy into 1-in. squares using a buttered knife. Wrap individually in waxed paper; twist ends.

Editor's Note: *Test your candy thermometer before each use. In boiling water, it should read 212°. Adjust your recipe temperature up or down based on your test.*

Apple Cobbler

A treasured family recipe, this cobbler is a delicious old-fashioned dessert. It travels well and slices nicely, so it's perfect for picnics.

—RITA REIFENSTEIN EVANS CITY, PENNSYLVANIA

YIELD: 12-16 SERVINGS.

    3   cups all-purpose flour
    1   cup sugar, divided
  1½   teaspoons baking powder
    ½   teaspoon salt
    ½   cup cold butter, cubed
    2   eggs
    1   tablespoon vanilla extract
    3   to 4 tablespoons milk
    8   cups thinly sliced peeled tart apples
    2   tablespoons quick-cooking tapioca
    ½   teaspoon ground cinnamon
TOPPING
    1   tablespoon milk
    ¾   teaspoon sugar
    ¼   teaspoon ground cinnamon

1. In a bowl, combine flour, ¼ cup sugar, baking powder and salt. Cut in butter until crumbly.

2. In another bowl, lightly beat eggs and vanilla; add to crumb mixture. With a fork, gently mix in milk to moisten. Stir until dough forms a ball. Press half of the dough into a greased 13-in. x 9-in. baking dish. Chill the remaining dough.

3. Toss apples with tapioca, cinnamon and remaining sugar; place over dough in pan. On a lightly floured surface, roll chilled dough to fit top of pan. Place over apples. Brush with milk. Combine sugar and cinnamon; sprinkle on top. Bake at 350° for 45-50 minutes or until apples are tender and crust is golden.

Coconut Cream Pudding

A golden baked meringue is the crowning touch for this mouthwatering dessert.

—VERONA KOEHLMOOS PILGER, NEBRASKA

YIELD: 9 SERVINGS.

  1¼   cups sugar, divided
    ¼   cup cornstarch
    3   cups milk
    4   eggs, separated
    1   cup flaked coconut
    1   teaspoon vanilla extract

1. In a large heavy saucepan, combine ¾ cup sugar and cornstarch; stir in milk until smooth. Cook and stir over medium heat until thick and bubbly; cook and stir 2 minutes more. Remove from heat.

2. In a bowl, beat egg yolks. Stir 1 cup hot milk mixture into yolks; return all to pan, stirring constantly. Bring to a gentle boil over medium heat; cook and stir 2 minutes longer. Remove from the heat. Stir in coconut and vanilla. Cool to lukewarm without stirring.

3. Pour into an ungreased 8-in. square baking dish. In a large bowl and with clean beaters, beat egg whites on medium speed until soft peaks form. Gradually beat in remaining sugar, 1 tablespoon at a time, on high until stiff peaks form. Spread over pudding, sealing to edges. Bake, uncovered, at 350° for 10-15 minutes. Serve warm.

Blueberry Custard Parfait

I'm a retired nurse and my hobby is cooking. This refreshing dessert is one I turn to time and again.

—MILDRED STUBBS ROCKINGHAM, NORTH CAROLINA

YIELD: 4 SERVINGS.

    2   eggs, lightly beaten
  1½   cups milk
    ¼   cup sugar
    ¼   teaspoon salt
    1   teaspoon vanilla extract
    1   teaspoon grated lemon peel
    1   teaspoon grated orange peel
    ¼   teaspoon ground nutmeg
    ½   cup heavy whipping cream
    2   teaspoons confectioners' sugar
    2   cups fresh blueberries

1. In a saucepan, combine eggs, milk, sugar and salt. Cook over medium-low heat, stirring constantly, until custard is slightly thickened and coats the back of a spoon, about 18 minutes.

2. Remove from the heat. Stir in the vanilla, peels and nutmeg. Cool for 30 minutes, stirring occasionally.

3. In a small bowl, beat the cream and confectioners' sugar until stiff. Fold two-thirds into the custard. Layer custard and blueberries in parfait glasses. Garnish with remaining cream. Chill for 1 hour.

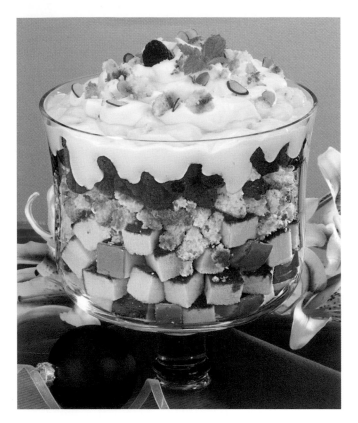

Raspberry Vanilla Trifle

When I was growing up, my English mother made this as the centerpiece at our traditional Christmas Day tea. Presented in a cut glass bowl, it's absolutely stunning.

—JOYCE TOTH WICHITA FALLS, TEXAS

YIELD: 10-12 SERVINGS.

- 2 **cups milk**
- 1 **package (3 ounces) cook-and-serve vanilla pudding mix**
- 1 **loaf (10¾ ounces) frozen pound cake, thawed**
- ¼ **cup seedless raspberry jam**
- ¼ **cup orange juice**
- 10 **soft macaroon cookies**
- 2 **cups fresh or frozen unsweetened raspberries, thawed and drained**
- 1 **cup heavy whipping cream**
- 2 **tablespoons confectioners' sugar**
- ¼ **cup sliced almonds, toasted**

1. In a small saucepan, combine milk and pudding mix. Cook and stir over medium heat until mixture comes to a full boil. Cool. Cut cake into 1-in. slices; spread with jam. Cut into 1-in. cubes. Place cubes jam side up in a 3-qt. trifle or glass bowl. Drizzle with orange juice.

2. Place macaroons in a food processor, cover and pulse until coarse crumbs form. Set aside ¼ cup crumbs for garnish; sprinkle remaining crumbs over cake cubes. Top with berries and pudding. Cover and refrigerate overnight.

3. Just before serving, in a small bowl, beat cream until thickened. Beat in confectioners' sugar until stiff peaks form. Spread over trifle. Sprinkle with almonds and reserved macaroon crumbs.

Fudgy Nut Coffee Pie

My mother served this pretty pie for my birthday dinner one year, and now it's one of my favorites. Fudge sauce, chopped pecans and coffee ice cream top the chocolate crumb crust. Sometimes I garnish the pie with dollops of whipped cream.

—AMY THEIS BILLINGS, MONTANA

YIELD: 8 SERVINGS.

- 1½ **cups confectioners' sugar**
- ½ **cup heavy whipping cream**
- 6 **tablespoons butter, cubed**
- 3 **ounces unsweetened chocolate**
- 3 **tablespoons light corn syrup**

Dash salt
- 1 **teaspoon vanilla extract**
- 1 **chocolate crumb crust (9 inches)**
- ¾ **cup coarsely chopped pecans, divided**
- 3 **pints coffee ice cream, softened**

1. In a small saucepan, combine the confectioners' sugar, cream, butter, chocolate, corn syrup and salt. Cook and stir over low heat until smooth. Remove from the heat. Stir in vanilla. Cool completely.

2. Spread ½ cup fudge sauce over the crust. Sprinkle with ¼ cup pecans. Freeze for 20 minutes or until set. Spread with half of the ice cream. Freeze for 1 hour or until firm. Repeat layers. Cover and freeze for 4 hours or until firm.

3. Just before serving, drizzle remaining fudge sauce over pie and sprinkle with remaining pecans.

Pinwheel Mints

Both my grandmother and my mom used to make these eye-catching confections as a replacement for ordinary mints at Christmas. When I offer them at parties, guests tell me the mints are wonderful, and then ask how I create the pretty swirl pattern.

—**MARILOU ROTH** MILFORD, NEBRASKA

YIELD: ABOUT 3 DOZEN.

- 1 **package (8 ounces) cream cheese, softened**
- ½ **to 1 teaspoon mint extract**
- 7½ **to 8½ cups confectioners' sugar**

Red and green food coloring

Additional confectioners' sugar

1. In a large bowl, beat cream cheese and mint extract until smooth. Gradually beat in as much confectioners' sugar as possible; knead in remaining confectioners' sugar until a firm mixture is achieved. Divide mixture in half; with food coloring, tint half pink and the other light green.

2. On waxed paper, lightly sprinkle remaining confectioners' sugar into a 12-in. x 5-in. rectangle. Divide pink portion in half; shape each portion into a 10-in. log.

3. Place one log on sugared waxed paper and flatten slightly. Cover with waxed paper; roll into a 12-in. x 5-in. rectangle. Repeat with remaining pink portion; set aside. Repeat with light green portion.

4. Remove top piece of waxed paper from one pink and one green rectangle. Place one over the other. Roll up jelly-roll style, starting with a long side. Wrap in waxed paper; twist ends. Repeat. Chill overnight.

5. To serve, cut into ½-in. slices. Store in an airtight container in the refrigerator for up to 1 week.

Pumpkin Bread Pudding

It may be old-fashioned, but this comforting dessert is never out of style. I got this recipe from an aunt who's a very experienced cook.

—LOIS FETTING NELSON, WISCONSIN

YIELD: 6-8 SERVINGS.

- 4 **cups cubed day-old whole wheat bread**
- ½ **cup chopped dates or raisins**
- ½ **cup chopped pecans, divided**
- 2 **cups milk**
- 1 **cup canned pumpkin**
- 2 **eggs, separated**
- ⅔ **cup packed brown sugar**
- 1½ **teaspoons ground cinnamon**
- ¾ **teaspoon ground nutmeg**
- ¼ **teaspoon salt**
- ⅛ **teaspoon ground cloves**

Half-and-half cream or whipped cream, optional

1. Combine bread cubes, dates and ⅓ cup pecans; place in a greased 2-qt. shallow baking dish.

2. In a bowl, combine milk, pumpkin, egg yolks, brown sugar, cinnamon, nutmeg, salt and cloves. In a small bowl and with clean beaters, beat the egg whites until stiff; fold into the pumpkin mixture. Pour over bread cubes and toss gently. Sprinkle with remaining nuts.

3. Bake, uncovered, at 350° for 1 hour or until a knife inserted near the center comes out clean. Serve warm or chilled with cream if desired.

Lemony Apple Dumplings

The first time I made this recipe, my guests included two little girls. They weren't sure about eating a dessert that looked so different. But after just one bite, they proclaimed it "yummy" and cleaned their plates.

—KRISTY DELOACH BAKER, LOUISIANA

YIELD: 4 SERVINGS.

- 1½ **cups all-purpose flour**
- 1¼ **teaspoons salt, divided**
- ⅓ **cup shortening**
- 4 **to 5 tablespoons cold milk**
- ½ **cup packed brown sugar**
- 3 **tablespoons butter, softened**
- ½ **teaspoon ground cinnamon**
- 4 **medium baking apples, peeled and cored**
- 1 **egg white, beaten**

LEMON SAUCE

- ½ **cup sugar**
- 4 **teaspoons cornstarch**
- 1 **cup cold water**
- 3 **tablespoons butter**
- 4 **teaspoons lemon juice**
- 2 **teaspoons grated lemon peel**
- ⅛ **teaspoon salt**

1. Combine flour and 1 teaspoon salt. Cut in shortening until crumbly. Stir in milk until pastry forms a ball; set aside. Stir brown sugar, butter, cinnamon and remaining salt to form a paste. Divide and press into center of each apple; pat any extra filling on outside of apples.

2. On a floured surface, roll pastry into a 14-in. square. Cut into four 7-in. squares. Place one apple in center of each square. Brush edges of pastry with egg white. Fold up corners to center; pinch to seal.

3. Place in a greased 9-in. square baking dish. Bake at 375° for 35-40 minutes or until golden brown.

4. Meanwhile, combine the sugar and cornstarch in a saucepan. Stir in water. Bring to a boil; cook and stir for 2 minutes or until thickened. Remove from the heat; stir in the remaining ingredients until smooth. Serve sauce warm over warm dumplings.

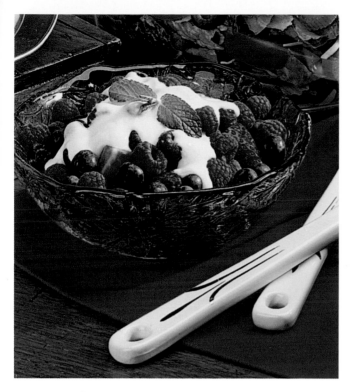

Berries in Custard Sauce

This refreshing treat showcases the fresh berries of summer. The custard is not overly sweet, so it doesn't overshadow the fruit.

—LEONA LUECKING WEST BURLINGTON, IOWA

YIELD: 6 SERVINGS.

- 1 **cup milk**
- 1 **egg, lightly beaten**
- 2 **tablespoons sugar**
- **Dash salt**
- ½ **teaspoon vanilla extract**
- 3 **cups fresh blueberries, raspberries and strawberries**

1. In a saucepan, heat milk over medium heat until bubbles form around sides of pan. Combine egg and sugar in a bowl; stir in a small amount of hot milk. Return all to saucepan. Cook over low heat, stirring constantly, until mixture coats a spoon, about 15 minutes. Remove from heat; stir in salt and vanilla. Chill at least 1 hour. Serve over berries.

Grandma's Chocolate Pudding

My grandmother always made this creamy, very chocolaty pudding when we visited.

—DONNA HUGHES ROCHESTER, NEW HAMPSHIRE

YIELD: 4-6 SERVINGS.

- 1 **cup sugar**
- ½ **cup baking cocoa**
- ¼ **cup all-purpose flour**
- 2 **cups water**
- ¾ **cup evaporated milk**
- 1 **tablespoon vanilla extract**
- **Dash salt**

1. In a saucepan, combine sugar, cocoa and flour. Add water and milk; stir until smooth. Cook over medium heat, stirring constantly, until mixture comes to a boil. Cook and stir for 1-2 minutes or until thickened.

2. Remove from heat; stir in vanilla and salt. Cool to room temperature, stirring several times. Pour into a serving bowl or individual dishes. Serve warm or chill.

Nutty Chocolate Fudge

Many years ago, when I was dating the man who is now my husband, his mother gave me this recipe for his favorite fudge. It's a tasty treat that's so simple to make.

—MAUREEN DREES MANNING, IOWA

YIELD: 2¼ POUNDS.

- 3 **tablespoons butter, divided**
- 12 **ounces German sweet chocolate, chopped**
- 2 **cups (12 ounces) semisweet chocolate chips**
- 1 **jar (7 ounces) marshmallow creme**
- 4½ **cups sugar**
- 1 **can (12 ounces) evaporated milk**
- 2 **cups pecans or walnuts, chopped**

1. Line a 13-in. x 9-in. pan with foil; butter the foil with 1 tablespoon butter and set aside. Break the German chocolate into 1-in. pieces; place in a bowl. Add the chocolate chips and marshmallow creme; set aside.

2. In a large saucepan, bring the sugar, milk and remaining butter to a boil over medium heat, stirring often. Reduce heat; simmer, uncovered, for 6 minutes, stirring occasionally. Slowly pour over chocolate mixture; stir until mixture is smooth and blended. Stir in nuts.

3. Pour into prepared pan. Let stand at room temperature until cool. Cut into squares. Store in an airtight container in the refrigerator.

General Recipe Index

This handy index lists every recipe by food category, major ingredient and/or cooking method, so you can easily locate recipes to suit your needs.

Appetizers & Snacks

Artichoke Spinach Dip in a Bread Bowl, 8
Blizzard Party Mix, 8
BLT Bites, 14
Caramel Corn, 19
Cheese Rye Appetizers, 7
Cheesy Sun Crisps, 11
Chunky Salsa, 11
Cinnamon-Raisin Granola, 10
Crisp and Nutty Mix, 20
Deviled Eggs with Bacon, 6
Easy Elephant Ears, 9
Easy Hummus, 12
Fresh Vegetable Dip, 16
Horseradish Cheese Spread, 21
Mini Apple Pizzas, 16
Mini Hamburgers, 13
Olive-Stuffed Celery, 21
Pepperoni Pizza Spread, 6
Puffed Wheat Balls, 18
Roast Beef Spirals, 9
Spiced Pecans, 12
Sweet Gingered Chicken Wings, 15
Sweet Minglers, 14
Tangy Meatballs, 10
Tater-Dipped Veggies, 19

Apples

Apple Bran Muffins, 112
Apple Cobbler, 297
Apple Fritters, 35
Apple Raisin Bread, 120
Apple-Topped Oatcakes, 40
Apple Turnovers with Custard, 289
Apple Walnut Cake, 224
Cookie Sheet Apple Pie, 249
Dutch Apple Bread, 111
Herbed Pork and Apples, 182
Lattice-Topped Apple Pie, 251
Lemony Apple Dumplings, 300
Mini Apple Pizzas, 16
Mulligatawny Soup, 51
Nutty Apple Muffins, 113
Oh-So-Good Oatmeal, 32
Overnight Apple French Toast, 28
Roasted Duck with Apple-Raisin Dressing, 163
Rustic Apple-Raisin Bread, 128
Rustic Autumn Fruit Tart, 256
Saucy Apple Cake, 228
Smoked Turkey and Apple Salad, 168
Sour Cream Apple Chicken, 155

Sour Cream Apple Pie, 255
Spicy Applesauce Cake, 241
Streusel-Topped Apple Cheesecake, 24
Summer Apple Salad, 72

Apricots

Apricot Baked Ham, 182
Apricot-Coconut Bars, 268
Apricot Walnut Bread, 107
Golden Apricot Pie, 261
Stuffed Apricot French Toast, 31

Asparagus

Asparagus Ham Rolls, 188
Asparagus with Sesame Butter, 90
Saucy Chicken and Asparagus, 169

Bacon

Bacon Swiss Bread, 113
BLT Bites, 14
Cheese Rye Appetizers, 7
Corn and Bacon Casserole, 87
Creamy German Potato Salad, 66
Deviled Eggs with Bacon, 6
Prosciutto Chicken Cacciatore, 166
Ranch Stuffed Baked Potatoes, 94
Sheepherder's Breakfast, 29
Spinach Bacon Quiche, 37
Tasty Tossed Salad, 65

Bananas

Banana Brunch Punch, 12
Banana Chip Pancakes, 35
Banana Cupcakes, 223
Banana Fruit Compote, 64
Banana Nut Layer Cake, 238
Banana Split Cream Puffs, 296
Creamy Banana Pie, 260
Layered Banana Pudding, 290

Bars & Brownies

Apricot-Coconut Bars, 268
Caramel Heavenlies, 284
Caramel-Pecan Dream Bars, 278
Chocolate Chip Brownies, 281
Chocolate Date Squares, 270
Chocolate Marshmallow Bars, 274
Frosted Cookie Brownies, 272
Fudge Brownies, 267
Grandma's Date Bars, 279
Lemon Bars, 273
Macaroon Brownies, 282

Peanut Butter Squares, 278
Pecan Squares, 277
Swedish Raspberry Almond Bars, 283
Turtle Bars, 275

Beans & Lentils
Chicken Provencale, 175
Five-Bean Soup, 53
Garden Bean Salad, 69
Maple Baked Beans, 84
Mushroom Barley Soup, 50
Red Beans and Rice, 202
Rocky Ford Chili, 50
Southwestern Rice Salad, 78
Three-Bean Soup, 44
U.S. Senate Bean Soup, 61
Western Beans, 94

Beef & Ground Beef
All-American Barbecue Sandwiches, 143
All-American Beef Stew, 150
Baked Spaghetti, 142
Baked Stuffed Tomatoes, 132
Barbecued Beef Sandwiches, 134
Barbecued Brisket, 147
Barbecued Short Ribs, 140
Beef and Mushroom Roll, 137
Beef Noodle Soup, 56
Blue Cheese Flank Steak, 151
Braciole, 137
Chipotle Beef Tenderloins, 151
Classic Beef Stew, 138
Corned Beef and Mixed Vegetables, 142
Cornish Pasties, 143
Grandma's Meat Loaf, 140
Grilled Asian Flank Steak, 148
Ground Beef Macaroni Casserole, 150
Hearty Lasagna, 134
Herbed Beef Stew, 144
Hungarian Goulash, 133
Italian Wedding Soup, 49
Mini Hamburgers, 13
Mom's Italian Beef Sandwiches, 136
Mozzarella Meat Loaf, 138
Old-Fashioned Cabbage Rolls, 141
Old-World Tomato Soup, 54
Peppered Ribeye Steaks, 132
Perfect Pot Roast, 145
Round Steak Italiano, 135
Salisbury Steak Deluxe, 138
Savory Pot Roast, 139
Savory Spaghetti Sauce, 146
Scotch Broth, 56
Spaghetti 'n' Meatballs, 149
Spicy Tomato Steak, 147
Standing Rib Roast, 146
Steak Potpie, 135
Stuffed Roast Pepper Soup, 61
Stuffed Zucchini, 144
Swedish Meatballs, 140
Tangy Meatballs, 10
Tex-Mex Beef Barbecues, 149
Vegetable Beef Casserole, 133
Vegetable Beef Chili, 145
Vegetable Beef Soup, 55

Beverages
Aunt Frances' Lemonade, 17
Banana Brunch Punch, 12
Buttermilk Shakes, 15
Cozy Hot Chocolate, 12
Cozy Hot Mocha, 12
Homemade Orange Refresher, 19
Jungle Float, 20
Maple Hot Chocolate, 12
Mock Champagne, 21
Strawberry Citrus Slushies, 6

Biscuits
Angel Biscuits, 123
Fluffy Whole Wheat Biscuits, 115
Glazed Cinnamon Biscuits, 108
Jellied Biscuits, 37
Mom's Buttermilk Biscuits, 105
Nutty Sweet Potato Biscuits, 116

Blueberries
Blueberry Custard Parfait, 297
Blueberry Grunt, 291
Blueberry Pie with Lemon Crust, 262
Blueberry Streusel Muffins, 110
Cherry-Berry Peach Pie, 252
Grandma's Berry Tart, 247
Lemon Blueberry Bread, 106
Lemon Blueberry Pie, 250
Overnight Blueberry Coffee Cake, 30
Watercress with Fennel & Berries, 67

Bread Pudding
Breakfast Bread Pudding, 41
Pumpkin Bread Pudding, 300

Breads
(also see Coffee Cakes; Corn Bread & Cornmeal;
Doughnuts & Pastries; Muffins; Rolls & Buns)
QUICK BREADS
Apricot Walnut Bread, 107
Cheddar-Dill Bread, 108
Chocolate Chip Cherry Bread, 105
Chocolate Mini Loaves, 109
Cranberry Nut Bread, 112
Dutch Apple Bread, 111
Irish Soda Bread, 106

Breads

QUICK BREADS (*continued*)

Lemon Blueberry Bread, 106
Lemon Bread, 115
Orange Date Bread, 114
Poppy Seed Bread, 111
Pumpkin Bread, 110

YEAST BREADS

Apple Raisin Bread, 120
Bacon Swiss Bread, 113
Butternut Squash Bread, 124
Caraway Rye Bread, 121
Cheese Twists, 120
Cinnamon Twists, 127
Country White Bread, 123
Danish Julekage, 119
English Muffin Bread, 127
Grandma Russell's Bread, 126
Herb Country White Bread, 123
Homemade Egg Bread, 121
Honey Wheat Bread, 117
Italian Easter Bread, 128
Lemon Cheese Braid, 124
Muenster Bread, 117
Poteca Nut Roll, 119
Rustic Apple-Raisin Bread, 128
Sally Lunn Batter Bread, 129

Breakfast & Brunch

Ambrosia Fruit, 26
Apple Fritters, 35
Apple-Topped Oatcakes, 40
Banana Chip Pancakes, 35
Breakfast Biscuit Cups, 40
Breakfast Bread Pudding, 41
Buttermilk Pecan Waffles, 38
Caramel-Pecan Monkey Bread, 34
Cherry Syrup, 25
Cinnamon Coffee Cake, 27
Cinnamon-Raisin Granola, 10
Cinnamon Twists, 127
Cream Cheese Coffee Cake, 33
Crunchy Granola, 28
Delicious Potato Doughnuts, 36
Elephant Ears, 25
English Muffin Bread, 127
Feather-Light Muffins, 26
Grandma's Cinnamon Rolls, 32
Ham 'n' Cheese Pie, 38
Hash Brown Quiche, 26
Hearty Egg Scramble, 29
Jellied Biscuits, 37
Oh-So-Good Oatmeal, 32
Overnight Apple French Toast, 28
Overnight Blueberry Coffee Cake, 30
Overnight Raisin French Toast, 24

Peanut Butter & Jelly Waffles, 25
Polynesian Parfaits, 24
Pork Patties, 41
Quiche Lorraine, 39
Sausage Gravy, 31
Sausage Hash, 35
Scrambled Egg Casserole, 37
Sheepherder's Breakfast, 29
Spinach Bacon Quiche, 37
Stuffed Apricot French Toast, 31
Sweet Broiled Grapefruit, 30
Sweet Potato Muffins, 34
Zucchini Scramble, 39

Broccoli

Broccoli Bake, 85
Broccoli-Ham Hot Dish, 190
Broccoli-Pasta Side Dish, 96
Broccoli Rice Casserole, 100
Broccoli Soup, 58
Broccoli-Stuffed Baked Potatoes, 94
Favorite Broccoli Salad, 70

Buns (*see Rolls & Buns*)

Buttermilk

Buttermilk Pecan Waffles, 38
Buttermilk Shakes, 15
Mom's Buttermilk Biscuits, 105
Soft Buttermilk Sugar Cookies, 267

Cabbage & Sauerkraut

Barbecued Beef Sandwiches, 134
Caraway Sauerkraut, 88
Creamy Cabbage-Pork Stew, 184
Country Pork 'n' Sauerkraut, 183
Oktoberfest Pork Roast, 180
Old-Fashioned Cabbage Rolls, 141
Overnight Coleslaw, 71
Pork Chops with Caraway Cabbage, 190
Sauerkraut 'n' Sausage, 186
Sweet 'n' Creamy Coleslaw, 67

Cakes & Tortes

(*also see Cheesecakes; Coffee Cakes; Cupcakes*)

Apple Walnut Cake, 224
Banana Nut Layer Cake, 238
Brittle Torte, 235
Carrot Cake, 239
Cherry Spice Cake, 240
Chocolate Almond Bundt, 232
Chocolate Potato Cake, 228
Decadent Fudge Cake, 237
Frozen Chocolate Torte, 288
Golden Chocolate Cake, 237
Grandma's Red Velvet Cake, 233
Great-Grandma's Ginger Cake, 227

Lemon Chiffon Cake, 243
Old-Fashioned Ice Cream Roll, 294
Orange Chiffon Cake, 240
Orange-Date Nut Cake, 229
Pineapple Bundt Cake, 226
Pineapple Cheese Torte, 290
Pumpkin Raisin Cake, 224
Pumpkin Sheet Cake, 229
Rhubarb Upside-Down Cake, 236
Sandy's Chocolate Cake, 225
Saucy Apple Cake, 228
Snowflake Cake, 236
Spiced Pudding Cake, 232
Spicy Applesauce Cake, 241
Toffee Poke Cake, 223
White Texas Sheet Cake, 227
Viennese Plum Cake, 238

Candies

Chocolate Caramels, 296
Nutty Chocolate Fudge, 301
Pinwheel Mints, 299

Caramel

Caramel Corn, 19
Caramel Heavenlies, 284
Caramel-Pecan Dream Bars, 278
Caramel-Pecan Monkey Bread, 34
Chocolate Caramels, 296
Texas Chocolate Cupcakes, 234
Toffee Poke Cake, 223
Turtle Bars, 275
Turtle Cheesecake, 233

Carrots

Carrot Cake, 239
Creamy Carrot Soup, 52
Root for Winter Vegetables, 82
Zesty Carrot Bake, 95

Casseroles *(also see Meat Pies)*
MAIN DISHES
Baked Spaghetti, 142
Broccoli-Ham Hot Dish, 190
Catch-of-the-Day Casserole, 216
Chicken and Dumpling Casserole, 172
Chicken 'n' Hash Brown Bake, 175
Chicken Cheese Lasagna, 162
Cordon Bleu Casserole, 174
Crescent Turkey Casserole, 164
Eggplant Parmigiana, 205
Florida Seafood Casserole, 207
Garden Vegetable Bake, 213
Ground Beef Macaroni Casserole, 150
Ham 'n' Cheese Pasta, 194
Ham 'n' Cheese Pie, 38
Hearty Lasagna, 134

Overnight Apple French Toast, 28
Overnight Raisin French Toast, 24
Parmesan Chicken, 172
Quiche Lorraine, 39
Scrambled Egg Casserole, 37
Smoked Sausage Potato Bake, 181
Three-Cheese Chicken Bake, 168
Tuna Mushroom Casserole, 209
Turkey Tetrazzini, 174
Vegetable Beef Casserole, 133
SIDE DISHES
Broccoli Bake, 85
Broccoli Rice Casserole, 100
Butternut Squash Bake, 87
Cheese Potato Puff, 86
Corn and Bacon Casserole, 87
Creamy Sweet Potatoes, 96
Delicious Corn Pudding, 88
Finnish Cauliflower, 99
Garden Casserole, 97
Party Potatoes, 92
Scalloped Pineapple Casserole, 93
Zesty Carrot Bake, 95

Cheese
APPETIZERS AND SNACKS
Cheese Rye Appetizers, 7
Cheesy Sun Crisps, 11
Horseradish Cheese Spread, 21
Olive-Stuffed Celery, 21
BREADS
Bacon Swiss Bread, 113
Breakfast Biscuit Cups, 40
Cheddar-Dill Bread, 108
Cheese Straws, 104
Cheese Twists, 120
Cream Cheese Coffee Cake, 33
Lemon Cheese Braid, 124
Muenster Bread, 117
Parmesan-Ranch Pan Rolls, 129
DESSERTS
Almond Pear Torte, 242
Butter Pecan Cheesecake, 222
Cherry Cheesecake Dessert, 242
Chocolate Caramel Cheesecake, 233
Fluffy Cranberry Cheese Pie, 251
Fresh Citrus Cheesecake, 230
Heavenly Surprise Mini Cupcakes, 231
Ladyfinger Cheesecake, 231
Luscious Almond Cheesecake, 226
New York-Style Cheesecake, 214
Pineapple Cheese Torte, 290
MAIN DISHES
Blue Cheese Flank Steak, 151
Budget Macaroni and Cheese, 202
Catch-of-the-Day Casserole, 216

Cheese

MAIN DISHES *(continued)*

Cheddary Chicken Potpie, 173
Chicken Cheese Lasagna, 162
Cordon Bleu Casserole, 174
Eggplant Parmigiana, 205
Garden Vegetable Bake, 213
Grilled Pizza Sandwiches, 199
Ground Beef Macaroni Casserole, 150
Ham 'n' Cheese Pasta, 194
Ham 'n' Cheese Pie, 38
Mozzarella Meat Loaf, 138
Mushroom Crab Melts, 204
Parmesan Chicken, 172
Parmesan Chicken Sandwiches, 154
Rocky Ford Chili, 50
Sheepherder's Breakfast, 29
Smoked Sausage Potato Bake, 181
Sourdough Chicken Sandwiches, 154
Spiral Stromboli, 185
Three-Cheese Chicken Bake, 168
Three-Cheese Spinach Calzones, 208

SIDE DISHES

Broccoli Rice Casserole, 100
Broccoli-Stuffed Baked Potatoes, 94
Cheddar-Almond Lettuce Salad, 77
Cheese Potato Puff, 86
Finnish Cauliflower, 99
Herb-Stuffed Baked Potatoes, 94
Parmesan Noodles, 99
Party Potatoes, 92
Ranch Stuffed Baked Potatoes, 94
Stuffed Baked Potatoes, 94
Tex-Mex Stuffed Baked Potatoes, 94
Zucchini Mozzarella Medley, 101

SOUPS

Cheesy Chicken Chowder, 46
Potato Cheese Soup, 54
Savory Cheese Soup, 59

Cheesecakes

Almond Pear Torte, 242
Butter Pecan Cheesecake, 222
Cherry Cheesecake Dessert, 242
Chocolate Caramel Cheesecake, 233
Fresh Citrus Cheesecake, 230
Ladyfinger Cheesecake, 231
Luscious Almond Cheesecake, 226
New York-Style Cheesecake, 214
Streusel-Topped Apple Cheesecake, 24

Cherries

Cherry-Berry Peach Pie, 252
Cherry Cheesecake Dessert, 242
Cherry Cobbler, 291
Cherry Pie, 261
Cherry Spice Cake, 240
Cherry Syrup, 25
Chocolate Chip Cherry Bread, 105
Duck with Cherry Sauce, 177

Chicken

Artichoke Chicken, 161
Barbecued Picnic Chicken, 156
Cheddary Chicken Potpie, 173
Cheesy Chicken Chowder, 46
Chicken and Dumpling Casserole, 172
Chicken 'n' Hash Brown Bake, 175
Chicken Cheese Lasagna, 162
Chicken Provencale, 175
Chicken Rice Dinner, 163
Chicken Soup with Spaetzle, 47
Cordon Bleu Casserole, 174
Cranberry Chicken, 157
Down-Home Chicken, 119
Fried Chicken Strips, 177
Fried Chicken with Pan Gravy, 164
Gnocchi Chicken Minestrone, 48
Grandma's Chicken 'n' Dumpling Soup, 55
Herbed Fried Chicken with Pan Gravy, 164
Honey-Glazed Chicken, 163
Honey-Grilled Chicken Breasts, 155
Hungarian Chicken Paprikash, 119
Italian Wedding Soup, 49
Mom's Chicken 'n' Buttermilk Dumplings, 166
Mulligatawny Soup, 51
Nutty Oven-Fried Chicken, 156
Oven Barbecued Chicken, 170
Parmesan Chicken, 172
Parmesan Chicken Sandwiches, 154
Prosciutto Chicken Cacciatore, 166
Roasted Chicken with Rosemary, 171
Sage Dressing for Chicken, 34
Saucy Chicken and Asparagus, 169
Savory Lemonade Chicken, 176
Sour Cream Apple Chicken, 155
Sourdough Chicken Sandwiches, 154
Sweet Gingered Chicken Wings, 15
Teriyaki Chicken, 167
Three-Cheese Chicken Bake, 168
Tropical Chicken Salad, 160

Chili *(see Stews & Chili)*

Chocolate

Blizzard Party Mix, 8
Chewy Brownie Cookies, 276
Chocolate Almond Bundt, 232
Chocolate Caramel Cheesecake, 233
Chocolate Chip Brownies, 281
Chocolate Chip Cherry Bread, 105
Chocolate Date Squares, 270
Chocolate-Filled Cream Puffs, 293

Chocolate Malted Cookies, 274
Chocolate Marshmallow Bars, 274
Chocolate Mini Loaves, 109
Chocolate-Peanut Butter Cookies, 273
Chocolate Potato Cake, 228
Chocolate Sauce, 288
Chocolaty Double Crunchers, 268
Cozy Hot Chocolate, 12
Cozy Hot Mocha, 12
Cupcake Cones, 234
Decadent Fudge Cake, 237
Frosted Cookie Brownies, 272
Frozen Chocolate Torte, 288
Fudge Brownies, 267
Golden Chocolate Cake, 237
Grandma's Chocolate Meringue Pie, 255
Grandma's Chocolate Pudding, 301
Grandma's Red Velvet Cake, 233
Heavenly Surprise Mini Cupcakes, 231
Jungle Float, 20
Macaroon Brownies, 282
Maple Hot Chocolate, 12
Mocha Cupcakes, 239
Mocha Pudding Cakes, 292
Nutty Chocolate Fudge, 301
Orange Cocoa Sandies, 279
Pecan Fudge Pie, 254
Sandy's Chocolate Cake, 225
Sweet Minglers, 14
Texas Chocolate Cupcakes, 234
Toffee Poke Cake, 223
Turtle Bars, 275

Cobblers
Apple Cobbler, 297
Cherry Cobbler, 291

Coconut
Apricot-Coconut Bars, 268
Coconut Cream Pudding, 297
Coconut-Pecan Pie, 257
Coconut Washboards, 271
Macaroon Brownies, 282
Raspberry Coconut Cookies, 285
Snowflake Cake, 236

Coffee Cakes
Caramel-Pecan Monkey Bread, 34
Cinnamon Coffee Cake, 27
Cream Cheese Coffee Cake, 33
Overnight Blueberry Coffee Cake, 30

Cookies *(also see Bars & Brownies)*
Chewy Brownie Cookies, 276
Chocolate Malted Cookies, 274
Chocolate-Peanut Butter Cookies, 273
Chocolaty Double Crunchers, 268

Coconut Washboards, 271
Cookie Jar Gingersnaps, 268
Gingerbread Cutouts, 280
Grandma's Polish Cookies, 282
Hazelnut Shortbread, 275
Icebox Cookies, 276
Iced Anise Cookies, 285
Mom's Soft Raisin Cookies, 271
Orange Cocoa Sandies, 279
Peanut Butter Cookies, 269
Pizzelle, 267
Raspberry Coconut Cookies, 285
Scotch Shortbread Cookies, 270
Soft Buttermilk Sugar Cookies, 267
Spiced Oatmeal Cookies, 266

Corn
Caramel Corn, 19
Corn and Bacon Casserole, 87
Creamy Corn Chowder, 58
Delicious Corn Pudding, 88
Succotash, 83
Summer Risotto, 83

Corn Bread & Cornmeal
Corn Bread Layered Salad, 69
Corn Bread Squares, 113
Mexican Corn Bread, 114
Turkey with Corn Bread Dressing, 160

Cranberries
Citrus Cranberry Pie, 249
Cran-Raspberry Pie, 257
Cranberry Chicken, 157
Cranberry-Glazed Pork Roast, 191
Cranberry Nut Bread, 112
Fluffy Cranberry Cheese Pie, 251

Cupcakes
Banana Cupcakes, 223
Cupcake Cones, 234
Heavenly Surprise Mini Cupcakes, 231
Mocha Cupcakes, 239

Dates *(see Raisins & Dates)*

Desserts
(also see Bars & Brownies; Cakes & Tortes; Candies; Cheesecakes; Coffee Cakes; Cookies; Cupcakes; Puddings & Parfaits)
Almond Pear Torte, 242
Apple Turnovers with Custard, 289
Banana Split Cream Puffs, 296
Berries in Custard Sauce, 301
Blueberry Custard Parfait, 297
Blueberry Grunt, 291
Butterfinger Delight, 295

Desserts *(continued)*

Chocolate-Filled Cream Puffs, 293
Chocolate Sauce, 288
Ice Cream Cookie Dessert, 292
Lemony Apple Dumplings, 300
Mocha Pudding Cakes, 292
Old-Fashioned Ice Cream Roll, 294
1-2-3 Blackberry Sherbet, 289
Raspberry Vanilla Trifle, 298

Doughnuts & Pastries

Apple Fritters, 35
Delicious Potato Doughnuts, 36
Elephant Ears, 25

Dressing *(see Stuffing & Dressing)*

Dumplings

Chicken and Dumpling Casserole, 172
Dumpling Vegetable Soup, 57
Grandma's Chicken 'n' Dumpling Soup, 55
Knoephla Soup, 49
Mom's Chicken 'n' Buttermilk Dumplings, 166
Tomato Dumplings, 85

Eggs *(also see Quiche)*

Curried Egg Salad, 215
Deviled Eggs with Bacon, 6
Ham 'n' Cheese Pie, 38
Hearty Egg Scramble, 29
Homemade Egg Bread, 121
Scrambled Egg Casserole, 37
Sheepherder's Breakfast, 29
Zucchini Scramble, 39

Fish *(also see Seafood)*

Baked Lemon Haddock, 217
Broiled Fish, 202
Catch-of-the-Day Casserole, 216
Catfish Cakes, 216
Catfish with Lemon-Butter Sauce, 214
Crispy Cajun Panfish, 219
Florida Seafood Casserole, 207
Grandma's French Tuna Salad Wraps, 205
Grilled Salmon, 217
Honey Walleye, 206
Lemon Herbed Salmon, 206
Lime Broiled Catfish, 203
Mock Lobster, 211
Puff Pastry Salmon Bundles, 215
Simple Pan-Fried Trout, 214
Sole in Herbed Butter, 219
Stuffed Sole, 210
Stuffed Trout, 208
Tuna Burgers, 209
Tuna Dill Spread, 214
Tuna Mushroom Casserole, 209

French Toast

Overnight Apple French Toast, 28
Overnight Raisin French Toast, 24
Stuffed Apricot French Toast, 31

Fruit *(also see specific kinds)*

Ambrosia Fruit, 26
Banana Fruit Compote, 64
Berries in Custard Sauce, 301
Crisp and Nutty Mix, 20
Festive Fruit Salad, 79
Four-Fruit Pie, 254
Layered Fruit Salad, 74
1-2-3 Blackberry Sherbet, 289
Polynesian Parfaits, 24
Rhubarb Meringue Pie, 262
Sweet Broiled Grapefruit, 30
Tropical Chicken Salad, 160
Viennese Plum Cake, 238

Garlic

Garlic Pork Roast, 182
Spinach Garlic Soup, 52

Ginger

Cookie Jar Gingersnaps, 268
Gingerbread Cutouts, 280
Great-Grandma's Ginger Cake, 227
Sweet Gingered Chicken Wings, 15

Grilled & Broiled

Barbecued Picnic Chicken, 156
Blue Cheese Flank Steak, 151
Broiled Fish, 202
Chipotle Beef Tenderloins, 151
Easy Grilled Squash, 89
Grilled Asian Flank Steak, 148
Grilled Ham Steak, 188
Grilled Salmon, 217
Honey-Grilled Chicken Breasts, 155
Lime Broiled Catfish, 203
Peppered Ribeye Steaks, 132

Ham

Apricot Baked Ham, 182
Asparagus Ham Rolls, 188
Barbecue Ham Sandwiches, 183
Broccoli-Ham Hot Dish, 190
Cordon Bleu Casserole, 174
Dandy Ham Sandwiches, 199
Festive Ham Glaze, 196
Grilled Ham Steak, 188
Ham a la King, 194
Ham 'n' Cheese Pasta, 194
Ham 'n' Cheese Pie, 38
Ham Buns, 197
Ham Loaves, 189

Ham-Stuffed Manicotti, 187
Hearty Egg Scramble, 29
Spiral Stromboli, 185
Sugar-Glazed Ham, 193
Turkey with Country Ham Stuffing, 157
U.S. Senate Bean Soup, 61

Lasagna
Chicken Cheese Lasagna, 162
Hearty Lasagna, 134

Lemon
Aunt Frances' Lemonade, 17
Baked Lemon Haddock, 217
Catfish with Lemon-Butter Sauce, 214
Lemon Bars, 273
Lemon Blueberry Bread, 106
Lemon Blueberry Pie, 250
Lemon Bread, 115
Lemon Butter Cookies, 280
Lemon Cheese Braid, 124
Lemon Chiffon Cake, 243
Lemony Apple Dumplings, 300
Raspberry Lemon Muffins, 108

Lime
Lime Broiled Catfish, 203
Lime Gelatin Salad, 71

Meat Loaves
Grandma's Meat Loaf, 140
Mozzarella Meat Loaf, 138

Meat Pies
Cheddary Chicken Potpie, 173
Cornish Pasties, 143
Potato Pork Pie, 193
Steak Potpie, 135

Meatballs
Spaghetti 'n' Meatballs, 149
Swedish Meatballs, 140
Tangy Meatballs, 10

Meatless Entrees
Baked Vegetarian Stuffed Peppers, 212
Budget Macaroni and Cheese, 202
Eggplant Parmigiana, 205
Garden Vegetable Bake, 213
Homemade Pasta Sauce, 211
Red Beans and Rice, 202
Three-Cheese Spinach Calzones, 208
Tomato Pizza, 210
Tomato Quiche, 207
Vegetarian Stuffed Peppers, 212

Muffins
Apple Bran Muffins, 112
Blueberry Streusel Muffins, 110

Breakfast Biscuit Cups, 40
Feather-Light Muffins, 26
Grandma's Honey Muffins, 104
Nutty Apple Muffins, 113
Raspberry Lemon Muffins, 108
Sweet Potato Muffins, 34

Mushrooms
Beef and Mushroom Roll, 137
Mushroom and Potato Chowder, 53
Mushroom Barley Soup, 50
Mushroom Crab Melts, 204
Mushroom Rice Medley, 98
Peas with Mushrooms, 97
Sausage and Mushroom Stew, 198
Sausage Hash, 35
Tuna Mushroom Casserole, 209

Nuts (also see Peanut Butter)
Almond Pear Torte, 242
Apple Walnut Cake, 224
Apricot Walnut Bread, 107
Banana Nut Layer Cake, 238
Blizzard Party Mix, 8
Butter Pecan Cheesecake, 222
Buttermilk Pecan Waffles, 38
Caramel-Pecan Dream Bars, 278
Caramel-Pecan Monkey Bread, 34
Cheddar-Almond Lettuce Salad, 77
Chocolate Almond Bundt, 232
Chocolate Caramel Cheesecake, 233
Club Pie, 246
Coconut-Pecan Pie, 257
Cranberry Nut Bread, 112
Crisp and Nutty Mix, 20
Curried Walnut Rice Salad, 75
Hazelnut Shortbread, 275
Luscious Almond Cheesecake, 226
Orange-Date Nut Cake, 229
Nutty Apple Muffins, 113
Nutty Chocolate Fudge, 301
Nutty Oven-Fried Chicken, 156
Pecan Fudge Pie, 254
Pecan Sandies Cookies, 281
Pecan Squares, 277
Poteca Nut Roll, 119
Southwestern Rice Salad, 78
Spiced Pecans, 12
Strawberry-Pecan Pie, 258
Swedish Raspberry Almond Bars, 283
Toffee Almond Tart, 253
Tropical Chicken Salad, 160

Oatmeal
Apple-Topped Oatcakes, 40
Cinnamon-Raisin Granola, 10

Oatmeal *(continued)*

Crunchy Granola, 28
Oh-So-Good Oatmeal, 32
Spiced Oatmeal Cookies, 266

Onions & Leeks

Creamed Onions, 90
French Onion Soup, 47
Italian-Style Onion Soup, 45
Onion Potato Pancakes, 84
Special Garden Medley, 95

Orange

Grandma's Orange Rolls, 122
Homemade Orange Refresher, 19
Orange Chiffon Cake, 240
Orange Cocoa Sandies, 279
Orange Date Bread, 114
Orange-Date Nut Cake, 229
Strawberry Citrus Slushies, 6

Pasta & Noodles *(also see Lasagna; Spaghetti)*

Beef Noodle Soup, 56
Broccoli-Pasta Side Dish, 96
Budget Macaroni and Cheese, 202
Ground Beef Macaroni Casserole, 150
Ham 'n' Cheese Pasta, 194
Ham-Stuffed Manicotti, 187
Hungarian Noodle Side Dish, 92
Parmesan Noodles, 99
Shrimp Shell Salad, 213
Spaetzle Dumplings, 100
Sweet and Tangy Pasta Salad, 76
Tomato Soup with Cheese Tortellini, 45
Vegetable Pasta Salad, 75

Pastries *(see Doughnuts & Pastries)*

Peaches

Cherry-Berry Peach Pie, 252
Molded Peach Gelatin, 72
Mom's Peach Pie, 248
Peach Cream Pie, 260

Peanut Butter

Chocolate-Peanut Butter Cookies, 273
Peanut Butter & Jelly Waffles, 25
Peanut Butter Cookies, 269
Peanut Butter Pie, 246
Peanut Butter Squares, 278
Sweet Minglers, 14

Pears

Almond Pear Torte, 242
Fall Pear Pie, 258
Rustic Autumn Fruit Tart, 256

Peas

Creamed Peas, 89
Peas with Mushrooms, 97

Pies

Blueberry Pie with Lemon Crust, 262
Cherry-Berry Peach Pie, 252
Cherry Pie, 261
Citrus Cranberry Pie, 249
Club Pie, 246
Coconut-Pecan Pie, 257
Cookie Sheet Apple Pie, 249
Cran-Raspberry Pie, 257
Creamy Banana Pie, 260
Creamy Pineapple Pie, 253
Fall Pear Pie, 258
Fluffy Cranberry Cheese Pie, 251
Four-Fruit Pie, 254
Freezer Pumpkin Pie, 248
Golden Apricot Pie, 261
Grandma's Berry Tart, 247
Grandma's Chocolate Meringue Pie, 255
Grandma's Sour Cream Raisin Pie, 250
Irish Coffee Pie, 263
Lattice-Topped Apple Pie, 251
Lemon Blueberry Pie, 250
Mom's Peach Pie, 248
Peach Cream Pie, 260
Peanut Butter Pie, 246
Pecan Fudge Pie, 254
Praline Pumpkin Pie, 261
Raspberry Ribbon Pie, 259
Rhubarb Meringue Pie, 262
Rustic Autumn Fruit Tart, 256
Sky-High Strawberry Pie, 256
Sour Cream Apple Pie, 255
Strawberry-Pecan Pie, 258
Toffee Almond Tart, 253
Vanilla Custard Pie, 252

Pineapple

Creamy Pineapple Pie, 253
Pineapple Bundt Cake, 226
Pineapple Cheese Torte, 290
Pineapple Gelatin Salad, 69
Scalloped Pineapple Casserole, 93

Pizzas

Mini Apple Pizzas, 16
Tomato Pizza, 210

Pork *(also see Bacon; Ham; Sausage)*

Barbecued Spareribs, 197
Country Pork 'n' Sauerkraut, 183
Cranberry-Glazed Pork Roast, 191
Creamy Cabbage-Pork Stew, 184
Garlic Pork Roast, 182
Grandma Edna's Cajun Pork, 181
Ham Loaves, 189
Herbed Pork and Apples, 182

Maple Country Ribs, 192
Oktoberfest Pork Roast, 180
One-Dish Pork Chop Dinner, 199
Pepperoni Pizza Spread, 6
Pork and Spinach Salad, 191
Pork Chops with Caraway Cabbage, 190
Pork Chow Mein, 196
Pork Patties, 41
Potato Pork Pie, 193
Scalloped Potatoes and Pork Chops, 189
Skillet Pork Chops with Zucchini, 192
Sweet-and-Sour Pork, 187
Tuscan Pork Roast, 198

Potatoes *(also see Sweet Potatoes)*

Breakfast Biscuit Cups, 40
Broccoli-Stuffed Baked Potatoes, 94
Cheese Potato Puff, 86
Chicken 'n' Hash Brown Bake, 175
Chocolate Potato Cake, 228
Creamy German Potato Salad, 66
Delicious Potato Doughnuts, 36
Dilly Bean Potato Salad, 79
Easy Potato Rolls, 125
Grandma Russell's Bread, 126
Hash Brown Quiche, 26
Hearty Egg Scramble, 29
Hearty Potato Soup, 60
Herb-Stuffed Baked Potatoes, 94
Knoephla Soup, 49
Mashed Horseradish Potatoes, 91
Mushroom and Potato Chowder, 53
Norwegian Parsley Potatoes, 88
Onion Potato Pancakes, 84
Paprika Potatoes, 86
Party Potatoes, 92
Pat's Potato Salad, 74
Potato Cheese Soup, 54
Potato Gnocchi, 101
Potato Pork Pie, 193
Ranch Stuffed Baked Potatoes, 94
Sausage Hash, 35
Scalloped Potatoes and Pork Chops, 189
Sheepherder's Breakfast, 29
Special Potato Salad, 72
Stuffed Baked Potatoes, 94
Tater-Dipped Veggies, 19
Tex-Mex Stuffed Baked Potatoes, 94

Poultry *(also see Chicken; Turkey)*

Cornish Hens with Rice Dressing, 155
Duck with Cherry Sauce, 177
Roasted Duck with Apple-Raisin Dressing, 163
Wild Goose with Giblet Stuffing, 170

Puddings & Parfaits

Blueberry Custard Parfait, 297
Coconut Cream Pudding, 297
Grandma's Chocolate Pudding, 301
Homemade Butterscotch Pudding, 295
Layered Banana Pudding, 290
Seven-Minute Pudding, 289

Pumpkin

Freezer Pumpkin Pie, 248
Praline Pumpkin Pie, 261
Pumpkin Bread, 110
Pumpkin Bread Pudding, 300
Pumpkin Sheet Cake, 229

Quiche

Hash Brown Quiche, 26
Quiche Lorraine, 39
Spinach Bacon Quiche, 37
Tomato Quiche, 207

Raisins & Dates

Apple Raisin Bread, 120
Chocolate Date Squares, 270
Cinnamon-Raisin Granola, 10
Club Pie, 246
Grandma's Date Bars, 279
Grandma's Sour Cream Raisin Pie, 250
Mom's Soft Raisin Cookies, 271
Orange Date Bread, 114
Orange-Date Nut Cake, 229
Overnight Raisin French Toast, 24
Pumpkin Raisin Cake, 224
Roasted Duck with Apple-Raisin Dressing, 163
Rustic Apple-Raisin Bread, 128

Raspberries

Cran-Raspberry Pie, 257
Grandma's Berry Tart, 247
Raspberry Coconut Cookies, 285
Raspberry Lemon Muffins, 108
Raspberry Ribbon Pie, 259
Raspberry Vanilla Trifle, 298
Ruby Red Raspberry Salad, 78
Swedish Raspberry Almond Bars, 283

Rice & Wild Rice

Broccoli Rice Casserole, 100
Chicken Rice Dinner, 163
Cornish Hens with Rice Dressing, 155
Curried Walnut Rice Salad, 75
Herbed Rice Pilaf, 90
Mushroom Rice Medley, 98
Sausage over Rice, 184
Southwestern Rice Salad, 78
Summer Risotto, 83
Turkey with Herbed Rice Dressing, 167

Roasts

Barbecued Brisket, 147
Cranberry-Glazed Pork Roast, 191
Garlic Pork Roast, 182
Grandma Edna's Cajun Pork, 181
Oktoberfest Pork Roast, 180
Perfect Pot Roast, 145
Savory Pot Roast, 139
Standing Rib Roast, 146
Tex-Mex Beef Barbecues, 149
Tuscan Pork Roast, 198

Rolls & Buns

Buttery Crescents, 116
Cheese Straws, 104
Easy Potato Rolls, 125
Grandma's Cinnamon Rolls, 32
Grandma's Orange Rolls, 122
Honey Party Buns, 125
Parmesan-Ranch Pan Rolls, 129
Pop-Up Rolls, 107
Sour Cream Yeast Rolls, 118
Whole Wheat Refrigerator Rolls, 122

Salads

Banana Fruit Compote, 64
Caesar Salad, 75
Cheddar-Almond Lettuce Salad, 77
Corn Bread Layered Salad, 69
Creamy German Potato Salad, 66
Curried Egg Salad, 215
Curried Walnut Rice Salad, 75
Dilly Bean Potato Salad, 79
Emily's Spinach Salad, 73
Favorite Broccoli Salad, 70
Festive Fruit Salad, 79
Garden Bean Salad, 69
Gazpacho Salad, 68
Greens with Vinaigrette, 77
Hearty Eight-Layer Salad, 66
Layered Fruit Salad, 74
Lime Gelatin Salad, 71
Molded Peach Gelatin, 72
Overnight Coleslaw, 71
Pat's Potato Salad, 74
Pineapple Gelatin Salad, 69
Pork and Spinach Salad, 191
Ruby Red Raspberry Salad, 78
Seven-Layer Gelatin Salad, 64
Shrimp Shell Salad, 213
Smoked Turkey and Apple Salad, 168
Southwestern Rice Salad, 78
Special Potato Salad, 72
Summer Apple Salad, 72
Summer Squash Salad, 68
Sweet 'n' Creamy Coleslaw, 67

Sweet and Tangy Pasta Salad, 76
Tasty Tossed Salad, 65
Tomato Basil Salad, 70
Tomato Spinach Salad, 78
Tropical Chicken Salad, 160
Vegetable Pasta Salad, 75
Watercress with Fennel & Berries, 67

Sandwiches

All-American Barbecue Sandwiches, 143
Barbecue Ham Sandwiches, 183
Barbecued Beef Sandwiches, 134
Dandy Ham Sandwiches, 199
Grandma's French Tuna Salad Wraps, 205
Grilled Pizza Sandwiches, 199
Ham Buns, 197
Mini Hamburgers, 13
Mom's Italian Beef Sandwiches, 136
Mushroom Crab Melts, 204
Parmesan Chicken Sandwiches, 154
Sourdough Chicken Sandwiches, 154
Spiral Stromboli, 185
Tex-Mex Beef Barbecues, 149
Three-Cheese Spinach Calzones, 208
Tuna Burgers, 209

Sausage

Breakfast Biscuit Cups, 40
Country Italian Soup, 46
Grandma's Meat Loaf, 140
Grilled Pizza Sandwiches, 199
Hearty Minestrone, 52
Italian Wedding Soup, 49
Kielbasa Skillet Stew, 186
Oktoberfest Pork Roast, 180
Old-Fashioned Cabbage Rolls, 141
Sauerkraut 'n' Sausage, 186
Sausage and Mushroom Stew, 198
Sausage Gravy, 31
Sausage Hash, 35
Sausage over Rice, 184
Smoked Sausage Potato Bake, 181
Spiral Stromboli, 185
Sweet-Sour Franks, 195

Seafood

Clam Stuffing Bake, 206
Florida Seafood Casserole, 207
Mushroom Crab Melts, 204
North Carolina Shrimp Saute, 209
Shrimp Scampi, 218
Shrimp Shell Salad, 213

Side Dishes *(also see Casseroles)*

Asparagus with Sesame Butter, 90
Broccoli-Pasta Side Dish, 96
Broccoli-Stuffed Baked Potatoes, 94

Caraway Sauerkraut, 88
Continental Zucchini, 93
Creamed Onions, 90
Creamed Peas, 89
Easy Grilled Squash, 89
Finnish Cauliflower, 99
Garden Casserole, 97
German-Style Spinach, 91
Harvard Beets, 93
Herbed Rice Pilaf, 90
Hungarian Noodle Side Dish, 92
Maple Baked Beans, 84
Mashed Horseradish Potatoes, 91
Mushroom Rice Medley, 98
Norwegian Parsley Potatoes, 88
Onion Potato Pancakes, 84
Paprika Potatoes, 86
Parmesan Noodles, 99
Peas with Mushrooms, 97
Potato Gnocchi, 101
Ranch Stuffed Baked Potatoes, 94
Root for Winter Vegetables, 82
Sage Dressing for Chicken, 84
Spaetzle Dumplings, 100
Special Garden Medley, 95
Stuffed Baked Potatoes, 94
Succotash, 83
Summer Risotto, 83
Tex-Mex Stuffed Baked Potatoes, 94
Tomato Dumplings, 85
Western Beans, 94
Zesty Carrot Bake, 95
Zucchini Mozzarella Medley, 101

Skillet & Stovetop Suppers

All-American Beef Stew, 150
Budget Macaroni & Cheese, 202
Braciole, 137
Catfish Cakes, 216
Catfish with Lemon-Butter Sauce, 214
Corned Beef and Mixed Vegetables, 142
Cranberry Chicken, 157
Crispy Cajun Panfish, 219
Down-Home Chicken, 119
Fried Chicken Strips, 177
Fried Chicken with Pan Gravy, 164
Herbed Fried Chicken with Pan Gravy, 164
Honey Walleye, 206
Hungarian Chicken Paprikash, 119
Mock Lobster, 211
Mom's Chicken 'n' Buttermilk Dumplings, 166
North Carolina Shrimp Saute, 209
Parmesan Chicken Sandwiches, 154
Pork Chow Mein, 196
Prosciutto Chicken Cacciatore, 166
Red Beans and Rice, 202
Salisbury Steak Deluxe, 138
Savory Spaghetti Sauce, 146
Simple Pan-Fried Trout, 214
Skillet Pork Chops with Zucchini, 192
Sole in Herbed Butter, 219
Sour Cream Apple Chicken, 155
Sourdough Chicken Sandwiches, 154
Spaghetti 'n' Meatballs, 149
Spicy Tomato Steak, 147
Sweet-Sour Franks, 195
Turkey Stir-Fry, 160

Soups

Basic Turkey Soup, 57
Beef Noodle Soup, 56
Broccoli Soup, 58
Cheesy Chicken Chowder, 46
Chicken Soup with Spaetzle, 47
Country Italian Soup, 46
Creamy Carrot Soup, 52
Creamy Corn Chowder, 58
Creamy Squash Soup, 56
Creamy Vegetable Soup, 44
Dumpling Vegetable Soup, 57
Five-Bean Soup, 53
French Onion Soup, 47
Gnocchi Chicken Minestrone, 48
Grandma's Chicken 'n' Dumpling Soup, 55
Hearty Minestrone, 52
Hearty Potato Soup, 60
Italian-Style Onion Soup, 45
Italian Wedding Soup, 49
Knoephla Soup, 49
Mulligatawny Soup, 51
Mushroom and Potato Chowder, 53
Mushroom Barley Soup, 50
Old-World Tomato Soup, 54
Potato Cheese Soup, 54
Savory Cheese Soup, 59
Scotch Broth, 56
Spinach Garlic Soup, 52
Stuffed Roast Pepper Soup, 61
Three-Bean Soup, 44
Tomato Dill Bisque, 59
Tomato Soup with Cheese Tortellini, 45
U.S. Senate Bean Soup, 61
Vegetable Beef Soup, 55

Spaghetti

Baked Spaghetti, 142
Homemade Pasta Sauce, 211
Savory Spaghetti Sauce, 146
Spaghetti 'n' Meatballs, 149

Spinach

Artichoke Spinach Dip in a Bread Bowl, 8
Emily's Spinach Salad, 73

Spinach (continued)

German-Style Spinach, 91
Pork and Spinach Salad, 191
Spinach Bacon Quiche, 37
Spinach Garlic Soup, 52
Three-Bean Soup, 44
Three-Cheese Spinach Calzones, 208
Tomato Spinach Salad, 78

Squash

Butternut Squash Bake, 87
Butternut Squash Bread, 124
Continental Zucchini, 93
Creamy Squash Soup, 56
Easy Grilled Squash, 89
Skillet Pork Chops with Zucchini, 192
Stuffed Zucchini, 144
Summer Squash Salad, 68
Zucchini Mozzarella Medley, 101
Zucchini Scramble, 39

Stews & Chili

All-American Beef Stew, 150
Classic Beef Stew, 138
Creamy Cabbage-Pork Stew, 184
Herbed Beef Stew, 144
Hungarian Goulash, 133
Kielbasa Skillet Stew, 186
Rocky Ford Chili, 50
Sausage and Mushroom Stew, 198
Vegetable Beef Chili, 145

Strawberries

Grandma's Berry Tart, 247
Sky-High Strawberry Pie, 256
Strawberry Citrus Slushies, 6
Strawberry-Pecan Pie, 258

Stuffing & Dressing

Italian Christmas Turkey, 158
Roasted Duck with Apple-Raisin Dressing, 163
Sage Dressing for Chicken, 84
Turkey with Corn Bread Dressing, 160
Turkey with Country Ham Stuffing, 157
Turkey with Herbed Rice Dressing, 167
Turkey with Sausage Stuffing, 173
Wild Goose with Giblet Stuffing, 170

Sweet Potatoes

Creamy Sweet Potatoes, 96
Nutty Sweet Potato Biscuits, 116
Sweet Potato Muffins, 34

Tomatoes

Baked Stuffed Tomatoes, 132
BLT Bites, 14
Chunky Salsa, 11
Gazpacho Salad, 68
Old-World Tomato Soup, 54
Special Garden Medley, 95
Spicy Tomato Steak, 147
Succotash, 83

Tomato Basil Salad, 70
Tomato Dill Bisque, 59
Tomato Dumplings, 85
Tomato Pizza, 210
Tomato Quiche, 207
Tomato Soup with Cheese Tortellini, 45
Tomato Spinach Salad, 78
Zucchini Mozzarella Medley, 101

Turkey

Basic Turkey Soup, 57
Crescent Turkey Casserole, 164
Italian Christmas Turkey, 158
Marinated Turkey, 169
Rolled-Up Turkey, 165
Smoked Turkey and Apple Salad, 168
Turkey and Mushroom Casserole, 176
Turkey Stir-Fry, 160
Turkey Tetrazzini, 174
Turkey with Corn Bread Dressing, 160
Turkey with Country Ham Stuffing, 157
Turkey with Herbed Rice Dressing, 167
Turkey with Sausage Stuffing, 173

Vegetables (also see specific kinds)

Artichoke Chicken, 161
Artichoke Spinach Dip in a Bread Bowl, 8
Baked Vegetarian Stuffed Peppers, 212
Corn Bread Layered Salad, 69
Corned Beef and Mixed Vegetables, 142
Country Italian Soup, 46
Creamy Vegetable Soup, 44
Crescent Turkey Casserole, 164
Dilly Bean Potato Salad, 79
Dumpling Vegetable Soup, 57
Easy Hummus, 12
Eggplant Parmigiana, 205
Finnish Cauliflower, 99
Garden Casserole, 97
Garden Vegetable Bake, 213
Gnocchi Chicken Minestrone, 48
Greens with Vinaigrette, 77
Harvard Beets, 93
Hearty Eight-Layer Salad, 66
Root for Winter Vegetables, 82
Southwestern Rice Salad, 78
Succotash, 83
Sweet and Tangy Pasta Salad, 76
Tasty Tossed Salad, 65
Tater-Dipped Veggies, 19
Vegetable Beef Casserole, 133
Vegetable Beef Chili, 145
Vegetable Beef Soup, 55
Vegetable Pasta Salad, 75
Vegetarian Stuffed Peppers, 212
Viennese Plum Cake, 238
Watercress with Fennel & Berries, 67

Waffles

Buttermilk Pecan Waffles, 38
Peanut Butter & Jelly Waffles, 25

Alphabetical Index

This handy index lists every recipe in alphabetical order so you can easily find your favorite dish.

A

All-American Barbecue Sandwiches, 143
All-American Beef Stew, 150
Almond Pear Torte, 242
Ambrosia Fruit, 26
Angel Biscuits, 123
Apple Bran Muffins, 112
Apple Cobbler, 297
Apple Fritters, 35
Apple Raisin Bread, 120
Apple-Topped Oatcakes, 40
Apple Turnovers with Custard, 289
Apple Walnut Cake, 224
Apricot Baked Ham, 182
Apricot-Coconut Bars, 268
Apricot Walnut Bread, 107
Artichoke Chicken, 161
Artichoke Spinach Dip in a Bread Bowl, 8
Asparagus Ham Rolls, 188
Asparagus with Sesame Butter, 90
Aunt Frances' Lemonade, 17

B

Bacon Swiss Bread, 113
Baked Lemon Haddock, 217
Baked Spaghetti, 142
Baked Stuffed Tomatoes, 132
Baked Vegetarian Stuffed Peppers, 212
Banana Brunch Punch, 12
Banana Chip Pancakes, 35
Banana Cupcakes, 223
Banana Fruit Compote, 64
Banana Nut Layer Cake, 238
Banana Split Cream Puffs, 296
Barbecue Ham Sandwiches, 183
Barbecued Beef Sandwiches, 134
Barbecued Brisket, 147
Barbecued Picnic Chicken, 156
Barbecued Short Ribs, 140
Barbecued Spareribs, 197
Basic Turkey Soup, 57
Beef and Mushroom Roll, 137
Beef Noodle Soup, 56
Berries in Custard Sauce, 301
Blizzard Party Mix, 8
BLT Bites, 14
Blue Cheese Flank Steak, 151
Blueberry Custard Parfait, 297
Blueberry Grunt, 291
Blueberry Pie with Lemon Crust, 262
Blueberry Streusel Muffins, 110

Braciole, 137
Breakfast Biscuit Cups, 40
Breakfast Bread Pudding, 41
Brittle Torte, 235
Broccoli Bake, 85
Broccoli-Ham Hot Dish, 190
Broccoli-Pasta Side Dish, 96
Broccoli Rice Casserole, 100
Broccoli-Stuffed Baked Potatoes, 94
Broccoli Soup, 58
Broiled Fish, 202
Budget Macaroni and Cheese, 202
Butter Pecan Cheesecake, 222
Butterfinger Delight, 295
Buttermilk Pecan Waffles, 38
Buttermilk Shakes, 15
Butternut Squash Bake, 87
Butternut Squash Bread, 124
Buttery Crescents, 116

C

Caesar Salad, 75
Caramel Corn, 19
Caramel Heavenlies, 284
Caramel-Pecan Dream Bars, 278
Caramel-Pecan Monkey Bread, 34
Caraway Rye Bread, 121
Caraway Sauerkraut, 88
Carrot Cake, 239
Catch-of-the-Day Casserole, 216
Catfish Cakes, 216
Catfish with Lemon-Butter Sauce, 214
Cheddar-Almond Lettuce Salad, 77
Cheddar-Dill Bread, 108
Cheddary Chicken Potpie, 173
Cheese Potato Puff, 86
Cheese Rye Appetizers, 7
Cheese Straws, 104
Cheese Twists, 120
Cheesy Chicken Chowder, 46
Cheesy Sun Crisps, 11
Cherry-Berry Peach Pie, 252
Cherry Cheesecake Dessert, 242
Cherry Cobbler, 291
Cherry Pie, 261
Cherry Spice Cake, 240
Cherry Syrup, 25
Chewy Brownie Cookies, 276
Chicken and Dumpling Casserole, 172
Chicken 'n' Hash Brown Bake, 175
Chicken Cheese Lasagna, 162

Chicken Provencale, 175
Chicken Rice Dinner, 163
Chicken Soup with Spaetzle, 47
Chipotle Beef Tenderloins, 151
Chocolate Almond Bundt, 232
Chocolate Caramel Cheesecake, 233
Chocolate Caramels, 296
Chocolate Chip Brownies, 281
Chocolate Chip Cherry Bread, 105
Chocolate Date Squares, 270
Chocolate-Filled Cream Puffs, 293
Chocolate Malted Cookies, 274
Chocolate Marshmallow Bars, 274
Chocolate Mini Loaves, 109
Chocolate-Peanut Butter Cookies, 273
Chocolate Potato Cake, 228
Chocolate Sauce, 288
Chocolaty Double Crunchers, 268
Chunky Salsa, 11
Cinnamon Coffee Cake, 27
Cinnamon-Raisin Granola, 10
Cinnamon Twists, 127
Citrus Cranberry Pie, 249
Clam Stuffing Bake, 206
Classic Beef Stew, 138
Club Pie, 246
Coconut Cream Pudding, 297
Coconut-Pecan Pie, 257
Coconut Washboards, 271
Continental Zucchini, 93
Cookie Jar Gingersnaps, 268
Cookie Sheet Apple Pie, 249
Cordon Bleu Casserole, 174
Corn and Bacon Casserole, 87
Corn Bread Layered Salad, 69
Corn Bread Squares, 113
Corned Beef and Mixed Vegetables, 142
Cornish Hens with Rice Dressing, 155
Cornish Pasties, 143
Country Italian Soup, 46
Country Pork 'n' Sauerkraut, 183
Country White Bread, 123
Cozy Hot Chocolate, 12
Cozy Hot Mocha, 12
Cran-Raspberry Pie, 257
Cranberry Chicken, 157
Cranberry-Glazed Pork Roast, 191
Cranberry Nut Bread, 112
Cream Cheese Coffee Cake, 33
Creamed Onions, 90
Creamed Peas, 89
Creamy Banana Pie, 260
Creamy Cabbage-Pork Stew, 184
Creamy Carrot Soup, 52
Creamy Corn Chowder, 58

Creamy German Potato Salad, 66
Creamy Pineapple Pie, 253
Creamy Squash Soup, 56
Creamy Sweet Potatoes, 96
Creamy Vegetable Soup, 44
Crescent Turkey Casserole, 164
Crisp and Nutty Mix, 20
Crispy Cajun Panfish, 219
Crunchy Granola, 28
Cupcake Cones, 234
Curried Egg Salad, 215
Curried Walnut Rice Salad, 75

D

Dandy Ham Sandwiches, 199
Danish Julekage, 119
Decadent Fudge Cake, 237
Delicious Corn Pudding, 88
Delicious Potato Doughnuts, 36
Deviled Eggs with Bacon, 6
Dilly Bean Potato Salad, 79
Down-Home Chicken, 119
Duck with Cherry Sauce, 177
Dumpling Vegetable Soup, 57
Dutch Apple Bread, 111

E

Easy Elephant Ears, 9
Easy Hummus, 12
Easy Potato Rolls, 125
Eggplant Parmigiana, 205
Elephant Ears, 25
Emily's Spinach Salad, 73
English Muffin Bread, 127

F

Fall Pear Pie, 258
Favorite Broccoli Salad, 70
Feather-Light Muffins, 26
Festive Fruit Salad, 79
Festive Ham Glaze, 196
Finnish Cauliflower, 99
Five-Bean Soup, 53
Florida Seafood Casserole, 207
Fluffy Cranberry Cheese Pie, 251
Fluffy Whole Wheat Biscuits, 115
Four-Fruit Pie, 254
Freezer Pumpkin Pie, 248
French Onion Soup, 47
Fresh Citrus Cheesecake, 230
Fresh Vegetable Dip, 16
Fried Chicken Strips, 177
Fried Chicken with Pan Gravy, 164
Frosted Cookie Brownies, 272
Frozen Chocolate Torte, 288
Fudge Brownies, 267

G

Garden Bean Salad, 69
Garden Casserole, 97
Garden Vegetable Bake, 213
Garlic Pork Roast, 182
Gazpacho Salad, 68
German-Style Spinach, 91
Gingerbread Cutouts, 280
Glazed Cinnamon Biscuits, 108
Gnocchi Chicken Minestrone, 48
Golden Apricot Pie, 261
Golden Chocolate Cake, 237
Grandma Edna's Cajun Pork, 181
Grandma Russell's Bread, 126
Grandma's Berry Tart, 247
Grandma's Chicken 'n' Dumpling Soup, 55
Grandma's Chocolate Meringue Pie, 255
Grandma's Chocolate Pudding, 301
Grandma's Cinnamon Rolls, 32
Grandma's Date Bars, 279
Grandma's French Tuna Salad Wraps, 205
Grandma's Honey Muffins, 104
Grandma's Meat Loaf, 140
Grandma's Orange Rolls, 122
Grandma's Polish Cookies, 282
Grandma's Red Velvet Cake, 233
Grandma's Sour Cream Raisin Pie, 250
Great-Grandma's Ginger Cake, 227
Greens with Vinaigrette, 77
Grilled Asian Flank Steak, 148
Grilled Ham Steak, 188
Grilled Pizza Sandwiches, 199
Grilled Salmon, 217
Ground Beef Macaroni Casserole, 150

H

Ham a la King, 194
Ham 'n' Cheese Pasta, 194
Ham 'n' Cheese Pie, 38
Ham Buns, 197
Ham Loaves, 189
Ham-Stuffed Manicotti, 187
Harvard Beets, 93
Hash Brown Quiche, 26
Hazelnut Shortbread, 275
Hearty Egg Scramble, 29
Hearty Eight-Layer Salad, 66
Hearty Lasagna, 134
Hearty Minestrone, 52
Hearty Potato Soup, 60
Heavenly Surprise Mini Cupcakes, 231
Herb Country White Bread, 123
Herb-Stuffed Baked Potatoes, 94
Herbed Beef Stew, 144
Herbed Fried Chicken with Pan Gravy, 164

Herbed Pork and Apples, 182
Herbed Rice Pilaf, 90
Homemade Butterscotch Pudding, 295
Homemade Egg Bread, 121
Homemade Orange Refresher, 19
Homemade Pasta Sauce, 211
Honey-Glazed Chicken, 163
Honey-Grilled Chicken Breasts, 155
Honey Party Buns, 125
Honey Walleye, 206
Honey Wheat Bread, 117
Horseradish Cheese Spread, 21
Hungarian Chicken Paprikash, 119
Hungarian Goulash, 133
Hungarian Noodle Side Dish, 92

I

Ice Cream Cookie Dessert, 292
Icebox Cookies, 276
Iced Anise Cookies, 285
Irish Coffee Pie, 263
Irish Soda Bread, 106
Italian Christmas Turkey, 158
Italian Easter Bread, 128
Italian-Style Onion Soup, 45
Italian Wedding Soup, 49

J

Jellied Biscuits, 37
Jungle Float, 20

K

Kielbasa Skillet Stew, 186
Knoephla Soup, 49

L

Ladyfinger Cheesecake, 231
Lattice-Topped Apple Pie, 251
Layered Banana Pudding, 290
Layered Fruit Salad, 74
Lemon Bars, 273
Lemon Blueberry Bread, 106
Lemon Blueberry Pie, 250
Lemon Bread, 115
Lemon Butter Cookies, 280
Lemon Cheese Braid, 124
Lemon Chiffon Cake, 243
Lemon Herbed Salmon, 206
Lemony Apple Dumplings, 300
Lime Broiled Catfish, 203
Lime Gelatin Salad, 71
Luscious Almond Cheesecake, 226

M

Macaroon Brownies, 282
Maple Country Ribs, 192

Maple Hot Chocolate, 12
Marinated Turkey, 169
Mashed Horseradish Potatoes, 91
Mexican Corn Bread, 114
Mini Apple Pizzas, 16
Mini Hamburgers, 13
Mocha Cupcakes, 239
Mocha Pudding Cakes, 292
Mock Champagne, 21
Mock Lobster, 211
Molded Peach Gelatin, 72
Mom's Buttermilk Biscuits, 105
Mom's Chicken 'n' Buttermilk Dumplings, 166
Mom's Italian Beef Sandwiches, 136
Mom's Peach Pie, 248
Mom's Soft Raisin Cookies, 271
Mozzarella Meat Loaf, 138
Muenster Bread, 117
Mulligatawny Soup, 51
Mushroom and Potato Chowder, 53
Mushroom Barley Soup, 50
Mushroom Crab Melts, 204
Mushroom Rice Medley, 98

N

New York-Style Cheesecake, 214
North Carolina Shrimp Saute, 209
Norwegian Parsley Potatoes, 88
Nutty Apple Muffins, 113
Nutty Chocolate Fudge, 301
Nutty Oven-Fried Chicken, 156
Nutty Sweet Potato Biscuits, 116

O

Oh-So-Good Oatmeal, 32
Oktoberfest Pork Roast, 180
Old-Fashioned Cabbage Rolls, 141
Old-Fashioned Ice Cream Roll, 294
Old-World Tomato Soup, 54
Olive-Stuffed Celery, 21
One-Dish Pork Chop Dinner, 199
1-2-3 Blackberry Sherbet, 289
Onion Potato Pancakes, 84
Orange Chiffon Cake, 240
Orange Cocoa Sandies, 279
Orange Date Bread, 114
Orange-Date Nut Cake, 229
Oven Barbecued Chicken, 170
Overnight Apple French Toast, 28
Overnight Blueberry Coffee Cake, 30
Overnight Coleslaw, 71
Overnight Raisin French Toast, 24

P

Paprika Potatoes, 86
Parmesan Chicken, 172

Parmesan Chicken Sandwiches, 154
Parmesan Noodles, 99
Parmesan-Ranch Pan Rolls, 129
Party Potatoes, 92
Pat's Potato Salad, 74
Peach Cream Pie, 260
Peanut Butter & Jelly Waffles, 25
Peanut Butter Cookies, 269
Peanut Butter Pie, 246
Peanut Butter Squares, 278
Peas with Mushrooms, 97
Pecan Fudge Pie, 254
Pecan Sandies Cookies, 281
Pecan Squares, 277
Peppered Ribeye Steaks, 132
Pepperoni Pizza Spread, 6
Perfect Pot Roast, 145
Pineapple Bundt Cake, 226
Pineapple Cheese Torte, 290
Pineapple Gelatin Salad, 69
Pinwheel Mints, 299
Pizzelle, 267
Polynesian Parfaits, 24
Pop-Up Rolls, 107
Poppy Seed Bread, 111
Pork and Spinach Salad, 191
Pork Chops with Caraway Cabbage, 190
Pork Chow Mein, 196
Pork Patties, 41
Potato Cheese Soup, 54
Potato Gnocchi, 101
Potato Pork Pie, 193
Poteca Nut Roll, 119
Praline Pumpkin Pie, 261
Prosciutto Chicken Cacciatore, 166
Puff Pastry Salmon Bundles, 215
Puffed Wheat Balls, 18
Pumpkin Bread, 110
Pumpkin Bread Pudding, 300
Pumpkin Raisin Cake, 224
Pumpkin Sheet Cake, 229

Q

Quiche Lorraine, 39

R

Ranch Stuffed Baked Potatoes, 94
Raspberry Coconut Cookies, 285
Raspberry Lemon Muffins, 108
Raspberry Ribbon Pie, 259
Raspberry Vanilla Trifle, 298
Red Beans and Rice, 202
Rhubarb Meringue Pie, 262
Rhubarb Upside-Down Cake, 236
Roast Beef Spirals, 9

Roasted Chicken with Rosemary, 171
Roasted Duck with Apple-Raisin Dressing, 163
Rocky Ford Chili, 50
Rolled-Up Turkey, 165
Root for Winter Vegetables, 82
Round Steak Italiano, 135
Ruby Red Raspberry Salad, 78
Rustic Apple-Raisin Bread, 128
Rustic Autumn Fruit Tart, 256

S

Sage Dressing for Chicken, 84
Salisbury Steak Deluxe, 138
Sally Lunn Batter Bread, 129
Sandy's Chocolate Cake, 225
Saucy Apple Cake, 228
Saucy Chicken and Asparagus, 169
Sauerkraut 'n' Sausage, 186
Sausage and Mushroom Stew, 198
Sausage Gravy, 31
Sausage Hash, 35
Sausage over Rice, 184
Savory Cheese Soup, 59
Savory Lemonade Chicken, 176
Savory Pot Roast, 139
Savory Spaghetti Sauce, 146
Scalloped Pineapple Casserole, 93
Scalloped Potatoes and Pork Chops, 189
Scotch Broth, 56
Scotch Shortbread Cookies, 270
Scrambled Egg Casserole, 37
Seven-Layer Gelatin Salad, 64
Seven-Minute Pudding, 289
Sheepherder's Breakfast, 29
Shrimp Scampi, 218
Shrimp Shell Salad, 213
Simple Pan-Fried Trout, 214
Skillet Pork Chops with Zucchini, 192
Sky-High Strawberry Pie, 256
Smoked Sausage Potato Bake, 181
Smoked Turkey and Apple Salad, 168
Snowflake Cake, 236
Soft Buttermilk Sugar Cookies, 267
Sole in Herbed Butter, 219
Sour Cream Apple Chicken, 155
Sour Cream Apple Pie, 255
Sour Cream Yeast Rolls, 118
Sourdough Chicken Sandwiches, 154
Southwestern Rice Salad, 78
Spaetzle Dumplings, 100
Spaghetti 'n' Meatballs, 149
Special Garden Medley, 95
Special Potato Salad, 72
Spiced Oatmeal Cookies, 266
Spiced Pecans, 12

Spiced Pudding Cake, 232
Spicy Applesauce Cake, 241
Spicy Tomato Steak, 147
Spinach Bacon Quiche, 37
Spinach Garlic Soup, 52
Spiral Stromboli, 185
Standing Rib Roast, 146
Steak Potpie, 135
Strawberry Citrus Slushies, 6
Strawberry-Pecan Pie, 258
Streusel-Topped Apple Cheesecake, 241
Stuffed Apricot French Toast, 31
Stuffed Baked Potatoes, 94
Stuffed Roast Pepper Soup, 61
Stuffed Sole, 210
Stuffed Trout, 208
Stuffed Zucchini, 144
Sugar-Glazed Ham, 193
Summer Apple Salad, 72
Summer Squash Salad, 68
Swedish Meatballs, 140
Swedish Raspberry Almond Bars, 283
Sweet 'n' Creamy Coleslaw, 67
Sweet-and-Sour Pork, 187
Sweet and Tangy Pasta Salad, 76
Sweet Broiled Grapefruit, 30
Sweet Gingered Chicken Wings, 15
Sweet Minglers, 14
Sweet Potato Muffins, 34
Sweet-Sour Franks, 195

T

Tangy Meatballs, 10
Tasty Tossed Salad, 65
Tater-Dipped Veggies, 19
Teriyaki Chicken, 167
Tex-Mex Beef Barbecues, 149
Tex-Mex Stuffed Baked Potatoes, 94
Texas Chocolate Cupcakes, 234
Three-Bean Soup, 44
Three-Cheese Chicken Bake, 168
Three-Cheese Spinach Calzones, 208
Toffee Almond Tart, 253
Toffee Poke Cake, 223
Tomato Basil Salad, 70
Tomato Dill Bisque, 59
Tomato Dumplings, 85
Tomato Pizza, 210
Tomato Quiche, 207
Tomato Soup with Cheese Tortellini, 45
Tomato Spinach Salad, 78
Tropical Chicken Salad, 160
Tuna Burgers, 209
Tuna Dill Spread, 214
Tuna Mushroom Casserole, 176

Turkey Stir-Fry, 160
Turkey Tetrazzini, 174
Turkey with Corn Bread Dressing, 160
Turkey with Country Ham Stuffing, 157
Turkey with Herbed Rice Dressing, 167
Turkey with Sausage Stuffing, 173
Turtle Bars, 275
Tuscan Pork Roast, 198

U

U.S. Senate Bean Soup, 61

V

Vanilla Custard Pie, 252
Vegetable Beef Casserole, 133
Vegetable Beef Chili, 145
Vegetable Beef Soup, 55
Vegetable Pasta Salad, 75
Vegetarian Stuffed Peppers, 212

W

Watercress with Fennel & Berries, 67
Western Beans, 94
White Texas Sheet Cake, 227
Whole Wheat Refrigerator Rolls, 122
Wild Goose with Giblet Stuffing, 170

Z

Zesty Carrot Bake, 95
Zucchini Mozzarella Medley, 101
Zucchini Scramble, 39

Photo Credits

COOKING UTENSILS IN CROCK, page 4
Graeme Dawes/Shutterstock.com

WOMAN LEANING OVER COUNTER, page 4
Susan Colbert

COFFEE GRINDER, page 22
Ronald Sumers/Shutterstock.com

WOMAN FLIPPING EGGS, page 22
Everett Collection/Shutterstock.com

KITCHEN UTENSILS, page 42
Danie Nel/Shutterstock.com

WOMAN AT STOVE, page 42
Everett Collection/Shutterstock.com

VINTAGE DISHES, page 62
Karuka/Shutterstock.com

FARM FRESH EGGS, page 62
Kathy Ridder

DISHES ON WOOD SHELVES, page 80
patpitchaya/Shutterstock.com

CANNING, page 80
Rose Cunningham

ROLLING PIN, page 102
Nik_Merkulov/Shutterstock.com

MAKING POTATO PANCAKES, page 102
Melanie Longenecker

ROCKING CHAIRS, page 130
Rob Byron/Shutterstock.com

MOM'S KITCHEN, page 130
Mary Compagnomi

VINTAGE SILVERWARE, page 152
Gyorgy Barna/Shutterstock.com

PULLING OUT TURKEY, page 152
Mike Simko

RICE, page 178
Bienchen-s/Shutterstock.com

WOMAN AT STOVE, page 178
Everett Collection/Shutterstock.com

SPICES, page 200
Vasil Vasilev/Shutterstock.com

WOMAN CUTTING FOOD, page 200
Everett Collection/Shutterstock.com

CUPCAKE LINERS, page 220
alexsalcedo/Shutterstock.com

PULLING FOOD FROM OVEN, page 220
Gene Marsh

MAKING PIE, page 244
jocic/Shutterstock.com

WOMAN TRIMMING CRUST, page 244
Everett Collection/Shutterstock.com

VINTAGE STAR COOKIE CUTTER, page 264
Donna Smith Photography/Shutterstock.com

COOKING POPCORN, page 264
Donna Deem

TEACUP AND SAUCERS, page 286
Cheryl E Davis/Shutterstock.com

WOMAN COOKING AT STOVE, page 286
Everett Collection/Shutterstock.com